Beyond the Evangelical Impasse
Spirit Baptism and the Quest for Authentic Spiritual Experience

D. Alan Blanc

FOOTHILLS PUBLICATIONS
Gloversville, New York

ISBN

FOOTHILLS PUBLICATIONS
Gloversville, NY 12078

Library of Congress Cataloguing-in-Publication Data

Printed in the United States of America

"He must increase, but I must decrease."

John 3:30 ESV

To my loving wife and best friend

Sally

TABLE OF CONTENTS

ENDORSEMENTS iii

FORWARD v

PREFACE... vi

LIST OF TABLES.. vii

ABBREVIATIONS viii

INTRODUCTION 1

CHAPTER 1

DEFINING THE COMMON HERITAGE..5

1. Introduction 5

2. Evangelicals and Evangelicalism: The Search for an Identity-Based Consensus..7

3. Concretizing the BHS Metaphor 17

4. Conclusion..32

CHAPTER 2

PENTECOSTAL SPIRITUALITY:
MULTIPLE MOVEMENTS WITH A COMMON ROOT 34

1. Introduction 34

2. Historical Excursus: Successive Waves and Divergent Streams.........36

3. Encounter: The Locus of P/C Spirituality 61

4. Conclusion..67

CHAPTER 3

AN AMERICAN BAPTIST RATIONALE FOR CONSENSUS......................68

1. Introduction 68

2. Encounter-Oriented Spirituality: Adducing American Baptist Identity 72

3. Beyond Identity: The Case for Doctrinal Consensus............91

4. Neo-Pentecostalism and the American Baptist Odyssey 97

5. Conclusion..107

CHAPTER 4

AMERICAN BAPTIST PERSPECTIVES ON SPIRIT BAPTISM.................109

1. Introduction 109

2. Textual Evidence Supporting BHS Perspectives.............................109

3. Historic American Baptist Perspectives on BHS.............................150

4. Conclusion...156

CHAPTER 5

SPIRIT BAPTISM DOCTRINAL CONSTRUCTS WITHIN
THE P/C MOVEMENT...158

1. Introduction 158

2. Classical Pentecostalism: Two-Stage Pneumatology Accompanied
by Initial Evidence...158

3. Charismatic Renewal...189

4. The Third Wave...194

5. Conclusion...198

CHAPTER 6

STEMMING THE HERMENEUTICAL DIVIDE: LUKE-ACTS AS
THE DOCTRINAL FOUNDATION FOR SPIRIT BAPTISM 200

1. Introduction 200

2. The Evangelicalization of the Classical Pentecostal Hermeneutic:
Toward a Common Ground for Doctrinal Consensus 201

3. A Dialogical Approach to Lukan Theological Intent 214

4. BHS and the New Spirit-Empowered Eschatological Community 222

5. Conclusion...237

CHAPTER 7

CONCLUSIONS 239

1. Introduction 239

2. Fidelity to the Thesis Aim 239

3. Summary of the Research Findings...240

4. The Significance of the Thesis 243

5. Remaining Questions...243

BIBLIOGRAPHY...245

ENDORSEMENTS

Few doctrinal issues have caused more division among believers than the Baptism in the Holy Spirit. In BEYOND THE EVANGELICAL IMPASSE, Doug Blanc seeks common ground upon which charismatics and non-charismatics can agree. He accomplishes this goal by turning to biblical theology rather than to systematic theology. Blanc bases his study on the Lukan corpus alone and refuses to interpret it through the grid of Pauline or Johannine literature. By eliminating the possibility of playing one NT writer against the other, most disagreements about "the Baptism" dissolve between the two sides, making dialogue possible.

Blanc points out that in Luke-Acts, the Baptism in the Spirit is eschatological in nature, which was uniquely given on the Day of Pentecost to the corporate body of the church for empowerment; yet, still available to individual believers on an ongoing basis so they might live and work for Christ. Upon this all can agree.

Doug Blanc has succeeded in doing what few others have even attempted to do. A SIGNIFICANT STUDY!

–R. Alan STREETT (PhD, University of Wales Trinity Saint David) is Senior Research Professor of Biblical Exegesis and the W. A. Criswell Endowed Chair of Expository Preaching at Criswell College, Dallas, Texas.

This innovative work is the outcome of careful scholarly research successfully undertaken for a doctoral degree. Its goal is to offer a possible way for Pentecostals and Baptists to dialogue with each other, identifying a common basis in personal spiritual experience. It represents a most helpful and readable contribution towards mutual understanding and harmony.

–JENNY READ-HEIMERDINGER (PhD, LicDD), Director of Studies, University of Wales Trinity Saint David, Lampeter, UK.

One does not have to agree with all the details of this book to appreciate its very fine treatment on the doctrine of the Baptism of the Holy Spirit. The research is extensive and the balance in analysis is a model of good scholarship. And, the book is a very enjoyable read. Dr. Blanc hopes to help bridge a divide within the evangelical community and engender respectful conversation and dialogue. His goal is more than met. I am delighted to commend this book to anyone serious about understanding the playing field of this important biblical and theological doctrine.

–DANIEL L. AKEN (PhD, University of Texas at Arlington) is president of Southeastern Baptist Theological Seminary, Wake Forest, North Carolina.

Doug Blanc is concerned about developing unity in contexts of diversity and desirous of establishing unity where disunity is present. Such aims are admirable and Biblical. In pursuit of these aspirations, he has carefully, and courageously, chosen to explore the Baptism of the Holy Spirit in order to determine if there is the possibility of consensus, and certainly dialogue, between groups of believers who initially appear to hold to very different perspectives with regard to this belief. In so doing, he identifies broader areas of belief that are shared by different believers that help to contextualize their views on the Baptism of the Holy Spirit. The process is marked by intellectual integrity, careful research methodology and an authentic and balanced critique throughout. It is scholarly and pastorally sensitive...and, even more importantly, has the potential of facilitating friendship, conversation, and the increasing appreciation of centrally important issues that can bring about relational healing, harmony, and wholeness.

–KEITH WARRINGTON (PhD, King's College, University of London) is Reader in Pentecostal Studies at Regents Theological College, Cheshire, England.

FORWARD

When I was a young pastor I attended a conference. The speaker, Dr. Lee Roberson, pastor of Highland Park Baptist Church, Chattanooga, Tennessee asked the question, "Are you filled with the Holy Spirit right now?" I was fascinated by the thought-provoking question and wondered how a person could really know the answer. I began a personal study on the Holy Spirit. I quickly learned that although it appears to be God's intention that the Holy Spirit unites followers of Christ, there is a vast disagreement that can produce disunity in the body of Christ. I have no doubt that sincere Christians desire to see God the Holy Spirit work in their lives. I know I do. When I heard the question in the conference I wished the book you are about to read was available.

Davis College started in 1900. It is a college dedicated to training men and women to serve the Lord around the world. Davis College has a world class faculty fulfilling that mission. One of those professors is Doug Blanc, Chair of the Intercultural Ministries Concentration. With years of study and research, my esteemed colleague has written a balanced and thought-provoking book. It designs a sense of unity by taking the doctrinal and the practical issues of the work of the Holy Spirit in a scholarly yet very practical way.

Doug is a scholar with two earned and one honorary doctorate and yet he is a very practical visionary with a heartbeat for the world. His heart is to reach people with the gospel of Jesus Christ and he has the time and ability to aid all of us on this unique and timely topic. His approach of bringing a theological construct of consensus between Baptists and Pentecostals in the USA on Spirit Baptism is noble, lofty, and brave. In a thoughtful fashion, he clearly introduces us to the blessed work of the Holy Spirit.

I reviewed in my own library a number of books on the Holy Spirit, and have concluded this book will be right at the top of the list. Thank you, my fellow educator and friend, for helping all of us to attempt to unite around that person of the Godhead, the Holy Spirit, which has always been his desire... *"Endeavoring to keep the unity of the Spirit in the bond of peace"* (Eph 4:3 AV). To the readers...Read, be blessed, and even when we disagree, let's unite together in the great work of God's kingdom through the work of the Holy Spirit.

Dino Pedrone, D. Min.
Chancellor
Davis College
Pottersville, New York

PREFACE

The term Baptism of the Holy Spirit means many things to many evangelical Christians. For some it represents a non-experienced event that coincides with conversion. For others it identifies a second work of grace, a reception of the Holy Spirit resulting in a deeply personal and empowering spiritual experience, one that is marked by evidence and integral to Christian service. A much debated and often polarizing doctrine, BHS is the subject of scores of books and numerous scholarly papers. Until now, no mediating path toward evangelical consensus has been attempted. This study is an effort to find a path toward BHS consensus between two polarized evangelical traditions, namely, American Baptists and Classical Pentecostals. It provides Baptists and other like-minded evangelicals with a rationale for understanding BHS as more than a formalized doctrine. This study offers the reader a foundation for discerning authentic spiritual experience in order to engage in effective missional pursuits. The study also provides Pentecostal and charismatic evangelicals with a fresh perspective on a phenomenon that not only defines, but is also integral to their traditions. However BHS is termed, the phenomenon is a significant resource for every Christian concerned with authentic spiritual experience. Such is the quest of this study.

LIST OF TABLES

Comparison of BHS Conceptions 26

ABBREVIATIONS

ANCIENT TEXTS

Language Versions

LXX .... Septuagint
NT .... New Testament
MT .... Masoretic Text
OT .... Old Testament
Nestle-Aland[27] .... *Novum Testamentum Graece* 27th ed.

Hebrew Bible/Old Testament

Gen .... Genesis
Ex .... Exodus
Lev .... Leviticus
Num .... Numbers
Deut .... Deuteronomy
Josh .... Joshua
Judg .... Judges
Ruth .... Ruth
1–2 Sam .... 1–2 Samuel
1–2 Kgs .... 1–2 Kings
1–2 Chr .... 1–2 Chronicles
Ezra .... Ezra
Neh .... Nehemiah
Esth .... Esther
Job .... Job
Ps/Pss .... Psalms
Prov .... Proverbs
Eccl (or Qoh) .... Ecclesiastes (or Qoheleth)
Song or (Cant) .... Song of Songs (Song of Solomon, or Canticles)
Isa .... Isaiah
Jer .... Jeremiah
Lam .... Lamentations

Ezek .... Ezekiel
Dan .... Daniel
Hos .... Hosea
Joel .... Joel
Amos .... Amos
Obad .... Obadiah
Jonah .... Jonah
Mic .... Micah
Nah .... Nahum
Hab .... Habakkuk
Zeph .... Zephaniah
Hag .... Haggai
Zech .... Zechariah
Mal .... Malachi

New Testament

Matt. .... Matthew
Mark .... Mark
Luke .... Luke
John .... John
Acts .... Acts
Rom .... Romans
1–2 Cor .... 1–2 Corinthians
Gal .... Galatians
Eph .... Ephesians
Phil .... Philippians
Col .... Colossians
1–2 Thess .... 1–2 Thessalonians
1–2 Tim. .... 1–2 Timothy
Titus .... Titus
Phlm .... Philemon
Heb .... Hebrews
Jas .... James
1–2 Pet. .... 1–2 Peter
1–2–3 John .... 1–2–3 John
Jude .... Jude

Rev .... Revelation

Old Testament Pseudepigrapha

Jub. .... *Jubilees*
T. Jud. .... *Testament of Judah*

Dead Sea Scrolls

1QH .... *Hodayot* or *Thanksgiving Hymns*
1QS .... *Serek Hayaḥad* or *Rule of the Community*

Rabbinic Works

Exod Rab .... *Exodus Rabbah*
Deut Rab .... *Deuteronomy Rabbah*

BIBLE TRANSLATIONS

NET .... New English Translation
NIV .... New International Version

JOURNALS, PERIODICALS, AND REFERENCE WORKS

AJPS .... *Asian Journal of Pentecostal Studies*
BECNT .... *Baker Exegetical Commentary on the New Testament*
BFM .... *Baptist Faith and Message*
BHH .... *Baptist History and Heritage*
BSac .... *Bibliotheca Sacra*
CenQ .... *Central Bible Quarterly*
CTR .... *Criswell Theological Review*
DBSJ .... *Detroit Baptist Seminary Journal*
DPCM .... *Dictionary of Pentecostal and Charismatic Movements*
EBC .... *The Expositor's Bible Commentary*
EQ .... *Evangelical Quarterly*
HTR .... *Harvard Theological Review*
IBMR .... *International Bulletin of Missionary Research*
JBL .... *Journal of Biblical Literature*

JEPTA ....*Journal of the European Pentecostal Theological Association*

JETS ....*Journal of the Evangelical Theological Society*

JPS ....*Journal of Pentecostal Studies*

JPT ....*Journal of Pentecostal Theology*

JSNT ....*Journal for the Study of the New Testament*

TMSJ .... *The Master's Seminary Journal*

EBC .... *Expositor's Bible Commentary*

ECNT... *Baker Exegetical Commentary on the New Testament*

EDNT... *Exegetical Dictionary of the New Testament*

EGT .... *Expositor's Greek Testament*

ICC .... *International Critical Commentary*

ISBE .... *International Standard Bible Encyclopedia*

NAC... *New American Commentary*

NIDNTT .... *New International Dictionary of the New Testament Theology*

NIDPCM... *New International Dictionary of Pentecostal and Charismatic Movements*

NIGTC .... *New International Greek Testament Commentary*

NovTest .... *Novum Testamentum*

NTS.. *New Testament Studies*

TDNT.. *Theological Dictionary of the New Testament*

RevExp .... *Review and Expositor*

WBC .... *Word Biblical Commentary*

DENOMINATIONS, SCHOOLS, AND MOVEMENTS

ABC... American Baptist Churches

ACCC .... American Council of Christian Churches

AG .... Assemblies of God

BGC... Baptist General Conference

BWA.. Baptist World Alliance

CBA... Conservative Baptists of America

CCR .... Catholic Charismatic Renewal

CM & A .... Christian Missionary & Alliance

ETS .... Evangelical Theological Society
GARBC .... General Association of Regular Baptist
                                                 Churches
HMB .... Home Mission Board
HSRM .... Holy Spirit Renewal Ministries
IMB .... International Mission Board
NAE .... National Association of Evangelicals
NAMB .... North American Mission Board
NAR .... New Apostolic Reformation
NSC .... National Service Committee
SBC .... Southern Baptist Convention
SBTS .... The Southern Baptist Theological Seminary
SWBTS .... Southwestern Baptist Theological Seminary
ORU .... Oral Roberts University
WCC .... World Council of Churches

INTRODUCTION

This project provides American Baptists[1] with a rationale for engaging with Pentecostal/charismatic (P/C)[2] spirituality to inform a biblically adduced understanding of Christian experience. Under consideration is the biblical metaphor identified as 'Spirit baptism' or 'baptism in the Holy Spirit' (BHS).[3] Though diversely understood in the movement and with varying degrees of emphasis, BHS is elemental to P/C spirituality. Although P/C spirituality is presented broadly in this study, the thesis will concentrate on the classical Pentecostal tradition and its BHS doctrine juxtaposing the American Baptist view.

The nature and function of BHS has enjoyed exhaustive scholarly investigation in response to the advent of Pentecostalism, the charismatic renewal, and the burgeoning Third Wave movement. No works epitomize this focus more than James D. G. Dunn's and Frederick Dale Bruner's 1970 appraisals of the Pentecostal understanding of the BHS doctrine.[4] These initial articulations responded to Pentecostalism's seminal doctrine and in turn have inspired numerous apologetic works by Pentecostal and charismatically-oriented scholars. Such works seek to correct excesses within the movement. At the same time, they mount a biblical defense against polemical works which challenge BHS as the

---

[1] Use of the term 'American Baptists' in this work does not refer to the American Baptist Churches USA denomination, but is a general reference to 'Baptists in America.'

[2] Margaret Poloma is exemplary of scholars using the 'P/C' notation to represent the diverse nature of the Pentecostal/charismatic movement. Margaret M. Poloma, *Main Street Mystics: The Toronto Blessing & Reviving Pentecostalism* (Oxford: AltaMira Press, 2003), 2. Alternatively, the term 'Spirit-filled movement' refers to trans-denominational 'charismatic non-Pentecostals' who exhibit particular spiritual gifts (primarily speaking in tongues). Corwin E. Smidt, Lyman A. Kellstedt, John C. Green, and James L. Guth, 'The Spirit-Filled Movements in Contemporary America: A Survey Perspective,' in Edith Blumhoefer, Russell P. Spittler, and Grant A. Wacker, eds., *Pentecostal Currents in American Protantism* (Chicago: University of Illinois Press, 1999), 112.

[3] The BHS notation accords with βαπτίσει ἐν πνεύματι ἁγίῳ and its similar biblical references (Matt 3:11; Mark 1:8; Luke 3:16; Acts 1:5; 11:16; 1 Cor 12:13a) and is conceptually neutral in this work. Referentially, 'Spirit baptism' or 'baptism in the Spirit' can function as 'concertina' expressions referring to actual acts, rites, or their constituent parts, until the term embraces the whole. See James D. G. Dunn, *Baptism in the Holy Spirit: A Re-examination of the New Testament Teaching on the Gift of the Spirit in Relation to Pentecostalism Today, 2nd ed.* ([original work published 1970] London: SCM Press, 2010), 5.

[4] James D. G. Dunn, *Baptism in the Holy Spirit: A Re-examination of the New Testament Teaching on the Gift of the Spirit in Relation to Pentecostalism Today* (Philadelphia: The Westminster Press, 1970). Frederick Dale Bruner, *A Theology of the Holy Spirit: The Pentecostal Experience and the New Testament Witness* (London: Hodder and Stoughton, 1970).

basis for miraculous *charismata* deemed normative for the contemporary church by Pentecostals and many within the charismatic renewal.

Methodology

This thesis considers an aspect of the BHS debate hitherto unexplored. A thorough review of the relevant literature is conducted throughout the thesis to represent both points of view where appropriate. Rather than engaging the body of scholarly works to further explore the nature and function of BHS, the thesis will present a focused comparison of two opposing traditions for the purpose of achieving doctrinal consensus. Thus, it isolates the spiritual traditions of American Baptists and the most ardent proponent of BHS, the P/C movement. American Baptists and P/C Christians hold polarizing BHS doctrinal constructs. Written from an American Baptist point of view, this thesis investigates reasons for the differing doctrinal assessments of BHS embraced by each tradition in order to adduce the existence of common ground. Intended for the benefit of American Baptists, the thesis acknowledges that the Pentecostal doctrine of 'the baptism in the Spirit' represents the greatest obstacle to inter-tradition dialogue. The thesis functions to point the way forward through textual and theological differences related to 'the baptism in the Spirit' and stipulates that although ultimate doctrinal consensus is unlikely, a path exists by which American Baptists may dialogue with Pentecostals and members of the charismatic renewal in order to inform the experiential core of their tradition. The formation of a rationale for inter-tradition (also described in this work as 'intra-evangelical') dialogue is the unique contribution of this work. The path for the dialogue advanced by the thesis builds on the premise that American Baptists and Pentecostals are encounter-oriented and experience-based spiritual traditions with a common evangelical heritage. It thus emerges that the common ground for dialogue is found to have a wider basis than the specific issue of Spirit baptism. An important outcome of the research is the conclusion that moving towards BHS consensus depends on establishing and acknowledging broader areas of commonality between the traditions. Emerging from this study is a path toward doctrinal consensus, a path that is based on a mutually accepted and qualified redaction-critical hermeneutical approach to Luke-Acts. Since Pentecostal/charismatic BHS constructs emphasize the unique contribution of Lukan pneumatology, Luke-Acts is preferred over the Synoptics since it represents the most advantageous point of dialogical engagement with Pentecostal scholarship by American Baptists.

The thesis is organized into seven chapters. Chapter 1 is foundational in that it establishes American Baptists and the P/C movement as mutually evangelical traditions. Chapters 2 and 3 evaluate the respective experiential loci of American Baptist and P/C spirituality. Together, the first three chapters articulate an American Baptist rationale for moving toward Spirit baptism consensus with the P/C movement. Chapters 4 and 5 present BHS doctrinal constructs relative to American Baptists and the P/C movement. Chapter 6 utilizes the redaction-critical hermeneutic to adduce a BHS construct via a dialogical approach to Luke-Acts. Chapter 7 summarizes the main points of the thesis and addresses their implications.

Significance of the Research

This study contends that as evangelicals, American Baptists and P/C Christians are mutually committed to a personal conversion experience-based spirituality. The role of experience in American Baptist spirituality, though markedly less prominent than among Pentecostals, is none-the-less encounter-oriented and part of the tradition's heritage. This study further contends that American Baptists benefit from doctrinally engaging the P/C movement to inform spiritual experience via a biblically-adduced understanding of BHS. The result is a doctrinal construct which posits BHS as an eschatologically unique and unrepeatable corporate reception of the Spirit by the body of Christ on the Day of Pentecost, one that provides ongoing evidential charismatic equipping for Christian life and ministry. The significance of this once and for all completed corporate event to American Baptists is its relevance to personal encounter-oriented spiritual experience. Though a definitive text-based Spirit baptism inter-tradition consensus remains elusive, the path toward the target reveals a mutual appreciation for experiential encounters with God as its common ground.

Precedence for this unique approach to inter-tradition American Baptist and Pentecostal dialogue is established by the ongoing Roman Catholic and classical Pentecostal dialogue attempted in recent decades.[5] Desire for mutual understanding and acceptance has led to active collaboration between Pentecostals and Roman Catholics in worship and evangelism, initiated notably by Cecil Robeck, a minister with the US Assemblies of God (AOG)

---

[5] Full text reports of the dialogues which began in 1969 and 1970 with a series of talks are available online. See Centro Pro Unione, 2012. 'Pentecostal-Roman Catholic Dialogue,' n.p. Available from: http://www.prounione.urbe.it/dia-int/pe-rc/e_pe-rc-info.html. [Accessed 20 April 2012]. For a helpful bibliographic reference, including numerous cited works by Cecil M. Robeck, see European Pentecostal Charismatic Research Association Conference, 2009. 'Cracked or Broken: Pentecostal Unity' by Keith Warrington, 1-22. Available online from: http://www.epcra.ch/papers_pdf/ oxford/keith_warrington.pdf. [Accessed 28 June 2013].

denomination.[6] According to Robeck, improving interecclesial relations involves an ongoing collaborative effort that he essentially describes as 'snapshots along the process of discovery.'[7] The present thesis is similar in that its approach does not achieve 'common consensus,'[8] but rather offers a path toward consensus.

The following research is important for several reasons:

1) A case for convergence, if not actual consensus, is made from identifying critical points of commonality between the traditions (e.g. evangelicalism and personal conversion-based spiritual experience).

2) American Baptist models for intra-denominational consensus are evaluated for transferability to the broader P/C Spirit baptism debate.

3) American Baptist Spirit baptism constructs are catalogued and articulated to identify the potential for consensus and the nature of the existing impasse.

4) A dialogical method is used to move American Baptists toward finding common ground for discussion with Pentecostals about BHS.

5) The path which opens up the way toward a consensus on Spirit baptism as presented in this study allows American Baptists not only to cooperate more fully with Pentecostal Christians, but also with members of the charismatic renewal within their own tradition.

6) The thesis contributes to the existing Spirit baptism scholarly debate by demonstrating the plausibility of devising a path leading toward achieving a consensus view between two opposing theological traditions.

7) The thesis acknowledges that additional work is needed to assess the impact of this study on the cessationist-noncessationist debate.

8) The thesis further concedes that exploring the nature and function of the specific topic of the 'Spirit of prophecy' is beyond the scope of this study.

---

[6] See Fuller Theological Seminary, 2008. 'Cecil M. Robeck, Jr.,' n.p. Available from: http://www.fuller.edu/academics/faculty/cecil-robeck.aspx. [Accessed 1 August, 2013].

[7] Jelle Creemers, 'The Intertwined Problems of Representation and Reception in Pentecostal Ecumenical Involvement: A Case Study,' in *One in Christ* (2011), 14.

[8] Ibid.

-1-

DEFINING THE COMMON HERITAGE

1. Introduction

The purpose of this chapter is to examine the spiritual traditions of American Baptists and adherents of the P/C movement and, in particular, to situate them within the larger tradition of evangelicalism. Linking the two traditions to the more inclusive and comprehensive movement will demonstrate that Baptists in America[1] and the P/C movement are diverse spiritual traditions[2] with polarizing views on certain matters. Among these views is the role of BHS in relation to spiritual experience, which will be examined in detail with respect to the two groups in chapters 2 and 3. Meanwhile, it will be found in this chapter that the issue of BHS may be classed as nonessential to the shared tenets of evangelical belief and praxis. That is true even though the disagreement is often perceived as a fundamental reason for the division between the two groups. Furthermore, it is important to note that many P/C adherents (notably classical Pentecostals and renewalists) who consider BHS to be a definite post-conversion event, also consider it to be 'essential' (foundational) for authentic spiritual experience. It is not common among evangelicals to refer to BHS as 'essential' to the definitional

---

[1] Lydia Huffman Hoyle, 'Baptist Americanus,' in W. Glenn Jonas, Jr., ed., *The Baptist River: Essays on Many Tributaries of a Diverse Tradition* (Macon: Mercer University Press, 2006), 269. Hoyle cites Barrett (2001) who totals 322 Baptist denominations globally. David B. Barrett, George T. Kurian, and Todd M. Johnson, 'World Summary,' in David B. Barrett, George T. Kurian, and Todd M. Johnson, eds., *World Christian Encyclopedia: A Contemporary Survey of Churches and Religions in the Modern World, 2nd ed., Vol. 1* (New York, Oxford Press, 2001), 741-50. Hoyle estimates Baptist denominations in the USA at 60, but identifies their status as 'in flux.'

[2] D. A. Carson, *Showing the Spirit: A Theological Exposition of 1 Corinthians 12-14* ([original work published 1987] Grand Rapids: Baker Books, 2003), 11. Land estimates 11,000 Pentecostal denominations and 3,000 independent charismatic denominations comprising (1997) 21% of global Christianity. Stephen L. Land, *Pentecostal Spirituality: A Passion for the Kingdom* ([original work published 1997] Sheffield: Sheffield Academic Press, 2001), 21.

criteria and core beliefs of evangelicalism. There are significant areas of agreement between American Baptists and P/C adherents concerning the core tenets of evangelical belief and praxis. This agreement provides the biblical and theological rationale for American Baptists to exegetically engage P/C adherents on matters nonessential to orthodoxy and to move toward doctrinal consensus.

As a corollary, the NT concept of κοινωνία ('fellowship,' 'association,' 'close relationship,' 'communion,' 'participation' and 'sharing'),[3] when understood in relation to the 'body of Christ' metaphor,[4] provides a biblical impetus for American Baptists to seek doctrinal consensus with the P/C movement.[5] It will be demonstrated that the ground on which this consensus can be explored is spiritual in nature. American Baptists and P/C adherents all belong to historically experienced-based traditions. Given that spiritual experience is foundational to American Baptist spirituality, the significance of an experienced BHS to many adherents within the P/C movement represents a legitimate point of common interest.[6]

---

[3] Walter Bauer, William F. Arndt, F. Wilbur Gingrich, and Frederick W. Danker, *A Greek-English Lexicon of the New Testament and Other Early Christian Literature,* 2nd ed. (Chicago: The University of Chicago Press, 1979), 438-39.

[4] Acts 2:42; 1 Cor 10:16-17; Phil 2:1; 1 John 1:7.

[5] To merely affirm that a mystical union exists within the body of Christ without also affirming that each constituent part makes a substantive contribution to the function and well-being of the whole, is to deny the essential teaching of the metaphor. A dynamic relationship exists among members of the body of Christ (Rom 12:5; 1 Cor 12:12, 27; Eph 2:16; 4:4, 16; Col 3:15).

[6] While an abundance of BHS literature has been produced by P/C scholars, the impetus behind the modern BHS debate is attributed to James D. G. Dunn and his seminal work, *Baptism in the Holy Spirit: A Re-examination of the New Testament Teaching on the Gift of the Spirit in Relation to Pentecostalism Today,* 2nd ed. ([original work published 1970] London: SCM Press, 2010). Other BHS works by Dunn include, 'Spirit-and-Fire Baptism,' in *NovTest* (1972), 81-92; 'Baptism in the Spirit: A Response to Pentecostal Scholarship on Luke-Acts,' in *JPT* (1993), 3-27; 'Baptism in the Holy Spirit...Yet Once More,' in *JEPTA* (1998), 3-25; 'Baptism in the Holy Spirit: Yet Once More...Again,' in *JPT* (2010), 23-43. The following works are exemplary of the attention to Dunn given by the Pentecostal scholarly community. Though now conceding much of Dunn's thesis (see Max Turner, 'James Dunn's *Baptism in the Holy Spirit*: Appreciation and Response,' in *JPT* (2010), 25-31) Max Turner was the first to offer a Pentecostal response to Dunn in, 'Luke and the Spirit: Studies in the Significance of Receiving the Spirit in Luke-Acts' (PhD diss., University of Cambridge, 1980). Howard Ervin engaged Dunn in *Conversion-Initiation and the Baptism in the Holy Spirit: An Engaging Critique of James D. G. Dunn's Baptism in the Holy Spirit* (Peabody: Hendrickson Publishers, 1984). David Petts critiqued Dunn in 'The Baptism in the Holy Spirit in Relation to Christian Initiation' (MA thesis, University of Nottingham, 1987). James B. Shelton interacted with Dunn in 'A Reply to James D. G. Dunn's *Baptism in the Spirit: A Response to Pentecostal Scholarship on Luke-Acts*,' in *JPT* (1994), 139-43. William Atkinson critiqued Dunn in 'Pentecostal Responses to Dunn's *Baptism in the Holy* Spirit: Pauline Literature,' in *JPT* (1995), 49-72; 'Pentecostal Responses to Dunn's *Baptism in the Holy Spirit*: Luke-Acts,' in *JPT* (1995), 87-131; *Baptism in the Spirit: Luke-Acts and the Dunn Debate* (Eugene: Pickwick Publications, 2011).

2. Evangelicals and Evangelicalism: The Search for an Identity-Based Consensus

This section demonstrates the evangelical common ground shared by American Baptists and adherents of the P/C movement. Both traditions embrace the same elemental doctrines crucial to Christian orthodoxy and each affirms identifying beliefs and praxis that uniquely characterize expressions of their faith.[7] The terms 'evangelical' and 'evangelicalism' are defined herein according to their theological, historical, and contemporary senses of meaning. The defining features of evangelicalism will demonstrate a meaningful degree of consensus concerning what American Baptist and P/C consider to be essential beliefs and praxis. It will emerge from this study that while not an essentially shared doctrine within the evangelical communion, agreement on essential core beliefs can provide a rationale for American Baptists to exegetically engage the P/C movement with regard to BHS. It is stipulated that many Pentecostals holding to a fourfold or fivefold creedal typology consider BHS to be an essential and primary doctrine. However, it is the contention of this thesis that this need not impede the path for American Baptists seeking to understand the P/C position and thereby move toward doctrinal consensus. In other words, a domain of essential doctrines exists for a common exploration of the issue.[8] Just as the quest undertaken by Catholics and Pentecostals is discovering new areas of agreement previously unrecognized,[9] it is expected that harmonious dialogue between American Baptists and P/C adherents will uncover fresh ground on which there is significant convergence if not total consensus.

Roger Stronstad commented on Dunn in, 'Forty Years On: An Appreciation and Assessment of *Baptism in the Holy Spirit* by James D. G. Dunn,' in *JPT* (2010), 3-11.

[7] Christian Smith, *American Evangelicalism: Embattled and Thriving* (Chicago: University of Chicago Press, 1998), 14.

[8] Donald W. Dayton, *The Theological Roots of Pentecostalism* ([original work published 1987] Peabody: Hendrickson Publishers, 2000), 19-21.

[9] A notable example concerns the citation of Patristic writings by classical Pentecostals to support the normative character of the NT church. This methodological shift for classical Pentecostals is mentioned with approval in the Final Report of the fifth Pentecostal-Roman Catholic dialogue phase. See Creemers, 'The Intertwined Problems of Representation and Reception in Pentecostal Ecumenical Involvement: A Case Study,' 14.

2.1   Definitional Challenges

2.1.1   The Traditional Understanding of 'Evangelical'

Historically, the terms 'evangelical' and 'evangelicalism' apply to active protest movements within Christianity during three eras (16th century Reformation, 17th-19th century Pietism, and 20th century Fundamentalism).[10] In the present day, the terms 'evangelical' and 'evangelicalism'[11] represent a broad semantic range of meaning.[12] This range of meaning does not permit the univocal use of the terms to describe a plurality of Christian traditions.[13] This study uses the terms in their broadest sense of meaning. Etymologically, 'evangelical' is derived from the Greek noun εὐαγγέλιον (verb, εὐαγγελίζομαι) referring to the message of 'good news' announced by the early disciples.[14] The term implies missionary emphasis and the act of proclaiming 'the good news of salvation.' An 'evangelical' is a Christian whose identity adheres to the 'gospel message.'[15] A movement of evangelical Christians committed to 'the good news of Jesus Christ' is properly referred to as 'evangelicalism.'[16] The most enduring description of

---

[10] Robert K. Johnson, 'Evangelicalism,' in Adrian Hastings, Alistair Mason, and Hugh S. Pyper, eds., *The Oxford Companion to Christian Thought* (Oxford: Oxford University Press, 2000), 219.

[11] Marsden identifies fourteen 'evangelicalisms.' See George M. Marsden, *Understanding Fundamentalism and Evangelicalism* (Grand Rapids: William B. Eerdmans Publishing, 1991), 110.

[12] Roger E. Olson, *The Westminster Handbook to Evangelical Theology* (Louisville: Westminster John Knox Press, 2004), 6; Mark A. Noll, *The Rise of Evangelicalism: The Age of Edwards, Whitefield and the Wesleys* (Downers Grove: InterVarsity Press, 2003), 15-21.

[13] Olson, *The Westminster Handbook to Evangelical Theology*, 6.

[14] The noun εὐαγγέλιον (Mark 1:1; Rom 1:16) and the verb εὐαγγελίζομαι (Luke 4:18) occur 76 times and 54 times respectively in the NT. The English derivation comes through the Latin *evangelium*. See R. V. Pierard, 'Evangelicalism,' in Walter A. Elwell, ed., *Evangelical Dictionary of Theology* (Grand Rapids: Baker Book House, 1984), 382-84.

[15] Donald G. Bloesch, *Essentials of Evangelical Theology: God, Authority, & Salvation, Vol. 1* (New York: Harper & Row, 1978), 7.

[16] Garrett refers to Evangelicals as an association of 'gospel people.' See James Leo Garrett, Jr., 'Who are the Evangelicals?,' in James L. Garrett, Jr., E. Glenn Hinson, and James E. Tull, eds., *Are Southern Baptists Evangelicals?* (Macon: Mercer University Press, 1983), 34.

evangelicalism is the four-fold typology (or 'quadrilateral')[17] offered by Bebbington and adopted by this study:[18]

1) *conversionism*, the belief that lives need to be changed;

2) *activism*, the expression of the gospel in effort;

3) *biblicism*, a particular regard for the Bible, and

4) *crucicentrism*, a stress on the sacrifice of Christ on the cross.[19]

Using the terms 'evangelical' and 'evangelicalism' with this sense of meaning distinguishes evangelical and non-evangelical traditions according to the essential features of authentic Christianity.[20]

Another important nuance of evangelical identity concerns what is deemed essential to Christian orthodoxy, while allowing for nonessential tradition-specific convictions. A current practice among churches affiliated with the Southern Baptist Convention (SBC) is to modify the term 'evangelicals' with the additional descriptive term 'denominational.'[21] Labeling SBC churches in this manner differentiates them denominationally from broader association with evangelicals 'outside their class' (classification). This narrowing of evangelical association avoids the brand of ecumenism. This results in increased scrutiny of other evangelicals outside the SBC 'denominational' structure, referring at times to the 'questionable associations' represented by the more inclusive 'movement

---

[17] A series of essays presented at the 2005 annual meeting of the *Evangelical Theological Society* (Valley Gorge, PA) and subsequently published as a response to Bebbington's seminal work is a testament to the enduring nature of his thesis. Michael A. G. Haykin and Kenneth J. Stewart, 'Preface,' in Michael A. G. Haykin and Kenneth J. Stewart, eds., *The Advent of Evangelicalism: Exploring Historical Continuities* (Nashville: B & H Academic, 2008), 18.

[18] Compare Bebbington with the 'great evangelical principles' articulated by the 1846 Evangelical Alliance, offering no less than nine affirmations. Garrett, 'Who are the Evangelicals?,' 40-41.

[19] D. W. Bebbington, *Evangelicalism in Modern Britain: A History from the 1730s to the 1980s* (London: Routledge, 2005), 2-3. Brian Harris emphasizes the adaptability of evangelicalism and characterizes the movement as a 'community of passionate piety.' Brian Harris, 'Beyond Bebbington: The Quest for Evangelical Identity,' in *Churchman* (2008), 201-219.

[20] Bloesch effectively identifies areas of discontinuity between evangelicalism, Catholicism, and liberalism. See Bloesch, *Essentials of Evangelical Theology*, 9-15.

[21] Garrett defines the SBC as 'denominational evangelicals' in the sense that 'they belong to and exemplify the great heritage of Scriptural authority, Christocentric doctrine, gospel proclamation, experience of grace, and evangelistic endeavor which is evangelicalism.' Garrett, 'Are Southern Baptists Evangelicals?,' 126.

evangelicalism.'[22] The 'denominational' versus 'movement' dichotomy is not helpful to attaining broader evangelical dialogue, because it seeks to justify the practice of partitioning evangelicals on the basis of what is generally considered to be secondary or nonessential doctrines or praxis. The term 'evangelical' is better represented etymologically by the post-Reformation Protestant emphasis on personally appropriating the redeeming work of Christ and propagating the message of 'good news.'[23] Specifically, 'evangelical' is often used as a reference to a personal conversion experience expressed in terms of 'a life-changing encounter with Jesus Christ' which is viewed as the necessary condition for spiritual salvation.[24] Following what Bebbington notes as a focus on the importance of the Bible, others modify 'evangelical' to include 'a high view of Scripture, its divine inspiration, and therefore its infallibility and its authority.'[25] Such modifications, however, exceed the etymological limits of the term and narrow its application to a particular theological perspective within evangelicalism as seen above in the 'denominational' versus 'movement' dichotomy.

The *sine qua non* of evangelicalism is the desire to recapture the original impulses of Christianity as represented in the NT (the apostolic Christian movement), the early documents of the church, and the critical Reformation ideals, as summed up in the criteria identified by Bebbington and listed above.[26] Evangelical passion for authentic Christianity can be described as a reaction to the perceived 'dead orthodoxy' in churches characterized by correctly confessed doctrine without the accompanying transformative power of God. Luther's 'evangelical experience' is self-described as a personal encounter with God.[27] On this basis, he and other Reformers opposing the Roman Catholic Church became

---

[22] Nathan A. Finn, 'Southern Baptists and Evangelicals: Passing on the Faith to the Next Generation,' in David S. Dockery, ed. with Ray Van Neste and Jerry Tidwell, *Southern Baptists, Evangelicals, and the Future of Denominationalism* (Nashville: B & H Academic, 2011), 240.

[23] Mark Noll, 'What is an Evangelical?,' in Gerald R. McDermott, ed., *The Oxford Handbook of Evangelical Theology* (Oxford: Oxford University Press, 2010), 21.

[24] Nancy Tatom Ammerman, *Baptist Battles: Social Change and Religious Conflict in the Southern Baptist Convention* (London: Rutgers University Press, 1990), 16.

[25] David Pawson, *The Fourth Wave: Charismatics and Evangelicals, are we Ready to Come Together?* (London: Hodder & Stoughton, 1993), 44.

[26] Roger E. Olson, 'Confessions of a Post-Pentecostal Believer in the Charismatic Gifts,' in *CTR* (2006), 31-40.

[27] Roland H. Bainton, *Here I Stand: A Life of Martin Luther* (New York: Meridian, 1955), 45-50.

known as 'evangelicals.'[28] Evangelicals are historically sympathetic to periods of revival which they understand in encounter-oriented terms as God prevailing upon the intellect and stirring the affections into life-changing commitments to Jesus Christ.[29] The role of the Holy Spirit is commonly acknowledged and praised by those who attribute times of revival to divine intervention. Indeed, it may be said that as a set of defining beliefs and practices, evangelicalism emerged from a 'common original commitment to revival and from the strength of shared convictions.'[30]

2.1.2   Contemporary Understanding: Evangelicalism Redivivus

The Pew Forum on Religion & Public Life conducted the 'U.S. Religious Landscape Survey' involving more than 35,000 adults between 8 May and 13 August 2007. Results of the survey indicated that 26.3% of adults in the USA belong to evangelical Protestant churches.[31] Respondents to the survey represented a diverse evangelical affiliation which encompassed sixteen statistical categories consisting of mainline denominations and nondenominational churches.[32] Baptist, Nondenominational, and Pentecostal Christians represent an additional twenty-five subcategories.[33] This aggregation of evangelicals indicates that a degree of unity exists among a diverse group of members. The survey attributes evangelical unity to agreement on essential beliefs and conversely

---

[28] Collin Hansen, 'Introduction,' in David Nasellli and Collin Hansen, eds., *Four Views on the Spectrum of Evangelicalism* (Grand Rapids: Zondervan, 2011), 13.

[29] Olson, *The Westminster Handbook to Evangelical Theology*, 7-8.

[30] Noll, *The Rise of Evangelicalism*, 21.

[31] The Pew Forum on Religion & Public Life, 2010. 'U.S. Religious Landscape Survey,' n.p. Available from: http://religions.pewforum.org/affiliations. [Accessed 5 July 2011].

[32] The following categories are represented in the survey order as Protestant churches of evangelical tradition: Baptist, Methodist, Nondenominational, Lutheran, Presbyterian, Pentecostal, Anglican/Episcopal, Restorationist, Congregationalist, Holiness, Reformed, Adventist, Anabaptist, and Pietist. The survey also includes as evangelical tradition: Other, Evangelical/Fundamentalist, and Protestant nonspecific. See The Pew Forum on Religion & Public Life, 2010. 'U.S. Religious Landscape Survey,' n.p. Available from: http://religions.pewforum.org/affiliations. [Accessed 5 July 2011].

[33] The Religious Landscape Survey provides data on 'Mainline Protestant Churches.' Potential for greater diversity occurs when overlapping between 'evangelical' and 'mainline' categories is taken into account. For example, American Baptist Churches USA are listed as 'mainline' and not 'evangelical' (The Pew Forum on Religion & Public Life, 2010. 'U.S. Religious Landscape Survey,' n.p. Available from: http://religions.pewforum.org/affiliations. [Accessed 5 July 2011]).

regards ecumenism as a divisive force within the movement.[34] The divisive nature of ecumenism is evident by concessions which leave evangelicals doubting the authenticity of other Christians in the movement.[35] The suspicion is based on the perceived lack of 'experienced faith' as the necessary corollary to stated core beliefs. Evangelicals consider such evidence among non-evangelicals to be obscured by church dogma, intricately performed rituals, and appeals to religious experience which cannot be corroborated with Scripture.[36]

There is, in reality, some division among evangelicals concerning the importance of experience in the life of a Christian. This factor tends to be obscured by the focus of evangelical statements on assent to a set of beliefs. Typical is the list of descriptive criteria set out in the updated edition of *Operation World: The Definitive Prayer Guide to Every Nation (7th edition 2010)*[37], and based on the earlier definition of Bebbington:

> (1) Jesus Christ as the exclusive source and means of salvation; (2) The exercise of personal faith with conversion as the regenerating work of the Holy Spirit; (3) The Word of God as inspired and the final authority for Christian living; and (4) A commitment to a biblical witness that brings others to faith in Christ.[38]

The above description defines 'evangelical' theologically, not experientially. However, there is a real distinction between evangelicals who 'confess' a given set of doctrinal affirmations and those who 'profess' the same from personal experience. The latter, having experienced a transformational encounter with God

---

[34] The Religious Landscape Survey queries respondents according to the following topics: (1) Belief in God or Universal Spirit; (2) Importance of Religion in One's Life; (3) Frequency of Attendance at Religious Services; (4) Frequency of Prayer; (5) Frequency of Receiving Answers to Prayer; (6) Literal Interpretation of Scripture; (7) Interpretation of Religious Teachings; and (8) Views of One's Religion as the One Faith. Concerning the final topic, only 36% of the respondents identified as 'evangelical Protestant' hold to their religion as 'the one, true faith leading to eternal life.' Fully 57% of respondents believe that 'many religions can lead to eternal life.' While this does not square with orthodox evangelical doctrine, it strongly indicates a discontinuity between how 'evangelicals' are popularly perceived and the true nature of their personal identity. Also indicated are a much smaller percentage of 'born again' evangelicals (or 'those who profess a personal conversion experience') within 'evangelicalism.' This phenomenon results in an equivocation of the term 'evangelical' as traditionally defined in terms of the new birth. See The Pew Forum on Religion & Public Life, 2010. 'U.S. Religious Landscape Survey,' n.p. Available from: http://religions. pewforum .org/affiliations. [Accessed 5 July 2011].

[35] Erickson, *Christian Theology*, 1143.

[36] Bloesch, *Essentials of Evangelical Theology*, 15-17.

[37] Jason Mandryk, *Operation World: The Definitive Prayer Guide to Every Nation, 7th ed.* (Colorado Springs: Biblica Publishing, 2010).

[38] Ibid., 959.

(variously referred to as a 'born again' or 'conversion' experience'), represent only 10-40 percent of evangelicalism.[39] American Baptists and P/C adherents fall into this 10-40 percent evangelical subgroup. The result is a narrow application of the term 'evangelical' by American Baptists and P/C adherents who are keen to differentiate between their 'born again' movements and other 'non-conversional' evangelical groups. This qualification of core beliefs within evangelicalism, shared by American Baptists and P/C adherents, further demonstrates that the common value accorded to spiritual experience is a significant factor in furnishing appropriate grounds for effective doctrinal engagement.

2.2   *Methodology: Centered Set vs. Bounded Set Evangelicalism*

This study acknowledges the shared evangelical 'essentials' presented above as the locus of American Baptist and P/C engagement. It considers other elements of traditional Christian faith to be valid topics for intra-evangelical dialogue toward consensus. This approach to intra-evangelical dialogue is reflected in the Augustinian dictum adopted by the Baptist General Conference (Arlington Heights, IL),[40] 'in essentials unity, in nonessentials liberty, in everything charity.'[41] The task envisaged by this project is to extend the American Baptist-P/C dialogue beyond the core essentials to include BHS as a secondary (evangelical) doctrinal issue. Since the American Baptist and P/C movements are both conversion experience-based traditions, it remains for this study to establish biblically the P/C relevance of BHS to the experience of American Baptists. The assertion of a valid personal conversion experience, contra mere intellectual assent, forms the locus of a 'centered set' versus 'bounded set' (Hiebert) understanding of evangelicalism as a dynamic movement.[42]

As evangelicals, both American Baptists and P/C adherents have a common and shared belief in the existence of the Holy Spirit as part of the triune God. Both traditions are committed to the Holy Spirit's continued work in the life of the believer following conversion experience. Though these beliefs are shared by both

---

[39] Ibid.

[40] The BGC is now 'Converge Worldwide.'

[41] Bethel Seminary, 2010. 'The Baptist Pietist Clarion,' n.p. Available from: http://www. bethel.edu/cas/dept/history/Baptist_Pietist_Clarion_Issues/BPC_May_2011.pdf. [Accessed 26 December 2011].

[42] Paul G. Hiebert, 'Conversion, Culture and Cognitive Categories,' in *Gospel in Context* (1978), 24-29.

traditions, American Baptists remain wary of charismatic phenomena attributed to the Spirit's working by Pentecostals and many renewalists.

As a movement, evangelicalism is not organizational in structure, is without boundaries, and therefore does not have a definitive membership.[43] Conceived as a 'bounded set,' evangelicalism is reduced to a delimited set of beliefs (orthodoxy) and practices (orthopraxy) which distinguish a Christian from a non-Christian. Taking this view, however, is problematic due to the uncertain nature of the type and number of elements needed to be considered Christian. It is possible to construct a continuum ranging from simple to complex identifying criteria. By contrast, 'centered set' evangelicalism locates an essential center and determines 'the relationship of [non-essential] things to that center.'[44] The diffused parts of the movement, the non-essentials, are oriented in motion toward the center (the shared essentials). In other words, evangelicalism as a 'centered set' does not reduce 'to a single uniformity within the category.'[45] This is illustrated when the concept 'Christian' is considered in terms of the 'centered set' model. Christ is the determined center which includes anyone, regardless of distance (i.e. those who know much or little), to whom Christ is 'the center around which their life revolves' (e.g. 'they have made Christ their Lord').[46] This 'centered set' terminology attempts to portray the dynamic nature of evangelicalism by taking into account 'the turnaround' of those moving away from the center (non-Christian) and the post-conversion growth of those moving toward the center. The strength of the model is to reduce evangelical essentials to a core toward which nonessentials are oriented. Nonessentials are significant to the authentic Christian life as their purported spiritual experience offers the potential for enhancing life at the center. American Baptists, therefore, have a rational for considering relevant P/C BHS doctrinal formations in motion toward the evangelical center (i.e. the authentic Christian life is expressed in the spiritual experience of the believer).

Alternatively, 'bounded set' evangelicals represented, for example, by fundamentalists,[47] separate from others in the movement on the basis of tradition-

---

[43] Roger E. Olson, 'Postconservative Evangelicalism,' in David Nasellli and Collin Hansen, eds., *Four Views on the Spectrum of Evangelicalism* (Grand Rapids: Zondervan, 2011), 163.

[44] Hiebert, 'Conversion, Culture and Cognitive Categories,' 27-28.

[45] Ibid.

[46] Ibid.

[47] Understood relative to evangelical Christianity, the term 'fundamentalism' refers to a 'subgroup within evangelicalism that accepts biblical authority, salvation through Christ, and a commitment to spreading the faith.' Lyman A. Kellstedt and Corwin L. Smidt, 'Measuring

specific doctrinal nonessentials.[48] This separation-oriented thinking occurs when evangelicals focus on secondary issues and equate the derivatives of dogma with the dogma itself.[49] Applied to 'centered set' evangelicalism, 'the dogma' is personal conversion experience (the center) and it is this that serves as the basis for intra-evangelical dialogue. The 'derivatives of the dogma' are issues open to intra-evangelical dialogue (the non-uniform elements within the set). BHS is among the non-uniform elements within this set for American Baptists in dialogue with P/C adherents. From the point of view of the American Baptists, it can be said that BHS is an inference derived from the central core and as such represents an occasion for both traditions to coalesce around 'gospel proclamation and gospel living.'[50] It is when 'bounded set' evangelicalism, manifesting itself as exclusivist fundamentalism, is adopted as a position within the American Baptist movement, that meaningful 'centered set' P/C dialogue is compromised by an intractable commitment to a growing set of essentials.

Within the recent history of the evangelical movement, particularly with reference to the American Baptists, there is a clear intent to move away from rigid fundamentalism to acceptance and dialogue with other movements. This has been witnessed in the rise of the 'neo-evangelicals' under the leadership of Carl F. H. Henry and Harold John Ockenga. Neo-evangelicals have emphasized the need for reestablishing contact with the world beyond the evangelical church, including engagement with secular society.[51] This openness to communicate with those outside the confines of the immediate circle counters the adverse effects of fundamentalist separatism. The movement gives further impetus for American

---

Fundamentalism: An Analysis of Different Operational Strategies,' in *JSSR* (1991), 259-78. Expressed discursively, the term refers to those who possess (1) an orientation toward biblical literalism, (2) the experience of being reborn in faith, (3) 'evangelicalism' (the obligation to convert others), and (4) an apocalypticism in its specifically end time form. Charles B. Strozier, *Apocalypse: On the Psychology of Fundamentalism in America* (Boston: Beacon Press, 1994), 5.

[48] Olson, 'Postconservative Evangelicalism,' 161-62.

[49] Bloesch refers to demarcating on the basis of secondary issues and nonessentials, 'the bane of latter day evangelicalism.' See Bloesch, *Essentials of Evangelical Theology*, 20.

[50] Hansen, 'Introduction,' 10.

[51] Carl F. H. Henry, *The Uneasy Conscience of Modern Fundamentalism* (Grand Rapids: William B. Eerdmans Publishing, 1947). See George M. Marsden, *Fundamentalism and American Culture: The Shaping of Twentieth-Century Evangelicalism, 1870-1925* (London: Oxford University Press, 1980), xiv. See also, Harold Lindsell, *The Battle for the Bible: The Book that Rocked the Evangelical World* (Grand Rapids: Zondervan Publishing, 1976), 8.

Baptists to dialogue concerning BHS in order to inform Christian experience by a biblically adduced perspective.[52]

2.3 Summary

Evangelicalism is a historical movement rooted in the theological renewal of NT Christianity.[53] American Baptists and P/C adherents exist as evangelical subgroups joined at the center by a commitment to personal conversional experience and the proclamation of the good news. American Baptists and P/C adherents mutually desire to embody and to promote authentic Christianity. Use of the term 'authentic' to qualify Christian experience is for some within the American Baptist movement an equation with a 'bounded set' fundamentalist orientation to evangelicalism. This theme is developed in Chapter 3 which contains a discussion on American Baptists and the charismatic renewal. The resultant deviation from the inclusive nature of evangelicalism represents a methodological impasse for American Baptist intra-evangelical dialogue. When understood within the framework of 'centered set' evangelicalism, the BHS metaphor articulated by P/C adherents is a nonessential doctrine consistent with and in motion toward the core element of personal conversion experience. BHS is therefore relevant to the interests of American Baptists seeking to articulate biblically an authentic Christian experience. American Baptists can appreciate the historic and enduring commitment of Pentecostalism to its biblical basis[54] and emphasis on a living faith.[55] Early evidence of acceptance of the Pentecostal

---

[52] According to Ellingsen, neo-evangelicals desire to present the fundamentals of the faith to their own denominations, capitulating to liberalism in a positive and not merely defensive way. For Ellingsen, this paves the way for 'the emergence of evangelicalism out of its original fundamentalist heritage' See Mark Ellingsen, *The Evangelical Movement: Growth, Impact, Controversy, Dialogue* (Minneapolis: Augsburg Press, 1988), 99.

[53] According to Hansen, 'evangelicals have [historically] called moribund ministers to theological renewal and called on God to send revival by the power of the Holy Spirit' (Hansen, 'Introduction,' 10).

[54] Spittler writes: 'For evangelicalized Pentecostals, the Bible ranks as the sole and final authority for belief and practice.' Spittler, 'Corinthian Spirituality,' 16. In his discussion on the role of the Bible in Pentecostalism, Massey interprets the evidence as pointing to 'the central position of the Bible in all aspects of Pentecostal belief and practice.' Richard D. Massey, 'The Word of God: Thus Saith the Lord' in Keith Warrington, ed., *Pentecostal Perspectives* (Carlisle: Paternoster Press, 1998), 64-79.

[55] Pentecostalism offers a 'theology of the dynamic, seen through the lens of experience. It is a functional theology that exists to operate in life and to incorporate an experiential dimension...it insists on exploring [beliefs] in the context of praxis.' Warrington, *Pentecostal Theology*, 16.

position is seen in the scholarly writings of an American Baptist apologist who embraced the same evangelical ethos.[56]

3. Defining the Terms of the BHS Metaphor

A detailed analysis of BHS positions held by American Baptist and P/C adherents[57] is investigated in Chapters 4 and 5 of this study. This present section provides semantic clarification for the BHS metaphor used by American Baptists and members of the P/C movement.[58] While American Baptists possess a more univocal conception of BHS than do P/C adherents, both traditions identify the metaphor in terms of a personal 'event' or 'experience' for the Christian. Common expressions for BHS appear as part of the theological discourse and include: 'Spirit baptism,' 'the baptism of the Spirit,' or 'the baptism in/with/by the Spirit.' The following succinct analysis concretizes the commonly held BHS conceptions of American Baptists and the P/C movement.

3.1   The P/C Movement and the Pentecostal Experience

The noun phrase, 'baptism in the Spirit,' or the noun, 'Spirit baptism,' is an often-used referent for the NT occurrences of the BHS metaphor. In point of fact, neither the noun phrase, nor the noun appear in the NT.[59] The NT grammatical construction common to the seven NT references to BHS express the metaphor in terms of the verb βαπτίζω ('I baptize') with the prepositional phrase ἐν πνεύματι ἁγίῳ ('in [with/by] the Holy Spirit').[60] The verbal phrase appears in the active voice and present tense, 'baptizes in Holy Spirit' (John 1:33); the active voice and

---

[56] As an ABCUSA minister, Ervin was first to engage Dunn, defending the two-stage pneumatology of classical Pentecostalism. See Howard M. Ervin, *Conversion-Initiation and the Baptism in the Holy Spirit: An Engaging Critique of James D. G. Dunn's Baptism in the Holy Spirit* (Peabody: Hendrickson Publishers, 1984), vii-viii. See also, Howard M. Ervin, *Spirit Baptism: A Biblical Investigation* (Peabody: Hendrickson Publishers, 1987).

[57] A detailed presentation of the diverse BHS positions represented in the P/C movement is Henry I. Lederle, *Treasures Old and New: Interpretations of "Spirit-Baptism" in the Charismatic Renewal Movement* (Peabody: Hendrickson Publishers, 1988).

[58] For an example of the term 'baptized in Spirit' used as a metaphor relative to the water rite in the ministry of John the Baptist, see James D. G. Dunn, *The Christ & The Spirit: Pneumatology, Vol. 2* (Grand Rapids: William B. Eerdmans, 1998), 103-17; See also *Christianity in the Making: Jesus Remembered, Vol. 1* (Grand Rapids: William B. Eerdmans Publishing, 2003), 367-68, 802-3, 808-9.

[59] Dunn, *The Christ & The Spirit: Pneumatology, Vol. 2*, 224 n. 11.

[60] Wayne Grudem, *Systematic Theology: An Introduction to Biblical Doctrine* (Grand Rapids: Zondervan Publishing, 1994), 766 n. 9.

future tense, 'will baptize in Holy Spirit' (Matt 3:11; Mark 1:8; Luke 3:16); the passive voice and future tense, 'will be baptized in Holy Spirit' (Acts 1:5; 11:16); or the passive voice and the aorist tense, 'were...baptized in one Spirit' (1 Cor 12:13).[61] This lack of NT support for the designations 'baptism in the Spirit' and 'Spirit baptism' is not contested by P/C scholars.[62] Nevertheless, though there are differences concerning its timing and evidence[63] within the P/C movement, classical Pentecostals and some charismatics consider BHS to be a post-conversional and life transforming event, or experience, referred to commonly as 'the baptism in the Holy Spirit.'[64] Referred to commonly as the 'second-blessing,' BHS is regarded as a distinct experience and subsequent to conversion. Though secondary, BHS is considered nearly as vital as conversion by Pentecostals and many within the charismatic renewal.

A brief mention of an additional lexical concern is warranted here. For some within the P/C movement, several biblical phrases represent a domain of comparable BHS metaphors. Wyckoff identifies predominately Acts-based phraseology, 'being filled with the Holy Spirit,' 'receiving the Holy Spirit,' 'the Holy Spirit being poured out,' 'the Holy Spirit falling upon,' 'the Holy Spirit coming upon,' and notes additional variants of these phrases.[65] He considers each biblical metaphor to be a reference to the identical experiences of the Holy Spirit, namely, the 'Pentecostal experience.'[66] The rationale behind such an assertion is

---

[61] Dunn, *The Christ & The Spirit: Pneumatology, Vol. 2,* 224 n. 11.

[62] John W. Wyckoff, 'The Baptism in the Holy Spirit,' in Stanley M. Horton, ed., *Systematic Theology: A Pentecostal Perspective* (Springfield: Logion Press, 1994), 425; Keith Warrington, *Pentecostal Theology: A Theology of Encounter* (London: T & T Clark, 2008), 95; French Arrington, 'The Indwelling, Baptism, and Infilling with the Holy Spirit,' in *Pneuma* (1981), 5 n. 1; John Wimber with Kevin Springer, *Power Evangelism* (San Francisco: Harper & Row Publishers, 1986), 145.

[63] William P. Atkinson, *Baptism in the Spirit: Luke-Acts and the Dunn Debate* (Eugene: Pickwick Publications, 2011), 2-3; Wimber with Springer, *Power Evangelism*, 146; Kilian McDonnell, 'Baptism in the Holy Spirit as an Ecumenical Problem,' in Killian McDonnell and Arnold Bittlinger, eds., *The Baptism in the Holy Spirit as an Ecumenical Problem* (Notre Dame: Catholic Renewal Services, 1972), 33.

[64] Grant Wacker, 'Wild Theories and Mad Excitement,' in Harold B. Smith, ed., *Pentecostals from the Inside Out* by (Wheaton: Victor Press, 1990), 21. Warrington, *Pentecostal Theology*, 100. Addressing the decline of BHS from central prominence among Pentecostals, Macchia calls for a thorough reexamination of what he calls 'the crown jewel of our theological distinctives.' See Frank D. Macchia, *Baptized in the Spirit: A Global Pentecostal Theology* (Grand Rapids: Zondervan Publishing House, 2006), 28.

[65] Wyckoff, 'The Baptism in the Holy Spirit,' 426.

[66] Howard M. Ervin, *Spirit Baptism: A Biblical Investigation* (Peabody: Hendrickson Publishers, 1987), 35. Lederle refers to the so-called 'Pentecostal experience' accurately as an 'experiential faith dimension' of the Christian life. Lederle, *Treasures Old and New*, 227.

that no single term is capable of capturing the multi-faceted nature of the Pentecostal experience.[67] There is, however, an inherent difficulty with this reasoning in that no semantic allowance exists for distinguishing BHS from 'being filled with the Spirit.' That is, BHS understood to be a completed conversion-like personal event does not reconcile with iterative Spirit filings such as are mentioned, for example, in Eph 5:18. This leaves one to conclude that either multiple BHS experiences must occur or that BHS and Spirit fillings are two distinctly experienced phenomena. Additionally, Williams believes the preference for the phrase 'baptism in the Holy Spirit' within the P/C movement is due to its linguistic connection to the term 'baptism' as a technical reference to water baptism.[68] This suggests that being '*baptized* in the Holy Spirit' is being 'totally enveloped in and saturated with the dynamic Spirit of the living God.'[69] Perhaps a simpler explanation is behind the expression, one that is derived from the language employed by Jesus (Acts 1:5).[70]

The biblical phrases are complementary and aid in conceptualizing the event, or experience, in terms of God being dynamically present in the Holy Spirit. However, Warrington is right to call for articulating BHS with 'terminology other than that historically used' and to offer a defense 'from a different perspective other than a strictly biblical one based on the book of Acts.'[71] The appeal of Warrington's position is that it avoids reading one's tradition into the metaphor, focuses on the nature of the experience, and opens the door for the broader acceptance of new conceptual terminology. Characteristic of the P/C movement is an emphasis on the experience of BHS rather than its comprehensive explanation.[72] This emphasis on experience over explanation does not imply that BHS is not articulated biblically or defended capably by P/C scholars.[73] On the

---

[67] Stanley M. Horton, *The Book of Acts* (Springfield: Gospel Publishing House, 1981), 32.

[68] J. Rodman Williams, *Renewal Theology: Systematic Theology from a Charismatic Perspective, 3 Vols.* (Grand Rapids: Zondervan, 1996), 199-203.

[69] Ibid.

[70] Wyckoff, 'The Baptism in the Holy Spirit,' 427.

[71] Warrington, *Pentecostal Theology*, 97.

[72] Ibid., 96.

[73] Atkinson, *Baptism in the Spirit*, 92-138; Howard M. Ervin, *Spirit Baptism: A Biblical Investigation* (Peabody: Hendrickson Publishers, 1987); David Petts, 'The Baptism in the Holy Spirit: The Theological Distinctive,' in Keith Warrington, ed., *Pentecostal Perspectives* (Carlisle: Paternoster Press, 1998), 98-119; William W. and Robert P. Menzies, *Spirit and Power: Foundations of Pentecostal Experience* (Grand Rapids: Zondervan Publishing House, 2000), 109-44, 189-208; Stanley M. Horton, 'Spirit Baptism: A Pentecostal Perspective,' in Chad Owen Brand, ed., *Perspectives on Spirit Baptism: Five Views* (Nashville: Broadman & Holman Publishers, 2004), 47-

contrary, the P/C emphasis on experience provides balance to what is perceived by many outside the tradition to be an imbalanced approach to understanding the BHS phenomenon.[74]

The relevance of new conceptual terminology is evident when the biblical articulation of the doctrine by some within the P/C movement involves a pneumatological distinction[75] between Lukan 'baptism *in* the Holy Spirit'[76] and Pauline 'baptism *of* the Holy Spirit.' On this view, the 'baptism *in* the Holy Spirit' is a distinct event, or experience, initiated by Christ who baptizes the believer into the Spirit (Acts 2:33). Conversely, 'the baptism *of* the Holy Spirit' is an event, or experience, linked to conversion (i.e. when the Spirit baptizes the believer into the Church, 1 Cor 12:13).[77] For some Pentecostals, both phenomena are discernible in 1 Cor 12:13;[78] Atkinson, however, strongly contests this attempt to read both phenomena into Paul (1 Cor 12:13),[79] and persuasively argues that the Lukan 'in' versus Pauline 'of' dichotomy is a false one.

Beyond identifying terminology is the relevance of reception-validating phenomena. Though glossolalia[80] is not universally regarded as the exclusive

---

94; Larry Hart, 'Spirit Baptism: A Dimensional Charismatic Perspective,' in Chad Owen Brand, ed., *Perspectives on Spirit Baptism: Five Views* (Nashville: Broadman & Holman Publishers, 2004), 105-69; Frank D. Macchia, *Baptized in the Spirit: A Global Pentecostal Theology* (Grand Rapids: Zondervan Publishing House, 2006).

[74] Warrington, *Pentecostal Theology*, 95; Arrington, 'The Indwelling, Baptism, and Infilling with the Holy Spirit,' 5 n. 1.

[75] Arrington cites Matt 3:11; Mark 1:8; Luke 3:16; John 1:33; Acts 1:5 and 11:16 for the 'baptism *in* the Spirit' and 1 Cor 12:13 for the 'baptism *of* the Spirit.' Arrington, 'The Indwelling, Baptism, and Infilling with the Holy Spirit,' 5 n. 1. According to Garrett, 'the question of a baptism *by* the Holy Spirit rests on the interpretation of 1 Cor 12:13a.' See James Leo Garrett, Jr., *Systematic Theology: Biblical, Historical, and Evangelical, Vol. 2* (Grand Rapids: William B. Eerdmans Publishing, 1990), 166.

[76] Ibid., 107. Ervin, *Conversion-Initiation and the Baptism in the Holy Spirit*, 79. Robert P. Menzies, *The Development of Early Christian Pneumatology with Special Reference to Luke-Acts* (Sheffield: Sheffield Academic Press, 1991), 135-45; Robert P. Menzies, *Empowered for Witness: The Holy Spirit in Luke-Acts* (Sheffield: Sheffield Academic Press, 1994), 123-31; Roger Stronstad, *The Charismatic Theology of St. Luke* ([original work published 1984] Peabody: Hendrickson Publishers, 2002), 10-12, 35, 39, 51-52; *The Prophethood of All Believers: A Study in Luke's Charismatic Theology* ([original work published 1999] Sheffield: Sheffield Academic Press, 2003), 54-70. Atkinson devotes an entire volume to BHS, Luke-Acts, and the Pentecostal response to James D. G. Dunn. See William P. Atkinson, *Baptism in the Spirit: Luke-Acts and the Dunn Debate* (Eugene: Pickwick Publications, 2011).

[77] Warrington, *Pentecostal Theology*, 100.

[78] Ervin, *Conversion-Initiation and the Baptism in the Holy Spirit*, 98-102.

[79] Atkinson, *Baptism in the Spirit*, 93-100.

[80] The term is based on the biblical expression 'to speak in ['with' or 'by'] tongues' (γλῶσσης λαλεῖν) appearing in the NT (Mark 16:17). 'Glossolalia' is a transliteration of a

evidential sign of BHS reception,[81] certain religious gifts and experiences (e.g. prophecy, healing, miracles, and other paranormal phenomena) are universally identified by Pentecostals and charismatics as uniquely valid indicators for the reception of the baptism and power of the Holy Spirit.[82] Biblical evidence appealed to for such manifestations of the Holy Spirit is drawn from a range of NT writings, notably Luke 24:49, Acts 1:4-8, and 1 Cor 12:1-31. The operation of spiritual gifts, referred to as 'charismata,' is a practical issue that frequently divides American Baptists from P/C adherents.

3.2   Baptists: Placement into the Body of Christ

In contrast to the extensive range of Pentecostal and charismatic writings on the topic of BHS, American Baptists have not devoted entire volumes to discussions on BHS.[83] This is a striking difference between the two traditions, and it means that there is a lack of written material to draw from to describe the American Baptist BHS position. Since this study seeks to view the possibility for dialogue from a Baptist perspective, it is important to present a clear and effective summary of the Baptist position. Analyses provided generally occur in theological publications and pneumatological references. This demonstrates the non-essential nature of the BHS doctrine among American Baptists, who frequently depend on non-Baptist writers for its articulation. Endorsement of these writers by American Baptist pastors and scholars results in BHS views adopted by denominational institutions and among local church affiliates.

---

compound Greek term (γλῶσσα + λαλέω). See Russell P. Spittler, 'Glossolalia,' in Stanley M. Burgess and Eduard M. Van Der Maas, eds., *NIDPCM* (Grand Rapids: Zondervan, 2002), 670. Horton believes the 1 Cor 13:1 reference to 'tongues of angels' to be a hyperbole due to the Corinthians high regard for speaking in tongues. See Stanley M. Horton, *I and II Corinthians* (Springfield: Gospel Publishing House, 1999), 125. See also, Mark J. Cartledge, 'The Nature and Function of New Testament Glossolalia,' in *EQ* (2000), 135-50.

[81] According to Smidt, Kellstedt, Green, and Guth, while many within the P/C movement hold that glossolalia (tongues) is a 'valid indicator' of BHS, 'it is not an adequate defining characteristic.' Smidt, Kellstedt, Green, and Guth, 'The Spirit-Filled Movements in Contemporary America: A Survey Perspective,' 112-13.

[82] Margaret M. Poloma, 'Pentecostals and Politics in North and Central America,' Jeffrey K. Hadden and Anson Shupe, eds., *Prophetic Religions and Politics* (New York: Paragon, 1986), 330. Smidt, Kellstedt, Green, and Guth, 'The Spirit-Filled Movements in Contemporary America: A Survey Perspective,' 112-13.

[83] Criswell is a notable exception. W.A. Criswell, *The Holy Spirit in Today's World* (Grand Rapids: Zondervan Publishing, 1966). See also, *The Baptism, Filling & Gifts of the Holy Spirit* (Grand Rapids: Zondervan Publishing, 1973). Merrill F. Unger wrote *The Baptism & Gifts of the Holy Spirit* (Chicago: Moody Press, 1974) which was widely accepted among American Baptists.

In his seven-fold BHS typology, Brand refers to scholars of the Reformed tradition who intensely address the Augustinian notion 'that Christians receive the full benefits of salvation at regeneration.'[84] SBC theologian Yarnell affirms this correspondence of BHS to conversion. He finds contemporary support for this view from British Methodist theologian James Dunn and fellow SBC scholar James Garrett.[85] This eclectic comingling of traditions suggests the range of scholarship used by American Baptists to conceptualize BHS. In addition, some American Baptists[86] utilize the works of dispensational[87] scholars such as MacArthur[88] and former Dallas Theological Seminary (Dallas, TX) faculty, including Ryrie, Pentecost, Unger, and Walvoord.[89]

American Baptists primarily regard BHS as an unrepeatable non-affective event performed historically on the body of Christ by the Holy Spirit on the Day of Pentecost.[90] One Pauline text, namely 1 Cor 12:13, often dominates American Baptist formulations of a BHS doctrinal construct.[91] Gromacki considers the apostle Paul to be the definitive NT writer on BHS and 1 Cor 12:13 as the key to

---

[84] Chad Owen Brand, 'Introduction,' in Chad Owen Brand, ed., *Perspectives on Spirit Baptism: Five Views* (Nashville: Broadman & Holman Publishers, 2004), 13.

[85] Malcolm B. Yarnell, III, 'The Person and Work of the Holy Spirit,' in Daniel L. Akin, ed., *A Theology for the Church* (Nashville: B & H Academic, 2007), 670; Dunn, *Baptism in the Holy Spirit*, 1-7; Garrett, *Systematic Theology, Vol. 2*, 181.

[86] Particularly, but not limited to, those affiliated with the Southern Baptist Convention.

[87] The term 'dispensational' in this work is used descriptively as a general reference to God's stewardship of dispensing or administering his program (will) via human history in a succession of stages (economies). Dispensationalists believe that these stages (economies) are distinguishable from the written revelation of God in Scripture. Dispensationalists have historically embraced the grammatical-historical hermeneutical school common among American Baptists. Charles C. Ryrie, *Dispensationalism* ([original work published 1966] Moody Press: Chicago, 1995), 23-43. A variety of doctrinal distinctives embraced by dispensationalists are traceable to the movement's progenitor John Nelson Darby (1800-82). The distinctives are summarized in James Leo Garrett, Jr., *Baptist Theology: A Four-Century Study* (Macon: Mercer University Press, 2009), 561.

[88] John F. MacArthur, Jr. is pastor-teacher at Grace Community Church (Sun Valley, CA).

[89] Dallas Theological Seminary is of the evangelical and dispensational tradition.

[90] Jerry Vines in *Spirit Works: Charismatic Practices and the Bible* (Nashville: Broadman & Holman Publishers, 1999), 72-82; John F. Walvoord, *The Holy Spirit: A Comprehensive Study of the Person and Work of the Holy Spirit* ([original work published 1954] Findlay: Dunham Publishing Company, 1958), 146-47; Charles C. Ryrie, *The Holy Spirit* (Chicago: Moody Press, 1965), 77.

[91] John S. Hammett, *Biblical Foundations for Baptist Churches: A Contemporary Ecclesiology* (Grand Rapids: Kregel Publications, 2005), 38.

its understanding.[92] BGC minister Millard Erickson refers to the primacy of Paul in 1 Cor 12:13[93] as the 'normal pattern' (in his view, the book of Acts is transitional) for the coincidence of 'conversion/regeneration and the baptism of the Holy Spirit.'[94] American Baptists uniformly consider 1 Cor 12:13 to be Paul's description of how believers[95] become members of the body of Christ.[96] Influential among American Baptists is evangelical scholar Ryrie who attributes incorporation into the body of Christ to be the result of a baptism performed 'by the Spirit.'[97] Though historically performed corporately on the body of Christ at Pentecost, Conservative Baptist Association (CBA) pastor Stanley Grenz believes that individual incorporation into the body of Christ occurs at conversion.[98] Erickson also regards BHS as occurring simultaneously with conversion or as the functional equivalent of conversion.[99] The complete analysis of American Baptist BHS perspectives is the subject of Chapter 4 and incorporates a wider range of American Baptist scholars.

---

[92] Robert Gromacki, *The Holy Spirit* (Nashville: Word Publishing, 1999), 167-71. Gromacki is pastor emeritus of Grace Community Baptist Church (Washington Court House, OH). GCBC is affiliated with the General Association of Regular Baptist Churches (Schaumburg, IL).

[93] J. Dwight Pentecost, *The Divine Comforter: The Person and Work of the Holy Spirit* (Westwood: Fleming H. Revell, 1963), 136. Charles C. Ryrie, *A Survey of Bible Doctrine* (Chicago: Moody Press, 1972), 78; *The Holy Spirit* (Chicago: Moody Press, 1965), 77; *Basic Theology: A Popular Systematic Guide to Understanding Biblical Truth* (Wheaton: Victor Books, 1986), 363; Vines, *Spirit Works,* 78.

[94] Millard J. Erickson, *Christian Theology* (Grand Rapids: Baker Book House, 1986), 880; Ryrie, *The Holy Spirit*, 78-79. Vines, *Spirit Works,* 79.

[95] Use of the term 'believer' in this work refers to the NT doctrine of faith as trust in God's mercy in Christ apprehended by the individual (John 20:31; Rom 3:22). There is NT textual basis to support the use of the term 'believer' as a technical title for the Christian (2 Cor 6:15; 1 Tim 4:10, 12). Robert S. Rayburn, 'Christian, Names of,' in Walter A. Elwell, ed., *Evangelical Dictionary of Theology* ([original work published 1984] Grand Rapids: Baker Book House, 1985), 216-18.

[96] Erickson, *Christian Theology*, 880; Walvoord, *The Holy Spirit*, 141; Unger, *The Baptism & Gifts of the Holy Spirit*, 96-97; Pentecost, *The Divine Comforter*, 142; Criswell, *The Baptism, Filling & Gifts of the Holy Spirit*, 16-18; Vines, *Spirit Works,* 79.

[97] Ryrie, *Basic Theology*, 362-63. Ryrie explains the occurrence of dual Divine agency appearing in Acts 2:33 and 1 Cor 12:13 as 'different Persons in the Trinity' being 'involved in the same work.' Walvoord, *The Holy Spirit*, 147-48; Pentecost, *The Divine Comforter*, 136.

[98] Stanley J. Grenz, *Theology for the Community of God* (Nashville: Broadman & Holman Publishers, 1994), 550; Emery Bancroft, *Elemental Theology* ([original work published 1932] Grand Rapids: Zondervan Publishing, 1977), 220.

[99] Erickson, *Christian Theology*, 880. According to Walvoord, BHS and conversion are 'coextensive' phenomena. See Walvoord, *The Holy Spirit*, 139. For Unger and Criswell, BHS occurs simultaneously with conversion, but separate from regeneration as a distinct and complementary operation of the Spirit. See Unger, *The Baptism & Gifts of the Holy Spirit*, 22, 56; Criswell, *The Baptism, Filling & Gifts of the Holy Spirit*, 13-15.

The paradigmatic nature of the phenomena described in the book of Acts poses a hermeneutical challenge to the American Baptist view.[100] Specifically, do the cases involving the Jews as a group (Acts 2:1-4, 33), the Samaritans (Acts 8:14-17), the Gentiles (Acts 10:44-48), and the disciples of John the Baptist (Acts 19:1-7) indicate a separation between conversion-regeneration and BHS? American Baptists do not consider these internal case studies to be paradigmatic for contemporary believers. This view is justified by regarding Acts as a transitional NT book. The cases presented by Luke represent the experiences of 'the last of the OT believers.'[101] Alternatively, the cases reveal exceptional incidents within the early dissemination of the kerygma to ever-widening ethnic circles. Assessing BHS as an event linked to conversion is common among American Baptists and scholars whose works are influential within the tradition.[102]

While the majority of American Baptists identify the non-affective incorporation into the body of Christ as the primary function of BHS, advocates of the correspondence of BHS to spiritual experience do exist within the tradition. ABCUSA theologian Barnard Ramm considers Matt 3:11 to describe the empowering and renewing work of BHS performed by Jesus. On his view, BHS results in 'the impartation of spiritual life and moral quickening.'[103] Ramm does not separate BHS from conversion, but rather acknowledges the reception of spiritual power as a concomitant to regeneration (Gal 3:3).[104] D. A. Carson admonishes noncharismatic Christians against overreacting to second-blessing theology. According to Carson, they risk minimizing the 'further pursuit of God' in terms of 'profound [post-conversion] experience' by focusing too heavily on a single enduement theology.[105] Grenz considers Jesus to be the agent of BHS

---

[100] The use of the term paradigmatic here refers to Luke's intention to provide BHS case studies as the basis for doctrinal formulation.

[101] Erickson, *Christian Theology*, 880. For a complete analysis of this view, see Frederick Dale Brunner, *A Theology of the Holy Spirit* (Grand Rapids: William B. Eerdmans Publishing, 1970), 153-218.

[102] Ryrie, *Basic Theology*, 362-65. *A Survey of Bible Doctrine*, 78. *The Holy Spirit*, 74-79; Bancroft, *Elemental Theology*, 219-20; Walvoord, *The Holy Spirit*, 138-50; Unger, *The Baptism & Gifts of the Holy Spirit*, 21-38; Pentecost, *The Divine Comforter*, 136-43; Criswell, *The Baptism, Filling & Gifts of the Holy Spirit*, 7-19; *The Holy Spirit in Today's World*, 93-102.

[103] Bernard Ramm, *The Witness of the Spirit: An Essay on the Contemporary Relevance of the Internal Witness of the Holy Spirit* (Grand Rapids: William B. Eerdmans Publishing Company, 1960), 48-49.

[104] Ibid.

[105] Carson, *Showing the Spirit*, 159-60.

whose 'immersion in the Spirit' is the radical event occurring at conversion.[106] This immersion is instrumental to the believer's participation in the non-repeatable 'bestowal of the Spirit' at Pentecost.[107] This view characterizes 'participation' as the believer's consciousness of the communal obligation established on the Day of Pentecost. ABCUSA pastor-theologian A. J. Gordon similarly identifies the one-time historical occurrence of 'baptism in the Spirit' at Pentecost and its enduring individual experience by contemporary believers.[108]

The relationship of the *charismata* (spiritual gifts) to BHS is a correlative issue for American Baptists. The exercise of miraculous (or 'sign') *charismata* in the contemporary church places BHS at the center of the cessationism versus noncessationism (or 'continuationism')[109] debate.[110] American Baptists are predominately cessationists,[111] limiting the exercise of the 'miraculous'

---

[106] Grenz, *Theology for the Community of God*, 541-51.

[107] Ibid.

[108] A. J. Gordon, *The Ministry of the Spirit* ([original work published 1894] Philadelphia: The Judson Press, 1950), 66-67.

[109] A work featuring the general points in the cessationism-continuationism debate is Wayne Grudem, ed., *Are Miraculous Gifts for Today? Four Views* (Grand Rapids: Zondervan Publishing House, 1996). Carson offers a comprehensive work on issues relating to the charismatic movement BHS and the *charismata*. He challenges both cessationists and continuationists and provides an extensive bibliography of select resources. See D. A. Carson, *Showing the Spirit: A Theological Exposition of 1 Corinthians 12-14* ([original work published 1987] Grand Rapids: Baker Books, 2003). Another work challenging both cessationists and continuationists is M. James Sawyer and Daniel B. Wallace, eds. *Who's Afraid of the Holy Spirit? An Investigation into the Ministry of the Spirit of God Today* (Dallas: Biblical Studies Press, 2005).

[110] Unger, *The Baptism & Gifts of the Holy Spirit*, 74; Harold John Ockenga, *Power through Pentecost* (Grand Rapids: William B. Eerdmans Publishing, 1959), 21.

[111] Works and articles devoted to the defense of cessationism are: B. B. Warfield, *Counterfeit Miracles* ([original work published 1918] Carlisle: The Banner of Truth Trust, 1972). Warfield's book criticizes post-apostolic era miracle claims and pre-dates the modern Pentecostal and charismatic renewal movement. The work is often the object of refutation by continuationist authors. Richard B. Gaffin, Jr., *Perspectives on Pentecost: New Testament Teaching on the Gifts of the Holy Spirit* (Phillipsburg: Presbyterian and Reformed Publishing, 1979); John F. MacArthur, Jr., *The Charismatics: A Doctrinal Perspective* ([original work published 1978] Grand Rapids: Zondervan Publishing House, 1980) and *Charismatic Chaos* (Grand Rapids: Zondervan Publishing House, 1992); Frederick Dale Bruner, *A Theology of the Holy Spirit: The Pentecostal Experience and the New Testament Witness* (London: Hodder and Stoughton, 1970). The Master's Seminary Journal devoted an entire issue in defense of cessationism: James F. Stitzinger, 'Spiritual Gifts: Definitions and Kinds,' in *TMSJ* (2003), 143-76; Donald G. McDougall, 'Cessationism in 1 Cor 13:8-12,' in *TMSJ* (2003), 177-213; John F. MacArthur, 'Does God Still Give Revelation?,' in *TMSJ* (2003), 217-34; F. David Farnell, 'The Montanist Crisis: A Key to Refuting Third-Wave Concepts of NT Prophecy,' in *TMSJ* (2003), 235-62; Richard L. Mayhue, 'Cessationism, "The Gifts of Healings," and Divine Healing,' in *TMSJ* (2003), 263-86; Robert L. Thomas, 'The Hermeneutics of Noncessationism,' in *TMSJ* (2003), 287-310; Dennis M. Swanson, 'Bibliography of Works on Cessationism,' in *TMSJ* (2003), 311-27.

charismata (e.g. tongues, prophecy, and healing) to the apostolic era of the church.[112]

3.3   Summary

The above analysis presents opposing BHS viewpoints and establishes the range of issues resulting from differing conceptual models applied to the BHS metaphor. The following table is not a comprehensive description of the BHS positions held by American Baptists and P/C adherents. Rather, it summarizes the contrasting features of the primary BHS positions respectively held by American Baptists and the P/C movement.

Table 1. Comparison of BHS Conceptions

	P/C	Baptist
Agency	Jesus	Spirit
Medium	Spirit	Body of Christ/Christ
Purpose	Divine encounter	Union with Christ
Time	Post-conversion	Conversion
Evidence	Experience-based with charismatic function	Non-affective event without charismatic function
Lexical Range	Possibility of synonymous phrases	No synonymous phrases
Frequency	Range of views	Non-repeated
Correlative Functions	Charismatic function and Noncessationist	Separate from charismatic function and Cessationist
Theological Orientation	Lukan	Pauline

---

[112] Wayne A. Grudem, 'Preface,' in Wayne A Grudem, ed., *Are Miraculous Gifts for Today? Four Views* (Grand Rapids: Zondervan Publishing House, 1996), 10.

There is an important clarification to the summary information contained in the table. The lack of univocacy by American Baptist and P/C adherents when referring to the BHS metaphor renders the above table an incomplete depiction of the conceptual impasse between the two traditions. American Baptists and P/C adherents apply altogether different meanings to the BHS metaphor. Four additional points of clarification consider the equivocation of the term.

1) The differentiation of two baptisms, 'the baptism *in* the Spirit' and 'the baptism *of* the Spirit,' sometimes evoked among P/C adherents is a *non sequitur* for American Baptists[113] who do not consider 'the baptism *in* the Spirit' to be a biblical, and therefore doctrinal, reality.[114]

2) The Luke-Paul dichotomy represents an interpretive locus for the P/C-American Baptist BHS debate. American Baptists who engage the P/C doctrinal model for BHS require a biblical investigation of the relevant Luke-Acts texts.[115] This investigation is intended to identify and resolve areas of Lukan-Pauline theological continuity and discontinuity relative to BHS. The nature of the investigation concerns Luke's so-called 'Spirit of prophecy' that appears to be in contradistinction to Paul's 'soteriological Spirit.'

3) The emphasis of some P/C adherents on post-conversion 'second blessing' ('second grace') BHS is premised on a 'first blessing' ('the baptism *of* the Holy Spirit') conversion experience.[116] The metaphorical reference to 'the baptism *in* the Spirit' is linguistically equivalent to a

---

[113] Gordon, who holds a similar BHS position as his contemporary, Dutch Reformed theologian Andrew Murray, is a historical exception. Gordon uses 'baptism *in* the Spirit' to reference a post-conversion experience, though the reception of the Spirit is rooted in conversion. See Gordon, *The Ministry of the Spirit*, 67-76.

[114] Gromacki does use the expression 'the baptism *in* the Holy Spirit,' but his use of the term equivocates with the P/C meaning. See Gromacki, *The Holy Spirit*, 165-77. W. T. Conner, who taught theology at Southwestern Baptist Theological Seminary (Fort Worth, TX) from 1910 until his retirement in 1949, referenced 'the baptism *in* the Spirit' and noted its appearance in the Gospels and Acts as a work of the Spirit performed by Jesus. See W. T. Conner, *Christian Doctrine* (Nashville: Broadman Press, 1937), 114. Carroll mentions 'baptism *in* the Spirit' as a one-time corporate work performed upon the church by Christ occurring at Pentecost. See Carroll, *The Holy Spirit*, 32-33.

[115] P/C scholar Stronstad, for example, argues that a theological and methodological impasse is represented in the meaning of the Holy Spirit in Luke-Acts. He calls for a consensus-building resolution that is in part based upon dispensing 'self-serving methodological programs' that either 'silence or manipulate Luke's distinctive theology.' See Stronstad, *The Charismatic Theology of St. Luke*, 12.

[116] Ray H. Hughes, *What is Pentecost?* (Cleveland: Pathway Press, 1963), 23; Ernest S. Williams, *Systematic Theology, Vol. 3* ([original work published 1953] Springfield: Gospel Publishing House, 1991), 47.

post-conversion and radically transformative encounter with God.[117] American Baptists and many P/C adherents agree on the agency of the Spirit in conversion but disagree on referring to this phenomenon as BHS.[118]

4) The American Baptist concept of BHS as a non-affective event is challenged by the P/C concept of an 'encounter-based' experience. Exemplifying the latter is P/C theologian Amos Yong who advocates a 'dynamic pneumatological soteriology.' The dynamic nature of the Spirit's soteriological function occurs when BHS is instrumental to experiencing 'the graces of God' through a process of 'palpably felt and radically transformative crisis moments.'[119]

The contrasting views on the issue of BHS and its relation to spiritual experience question the ability of theology to keep pace with personal spiritual experience.[120] It is significant that, despite the concerns of American Baptists regarding the effects of the charismatic renewal, the historical roots of their tradition have included 'radical and transformative encounters with God.' American Baptist historian Gaustad considers such encounters to be 'immediate experiences of grace' evidenced by an 'objective and certain' Spirit baptism.[121]

---

[117] Warrington, *Pentecostal Theology*, 125.

[118] John F. MacArthur, Jr., *The Charismatics: A Doctrinal Perspective* ([original work published 1978] Grand Rapids: Zondervan Publishing, 1980), 119-29; *Charismatic Chaos* (Grand Rapids: Zondervan Publishing House, 1992), 173-93; Denominational leader in both the Baptist State Convention of Texas (SBC) and the Southern Baptist Convention, pastor-theologian B. H. Carroll also refers to 'baptism in the Spirit' as a work performed by Christ. See B. H. Carroll, *The Holy Spirit: Comprising a Discussion of the Paraclete, the Other Self of Jesus, and Other Phases of the Work of the Spirit of God* (Nashville: Broadman Press, 1939), 32-33. See also James Spivey, 'Benjamin Harvey Carroll,' in Timothy George and David S. Dockery, eds., *Theologians of the Baptist Tradition, Revised Ed.* (Nashville: B & H Publishing Group, 2001), 163-80.

[119] Amos Yong, *The Spirit Poured Out on all Flesh: Pentecostalism and the Possibility of Global Theology* (Grand Rapids: Baker Academic, 2005), 105-8.

[120] J. David Pawson, *The Normal Christian Birth: How to Give New Believers a Proper Start in Life* (London: Hodder & Stoughton, 1989), 285. Of mixed review are the works of Jack Deere which have proved influential in some American Baptist circles. See *Surprised by the Power of the Spirit: A Former Dallas Seminary Professor Discovers that God Speaks and Heals Today* (Grand Rapids: Zondervan Publishing House, 1993). See also, *Surprised by the Voice of God: How God Speaks Today through Prophecies, Dreams, and Visions* (Grand Rapids: Zondervan Publishing House, 1996). Also having influence among American Baptist is Henry Blackaby's *Experiencing God: Knowing and Doing the Will of God, Revised and Expanded* (Nashville: B & H Books, 2008).

[121] Edwin S. Gaustad, 'Baptists and Experimental Religion,' in *Chronicle: The Journal of the American Baptist Historical Society* (1952), 110-16.

3.4   The Basis for the Study: Three Systemic Realities

3.4.1   Evangelical Traditions in Tension

Organized in 1968, the 'American Baptist Charismatic Fellowship' is indicative of the spiritual plurality within the ABCUSA and demonstrates the potential acceptance of matters relating to BHS.[122] By the mid-1970s, however, SBC opposition to the charismatic renewal became a matter of open conflict. The conflict focused on the present-day exercise of 'tongues' among charismatic believers. Well-documented cases involving SBC churches and pastors expressed dispensational challenges to the exercise of tongues in the contemporary church, based on views discussed above. SBC members impacted by the charismatic renewal opposed the denomination's interpretation of 1 Cor 13:8. In their view the interpretation nullified the contemporary practice of tongues.[123] The relationship of BHS to evidential tongues (or 'glossolalia') resulted in 'much ferment in churches of many traditions.'[124] Carson avers that the presence of respectively cherished 'neat stereotypes' enables either side in the controversy to forge caricatures of the other's spirituality.[125] Charismatics viewed noncharismatics as tradition-bound, dubious of the Bible's teachings, and lacking fervor for the Lord. Non-charismatics accused advocates of renewal for being zealous for experience at the expense of the truth. These caricatures offer no useful purpose toward resolving the controversy except to expose the profound suspicions on both sides of the debate. Appeals to biblical authority as the basis for belief and praxis effectively polarized the disputing sides. Carson rightly presents the existence of three possible outcomes:

> [1]…one side or the other is right in its interpretation of Scripture on this point, and the other is correspondingly wrong; [2] both sides are in some degree wrong, and some better way of understanding the Scripture must be found; or [3] the Bible simply does not speak clearly and univocally to these issues, and both sides of the dispute have

---

[122] Douglas Weaver, *In Search of the New Testament Church: The Baptist Story* (Macon: Mercer University Press, 2008), 184.

[123] Albert Frederick Schenkel, 'New Wine and Baptist Wineskins: American and Southern Baptist Denominational Responses to the Charismatic Renewal,' in Edith Blumhoefer, Russell P. Spittler, and Grant A. Wacker, eds., *Pentecostal Currents in American Protestantism* (Chicago: University of Illinois Press, 1999), 157-61.

[124] Grenz, *Theology for the Community of God*, 541-42.

[125] Carson, *Showing the Spirit*, 12.

extrapolated the Bible's teachings to entrenched positions not themselves defensible in Scripture.[126]

This three-option typology is useful for evaluating whether American Baptists have 'extrapolated the Bible's teachings' and are advocating an entrenched and biblically indefensible [BHS] position. This scrutiny of the American Baptist tradition does not correspondingly exonerate the theological methods and conclusions of the P/C movement. However, consideration of the process by which American Baptists engage biblically adduced P/C BHS conceptions will expose potential theological deficiencies as entrenched, biblically indefensible, and extrapolated biblical teaching. Therefore, doctrinal consensus emerges when 'neat stereotypes' (e.g. *ad hominem* arguments) are dismissed from intra-tradition dialogue.[127]

3.4.2   Existential Longing

Evangelicalism may be represented as a movement typified by the yearning of its participants for greater spiritual experience.[128] P/C adherents are representative of evangelicals who associate BHS with deep spiritual experience.[129] While evangelicals outside the P/C movement articulate depth of spiritual experience apart from BHS language, instances exist of individuals longing for personal experience of the divine presence mediated by the Holy Spirit. Biblical scholar Daniel Wallace experienced personal heartbreak from a family crisis that prompted a realization that 'the Bible alone' is an inadequate means for achieving greater spiritual experience. Wallace longed for what he

---

[126] Ibid.

[127] Nathan and Wilson, *Empowered Evangelicals*, 7. Grudem, 'Preface,' ii-iii.

[128] Harris, 'Beyond Bebbington,' 201-219.

[129] Warrington, *Pentecostal Theology*, 100. Donald Gee, *Wind and Flame* (Croydon: Heath Press, Ltd., 1967), 8; Gordon D. Fee, 'Baptism in the Holy Spirit: The Issue of Separability and Subsequence,' *Pneuma* (1985), 88, 96-98; Walter J. Hollenweger, *The Pentecostals: The Charismatic Movement in the Churches* (Minneapolis: Augsburg Publishing House, 1972), 9; Macchia, *Baptized in the Spirit*, 13; Ray H. Hughes, 'The New Pentecostalism: Perspective of a Pentecostal Administrator,' in Russell P. Spittler, ed., *Perspectives on the New Pentecostalism* (Grand Rapids: Baker Book House, 1976), 168-69; Petts, 'The Baptism in the Holy Spirit: The Theological Distinctive,' 109. See also the correlation of BHS to spiritual experience prior to the rise of the P/C movement within the Christian Missionary and Alliance (CM & A), A. B. Simpson, 'The Baptism of the Holy Spirit: a Crisis or an Evolution?' in *Living Truths* (1905), 705, 715-15, the Methodists, Asa Mahan, *The Baptism of the Holy Ghost* (New York: Hughes and Palmer, 1870), 55-73, and Congregationalists, R. A. Torrey, *The Baptism with the Holy Spirit* (New York: Fleming H. Revell, 1985), 9-20.

termed 'an existential experience of the Holy One.'[130] Presbyterian minister Kirk Bottomly reacted to reports of supernatural phenomena occurring within the P/C movement by reflecting on the existential nature of his own Christian experience.[131] He characterized his spiritual experience as 'devoid of supernatural reality' and insisted 'either those experiences are sub-Christian' (phony, self-induced) or he was 'sub-Christian.'[132] BGC pastor-theologian John Piper discovered discontinuity between Acts 4:29-31 and his own personal experience.[133] Piper gained a desire to possess the 'fullness of the power of the gospel' and deliverance from a 'preoccupation with secondary things, no matter how spectacular.'[134] While teaching at a leading evangelical seminary, OT scholar Jack Deere[135] became convinced that studying Scripture was not 'to discover what they taught about the gifts of the Spirit,' but 'to gather more reasons why God was not doing those things today.'[136] These examples from scholars conversant with the biblical record, express the need for theological language to describe personal spiritual experience.

---

[130] Daniel B. Wallace, 'Introduction: Who's Afraid of the Holy Spirit? The Uneasy Conscience of a Non-Charismatic Evangelical,' in Daniel B. Wallace and M. James Sawyer, eds., *Who's Afraid of the Holy Spirit: An Investigation into the Ministry of the Spirit of God Today,* (Dallas: Biblical Studies Press, 2005), 7.

[131] Kirk Bottomly, 'Coming out of the Hanger: Confessions of an Evangelical Deist,' in Gary S. Greig and Kevin N. Springer, eds., *The Kingdom and the Power: Are Healing and the Spiritual Gifts Used by Jesus and the Early Church Meant for the Church Today?* (Ventura: Regal Books, 1993), 258-74.

[132] Ibid.

[133] John Piper, 1990. 'Are Signs and Wonders for Today?,' n.p. Available from: http://www. desiringgod.org/resource-library/sermons/are-signs-and-wonders-for-today. (Accessed 22 June 2011).

[134] Ibid.

[135] Jack Deere is Senior Pastor of Wellspring Church (North Richland Hills, TX). Until 1986 Deere was professor of Old Testament at Dallas Theological Seminary (Dallas, TX). Deere reversed his cessationist views on the supernatural gifts of the Holy Spirit and left DTS in 1987 to join John Wimber and the staff of the Vineyard Christian Fellowship Church (Anaheim, CA). Wellspring Church, 2011. 'About Jack Deere,' n.p. Available from: http://www.wellspringdfw.org/jack-deere. [Accessed 22 June 2011].

[136] Deere, *Surprised by the Power of the Spirit*, 22.

3.4.3   The Rise of Pentecostal-charismatic Christianity

Longings for deeper spiritual experience are not unprecedented in the history of the church and are well-documented.[137] Contemporary expressions of deeper spiritual experience are common within the charismatic renewal. Often referred to as 'neo-Pentecostalism,' the charismatic renewal began in 1960 and manifests aspects of (classical) Pentecostal spirituality without preference for denominational affiliation.[138] Emerging from classical Pentecostalism, the charismatic renewal has contributed to the exponential rise of the P/C movement.[139] While Pentecostalism is a distinct movement, distinguishable from charismatic groups that exist on a broader and varied scale, it is important to note that the relationship between the tradition streams is sufficiently close with regard to BHS. The P/C movement has reached its present ascendency through successive waves of charismatic renewal. The result is a dominant spiritual milieu which emphasizes authentic biblically validated experience and challenges a variety of Christian traditions to consider its nature and source. American Baptists find themselves in this milieu and are challenged to reflect theologically upon the foundational role BHS plays among P/C adherents to produce authentic and biblically validated Christian experience.

4. Conclusion

As independent evangelical traditions, American Baptists and P/C adherents are united by a core commitment to personal conversion experience-based spirituality. Each tradition recognizes the role of BHS relative to personal conversion experience. However, significant equivocation exists concerning the

---

[137] D. D. Bundy, 'Keswick Higher Life Movement,' Stanley M. Burgess and Eduard M. Van Der Maas, eds., *NIDPCM* (Grand Rapids: Zondervan Publishing House, 2002), 820-21.

[138] Dennis Bennett, *Nine O'Clock in the Morning* (Plainfield: Bridge Publishing, 1970), 1-30; Vinson Synan, 'Charismatic Renewal Enters the Mainline Churches' in Vinson Synan, ed., *The Century of the Holy Spirit: 100 Years of Pentecostal and Charismatic Renewal, 1901-2001* (Nashville: Thomas Nelson Publishers, 2001), 149-76; Vinson Synan, 'The Charismatics: Renewal in Major Protestant Denominations' in Vinson Synan, ed., *The Century of the Holy Spirit: 100 Years of Pentecostal and Charismatic Renewal, 1901-2001* (Nashville: Thomas Nelson Publishers, 2001), 177-208.

[139] *IBMR*, 2011. 'Status of Global Mission, 2011, in Context of 20th and 21st Centuries,' n.p. Available from: http://www.gordonconwell.edu/sites/ default/ files/StatusOfGlobalMission.pdf. [Accessed 22 June 2011]. The statistical table tracks the rise of the P/C movement from 981,000 (1900), 67,021,000 (1970), 482,256,000 (mid-2000), 612,472,000 (mid-2011), and projects total adherent at 796,490,000 by 2025. With Christians representing fully 33% of the world's population in 2011, the P/C block represents 28% of all Christians. According to the *IBMR* report, this is an increase of 23% in just four decades.

meaning of the metaphor. In terms of applied doctrine or *praxis,* BHS is directly linked to personal piety and missional activity for P/C adherents, while American Baptists relegate the metaphor to the soteriological back waters of the *ordo salutis* (i.e. order of salvation). For the former tradition, BHS is a mediate phenomenon that is imminently impactful upon Christian living. For the latter, BHS represents a completed soteriological fact and is muted in terms of personal experience or missional efficiency. Many P/C adherents interpret the BHS metaphor as subsequent to conversion, the vital root of ongoing spirituality, and the necessary impetus for accomplishing tasks associated with the mission of the church. Conversely, American Baptists conceive the BHS metaphor as a non-affective and non-repeatable corporate event occurring on the Day of Pentecost. In their view, BHS is co-terminus with conversion and responsible for personal incorporation into the body of Christ.

This polarization of American Baptist and P/C BHS interpretations encompasses the agency, medium, purpose, correlative functions, timing, evidence, lexical range, frequency, relation to the *charismata,* and theological orientation of the metaphor, as summarized in Table 1. The nature of this polarization is manifested by equivocating American Baptist and P/C adherent BHS interpretations. Its basis is the lack of conceptual univocacy. Progress toward doctrinal consensus depends on a common BHS conception.

As conversion experience-based evangelical traditions unified by a common core, BHS represents one means for dynamic spiritual growth in motion toward the core (center). The BHS doctrine articulated by the P/C movement is neither opposed to orthodox evangelical belief and praxis, nor an impediment to evangelical communion. In the interest of authentic Christian spirituality, American Baptists benefit from exegetically engaging P/C adherents concerning the BHS metaphor. An impasse to constructive deliberation occurs at the point of applied doctrine or *praxis.* Whether or not BHS is the root of disputed miraculous *charismata* or personally experienced as a second work of grace need not be resolved in order to exegetically evaluate the phenomenon/metaphor commonly referred to as BHS.

-2-

PENTECOSTAL SPIRITUALITY: MULTIPLE MOVEMENTS WITH A COMMON ROOT

1. Introduction

The purpose of this and the following chapter is to present an analysis of two independent and unique spiritual traditions. The focus of this comparative analysis is the common experiential root which is the orientation identified in the previous chapter which is shared by American Baptists and P/C adherents. The notation 'P/C' represents a movement unified by independent spiritual traditions.[1] Beyond the evangelical ties demonstrated in the previous chapter, the following analyses establish more precisely the experiential dimension of American Baptist and P/C spirituality. This chapter investigates the P/C movement in order to adduce the central role of spiritual experience within the multi-faceted tradition. The data which follows is used to differentiate the various facets of the P/C movement while maintaining the integrity of each contributing spiritual tradition. This diversity illustrates the difficulty of forming discrete intellectual concepts for expressing in cognitive terms experiences that are embraced for non-cognitive reasons. While the core of P/C spirituality is presented in this chapter, its diversity is also highlighted. Existing within the movement is a range of nuanced and

---

[1] See the discussion in the Introduction. Smidt, Kellstedt, Green, and Guth distinguish the labels 'Pentecostal' and 'charismatic' in a manner useful for this study. 'Pentecostal' is a reference to 'those who are either members of Pentecostal denominations or who willingly label themselves as Pentecostals.' The 'charismatic' label is applied to 'non-Pentecostals who exhibit particular spiritual gifts (primarily speaking in tongues), subscribe to certain doctrines related to the workings of the Holy Spirit, or identify themselves as charismatics.' See Corwin E. Smidt, Lyman A. Kellstedt, John C. Green, and James L. Guth, 'The Spirit-Filled Movements in Contemporary America: A Survey Perspective,' in Edith L. Blumhofer, Russell P. Spittler, and Grant A. Wacker, eds., *Pentecostal Currents in American Protestantism* (Chicago: University of Illinois Press, 1999), 112.

conflicting views. It follows that the existing streams of P/C spirituality enhance the opportunity for dialogue with Christians outside the movement.

P/C unity contains a degree of evolution which defines the relation between the independent spiritual traditions. Classical Pentecostals[2] experienced early institutional fragmentation and evolved along racial, doctrinal, regional, and cultural lines. This institutional fragmentation resulted in scores of denominations, independent churches, and parachurch organizations. The spirituality exhibited by the early Pentecostals until the mid-1950s is the 'classical' expression of the P/C movement.[3] Later developments within the movement retained the core beliefs and praxis of nascent Pentecostalism. Scholars commonly distinguish between the spiritual traditions of the P/C movement in terms of a succession of 'waves.'[4] Classical Pentecostalism is the 'first wave' and is followed chronologically by 'second wave neo-Pentecostalism' ('charismatic renewal'). Adherents of the 'third wave' find expression through a variety of independent ministries.[5] Some have postulated a 'fourth wave' composed of charismatics and evangelicals reconsidering traditional beliefs in light of the biblical data.[6]

The 'waves' of Pentecostalism pose the difficult task of identifying a common spiritual root for the unified movement, though recent scholarship has

---

[2] August Cerillo, 'The Beginnings of American Pentecostalism: A Historiographical Overview,' in Edith L. Blumhofer, Russell P. Spittler, and Grant A. Wacker, eds., *Pentecostal Currents in American Protestantism* (Chicago: University of Illinois Press, 1999), 249. For bibliographic references see Warrington, *Pentecostal Theology*, 6-11. Jones' two volume bibliographic work on Pentecostalism is comprehensive up until 1983. See C. E. Jones, *A Guide to the Study of Pentecostalism, 2 Vols.* (Metuchen: Scarecrow Press, 1983). Mittelstadt's bibliography of Pentecostal literature on Luke-Acts is current up until 2010. See Martin William Mittelstadt, *Reading Luke-Acts in the Pentecostal Tradition* (Cleveland: CPT Press, 2010), 170-205. See also D. D. Bundy, 'Bibliography and Historiography' in Stanley M. Burgess and Eduard M. Van Der Mass, eds., *NIDPCM* (Grand Rapids: Zondervan, 2002), 382-417.

[3] Cerillo, 'The Beginnings of American Pentecostalism,' 249.

[4] Poloma refers to the P/C community as a diverse subculture that includes a 'first wave' of 'classic Pentecostals' occurring in the first quarter of the twentieth century, a 'second wave' of 'neo-Pentecostals' (or 'charismatics'), emerging during the 1960's and 1970's, and a 'third wave' of new churches and independent ministries (neo-charismatics) that 'revitalized the P/C movement during the 1980's and 1990's. Additionally, Poloma calls attention to 'countless syncretistic groups that have adapted Spirit-filled Christianity with their indigenous cultures.' See Poloma, *Main Street Mystics*, 20.

[5] C. Peter Wagner, *The Third Wave of the Holy Spirit: Encountering the Power of Signs and Wonders* (Ann Arbor: Servant Publications, 1988), 13-24; David B. Barrett and Todd M. Johnson, 'Global Statistics' in Stanley M. Burgess and Eduard M. Van Der Mass, eds., *NIDPCM* (Grand Rapids: Zondervan, 2002), 284.

[6] David Pawson, *Fourth Wave: Charismatics and Evangelicals, Are they Ready to Come Together?* (London: Hodder & Stoughton, 1993), 55-61.

successfully articulated fully-developed formulations of P/C spirituality.[7] The multidimensional nature of Pentecostalism(s)[8] contributes to the difficulty of identifying an adequate framework to accurately describe the P/C movement as a whole. Though differing in doctrinal emphases and praxis, the traditions contributing to P/C spirituality endorse a radically transformative experience of the Spirit. The research which follows strengthens the thesis of this study by providing American Baptists with a rationale for engaging P/C adherents in order to work together towards a biblically-adduced doctrinal BHS consensus. The rationale for engagement is an experiential orientation to spirituality that is mutually tethered to the core emphases of the P/C movement. Though discussed within the context of P/C spirituality, a thorough presentation of BHS views represented among the unique distinct traditions within the P/C movement is reserved for analysis in Chapter 5.

2. Historical Excursus: Successive Waves and Divergent Streams

2.1 Classical Pentecostalism

2.1.1 The Emergence of a Global Phenomenon

Pentecostalism achieved critical and scholarly acclaim during the 1950s.[9] The movement received endorsements from several prominent Christian leaders. Leslie Newbigin, director of the division of World Mission and Evangelism for

---

[7] Daniel E. Albrecht, *Rites in the Spirit: A Ritual Approach to Pentecostal/Charismatic Spirituality* (Sheffield: Sheffield Academic Press, 1999); Steven J. Land, *Pentecostal Spirituality: A Passion for the Kingdom* ([original work published 1997] Sheffield: Sheffield Academic Press, 2001).

[8] Spittler refers to 'twentieth-century Pentecostalisms.' See Russell P. Spittler, 'Corinthian Spirituality: How a Flawed Anthropology Imperils Authentic Christian Existence,' in Edith L. Blumhofer, Russell P. Spittler, and Grant A. Wacker, eds., *Pentecostal Currents in American Protestantism* (Chicago: University of Illinois Press, 1999), 13; See also Keith Warrington, *Pentecostal Theology: A Theology of Encounter* (London: T & T Clark, 2008), 12; Alan Anderson, 'Varieties, Taxonomies, and Definitions' in Alan Anderson, Michael Bergunder, André Droogers, Cornelius Van Der Laan, eds., *Studying Global Pentecostalism: Theories and Methods* (Berkley: University of California Press, 2010), 13; Veli-Matti Kärkkäinen, 'Pneumatologies in Systematic Theology' in Alan Anderson, Michael Bergunder, André Droogers, Cornelius Van Der Laan, eds., *Studying Global Pentecostalism: Theories and Methods* (Berkley: University of California Press, 2010), 224.

[9] According to Hocken, 'the designation "Pentecostal" indicated not so much an emphasis on particular teaching and church practice as with the Baptists, but the claim to a new experience of Pentecost.' See Peter D. Hocken, *The Challenge of the Pentecostal, Charismatic and Messianic Jewish Movements: The Tension of the Spirit* (Farnham: Ashgate Publishing, 2009), 4.

the World Council of Churches (WCC),[10] acclaimed Pentecostalism 'a third stream of Christian tradition.'[11] Union Theological Seminary (New York, NY) president Van Dusen heralded the burgeoning movement[12] a 'new reformation,' the 'Third Force in Christendom,'[13] and 'the most extra-ordinary religious phenomenon of our time.'[14] Princeton Theological Seminary (Princeton, NJ) president John Mackay officially recognized Pentecostal World Conference organizing secretary David Du Plessis as a fraternal delegate to the World Presbyterian Alliance at its 1959 meeting (Sao Paulo, Brazil). This event marked the first occasion by a confessional body to officially recognize the Pentecostal movement.[15] Pentecostalism emerged as a distinct tradition within the Christian movement. Deep differences separated Catholicism and orthodox Protestantism during this era, though each tradition attempted to safeguard the uniqueness, sufficiency, and finality of God's saving acts in Christ. As a 'third stream' in Christendom, Pentecostalism mingled and overlapped with the other two streams without compromising its distinctive character; the Christian life is a dynamic witness to the experienced power and presence of the Holy Spirit. Pentecostal assemblies frequently regard this spiritual intensity as existing in mere shell-like and lifeless form among Catholics and Protestants.[16] For its adherents, Pentecostalism is an answer to those who criticize Christianity for being rationalistic in form and without experiential substance.[17]

---

[10] J. Rodman Williams, 2003. 'The Upsurge of Pentecostalism' in *A Theological Pilgrimage,* n.p. Available from: http://www.cbn.com/spirituallife/BibleStudyAnd Theology/ DrWilliams/ bk_theopilgrim_ch03.aspx. (Accessed 22 September 2011).

[11] Newbigin identified the two existing streams as 'traditional Protestant' and 'Roman Catholic.' See Leslie Newbigin, *The Household of God: Lectures on the Nature of the Church* ([original work published 1953] New York: Friendship Press, 1954), 95, 121.

[12] According to statistical data provided by Barrett and Johnson, 'Denominational Pentecostals' (includes primarily classical Pentecostals) grew from 20,000 in 1910 to 15,382,330 by 1970. Barrett and Johnson, 'Global Statistics,' 286.

[13] Henry P. Van Dusen, 'Caribbean Holiday,' in *The Christian Century* (1955), 947-48.

[14] Henry P. Van Dusen, 'The Third Force in Christendom,' in *Life Magazine* (1958), 113-21.

[15] David Du Plessis, *The Spirit Bade Me Go: The Astounding Move of God in the Denominational Churches* ([original work published 1970] Gainesville: Bridge-Logos Publishers, 2004), 19.

[16] Newbigin, *The Household of God,* 94-95.

[17] Ibid., 94-122.

Claiming to be founded on biblical precedents[18] and deriving its dynamism from the Spirit, Pentecostalism soon gained the critical attention of the scholarly community.[19] The term 'Pentecostal' became an assigned name for spirituality with overlapping Catholic and Protestant elements. This distinctive spirituality disregards placing emphasis on visible form and structure and instead accentuates the transformative Spirit-based life that brings ontological change to the believer.[20] By incorporating values, beliefs, and practices into a distinctive religious lifestyle, Pentecostalism meets the spiritual criteria of a dynamically lived religion.[21]

In the name of orthodoxy and historical continuity, early American Pentecostal groups adopted doctrinal statements from the classical Christian traditions.[22] This practice denied Pentecostalism its status as a distinct movement within Christianity and relegated it to subgroup status within American fundamentalism[23] or evangelicalism.[24] The 1943 Statement of Faith adopted by

---

[18] Newbigin accredits the Pentecostal movement on the basis of biblical evidence he deems 'so abundant that I cannot do more than remind you of a few outstanding groups of passages.' Ibid., 96-102.

[19] In 1970, Dunn wrote a serious appraisal of the most distinctive aspect of Pentecostal theology, baptism in the Holy Spirit. James D. G. Dunn, *Baptism in the Holy Spirit: A Reexamination of the New Testament Teaching on the Gift of the Spirit in Relation to Pentecost Today* (Philadelphia: The Westminster Press, 1970). Another early significant and critical analysis of Pentecostal and neo-Pentecostal doctrine is Frederick Dale Bruner, *A Theology of the Holy Spirit: The Pentecostal Experience and the New Testament Witness* (London: Hodder and Stoughton, 1970).

[20] Newbigin, *The Household of God*, 95.

[21] Spittler, 'Corinthian Spirituality,' 3.

[22] Donald W. Dayton, *The Theological Roots of Pentecostalism* ([original work published 1987] Peabody: Hendrickson Publishers, 2000), 17.

[23] Pentecostals affirm the orthodox Christian beliefs held commonly with fundamentalists, though historic breaks with fundamentalism (a reference to specific occurrences in 1928 and 1943) 'freed the rising Pentecostals from the dead cultural and theological baggage of a discredited movement and opened up the way for unparalleled influence and growth in the last half of the twentieth century.' Vinson Synan, 'Fundamentalism' in Stanley M. Burgess and Eduard M. Van Der Mass, eds., *NIDPCM* (Grand Rapids: Zondervan, 2002), 820-21. Suurmond is more explicit when he describes the nature of fundamentalism and its corresponding effects on Pentecostal experience. According to Suurmond, fundamentalism is comprised of abstract conservative-Calvinist teachings, including cessationist views regarding the gifts of the Spirit and a pension for order that militates against the spontaneity of experiencing God in the present. See Jean-Jacques Suurmond, Trans. John Bowden, *Word and Play: Towards a Charismatic Theology* (ET Grand Rapids: William B. Eerdmans Publishing Company, 1995), 7.

[24] Pentecostalism's association with fundamentalism and evangelicalism is a debated issue. Faupel describes two competing visions regarding the historiography of Pentecostal doctrine. One view places Pentecostalism as a subgroup of evangelicalism and sharing its assumptions, agenda, and mission. A second view regards the first as abandoning many of the initial Pentecostal assumptions, 'the initial impulse which gave rise to the movement. See D. William Faupel, 'Whither Pentecostalism?' in *Pneuma* (1993), 26-27. The full participation of Pentecostals in NAE

the National Association of Evangelicals (NAE) is nearly identical to the one adopted by the Pentecostal Fellowship of North America in 1948.[25] The lone difference appears in Article 5 and is a significant exception. The exception identifies Pentecostalism as a 'full gospel' movement distinct from other evangelical and fundamental Protestant traditions.[26] It also describes 'full gospel' as including 'holiness of heart and life, healing for the body and baptism in the Holy Spirit with the initial evidence of speaking in other tongues as the Spirit gives evidence.'[27] Theologically, Pentecostalism followed the evangelical traditions,[28] but added BHS as a post-conversion experience evidenced by speaking in tongues.[29]

As a descriptive term applied to Pentecostalism, 'classical' denotes the earliest stage of the P/C movement.[30] The spiritual core and distinctive doctrines of the movement took definitive shape during this formative period.[31] A doctrinal

---

experienced initial resistance, but by 1987 Pentecostals numbered 3.1 million of the 5 million NAE members and Pentecostals served on three occasions as the NAE president. According to Hollenweger, what Pentecostals gained in terms of 'respectability' through the NAE affiliation, the subsequent 'evangelicalization' of the movement has resulted in the loss of 'certain distinctives' (e.g. pacifism, role of women) and being 'cut off from meaningful interaction with the conciliar sector of the church.' Walter J. Hollenweger, *Pentecostalism: Origins and Developments Worldwide* (Peabody: Hendrickson Publishers, 1997), 192-95.

[25] Dayton, *The Theological Roots of Pentecostalism*, 17-18.

[26] Hocken, *The Challenges of the Pentecostal, Charismatic and Messianic Jewish Movements*, 5-6.

[27] John Thomas Nichol, *Pentecostalism* (New York: Harper & Row, 1966), 4-5.

[28] Conn considers the 'bedrock of Pentecostal belief' to be 'five points of evangelical belief.' Charles W. Conn, *Pillars of Pentecost* (Cleveland: The Pathway Press, 1956), 26-27.

[29] Hollenweger, *Pentecostalism*, 19. According to Hathaway, 'the doctrine of initial evidence was axiomatic to most Pentecostals.' Malcolm R. Hathaway, 'The Elim Pentecostal Church: Origins, Development and Distinctives' in Keith Warrington, ed., *Pentecostal Perspectives* (Carlisle: Paternoster Press, 1998), 8.

[30] R. Hollis Gause, 'Issues in Pentecostalism' in Russell P. Spittler, ed., *Perspectives on the New Pentecostalism* (Grand Rapids: Baker Book House, 1976), 108.

[31] Michael Welker, Trans. John F. Hoffmeyer, *God the Spirit* (ET Minneapolis: Fortress Press, 1994), 9. Berends points to the 1908 outbreak of glossolalia among the First Fruit Harvesters of rural New Hampshire as exemplary of the restorationist tendencies of a holiness group. Former Free Methodist Joel Adams Wright proclaimed the twin themes of restorationism and millennialism, harkening back to the first-century church for the group's prototype. According to Wright, the apostolic church represented the apex of Christianity. The traits of the early church, in accordance with Wright's reading of the Bible, consisted of miraculous gifts, unity among the believers, and the outpouring of the Holy Spirit. Wright coupled these traits with a deep longing for the imminent return of Christ. See Kurt O. Berends, 'Social Variables and Community Response' in Edith L. Blumhofer, Russell P. Spittler, and Grant A. Wacker, eds., *Pentecostal Currents in American Protestantism* (Chicago: University of Illinois Press, 1999), 69-71. For restorationist themes in Pentecostalism, see also Blumhofer, *Restoring the Faith*, 11-34. Blumhofer identifies four elements of restorationist thought among early Pentecostals: (1) an ahistorical backward look to the NT

distinctive which differentiates classical Pentecostalism from other evangelicals is BHS as a post-conversion experience.[32] The arrival of the Spirit on the Day of Pentecost, as related in Acts 2,[33] is the historical and definitional marker for the movement.[34] BHS as the promised power associated with the Pentecostal gift of the Spirit (cf. Acts 1:8) is the experience which conceptually unifies the movement.[35] Classical Pentecostals have historically given priority to the BHS doctrine in modern theological discourse.[36] Some in the movement are critical of a discernible trend to ignore or even remove BHS from its functional center –i.e. as the means for theologically reflecting on the redemptive work of God in the world.[37] Classical Pentecostals consider BHS to be a direct and intense spiritual experience, overwhelming in nature, and centered on the person of Christ.[38]

Pentecostal origins are typically traced to Harriet Ozman, a student at Parham's Bethel Bible College (Topeka, KS). On 1 January 1901, Ozman is recorded as becoming the first to 'receive BHS' with the accompanying sign of glossolalia.[39] To many Pentecostals this event represents a providential,

---

church, (2) promotion of the unity of the body of Christ, (3) serious interest in eschatological issues, and (4) an anti-institutional 'come-outism.'

[32] William W. Menzies and Robert P. Menzies, *Spirit and Power: Foundations of Pentecostal Experience* (Grand Rapids: Zondervan, 2000), 11 n. 2.

[33] According to Petts, 'when Pentecostals talk about the Baptism in the Holy Spirit, they generally mean an experience of the Spirit's power accompanied by speaking in tongues as on the Day of Pentecost (Acts 2:4).' David Petts, 'The Baptism in the Holy Spirit: The Theological Distinctive' in Keith Warrington, ed., *Pentecostal Perspectives* (Carlisle: Paternoster Press, 1998), 98. See Gee, *Wind and Flame*, 7-8.

[34] Gause, 'Issues in Pentecostalism,' 107.

[35] Menzies and Menzies, *Spirit and Power*, 9-10.

[36] Veli-Matti Kärkkäinen, *Spiritus ubi vult spirat: Pneumatology in Catholic-Pentecostal Dialogue (1972-1989)* (Helsinki: Luther Agricola Society, 1998), 198.

[37] Frank D. Macchia, *Baptized in the Spirit: A Global Pentecostal Theology* (Grand Rapids: Zondervan, 2006), 19-20.

[38] Simon Chan, 'Evidential Glossolalia and the Doctrine of Subsequence,' in *AJPS* (1999), 198.

[39] The subject of Pentecostal origins has been thoroughly researched. Please refer to the list of representative works: Vinson Synan, 'The Pentecostal Century: An Overview' in Vinson Synan, ed., *The Century of the Holy Spirit: 100 Years of Pentecostal and Charismatic Renewal, 1901-2001* (Nashville: Thomas Nelson Publishers, 2001), 1-68; Dayton, *The Theological Roots of Pentecostalism*, 15-180; Gee, *Wind and Flame*, 11-19; Eddie L. Hyatt, *2000 Years of Charismatic Christianity: A 21st Century Look at Church History from a Pentecostal/Charismatic Perspective* (Lake Mary: Charisma House, 2002), 101-61; Stanley M. Horton, 'The Pentecostal Explosion: How the Fire Fell in 1906 and Spread,' in *Assemblies of God Heritage* (1982), 2-8; Hollenweger, *Pentecostalism*, 18-24 and *The Pentecostals*, 3-27; Cecil Roebeck, Jr., 'Pentecostal Origins from a Global Perspective' in Harold D. Hunter and Peter D. Hocken, eds., *All Together in One Place:*

spontaneous and restorative work of God; an eschatological 'latter rain'[40] outpouring of the Spirit attested by Scripture to precede the return of Christ.[41] Other Pentecostals consider the movement to be a fermentation of the nineteenth century antecedent influences[42] of Wesleyan (Holiness)[43] and non-Wesleyan (Reformed)[44] traditions. These traditions reflect the variety of influences which contributed to the emergence of Pentecostalism.[45] A summary of these influences include:

Theological Papers from the Brighton Conference on World Evangelization (Sheffield: Sheffield Academic Press, 1996), 166-80.

[40] Hocken, *The Challenge of the Pentecostal, Charismatic and Messianic Jewish Movements*, 4-5; Leonard Lovett, 'Black Origins of the Pentecostal Movement' in Vinson Synan, ed., *Aspects of Pentecostal-Charismatic Origins* (Gainesville: Bridge-Logos, 1975), 125-40; Vinson Synan, *In the Latter Days: The Outpouring of the Holy Spirit in the Twentieth Century* (Ann Arbor: Servant Publications, 1984), 9-48; Alan Anderson, *Spreading Fires: The Missionary Nature of Early Pentecostalism* (London: SCM Press, 2007), 290.

[41] Cerillo, 'The Beginnings of American Pentecostalism,' 229-59; Paul A. Pomerville, *The Third Force in Missions* (Peabody: Hendrickson Publishers, 1985), 5-20; Thomas F. Zimmerman, 'The Reason for the Rise of the Pentecostal Movement' in Grant McClung, ed., *Azusa Street and Beyond: 100 Years of Commentary on the Global Pentecostal/Charismatic Movement* (Gainesville: Bridge-Logos, 2006), 91; Hocken, *The Challenges of the Pentecostal, Charismatic and Messianic Jewish Movements*, 8-22; Cecil Roebeck, Jr., 'Pentecostal Origins from a Global Perspective,' 166-80.

[42] For a detailed survey of the roots of BHS in nineteenth century North American Evangelical Christianity, see Roland Wessels, 'The Spirit Baptism, Nineteenth Century Roots' in *Pneuma* (1992), 127-57. See also, Dayton, *The Theological Roots of Pentecostalism*, 63-113.

[43] The term 'Pentecostal' is a Wesleyan identification for the post-conversion experiences of sanctification and the infilling of the Spirit. See John Wesley, *A Plain Account of Christian Perfection* ([original work published 1844] London: The Epworth Press, 1952), 11-15. Wesley quotes his earlier tract, *The Character of a Methodist,* where he describes the attributes of the perfect Christian. See also Gause, 'Issues in Pentecostalism,' 108.

[44] The non-Wesleyan quest to attain renewal was expressed in terms of a 'deeper' or 'higher' life experience with God. From the non-Wesleyan perspective, sanctification was not complete or entire as the result of a crisis experience, but a life-long process. See Menzies and Menzies, *Spirit and Power*, 18. Hyatt, *2000 Years of Charismatic Christianity*, 124. In her doctoral dissertation, Blumhofer (now Waldvogel) attributed many Pentecostal emphases to non-Wesleyan evangelicals, including Holy Spirit baptism separate from conversion, sanctification as a progressive overcoming of sin and not a radical elimination of the sin nature, the premillennial return of Christ, and healing in the atonement. See Edith Lydia Waldvogel, 'The Overcoming Life: A Study in the Reformed Evangelical Origins of Pentecostalism' (PhD diss., Harvard University, 1977), 1-148.

[45] Warrington provides an extensive bibliography of the antecedents and influences contributing to the emergence of Pentecostalism. See Warrington, *Pentecostal Theology*, 2-5.

1) Hunger for the deeper experience of God evident in the teachings of John Wesley[46] and his followers.[47]

2) The higher life Keswick teaching.[48]

---

[46] Wesley's experiences recorded in his *Journal* include his conversion on the evening of May 14, 1738 at a meeting on Aldersgate Street in London and the mighty descent of the Spirit upon the convocation gathered for an all-night prayer meeting. See John Wesley, *The Journal of the Rev. John Wesley, 8 Vols.* in Nehemiah Curnock, ed., *The Journal of the Rev. John Wesley, Vol. 1* ([original work published 1911-12] London: Epworth, 1938), 476 and Nehemiah Curnock, ed., *The Journal of the Rev. John Wesley, Vol. 2* ([original work published 1911-12] London: Epworth, 1938), 122-25.

[47] The most influential leader in the nineteenth century Methodist renewal movement was Phoebe Worrall Palmer. Emphasis in her meetings was on the 'full baptism of the Holy Spirit as received by the one hundred and twenty disciples on the Day of Pentecost.' Phoebe Palmer, *Four Years in the Old World* (Boston: Foster & Palmer, 1965), 145; Hyatt, *2000 Years of Charismatic Christianity*, 124-26; D. William Faupel, 'The Everlasting Gospel: The Significance of Eschatology in the Development of Pentecostal Thought' (PhD diss., University of Birmingham, 1989), 110-12.

[48] Synan cites three British perfectionistic and charismatic movements antecedent to the American emergence of Pentecostalism; the Methodist holiness movement, the Catholic Apostolic movement of Edward Irving, and the British Keswick 'Higher Life' movement. See Synan, 'The Pentecostal Century,' 2-3. With a name taken from the English town hosting annual conventions beginning in 1875 for the purpose of cultivating the 'higher Christian life,' early Keswick teaching incorporated American Holiness evangelists in England (e.g. W. E. Boardman, Robert Pearsall Smith and Hannah Pearsall Smith) who rejected the 'absolutizing of sanctification' and emphasized a normative Christian life characterized by 'fullness of the Spirit.' For Keswickians, the 'fullness of the Spirit' is received in a manner distinct from and generally coincident with regeneration. The emphasis is upon the actualization of power to live the Christian life effectively. See D. D. Bundy, 'Keswick Higher Life Movement' in Stanley M. Burgess and Eduard M. Van Der Mass, eds., *NIDPCM* (Grand Rapids: Zondervan, 2002), 820-21. See also Hollenweger, *Pentecostalism*, 182-89 and Faupel, 'The Everlasting Gospel,' 147-51.

3) Fundamentalism existing in the dual manifestations of evangelical revivalism[49] owing to the era of Edwards[50] and represented in the ministries of Finney,[51] Moody,[52] Gordon,[53] Torrey,[54] and Simpson.[55]

4) The exegetically and apologetically oriented Princetonian scholastics (Warfield, Hodge, and Machen) who battled the encroachment of a German-inspired (Schleiermacher, Hegel, Kant, Ritschl, and Harnack) reshaping of liberalism into modernism which threatened the foundations of Christian orthodoxy.[56]

Ozman's eruption of glossolalia, purportedly speaking the Chinese language uncontrollably for four days,[57] came as a result of Parham imploring his students

---

[49] Hocken, *The Challenges of the Pentecostal, Charismatic and Messianic Jewish Movements*, 6-7.

[50] Jonathan Edwards, 'A Narrative of Surprising Conversions,' in *Jonathan Edwards on Revival* (Carlisle: Banner of Truth, 1984), 14.

[51] As professor of systematic theology at Oberlin College (1835), Finney and president Mahan framed what is known as 'Oberlin Theology,' a theological orientation including references to the second blessing as the baptism in the Holy Spirit. Rather than radically cleansing from sin, the baptism in the Holy Spirit provided power for Christian service. See Charles G. Finney, *An Autobiography* ([original work published 1876] Westwood: Fleming H. Revell Co., 1908), 55.

[52] Moody's life-altering experience of the Spirit is detailed in William Revell Moody, *The Life of Dwight L. Moody* (Chicago: Fleming H. Revell Co., 1900), 149.

[53] Gordon affirmed the post-conversion endowment of the Spirit and the viability of charismatic gifts. See A. J. Gordon, *The Ministry of Healing: Miracles of Cure in all Ages* (Chicago: Fleming H. Revell Co., 1882), 53. See also A. J. Gordon, *The Two-Fold Life* (Boston: Howard Garnett, 1884), 75-76.

[54] Though he did not recognize glossolalia as evidence for BHS, Torrey did testify to receiving the BHS experience subsequent to conversion and taught the doctrine in his ministry and writings. See R. A. Torrey, *The Baptism with the Holy Spirit* (Chicago: Fleming H. Revell Co, 1895), 9-67; *The Person & Work of the Holy Spirit* ([original work published 1910] Grand Rapids: Zondervan Publishing House, 1974), 146-224; *What the Bible Teaches* ([original work published 1898] New Kensington: Whitaker House, 1996), 269-81 and *The Holy Spirit: Who He is and What He Does* in Harold J. Chadwick, ed., ([original work published 1927] Alachua: Bridge-Logos, 2008), 119-206.

[55] Simpson, founder of the Christian and Missionary Alliance (CM & A), introduced the concept of a 'fourfold gospel.' The role of Jesus as sanctifier was for Simpson equated with Jesus baptizing in the Holy Spirit. Following Holiness teaching, he taught that BHS was a decisive experience of sanctification. See Charles W. Nienkirchen, *A. B. Simpson and the Pentecostal Movement* (Peabody: Hendrickson Publishers, 1993), 2 and Charles W. Nienkirchen, 'Simpson, Albert Benjamin' in Stanley M. Burgess and Eduard M. Van Der Mass, eds., *NIDPCM* (Grand Rapids: Zondervan, 2002), 1069-70. See also, A. B. Simpson, *Power from on High: An Unfolding of the Doctrine of the Holy Spirit in the Old and New Testaments, Part Two: The New Testament* (Harrisburg: Christian Publications, 1896), 77-79.

[56] Menzies and Menzies, *Spirit and Power*, 17-19.

[57] Hyatt, *2000 Years of Charismatic Christianity*, 139. Blumhofer describes the glossolalia phenomenon as lasting three days and speaks of Parham considering it not in terms of

to search for objective and biblical certainty to affirm the BHS experience.[58] What was significant to early Pentecostalism, however, was not the occurrence itself of glossolalia,[59] or the occasion of BHS by Holiness advocates previously identifying the experience with entire sanctification, but rather glossolalia as the validating evidence for the BHS experience.[60] Ozman's experience coincided with the theological understanding of BHS as an empowering of the Spirit for ministry subsequent to conversion and marked by the sign of speaking in other tongues.[61] Early Pentecostalism possessed distinguishing marks, both theological and behavioral,[62] but none more centrally identifiable[63] than BHS.[64] The

---

biblical evidence of BHS, but rather missiologically, as the divinely given ability to speak other languages for the purpose of preaching the gospel to all the nations. See Edith L. Blumhofer, *Restoring the Faith: The Assemblies of God, Pentecostalism, and American Culture* (Chicago: University of Illinois Press, 1993), 51-52.

[58] Sarah Parham, *The Life of Charles F. Parham, Founder of the Apostolic Faith Movement* ([original work published 1930] Joplin: Hunter Publishing House, 1969), 51-52.

[59] Dubious of its sporadic occurrence in the history of the church, Hinson views glossolalia as prospering only in the 20th century. See Stagg, Hinson, and Oates, *Glossolalia*, 45-46. See also Thomas R. Edgar, *Satisfied by the Promise of the Spirit: Affirming the Fullness of God's Provision for Spiritual Living* (Grand Rapids: Kregel Resources, 1996), 201-30. Conversely, Cox views glossolalia as a recovery of a vital spirituality having its roots in primal speech, primal piety, and primal hope suited in a timely fashion to the 'ecstasy deficit' of the twenty-first century and offering as a remedy a 'language of the heart.' See Harvey Cox, *Fire from Heaven: The Rise of Pentecostal Spirituality and the Reshaping of Religion in the Twenty-First Century* (New York: Addison-Wesley Publishing Company, 1995), 81-122.

[60] This view, though not uniformly held among Pentecostals globally, is the stated position of the Assemblies of God in the USA. In particular, see articles 7 and 8 of the 16 Fundamental Truths. See Assemblies of God USA, 2010, 'Our 16 Fundamental Truths,' n.p. Available from: http://ag.org/top/Beliefs/Statement_of_Fundamental_Truths/sft_full.cfm#8. (Accessed: 21 October 2011). Spittler attributes to the P/C movement the democratization of individual religious experience 'by holding out as a value an intensely personal religious experience, termed "baptism in the Holy Spirit," which can be known to have occurred by the audible manifestation of speaking in tongues.' Spittler, 'Corinthian Spirituality,' 6. See also, Suurmond, *Word & Spirit at Play*, 5.

[61] Menzies and Menzies, *Spirit and Power*, 16.

[62] Faupel, 'The Everlasting Gospel,' 6.

[63] See André Droogers, 'Essentialist and Normative Approaches' in Alan Anderson, Michael Bergunder, André Droogers, Cornelius Van Der Laan, eds., *Studying Global Pentecostalism: Theories and Methods* (Berkley: University of California Press, 2010), 41. See also Russell P. Spittler, 'Spirituality, Pentecostal and Charismatic' in Stanley M. Burgess and Eduard M. Van Der Mass, eds., *NIDPCM* (Grand Rapids: Zondervan, 2002), 1096-1102. According to Albrecht, 'Pentecostal spirituality' is a 'specific type of spirituality within the broader category of Christian spirituality.' Therefore, he concludes, it is not utterly unique and each characteristic has appeared in Christian spirituality through the ages. It is the combination, according to Albrecht, that is new. See Daniel E. Albrecht, 'Pentecostal Spirituality: Looking through the Lens of Ritual' in *Pneuma* (1992), 2 n. 5.

[64] Alan Anderson, *An Introduction to Pentecostalism* (Cambridge: Cambridge University Press, 2004), 10. Johnstone and Mandryk define the term 'Pentecostals' as 'those affiliated

importance of BHS is adduced from its historical and theological contexts. Parham's insistence on glossolalia as the biblical evidence for BHS was intended for global evangelization (properly speaking, this is xenolalia). Pentecostals understood BHS as a gift specially given by God for the days immediately preceding the return of Christ. This is represented by the Topeka Pentecostalism founded by Parham in 1901 which was influenced by millenarianism with a missionary emphasis.[65] Though there are global exceptions[66] to its interpretation, classical Pentecostals consider BHS to be a post-conversion, ministry-empowering, and tongues-validated experience.[67]

2.1.2   The Gestalt of the Theological Themes

Shaped in part by Wesleyan-Holiness and non-Wesleyan (Keswick) influences consistent with the theological milieu of nineteenth century revivalist evangelicalism, classical Pentecostalism's commitment to glossolalia as the biblical evidence for BHS represents 'a significant *novum*' (innovation) and establishes a point of discontinuity from this historical period.[68] Defining classical Pentecostalism in terms of a single distinctive (c.g. 'initial evidence') is debated.[69] Theological analysis centering on pneumatological questions concerning BHS and the *charismata* is preferred by some over strictly glossolalia-based

---

specifically to Pentecostal denominations committed to Pentecostal theology usually including a post-conversion experience of a baptism in the Spirit.' Patrick Johnstone and Jason Mandryk, *Operation World: 21ˢᵗ Century Edition* (Carlisle: Paternoster Press, 2005), 3, 21, 755, 757, 762.

[65] James R. Goff, Jr., *Fields White Unto Harvest: Charles F. Parham and the Missionary Origins of Pentecostalism* (Fayetteville: University of Arkansas Press, 1988), 15-16.

[66] See Anderson, *An Introduction to Pentecostalism*, 10-12. See also Dayton, *The Theological Roots of Pentecostalism*, 18-19; Frank D. Macchia, *Baptized in the Spirit: A Global Pentecostal Theology* (Grand Rapids: Zondervan, 2006), 20; Hocken, *The Challenges of the Pentecostal, Charismatic and Messianic Jewish Movements*, 23.

[67] Macchia, *Baptized in the Spirit*, 20-27; Walter J. Hollenweger, *The Pentecostals: The Charismatic Movement in the Churches* (Minneapolis: Augsburg Publishing House, 1972), 9; William W. Menzies, *Anointed to Serve: The Story of the Assemblies of God* (Springfield: Gospel Publishing House, 1971), 9.

[68] Dayton, *The Theological Roots of Pentecostalism*, 176. Dayton discusses at length the significance of BHS. He traces the chronological development of the classical Pentecostal doctrine of BHS within the nineteenth century milieu. According to Dayton, by the mid-1890s both Holiness and higher life wings of the renewal were 'teaching a variation…on the baptism of the Holy Spirit.' This teaching, coupled with the 'pervasiveness of the Pentecostal themes,' required only the proverbial 'spark' to 'ignite this volatile tinder.' See Dayton, *The Theological Roots of Pentecostalism*, 87-113.

[69] For a thorough discussion on the bibliographic material relating to the distinctives of Pentecostalism, see Harold D. Hunter, 2008. 'Orphans or Widows? Seeing Through a Glass darkly,' n.p. Available from: http://www.pctii.org/cyberj/cyberj17/Irenaeus.html. (Accessed 10 November 2011).

interpretations of the movement. Glossolalia as the definitive mark of the movement has been criticized for its failure to embrace the more complex *gestalt* of theological themes which constitute the movement.[70] This *gestalt*[71] is in the form of a common theological pattern which comprises the classical Pentecostal theological package[72] (e.g. 'the fourfold' or 'full gospel').[73] This 'full' or 'fourfold gospel'[74] expresses four fundamental teachings: salvation, healing, BHS, and the second coming of Christ.[75] Notable historical proponents of the 'fourfold' theological *gestalt* include the International Church of the Foursquare Gospel founder Aimee Semple McPherson[76] and Elim Foursquare Gospel Alliance founder George Jeffreys.[77] The fourfold pattern and its attending themes were represented separately or in various combinations during late nineteenth-century revivalism.[78] The experience of glossolalia, however, was conspicuously absent from both Wesleyan and non-Wesleyan revivalism teaching.[79] Pentecostals and radical evangelicals of the period could not be differentiated in terms of doctrine

---

[70] Dayton, *The Theological Roots of Pentecostalism*, 16. Land offers a threefold typology of Pentecostal experience which includes the crises of justification (salvation), sanctification, and Spirit-baptism. See Land, *Pentecostal Spirituality*, 82-94, 125-31.

[71] According to Macchia, *gestalt* is a reference to the theological *loci* of the movement, the original framework and grammar of Pentecostal theology. See Frank D. Macchia, 'Theology, Pentecostal' in Stanley M. Burgess and Eduard M. Van Der Mass, eds., *NIDPCM* (Grand Rapids: Zondervan, 2002), 1123.

[72] Initially delineated as (five-fold) Justification, Salvation, Sanctification, the Baptism of the Holy Ghost, Divine Healing, and the Second Coming. Apostolic Faith Mission Headquarters, *A Historical Account of the Apostolic Faith: Trinitarian-Fundamental Evangelistic Organization* (Portland: Apostolic Faith Mission Headquarters, 1965), 20-21.

[73] Dayton, *The Theological Roots of Pentecostalism*, 21-23.

[74] Hathaway, 'The Elim Pentecostal Church: Origins, Development and Distinctives,' 6-8.

[75] Stanley Horton, *Into all Truth: A Survey of the Course and Content of Divine Revelation* (Springfield: Gospel Publishing House, 1955), 13. Stanley Horton is professor emeritus at Assemblies of God Theological Seminary (Springfield, MS).

[76] According to Aimee Semple McPherson, 'Jesus saves us according to John 3:16. He baptizes us with the Holy Spirit according to Acts 2:4. He heals our bodies according to James 5:14-15. Jesus is coming again to receive us unto Himself according to 1 Thessalonians 4:16-17.' Raymond Cox, *The Foursquare Gospel* (Los Angeles: Foursquare Publications, 1969), 9.

[77] George Jeffreys, *The Miraculous Foursquare Gospel, Vol. 1* (London: Elim Publishing, 1929), 1-11.

[78] Dayton, *The Theological Roots of Pentecostalism*, 22, 167. This is expressed by Simpson who advocated Christ as 'Savior, Sanctifier, Healer, and Coming King.' A. B. Simpson, *The Fourfold Gospel* ([original work published in 1890] New York: Gospel Alliance Publishing, 1925), 7-142.

[79] Hathaway, 'The Elim Pentecostal Church: Origins, Development and Distinctives,' 8.

and lifestyle except for the specific question of tongues.[80] This is an important point to underline in preparing for dialogue with Christians outside the P/C traditions. The following characteristics distinguish (classical) Pentecostalism from other Protestant groups:

1) The experience first recorded in Acts 2 is enduring in the life of the church.

2) This experience is distinct from regeneration and subsequent to it.

3) This experience is the baptism in the Holy Spirit.

4) Speaking in other tongues is the initial and outward sign of BHS.

5) This experience is normative for every believer.[81]

Classical Pentecostalism is defined in relation to BHS. While not denying its centrality to the movement, BHS set in its broader doctrinal *gestalt* indicates that classical Pentecostal belief is more than one-dimensional. Non-Pentecostal evangelicals, who embrace similar doctrinal tenets of the fourfold Pentecostal *gestalt*,[82] would distance themselves from classical Pentecostalism on the issue of BHS and its corresponding doctrine of initial evidence.[83]

Further delineated, the classical Pentecostal *gestalt* includes an expressed Spirit-powered devotion to Jesus making the movement not only theologically cogent, but also Christocentric. The dynamic center of classical Pentecostal theology is the reality of the living Christ performing the will of the Father through the power of the Spirit. The movement's dialogical approach to Christocentric

---

[80] Wacker uses the term 'radical evangelical' to describe Wesleyan and Keswick spirituality. Grant A. Wacker, 'Travail of a Broken Family: Radical Evangelical Responses to the Emergence of Pentecostalism in America, 1906-16' in Edith L. Blumhofer, Russell P. Spittler, and Grant A. Wacker, eds., *Pentecostal Currents in American Protestantism* (Chicago: University of Illinois Press, 1999), 23-49.

[81] Gause, 'Issues in Pentecostalism,' 108.

[82] Wessels, 'The Spirit Baptism, Nineteenth Century Roots,' 127-29.

[83] Referred to by many classical Pentecostals as 'the doctrine of initial evidence,' the view is based primarily on four passages in Acts (2:1-21; 8:5-24; 10:34-48; 19:1-7). The passages are interpreted by classical Pentecostals to express instances of BHS with glossolalia being the one repeated phenomenon. This has led many classical Pentecostals to regard glossolalia (or 'speaking in tongues') as the initial evidence of BHS. See Petts, 'The Baptism in the Holy Spirit: The Theological Distinctive,' 101-15. See also Vinson Synan, 'The Role of Tongues as Initial Evidence' in Mark W. Wilson, ed., *Spirit and Renewal: Essays in Honor of J. Rodman Williams* (Sheffield: Sheffield Academic Press, 1994), 67-82. For a thorough investigation of the doctrine, see Gary B. McGee, ed., *Initial Evidence: Historical and Biblical Perspectives on the Pentecostal Doctrine of Spirit Baptism* (Peabody: Hendrickson Publishers, 1991). For a bibliographic source, see Gerald J. Flokstra, III, 'Sources for the Initial Evidence Discussion: A Bibliographic Essay,' in *AJPS* (1999), 243-59.

devotion is evidenced by a commitment to pluralism and ecumenism. The rationale for this commitment rests on the premise that cultural and ecclesiastical perspectives cannot independently represent the fullness of Christ. Classical Pentecostals encourage solidarity with other Christian traditions in order to achieve a Christocentric pneumatology. Such a pneumatology is devoted to the witness of Scripture, is faithful to the ministry of the kingdom of God (as evidenced by the person and work of Jesus), and functions in accordance with the ministry of the exalted Christ and the Holy Spirit.[84]

2.2   Charismatic Renewal

2.2.1   Transcending Denominational Boundaries with a Dynamic Move of the Spirit

A dynamic USA-based movement of the Holy Spirit for renewal began in 1960 as a second charismatic awakening (neo-Pentecostalism).[85] Though some see the charismatic renewal and neo-Pentecostalism as distinct traditions within the charismatic awakening, this work considers the terms to be synonymous.[86] The awakening produced an eruption of charismatic experience outside the established bounds of classical Pentecostalism[87] and into the mainline denominational churches.[88] This phenomenon was driven by renewalists[89]

---

[84] Macchia, 'Theology, Pentecostal,' 1123-24.

[85] J. Rodman Williams, *The Era of the Spirit* (Plainfield: Logos International, 1971), 9.

[86] Welker, *God the Spirit*, 9-10. Welker differentiates two movements, 'charismatic renewal' and 'neo-Pentecostalism,' the latter accepting the theology of its classical predecessor, including its fundamental understanding of the Bible, Baptist understanding of baptism, insistence on BHS and its close connection with speaking in tongues. For neo-Pentecostals, glossolalia represents an initiation into faith or the culmination of the path of faith after conversion and sanctification.

[87] The classical Pentecostal movement spawned in excess of 14,000 denominations worldwide. Synan, 'The Pentecostal Century,' 8. See Synan for detailed accounts of several Protestant renewal movements and the impact of the charismatic renewal on the major Protestant denominations. Vinson Synan, 'Charismatic Renewal Enters the Mainline Churches' in Vinson Synan, ed., *The Century of the Holy Spirit: 100 Years of Pentecostal and Charismatic Renewal, 1901-2001* (Nashville: Thomas Nelson Publishers, 2001), 149-76; Vinson Synan, 'The Charismatics: Renewal in Major Protestant Denominations' in Vinson Synan, ed., *The Century of the Holy Spirit: 100 Years of Pentecostal and Charismatic Renewal, 1901-2001* (Nashville: Thomas Nelson Publishers, 2001), 177-208.

[88] Synan, 'The Pentecostal Century,' 9. For a detailed case study see William J. Samarin, 'Religious Goals of a Neo-Pentecostal Group in a Non-Pentecostal Church' in Russell P. Spittler, ed., *Perspectives on the New Pentecostalism* by (Grand Rapids: Baker Book House, 1976), 134-49 and Cerillo, 'The Beginnings of American Pentecostalism: A Historiographical Overview,' 249.

[89] This evangelical block is labeled 'Renewalists' in the *IBMR* report, 'Status of Global Mission, 2011, in Context of 20th and 21st Centuries.' *IBMR*, 2011. 'Status of Global Mission, 2011,

determined to remain in their churches and to inspire revival.[90] The function of the charismatic renewal is summarized as follows:

1) Within the mainline churches, the charismatic renewal represents an element of the whole.

2) The renewing element is instrumental to the transformation of the entire church or denomination.

3) The charismatic renewal recognizes the value of preserving (while renewing) the core-tradition of the church or denomination.[91]

The strength of the renewal may be seen in its interaction with the entire heritage (or 'apostolic tradition') of a given church-tradition. It is also comprehensive and encompasses the full range of spiritual and ecclesial disciplines (e.g. worship, doctrine, evangelism and mission, catechesis, pastoral care, social outreach, and church polity).[92]

The renewal movement traces its origin to the 1960 BHS experience of Episcopalian pastor Dennis Bennett.[93] Prior to 1960 several mainline pastors experienced glossolalia, but Bennett forged a breakthrough into the mainline denominational churches by witnessing resolutely to the validity of his experience.[94] It was Bennett's initial followers who were labeled 'neo-

---

in Context of 20th and 21st Centuries,' n.p. Available from: http://www.gordonconwell.edu/sites/default/ files/StatusOfGlobalMission.pdf. [Accessed 22 June 2011]. The term 'renewalists' is applicable to members of a single movement composed of classical Pentecostals, charismatics, and neo-charismatics. See Todd Johnson, David B. Barrett and Peter Crossing, 'Status of Global Mission, 2011, in Context of 20th and 21st Centuries,' in *IBMR* (2011), 36-37. The term is used in this work to identify members of the charismatic (neo-Pentecostal) renewal.

[90] Synan, 'The Charismatics,' 178. For Olson, the 'Charismatic movement' shares commonality with evangelicalism as each represents a 'religious-spiritual' network without membership. Members of the renewal exist as a diverse group with common interests, but lacking a single spokesperson. See Roger E. Olson, 'Postconservative Evangelicalism' in David Naselli and Collin Hansen, eds., *Four Views on the Spectrum of Evangelicalism* (Grand Rapids: Zondervan, 2011), 162. Williams, *Era of the Spirit*, 35; Hocken, *The Challenges of the Pentecostal, Charismatic and Messianic Jewish Movements*, 53-74.

[91] All three elements are mentioned in Hocken, *The Challenges of the Pentecostal, Charismatic and Messianic Movements*, 78. See also Smidt, Kellstedt, Green, and Guth, 'The Spirit-Filled Movements in Contemporary America,' 122-25.

[92] Hocken, *The Challenges of the Pentecostal, Charismatic and Messianic Movements*, 78.

[93] Dennis Bennett, *Nine O'Clock in the Morning* (Plainfield: Bridge Publishing, 1970), 1-30.

[94] Synan statistically represents the expansion of the movement to 150 major protestant families in the first decade and reaching 55 million people by 1990. Synan, 'The Pentecostal Century,' 9. Synan, 'Charismatic Renewal Enters the Mainline Churches,' 151. According to statistical data provided by Barrett and Johnson, 'Charismatics' (defined as 'all who have

Pentecostals.'[95] Beginning with Episcopalians, the charismatic renewal made early inroads among Presbyterians, Lutherans, and Roman Catholics.[96] The term 'neo-Pentecostal' became a general reference to those practicing glossolalia,[97] but who wished to disassociate from some aspect of classical Pentecostalism.[98] The movement earned the label 'New Pentecostalism' because of its protestation against the perceived cold and impersonal formalism within some sectors of institutional evangelicalism.[99] As a result, Pentecostal religious experiences (e.g. glossolalia and other *charismata*) entered into mainline Protestant denominations,[100] Roman Catholic assemblies,[101] and evangelical Protestant groups.[102] Specifically, Pentecostal spirituality impacted the mainline churches by revitalizing (or actualizing) historic church doctrines, rites, and practices. Validating the new spiritual experience became the goal of the charismatic renewal. This was considered as having been achieved either by linking the experience to prior occurrence in church history, or demonstrating its implicit role within the traditional beliefs or sacramental rites of the church.[103] The charismatic

---

experienced Spirit-baptism but remain within non-Pentecostal mainline churches') grew from 3,349,400 in 1970 to 175,856,690 by 2000. The projected growth is 274,934,000 by 2025. Barrett and Johnson, 'Global Statistics,' 286.

[95] Synan, 'The Role of Tongues as Initial Evidence,' 67.

[96] Synan, 'The Charismatics,' 177; Peter D. Hocken, 'The Catholic Charismatic Renewal' in Vinson Synan, ed., *The Century of the Holy Spirit* (Nashville: Thomas Nelson Publishers, 2001), 209-32.

[97] Welker critiques the centrality of glossolalia among Pentecostals and the charismatic renewal, attributing the phenomenon in part to viewing the Spirit 'as something numinous…a force that evokes numinous feelings and corresponding experiences…mystical gifts and impressions.' These experiences, according to Welker, 'are placed at the center of piety and ecclesiastical life.' Welker, *God the Spirit*, 268.

[98] Gause, 'Issues in Pentecostalism,' 108-9.

[99] Clark H. Pinnock, 'The New Pentecostalism: Reflections of an Evangelical Observer' in Russell P. Spittler, ed., *Perspectives on the New Pentecostalism* (Grand Rapids: Baker Book House, 1976), 185 n. 3.

[100] Anderson, *Introduction to Pentecostalism*, 144.

[101] Hocken, 'Charismatic Movement,' 483. See also Anderson, *Introduction to Pentecostalism*, 151. According to statistical data provided by Barrett and Johnson, 'Catholic Charismatics' (defined as baptized RCs in the CCR) numbered 119,912,200 in 2000 and are projected to number 194,973,000 by 2025. See Barrett and Johnson, 'Global Statistics,' 286. For the influence of the Catholic Charismatic renewal on classical Pentecostal identity, see Frank D. Macchia, 'God Present in a Confused Situation: The Mixed Influence of the Charismatic Movement on Classical Pentecostalism in the United States' in *Pneuma* (1996), 35-37.

[102] Synan, 'The Pentecostal Century,' 8.

[103] Cerillo, 'The Beginnings of American Pentecostalism: A Historiographical Overview,' 250. Exemplary of this pattern is the Roman Catholic reaction to the charismatic renewal. This is best represented in Kilian McDonnell, ed., *Presence, Power, Praise: Documents on the Charismatic*

renewal made operative, whether again or more fully, previous traditional theological categories such as regeneration, sanctification, and confirmation.[104] Several formative factors[105] are attributed to the spiritual dynamism which characterized the renewal:

1) Openness and expectation for the Spirit's activity produced a corresponding sense of readiness.

2) An intense desire for the reality and presence of the Spirit resulted in importunate prayer for the manifestation of the Spirit's presence and power.

3) Humility produced the willingness to receive prayer for renewal from those walking in the Spirit.

4) A growing conviction that a move of the Spirit, i.e. the lively sense of God's presence and power, was required to resolve the prevailing inner weakness in the churches, measured as the lack of evangelistic fervor.

5) A critical and formative feature of the renewal concerned its global vision of a world filled with the knowledge and glory of God.[106]

Considered according to these formative factors, the charismatic renewal was not a containment movement, but one which expressed a desire for the powers of the age to become operative in the contemporary church.[107]

2.2.3   Extraordinary Manifestations of the Spirit

The purpose of this section is to explore the experienced phenomena occurring within the charismatic renewal. The phenomena approximate those often associated with BHS by classical Pentecostal assemblies. There is, however, an important distinction concerning the role of glossolalia considered by classical

---

Renewal, 3 Vols. (Collegeville: Liturgical Press, 1980). In *Presence, Power, Praise*, the validity of the renewal is accepted, cessationism is rejected, and pastoral guidelines for integrating the renewal into the life of the church are offered. See McDonnell, *Presence, Power, Praise, Vol. 3*, 13-69, 82-178, 291-357.

[104] Williams, *The Era of the Spirit*, 41.

[105] Hocken lists nine 'constant characteristics,' each enduring what he terms 'the ongoing evolution of the movement.' See Hocken, 'Charismatic Movement,' 514-15. From a Reformed perspective, Suurmond offers five 'characteristics of charismatic celebration.' See Suurmond, 'Word & Spirit at Play,' 22-26.

[106] Points 1-5 are summarized from Williams, *The Era of the Spirit*, 36-41.

[107] Ibid., 41.

Pentecostals to be 'the' initial evidence of BHS. Members of the charismatic renewal diverge from the classical Pentecostal timing and validation of BHS and hold that 'any' of the *charismata* constitute evidence of BHS.[108] At the same time, the role of BHS in issuing deep existential experience requires a brief look at the phenomena often associated with its manifestation within the renewal.[109] While not all classical Pentecostals agree that the *charismata* are solely dependent upon BHS,[110] its link to enduement with 'power for service' is shared with members of the renewal.[111] It is this link that anticipates the experienced empowering of the Spirit especially via miraculous *charismata* that contribute to an understanding of the experiential dimension of charismatic spirituality.

Jesus is considered by renewalists as the mediator of the plenitude of manifestations of the Spirit and the central focus of the charismatic renewal.[112] It is through his Spirit that renewalists claim to know with certainty the reality of Jesus as living Lord.[113] There is a corresponding yearning for the personal return of Jesus attended by an awakening to God's nearness by his Spirit.[114] By exhibiting a lifestyle of constant and joyous expressions of praise inspired by the Spirit, the new dimension of Spirit-occasioned experience militates against the rote performances of liturgical worship (e.g. Scripture reading and hymn singing).[115] Profound communal love and inward joy, an abounding Spirit-

---

[108] Gordon L. Anderson, 2005. 'Baptism in the Holy Spirit, Initial Evidence, and a New Model,' n.p. Available from: http://enrichmentjournal.ag.org/200501/200501_071_BaptismHS.cfm. (Accessed 10 November 2011). This article is updated from its original publication in *Paraclete* (1993), 1-10.

[109] Henry I. Lederle, *Treasures Old and New: Interpretations of "Spirit-Baptism" in the Charismatic Renewal Movement* (Peabody: Hendrickson Publishers, 1988), 37.

[110] Anderson, 'Baptism in the Holy Spirit, Initial Evidence, and a New Model,' n.p. Available from: http://enrichmentjournal.ag.org/200501/200501_071_BaptismHS.cfm. (Accessed 10 November 2011).

[111] Don Basham, *A Handbook on Holy Spirit Baptism* (New Kensington: Whitaker House, 1969), 24-27.

[112] Hocken, 'Charismatic Movement,' 514. Hocken places every defining aspect of the renewal subordinate to 'manifestations of the exercise of Jesus' lordship.' In his view, the palpable and immediate presence of Jesus is known through his present actions (e.g. speaking through his Word, delivering from evil, healing).

[113] Basham, *A Handbook on Holy Spirit Baptism*, 24-27.

[114] Williams, *Era of the Spirit*, 11-12.

[115] Hocken, 'Charismatic Movement,' 514-15. Hocken links the spontaneous flow of praise to the 'filling of the Holy Spirit.' In his view, this flow of praise from within the believer is a verification of John 7:38 and represents a new capacity for giving glory to God. He regards glossolalia as a symbol of this new capacity for praise and the explosion of new songs as its consequent.

directed freedom, a prevailing and indescribable atmosphere of peace, a deep and stirring spirit of unity –these are considered the byproducts of God living, moving, and multiplying a multi-faceted experience of his intimate and real presence.[116] A Spirit-borne love of the Scriptures is considered the means for transforming the corporate assembly which encounters God's vital presence in a manner rivaling anything in the biblical account.[117]

Renewalists identify the above manifestations as functions of the Spirit occurring within the assembly. In relation to the *charismata* there is readiness and corresponding desire to express the diverse operations of the Spirit.[118] Renewalists consider the exercise of the *charismata*[119] divinely intended for the revealing of the glory of God and for the building up of the fellowship.[120] It is necessary to delimit what is meant by the term *charismata* within the scope of this section. Turner is right when he confesses the near impossibility of determining 'a full semantic stereotype' of spiritual gifts.[121] There are, however, what he terms a few 'prototypical' examples of *charismata* generally associated with the classical Pentecostal and charismatic renewal movements.[122] Commonly referred to as 'the

---

[116] Williams, *Era of the Spirit*, 12-13.

[117] Hocken, 'Charismatic Movement,' 515. To members of the renewal, the Bible, formerly known only as an external norm or historical witness to the works of God in the past, becomes a witness to the present activity of God. The 'greater works' promise of Jesus (John 14:12) is an invitation to look expectantly forward on the basis of the biblical record. See Williams, *Era of the Spirit*, 16-17. In terms of practice, renewalists adopt the existential conviction that 'what God can do for you' is 'what God has done for me.' See Suurmond, *Word & Spirit at Play*, 22-23.

[118] Williams, *Era of the Spirit*, 34. Hocken refers to this urgency in terms of a concern for 'spiritual impact' and its associated power to transform a lifeless church: 'This power of the Spirit is experienced as a gift of the risen Lord Jesus, flowing from obedience to God's Word and manifested in every form of Christian ministry and service, in Word and in sacrament, in ministries within the body of Christ, and in service to those outside.' Hocken, 'Charismatic Movement,' 515.

[119] According to Hocken, renewal centers on 'the availability of the gifts as an intrinsic part of God's equipment of each local church for its mission.' He sees an escalation of the use of gifts in the church during the 1990s and a change in focus away from glossolalia to the gifts of prophecy and healing. See Hocken, 'Charismatic Movement,' 515.

[120] Williams, *Era of the Spirit*, 21. Suurmond agrees, citing 1 Cor 14:12 and noting that the *charismata* cannot be detached from their relation to each other, but together are meant to encourage the 'building up' of the community. See Suurmond, *Word & Spirit at Play*, 170.

[121] Max Turner, *The Holy Spirit and Spiritual Gifts* ([original work published 1996] Peabody: Hendrickson Publishers, 1998), 184; Max Turner, *Power from on High: The Spirit in Israel's Restoration and Witness in Luke-Acts* ([original work published 1996] Sheffield: Sheffield Academic Press, 2000), 91.

[122] Turner, *The Holy Spirit and Spiritual Gifts*, 184.

miraculous gifts of the Spirit,'[123] these *charismata* have special interest to participants of the charismatic renewal and are described below:

1) Evidence of the renewal of the Christian community is the prevalence of Spirit-granted spiritual 'wisdom and knowledge.' This *charisma* is unrelated to office and ability and is considered to provide supernatural guidance at opportune moments.[124] Despite the resistance to direct divine communication expressed by many Christians, renewalists do not consider such communication an infallible 'word' and the assembly is admonished to be discerning in validating the wisdom contained in the message.[125]

2) Extraordinary manifestations of 'healings and deliverance' through the Spirit are considered by renewalists to confirm the NT record. The same Lord who delivered many from oppressive forces is regarded as active among his people through the Spirit.[126] Spiritual blindness occasioned by modernity (e.g. the corresponding need for intellectual and empirical validation)[127] is the identified root cause for denying the viability of extraordinary works of the Spirit within the contemporary church. Conversely, renewalists view profound (miraculous) healings to be the Spirit operating either directly in the affected individual or through the indirect use of a human agent (i.e. a 'gifted' instrument).[128] Deliverance (i.e. setting one free) is a phenomenon distinguished from healing (i.e. making one whole) and is thought to occur when dominating forces are broken. When spiritual oppression (i.e. a demonic spirit) captivates the human spirit, deliverance ministry is performed by one in the fellowship

---

[123] Jon Mark Ruthven, *On the Cessation of the Charismata: The Protestant Polemic on Post-Biblical Miracles* ([original work published 1993] Tulsa: Word & Spirit Press, 2011), 6.

[124] Turner, *Power from on High*, 92-99.

[125] Hocken, 'Charismatic Movement,' 515.

[126] Williams, *Era of the Spirit*, 23.

[127] For Lederle, the charismatic agenda seems pre-eminently 'to challenge the mindset of secular modernity.' He makes a distinction between reason-based modernity and experience-based postmodernity. See Lederle, 'Life in the Spirit and Worldview,' 23-35. For an extended analysis of 'radical materialism' in relation to so-called 'Christian idealism' (thoughts and words influence the natural world to come) see William DeArteaga, *Quenching the Spirit: Examining Centuries of Opposition to the Moving of the Holy Spirit* (Lake Mary: Creation House, 1992), 131-212.

[128] Williams chooses to use the word 'miracles' rather than 'powers' to render the Greek *dunameis* in the context of this discussion. His rationale centers on the need to differentiate between the exercise and limitations of ordinary human power and the extraordinary operations of the Spirit's functioning to produce results beyond the exercise of ordinary human powers. See Williams, *Era of the Spirit*, 24-25.

who is specially 'gifted' by the Spirit.[129] Such demonological phenomena associated with the renewal have drawn critical attention from non-charismatic evangelical Christians. At the center of the 'deliverance' debate is the issue of whether or not the believer can become 'demon-possessed.' Unger is exemplary of a non-charismatic biblical scholar whose seminal work on demonology affirms that the believer's position in Christ makes impossible the likelihood of demon-possession.[130] He later reversed his view on demon-possession and the believer, citing abounding clinical evidence to support his new position.[131] This new position, favorable to charismatically-oriented Christians, was criticized for its perceived emphasis on subjective experience (observation) over the objective teaching of Scripture.[132] Unger concluded that Scripture did not expressly exclude believers from a demon-possessed state, but under certain conditions 'the powers of darkness may invade the believer.'[133]

3) Manifestations of 'prophecy with tongues' is considered by the renewal to provide direct communication with God by the Spirit, both as God's word to people and as their response to him. Because of its edifying capacity for the body, prophecy is often regarded as the most significant *charisma* of all the manifestations of the Spirit.[134] The absence of the prophetic function is attributed to ignorance and the misreading of the NT which, in the view of many renewalists, provides an unmistakable witness to prophets and prophetesses functioning in the early church (e.g. Acts 11:27; 13:1; 21:8-11; 1 Cor 14:1; 1 Thess 5:20). When viewed in

---

[129] Lederle attributes to charismatic spirituality the centrality of spiritual warfare and the corresponding view of the kingdom of God in an 'ongoing struggle' with Satan. In his view, the devil and his demonic spirits were decisively defeated through the atonement and resurrection of Christ, but this does represent 'the final victory' as the devil remains active (1 Pet 5:8). He points to a general agreement between charismatic and non-charismatic evangelicals on this point, though the latter have reservations concerning so-called 'deliverance ministry.' See Lederle, 'Life in the Spirit and Worldview,' 26-31.

[130] Merrill F. Unger, *Biblical Demonology: A Study of the Spiritual Forces Behind the Present World Unrest* (Wheaton: Van Kampen Press, 1952), 100, 122.

[131] Merrill F. Unger, *What Demons Can Do To Saints* ([original work published 1977] Chicago: The Moody Bible Institute, 1991), 37.

[132] See Stanford's critique of former C. Fred Dickason, *Demon Possession and the Christian* (Chicago: The Moody Bible Institute, 1987). Dickason served on the faulty of the Moody Bible Institute (Chicago, IL). Miles J. Stanford, 1996. 'Demon Possession and the Christian,' n.p. Available from: http://withchrist.org/MJS/dickasonf.pdf. [Accessed 11 April 2012].

[133] Unger, *What Demons Can Do To Saints*, 88.

[134] Lederle, 'Life in the Spirit and Worldview,' 26-27.

terms of pastoral functions (e.g. consolation, encouragement, stimulation, exhortation and strengthening), prophecy takes on an edifying role as the means for proper daily living in the presence of God. Prophecy thus understood is the voice of God heard through human language and occasioned by the Spirit of God. The occurrence of prophecy is the spontaneous operation of the Spirit for all renewalists to voice the direct utterances of God, having the dual effect of edifying believers and profoundly impressing non-believers with evidence of the reality of God's immediate presence. References to 'tongues' (glossolalia) encompasses the expressions 'speaking in tongues,' 'praying in tongues, 'praying with the Spirit,' and 'the language of the Spirit.' Two types of glossolalic utterance (public and private) are predominant among renewalists. The exercise of tongues in private is understood as utterances expressed directly to God and having devotional value (e.g. 'praying in tongues,' see Chapter 3 §3.1.2). Outward expressions of tongues are considered to be beneficial to the fellowship and understood to maintain openness to the presence of God and readiness to seek and carry out his will through his Word. Glossolalia is considered on equal authority with prophetic utterance when interpreted for the edification of the body. Differentiation is made between the 'Godward' and 'manward' aspects of tongues and prophecy. Tongues speech, even when supplied with interpretation, is always directed to God. There is no biblical support for tongues-speech being a (prophetic) communication from God to man (Acts 2:6, 11; 10:46; 1 Cor 14:2, 14-16, 28).[135] The phenomenon 'singing in the Spirit' is the result of 'charismatic improvisation' (i.e. humanly impossible) and similar in character and effect to tongues-speech. In sum, renewalists consider tongues, prophecy, and singing in the Spirit to be God-glorifying manifestations of the Holy Spirit uttered through the human spirit.[136]

2.2.4   *Classical Pentecostalism and the Charismatic Renewal*

The charismatic renewal brought confusion and suspicion to many classical Pentecostals ambivalent toward those formerly opposing the manifestation of

---

[135] Keith Warrington, 'The Message of the Holy Spirit: The Spirit of Encounter,' in Derek Tidball, ed., *The Bible Speaks Today* (Downers Grove: InterVarsity Press, 2009), 186-87.

[136] Williams, *Era of the Spirit*, 27-29, 30 n. 10, 32-33.

supernatural *charismata*.[137] Emerging from Holiness roots, many classical Pentecostals were suspicious of the renewal's authenticity, particularly concerning its depth of conversion experience and degree of moral transformation. These Holiness concerns intensified as practices once standard among earlier Pentecostals (e.g. 'tarrying for baptism,' intense soul-searching, and praying over penitent worshippers) were largely lacking among renewalists more concerned with realizing the more immediate BHS result. Rooted in the spiritual tradition of classical Pentecostalism, renewalists lacked the antecedent missionary fervor of the early Pentecostals. This comparative lack of missionary fervor is attributed to the inward focus of the renewal, compelling adherents to experience BHS.[138] Renewalists have, however, positively influenced classical Pentecostal churches in so far as they replaced the aforementioned missionary and eschatological fervor[139] for a here-and-now success-oriented mega church focus. Another effect of the renewal on classical Pentecostals came in the form of an identity crisis as manifestations of early Pentecostalism occurred within foreign spiritual traditions and liturgical contexts and so took on the appearance on an 'alternative' spirituality.[140]

The Spirit's role of bringing *koinonia* to the body of Christ is fundamental to the charismatic renewal.[141] Seen as its most significant influence,[142] ecumenism is deemed responsible for the worldwide scope and power of the renewal.[143] Dubious of this perceived corporate working of the Spirit, classical Pentecostals became skeptical of the mainline renewal,[144] though in recent years a robust attempt at seeking harmony and mutual understanding has formally existed in the form of the ongoing dialogue between classical Pentecostals and the Roman

---

[137] Macchia, 'God Present in a Confused Situation,' 33.

[138] Hocken, 'Charismatic Movement,' 515-17.

[139] See the works of Steven J. Land, *Pentecostal Spirituality: A Passion for the Kingdom* ([original work published 1997] Sheffield: Sheffield Academic Press, 2001) and D. William Faupel, 'The Everlasting Gospel: The Significance of Eschatology in the Development of Pentecostal Thought' (PhD diss., University of Birmingham, 1989).

[140] Macchia, 'God Present in a Confused Situation,' 33-35, 51.

[141] Hocken, 'Charismatic Movement,' 517.

[142] Macchia, 'God Present in a Confused Situation,' 49.

[143] Vinson Synan, *Charismatic Bridges* (Ann Arbor: Word of Life, 1974), 17.

[144] According to Synan, the past persecution and resistance of the mainline churches against Pentecostals made him skeptical of any renewal work of the Spirit within these churches. Synan, *Charismatic Bridges*, 16. See Edward O'Connor, *The Pentecostal Movement in the Catholic Church* (Notre Dame: Ave Maria Press, 1971), 214, 221, 239. See also, Kevin and Dorothy Ranaghan, *Catholic Pentecostals* (New York: Paulist Press, 1969), 154-55.

Catholic Church. Perhaps the greatest impact of the renewal on the mainline denominations is theological. Renewalists within traditions known for their rich theological inheritance (e.g. Catholic, Orthodox, Lutheran, Baptist, and Reformed) are more likely to base the BHS experience on coherent theological analysis than is the case with classical Pentecostals or independent renewalists.[145] The result has been an increase in scholarly reflection on BHS and the *charismata* within traditions influenced by the charismatic renewal.[146] This scholarly reflection has queried a variety of BHS related assumptions held by classical Pentecostals.[147] The result is a variety of BHS views that places the renewal in tension with classical Pentecostalism.[148] The basic elements differentiating the BHS views are presented in Chapter 5.

2.3   Third Wave

In order to complete a composite presentation of P/C spirituality, a brief overview of what is known as 'the third wave' is necessary. Of the three spirituality streams promoted by P/C adherents, the third wave does not rely on BHS to establish charismatic phenomena. The mention of the tradition has value to this study because it demonstrates that spiritual experience is validated apart from BHS within the P/C tradition. Mentioning the third wave is also necessary to demonstrate that within the P/C movement there is a tradition that does not make the *charismata* dependent upon the BHS experience. American Baptists also do not associate BHS with the manifestation of charismatic phenomena. From the perspective of American Baptists, the completed composite presentation of P/C

---

[145] Hocken, 'Charismatic Movement,' 517.

[146] In 1976, the National Service Committee (NSC) of the Catholic Charismatic Renewal (CCR) sponsored a symposium and published the papers as John C. Haughey, ed., *Theological Reflections on the Charismatic Renewal* (Ann Arbor: Servant Books, 1979). The CCR has also produced the work of Kilian McDonnell and George T. Montague, *Christian Initiation and Baptism in the Holy Spirit: Evidence from the First Eight Centuries* (Collegeville: Liturgical Press, 1991). Other scholarly works influenced by the charismatic renewal include: Larry Christenson, *Welcome, Holy Spirit: A Study of Charismatic Renewal in the Church* (Minneapolis: Augsburg Fortress Publications, 1987); Clark H. Pinnock, *Flame of Love: A Theology of the Holy Spirit* (Downers Grove: InterVarsity Press, 1996); Miroslav Volf, *After our Likeness: The Church as the Image of the Trinity* (Grand Rapids: William B. Eerdmans Publishing, 1998); Daniel B. Wallace and M. James Sawyer, eds., *Who's Afraid of the Holy Spirit? An Investigation into the Ministry of the Spirit of God Today* (Dallas: Biblical Studies Press, 2005).

[147] Warrington, *Pentecostal Theology*, 19.

[148] See Lederle for a detailed treatment of BHS embraced by the charismatic renewal. Lederle, *Treasures Old and New*, 37-103. See also Macchia, 'God Present in a Confused Situation,' 37. Warrington refers to these as 'divisive aspects related to this apparently central belief of Pentecostalism.' Warrington, *Pentecostal Theology*, 19.

spirituality is significant for emphasizing the role of charismatic experience rooted either in BHS (classical Pentecostal and charismatic renewal) or occurring independently of the phenomenon (third wave). The third wave is considered here briefly because of its relative de-emphasis on BHS for spiritual experience.

2.3.1   Non-Pentecostal and Non-charismatic

In the 1980s various P/C groups began to be identified according to their affiliation with first wave (classical Pentecostal), second wave (charismatics in the historic mainline churches) and third wave spirituality (non-Pentecostal, non-charismatic).[149] Third wave (also referred to as neo-charismatic) Christians have 'Pentecostal-like experiences,' but are without traditional Pentecostal or charismatic denominational affiliation.[150] These third wave participants are largely evangelical Christians with an affinity toward classical and neo-Pentecostalism,[151] but refrain from identifying with either tradition.[152] The emphasis of the third wave[153] is on experiencing the Holy Spirit[154] through charismatic-type manifestations (e.g. physical healing, casting out demons, and prophetic revelation).[155] For members of the third wave, these charismatic

---

[149] Stanley M. Burgess, 'Neocharismatics,' in Stanley M. Burgess and Eduard M. Van Der Mass, eds., *NIDPCM* (Grand Rapids: Zondervan, 2002), 928; Synan, *The Century of the Holy Spirit,* 395-405; Cox, *Fire from Heaven,* 281. The term 'third wave' gained prominence around 1983 after being coined by Wagner. See Hyatt, *2000 Years of Charismatic Christianity,* 180. Wagner wrote, 'I see the third wave of the eighties as an opening of the straight-line evangelicals and other Christians to the supernatural work of the Holy Spirit that the Pentecostals and charismatics have experienced, but without becoming either charismatic or Pentecostal.' C. Peter Wagner, 'The Third Wave?' in *Pastoral Renewal* (1983), 1-5.

[150] Cox, *Fire from Heaven,* 312.

[151] Gary S. Greig and Kevin N. Springer, 'Introduction,' in Gary S. Grieg and Kevin N. Springer, eds., *The Kingdom and the Power: Are Healing and the Spiritual Gifts Used by Jesus and the Early Church Meant for the Church Today?* (Wheaton: Regal Books, 1993), 20.

[152] C. Peter Wagner, 'Third Wave,' in Stanley M. Burgess and Eduard M. Van Der Mass, eds., *NIDPCM* (Grand Rapids: Zondervan, 2002), 1141.

[153] C. Peter Wagner,. *The Third Wave of the Holy Spirit: Encountering the Power of Signs and Wonders* (Ann Arbor: Servant Publications, 1988), 13-24.

[154] With reference to third wave expectations of the Holy Spirit, Storms advocates prayer 'for [the Spirit's] appearance with the expectation that he will minister *to* God's people *through* God's people by means of the full range of *charismata* listed in such passages as 1 Corinthians 12:7-10, 28-30. See C. Samuel Storms, 'A Third Wave View,' in Wayne A. Grudem, ed., *Are Miraculous Gifts for Today? Four Views* (Grand Rapids: Zondervan, 1996), 175.

[155] As a subgroup within evangelicalism, the third wave is sometimes referred to as the 'Signs and Wonders' movement due to these emphases. See Menzies and Menzies, *Spirit and Power,* 145. See also C. Peter Wagner, 'Wimber, John,' in Stanley M. Burgess and Eduard M. Van Der Mass, eds., *NIDPCM* (Grand Rapids: Zondervan, 2002), 1199-1200.

experiences differ from BHS which occurs without evidential signs at conversion. Third wavers constitute a relatively high number of Christians, since they outnumber classical Pentecostals and charismatics combined.[156] By the year 2000 third wavers totaled 295 million adherents worldwide, including 20 percent of all American Baptists.[157]

A wide range of experienced miraculous phenomena is emphasized by the third wave. Less emphasized is BHS which is comparatively more dominant among classical Pentecostals and renewalists. Third wavers, contra classical Pentecostalism and most renewalists, associate BHS with conversion and not with a post-faith 'second blessing.'[158] This association does not negate the necessity of post-faith experiences of the Spirit for continued filling and empowerment by the Spirit.[159] Contra the classical Pentecostal view, glossolalia is not considered evidentiary of BHS or the Spirit-filled life.[160] A complete analysis of the third wave BHS apologetic is found in Chapter 5.

---

[156] Barrett and Johnson note the activity of all three streams of the renewal in 80% of the world's 3,300 large metropolises. Members of the renewal number 27.7% of organized global Christianity. Charismatics are found in all 150 traditional non-Pentecostal ecclesiastical confessions, families and traditions. P/C Christians represent 9,000 ethnolinguistic groups, speak 8,000 languages, and cover 95% of the world's population. Participants in the renewal represent 740 Pentecostal denominations, 6,530 non-Pentecostal, and mainline denominations with large organized internal charismatic movements. For comparison purposes, there are 18,810 independent, neo-charismatic denominations and networks. See David B. Barrett and Todd M. Johnson, 'Global Statistics,' in Stanley M. Burgess and Eduard M. Van Der Mass, eds., *NIDPCM* (Grand Rapids: Zondervan, 2002), 284.

[157] Synan, *The Century of the Holy Spirit*, 9, 192. These statistics also include 200-300 'fullness congregations' within the Southern Baptist Convention. See Kenneth Kantzer, 'The Charismatics Among Us,' in *Christianity Today* (February, 1980), 25-29.

[158] Gary S. Greig and Kevin N. Springer, 'Introduction,' in Gary S. Grieg and Kevin N. Springer, eds., *The Kingdom and the Power: Are Healing and the Spiritual Gifts Used by Jesus and the Early Church Meant for the Church Today?* (Wheaton: Regal Books, 1993), 21. Greig and Springer cite the following passages to frame the third wave position: 1 Cor 12:13; Eph 1:13-14; Tit 3:5; John 3:3, 5-8; Rom 8:9; Gal 3:26 and 4:6; Hyatt, *2000 Years of Charismatic Christianity*, 181; Menzies and Menzies, *Spirit and Power*, 145; Albrecht, *Rites in the Spirit*, 65.

[159] Greig and Springer, 'Introduction,' 21. Greig and Springer cite the following passages as textual support for the third wave position: Eph 5:18; Acts 4:8, 31; 7:55; 13:9, 52. Storms, 'A Third Wave View,' 176.

[160] Greig and Springer, 'Introduction,' 21; Hyatt, *2000 Years of Charismatic Christianity*, 181.

3. Divine Encounter: The Locus of P/C Spirituality

The purpose of this section is to reduce the preceding analyses to an essential P/C spirituality. Dayton's 'full gospel' *gestalt* of spirituality encompasses conversion, BHS, bodily healing, and an eschatological expectation of the imminent return of Christ. Land, and Faupel, together with Macchia, attribute P/C emphases on holiness, empowered missionary witness, and revival of extraordinary gifts to a spirituality formed by eschatological passions.[161] Understood in terms of a vibrating and vitalizing energy-field emanating from God,[162] the Holy Spirit is the divine locus or medium of an expressive P/C spirituality.[163] P/C spirituality is not the result of mere mental assent to a range of biblical beliefs, but is a matter of encountering one's beliefs experientially.[164] P/C spirituality is deemed a comprehensive and radically transformative experience of the Spirit, in that it affects the believer's identity, perception, worship and service, mission and evangelism, reading and application of the Bible, and transforms relationships to other believers.[165] For classical Pentecostals and many within the charismatic renewal, BHS is a significant example of a believer encountering God. There is a tactile element to this encounter with God which is expressed in the BHS experience.

---

[161] Donald W. Dayton, *The Theological Roots of Pentecostalism* ([original work published 1987] Peabody: Hendrickson Publishers, 2000); D. William Faupel, 'The Everlasting Gospel: The Significance of Eschatology in the Development of Pentecostal Thought' (PhD dissertation, University of Birmingham, 1989); Steven J. Land, *Pentecostal Spirituality: A Passion for the Kingdom* ([original work published 1997] Sheffield: Sheffield Academic Press, 2001); Macchia, 'God Present in a Confused Situation,' 34.

[162] Jürgen Moltmann, 'The Spirit Gives Life: Spirituality and Vitality,' in Harold D. Hunter and Peter D. Hocken, eds., *All Together in One Place: Theological Papers from the Brighton Conference on World Evangelization* (Sheffield: Sheffield Academic Press, 1993), 22.

[163] Williams, *Renewal Theology,* 194.

[164] Warrington, *Pentecostal Theology,* 22.

[165] Donald L. Gelpi, *The Gracing of Human Experience: Rethinking the Relationship between Nature and Grace* (Collegeville: Liturgical Press, 2001), 355-59; Allan Anderson, 'Pentecostal-Charismatic Spirituality and Theological Education in Europe from a Global Perspective,' in *PentecoStudies* (2004), 9; Oliver McMahan, 'A Living Stream: Spiritual Direction within the Pentecostal/Charismatic Tradition,' in *Journal of Psychology and Theology* (2002), 336.

3.1   Expression in the Form of Encounter-based Piety

Spirituality identified by the expression 'the *gestalt* of piety'[166] is not exclusive to the P/C movement.[167] For example, a unified spirituality exists among the distinctive worship styles of not only classical Pentecostals, but also Quakers, Catholics, and Episcopalians.[168] Baer describes the expressional nature of this unifying spirituality:

> ...each of these three practices [glossolalia, silence, and liturgy] permits the analytical mind –the focused, objectifying dimension of man's intellect –to rest, thus freeing other dimensions of the person, what we might loosely refer to as man's spirit, for a deeper openness to divine reality...this goal is not achieved by a deliberate concentration on the emotions as over against the analytical mind... [Rather], the desire is to free man in the depth of his spirit to respond to the immediate reality of the living God.[169]

The ground of an expressional P/C spirituality is the immediate reality of the divine presence. Rituals and rites[170] play an integral role in P/C spirituality, providing the necessary means to express divine encounter[171] within the corporate worship experience. Rituals and rites are considered to possess efficacious properties to either induce experience or become experiences. By performing rites and rituals P/C spirituality is a participatory and enacted theology whereby one's salvation is encompassing the worshiper (i.e. beliefs, convictions, patterns of

---

[166] Spittler identifies 'five implicit values' (experience, orality, spontaneity, otherworldliness, and biblical authority) that form a 'constellation of characteristic practices' found in P/C spirituality. In his view, this 'constellation' is distinct from the central features of the movement (speaking in tongues, BHS, and prayer for divine healing). See Spittler, 'Spirituality, Pentecostal and Charismatic,' 1096-99. Cecil M. Robeck, Jr., 'The Nature of Pentecostal Spirituality,' in *Pneuma* (1992), 104.

[167] Spittler, 'Spirituality, Pentecostal and Charismatic,' 1096.

[168] Richard A. Baer, Jr., 'Quaker Silence, Catholic Liturgy, and Pentecostal Glossolalia: Some Functional Similarities,' in Russell P. Spittler, ed., *Perspectives on the New Pentecostalism* (Grand Rapids: Baker Book House, 1976), 152.

[169] Ibid.

[170] Albrecht defines 'rituals' as 'acts, actions, dramas and performances that a community creates, continues, recognizes and sanctions as ways of behaving that express appropriate attitudes, sensibilities, values, and beliefs within a given situation.' As a ritual, Albrecht identifies the 'worship service' as composed of a variety of rites which comprise a portion or phase of the service (e.g. sermon, the song service), a particular practice or specific act or enactment (e.g. the laying on of hands, prayer), or a set of actions (e.g. altar responses). See Albrecht, *Rites in the Spirit,* 22. See also Daniel E. Albrecht, 'Pentecostal Spirituality: Looking through the Lens of Ritual,' in *Pneuma* (1992), 107-23 and Daniel E. Albrecht, 'Pentecostal Spirituality: Ecumenical Potential and Challenge,' in *Cyberjournal for Pentecostal-Charismatic Research* (1997), 1-52.

[171] See sources quoted in Warrington, *Pentecostal Theology,* 20-27.

thought, emotions, and behavior) with respect to what is ultimate, or God.[172] An imminent sense of the divine is rudimentary to P/C spirituality.[173] This deep, mystical piety emphasizes an immanent sense of the divine that is integrally associated with the subjective experience of BHS.[174]

3.2   Spiritual Expression as Charismata in General and BHS in Particular

In addition to divine encounter, the 'trademarks' of the P/C movement are the objective gifts of the Spirit[175] as well as the subjective experience of BHS. These distinctives function normatively in the life of the church.[176] In his critical analysis of Pentecostal spirituality, Frederick Dale Bruner draws attention to the centrality, even the normativity, of the *charismata* and BHS to Pentecostal religious experiences and expressions.[177] The exercise of the full range of the *charismata* is indicative of the presence of renewal in an assembly. Close reference is made to Scripture to represent spirituality as a duality, where discipline is balanced by BHS.[178] On the one hand, there is an ascetic spirituality rooted in spiritual disciplines[179] and functioning as the 'training mode' of spirituality.[180] This ascetic component includes the formation of habits and exercises conducive to the process of sanctification (1 Cor 9:24-27). Its complement is the Pentecostal component epitomized by BHS which functions as

---

[172] Anne E. Carr, *Transforming Grace* (San Francisco: Harper & Row, 1988), 201-202.

[173] Warrington, *Pentecostal Theology,* 20-27.

[174] Albrecht, Rites in the Spirit, 24.

[175] According to Gelpi, 'the charisms of the Spirit play an indispensable role in the life of the church because they create the shared faith of the Christian community…[and] give the community a vivid sense of God's presence that nurtures charismatic openness to the Spirit.' See Donald L. Gelpi, 'The Theological Challenge of Charismatic Spirituality,' in *Pneuma* (1992), 193-94.

[176] Albrecht, *Rites in the Spirit,* 24.

[177] Frederick Dale Bruner, *A Theology of the Holy Spirit: The Pentecostal Experience and the New Testament Witness* (London: Hodder and Stoughton, 1970), 19-149.

[178] Richard Lovelace, 'Baptism in the Holy Spirit and the Evangelical Tradition,' in *Pneuma* (1985), 101-23.

[179] Foster articulates an ascetic spirituality in Richard Foster, *Celebration of Disciplines: The Path to Spiritual Growth* (San Francisco: Harper & Row, 1978), 125-71. Three spiritual disciples are identified: (1) inward disciplines (meditation, prayer, fasting and study), 13-66; (2) outward disciplines (simplicity, solitude, submission and service), 69-122; and (3) corporate disciplines (confession, worship, guidance and celebration).

[180] Rebecca Jaichandran and B. D. Madhav, 'Pentecostal Spirituality in a Postmodern World,' in *AJPS* (2003), 41.

the impetus for Spirit-based growth (Gal 3:2-3, 5). This duality is acknowledged as a Pauline witnesses to authentic Christian spirituality. The presence of extraordinary works of the Spirit is linked to those who have subjected themselves to ascetic disciplines in order to obtain a conscious awareness of the Holy Spirit.[181]

3.3   Invasion of the Supernatural

Emphasis on the supernatural, occasioned by the outpouring (gift/reception) of the Holy Spirit, is a hallmark of P/C spirituality.[182] Though occurring on the Day of Pentecost, the gift of the Spirit is presently realized in terms of continuous occurrence.[183] From one point of view, it could be said that the three streams of the P/C movement represent a single latter-day outpouring of the Holy Spirit.[184] The diversity of expressions describing the present-day operations of the Spirit (e.g. 'outpouring,' 'falling on,' 'coming on,' 'baptizing' and 'filling') depict the role of the Spirit relative to P/C spirituality. Whether this 'coming' of the Spirit is variously understood as invasion (e.g. 'poured out,' 'falling upon'), immersion ('baptized in'), or penetration (being 'filled with'), the various aspects of Spirit activity combine teleologically to exhibit a Christ-centered purpose which focuses on the manifestation of God's glory.[185] P/C rituals and corresponding rites assume an awareness of God and are often regarded in terms of a supernatural 'in-breaking' of God.[186] The supernatural is realized by P/C adherents when God intervenes miraculously or through an act of practical assistance.[187] Supernatural experience is further represented as being 'overwhelmed' by the Spirit[188] and BHS being its most common occurrence.[189]

---

[181] Lovelace, 'Baptism in the Holy Spirit and the Evangelical Tradition,' 103-104.

[182] Albrecht, *Rites in the Spirit,* 241; Grant Wacker, 'The Functions of Faith in Primitive Pentecostalism,' in *HTR* (1984), 353-75; Williams, *Renewal Theology,* 194.

[183] Williams, *Renewal Theology,* 184-85.

[184] Vinson Synan, *In the Latter Days: The Outpouring of the Holy Spirit in the Twentieth Century* ([original work published 1984] Fairfax: Xulon Press, 2001), vii.

[185] Williams, *Renewal Theology,* 190-205

[186] Stephen L. Land, *Pentecostal Spirituality: A Passion for the Kingdom* ([original work published 1997] Sheffield: Sheffield Academic Press, 2001), 58.

[187] Albrecht, *Rites in the Spirit,* 240-41 n. 42.

[188] Kilian McDonnell and George Montague, 'What Does Baptism in the Spirit have to do with Christian Initiation?' in Killian McDonnell and George Montague, eds., *Fanning the Flame* (Collegeville: Liturgical Press, 1991), 9.

[189] Albrecht, *Rites in the Spirit,* 241-42.

3.4 The Tactile Element of P/C Spirituality Realized in BHS

Is BHS accompanied by tactile experience? To determine the tactile nature of BHS experienced by classical Pentecostals and many within the charismatic renewal, the phenomenon must be isolated from the intense longing which precedes it, its validating mark (glossolalia), and the charismatic phenomena associated with its occurrence. Daniel Albrecht provides a descriptive typology of what he terms 'modes of sensibility' that refer to embodied attitudes, sensibilities, and affections which accompany performed Pentecostal rituals.[190] According to Albrecht, BHS, among other desired encounters such as healing and miracles, occurs pragmatically within the context of a rite or prayer that incorporates an attitude toward a transcendent reality, specifically God, in order to produce the anticipated effect (BHS).[191] This 'transcendental efficacious mode' of sensibility is an experience of earnest expectation which focuses more on the consequence than on the meaning.[192] Land associates the reception of the Spirit by the early Pentecostals with tasting of the 'powers of the age to come' (Heb 6:5).[193] In this context, γεύομαι ('to taste') is a figurative expression for experience, either cognitive or emotional.[194] It is Bruner, however, who offers more directly a tactile description of the BHS experience through a series of historical personal accounts.[195] There is difficultly when seeking to locate descriptions of BHS (i.e. the experience itself) from among the discrete testimonies recorded by Bruner. This difficulty is primarily due to the comingling of testimony to the events preceding and the related effects following BHS. The most common tactile (physiological) elements of reported BHS experience are physical tremors and a sense of being seized by the power of God, an ecstatic sensation of joy and glory, a sensation of perspiration-resulting heat, and a sense of the depth of the presence of the Lord flowing from within one's being. For Pentecostals, the 'full' BHS experience has not occurred until one has 'pressed through' to the utterance of glossolalia.

---

[190] Ibid., 179-89.

[191] Ibid., 182.

[192] Ibid.

[193] Land, *Pentecostal Spirituality*, 60.

[194] Walter Bauer, William F. Arndt, F. Wilbur Gingrich, and Frederick W. Danker, *A Greek-English Lexicon of the New Testament and Other Early Christian Literature*, 2nd ed. (Chicago: The University of Chicago Press, 1979), 157.

[195] Bruner, *A Theology of the Holy Spirit*, 118-29.

Though recognizing the person and work of the Spirit in their doctrinal formulation, many American Baptists find it difficult to attribute profound emotional and physical experiences to the working of the Spirit. This may be the result of cultural conditioning, the lack of familiarity with bodily expressions of worship, the fear of things getting out of control, or the need to maintain order (cf. 1 Cor 14:40). American Baptist aversion to emotional displays of Spirit encounter may also be the result of the lack of theological language within their tradition to account for manifestations of the Spirit. American Baptists do admit to being moved emotionally in worship by a sermon or song, being led intuitively by the Spirit through prayer and personal Bible study, falling under the conviction of the Spirit, sensing the hand and/or blessing of God upon their life, and responding to the invitation by means of an altar call. These affective dimensions of American Baptist corporate worship anticipate and manifest the ongoing work of the Spirit. The need for renewal in worship has recently been expressed by SBC leader David Dockery:

> Baptist worship needs renewal because our church services tend to be human-centered…worship is only possible in and by the Holy Spirit, who prompts our love and praise to God…Much that is often easily dismissed as merely tradition can be rebaptized by the Holy Spirit to shape our congregational worship…Let us pray that the blowing of the Holy Spirit will indeed bring renewal to our worship…may the Spirit of God enable Southern Baptists to recover the significance and vitality of authentic biblical worship for our individual lives and for local churches across our convention.[196]

American Baptist scholar Elmer Towns similarly calls for renewal when he writes, 'we must invite everyone to worship God, to touch God, and have God touch them.'[197] This is the language of spiritual encounter and suggests the need for American Baptist worshippers to take account of such phenomena in relation to understanding the spiritual experiences associated with the ongoing work of the Spirit in other traditions, such as those manifested among Pentecostals. This step opens the way for additional points of convergence between American Baptists and P/C adherents.

---

[196] David S. Dockery, *Southern Baptist Consensus and Renewal: A Biblical, Historical, and Theological Proposal* (Nashville: B & H Academic, 2008), 122, 125, 128-29.

[197] Elmer Towns, *Putting an End to the Worship Wars* (Nashville: B & H Publishers, 1996), 112.

4. Conclusion

This chapter has demonstrated the presence of an encounter-oriented spirituality which unites the differentiated traditions within the P/C movement. The Pentecostal movement emerged from diverse influential stimuli (Holiness, Keswick, fundamentalism, and modernism) to emphasize transformative Spirit-based living and to oppose the dead orthodoxy embodied by formal and rationalistic Christian traditions. Pentecostals embraced a Scripture-based full gospel orientation to the Christian life (salvation, healing, BHS, and the second coming of Christ) which prioritized BHS as a Christ-centered and post-conversion personal experience validated by evidential tongues. The charismatic renewal marked the appearance of Pentecostal phenomena in the mainline churches resulting in an awakening of intense desire for the manifested presence and power of the Spirit. The exercise of the miraculous *charismata* (extraordinary manifestations of the Spirit) revitalized inert traditional beliefs (theological categories) and sacramental rites. Third wave proponents are largely evangelical Christians who emphasize supernatural phenomena, but refrain from association with (classical) Pentecostalism and the charismatic renewal. Though practicing charismatic-type manifestations of the Spirit, the third wave emphasizes BHS the least among P/C adherents.

These diverse P/C traditions are equally committed to a demonstratively expressed spirituality whereby participation in worship (i.e. enacted theology via rites and rituals) is directly related to divine encounter. For classical Pentecostals and many renewalists, BHS is a tactile experience that is necessary to the exercise of the full range of *charismata*, is the impetus for Spirit-based growth, and the primary witness to the supernatural in-breaking of God. Even charismatics of the third wave who refrain from using such language to describe BHS, do consider the gifts associated with BHS to be integral to Spirit-based growth and expressed spirituality.

United with P/C adherents by a common evangelical core, and in the interest of demonstratively expressed Spirit-based growth, American Baptists should inform their BHS apologetic by doctrinally engaging P/C adherents. The pursuit of experience-based intra-evangelical common ground continues with an analysis of the nature of American Baptist spiritual experience in the next chapter.

-3-

AN AMERICAN BAPTIST RATIONALE FOR CONSENSUS

1. Introduction

The task of this chapter is to explore commonality between the P/C and American Baptist traditions. The research will establish that inter-tradition commonality is rooted historically in spiritual experience. The focus of the study is to determine the formative nature of encounter-oriented personal spiritual experience to the American Baptist tradition and to discover to what extent and in what ways it may be compared to the profoundly intense BHS experience claimed by Pentecostals and many renewalists. The chapter does not intend to suggest that the palpable features of Pentecostal BHS are identical to phenomena experienced within the American Baptist tradition. Rather, the chapter is intended to demonstrate that the spiritual experience which grounds both traditions is encounter-oriented. This nuance permits the following analysis to avoid equivocation where the terms 'experience' or 'encounter' occur. The intensity of personal spiritual experience may differ radically between the traditions (e.g. tactile-physiological, psychological-emotional, intellectual-mental), but the fact that it is the result of divine encounter is sufficient to establish commonality.

The analysis also provides context for evaluating American Baptist reactions to the eruption of Pentecostal-like religious experiences (e.g. glossolalia and other *charismata*) within their own tradition. The charismatic renewal within American Baptist churches is a single schism within a larger field of doctrinal controversy. Doctrinal fragmentation has led the SBC to seek intra-denominational doctrinal consensus. Efforts to achieve consensus on doctrines that are deemed essential to SBC denominational unity are adaptable to intra-evangelical consensus. This relates specifically to BHS when it is conceived as a nonessential doctrine that promotes authentic spiritual experience (i.e. encounter-oriented religion). Once the common ground of encounter-oriented spiritual experience is established between the traditions, a rationale exists for American Baptists to dialogue with

Pentecostals and renewalists regarding BHS and to move toward a consensus view that will inform their spiritual experience.

1.1   The Nature of Encounter-Oriented Religion

Encounter-oriented religion is evidential in nature and involves a personal history of religious experience that corresponds to ethical transformation. Religious experience is the intimate and personal creature-Creator relation. The evidential nature of encounter-oriented religion makes visible the spiritually authentic life of the invisible church of Jesus Christ. Identified historically by the archaic term 'experimental,' the identity of American Baptist encounter-oriented spirituality is traced to the earliest developments of the tradition.[1]

1.2   Contemporary American Baptists and Experience-based Spirituality

According to American Baptist historian Edwin Gaustad, 'radical and transformative encounters with God' were once foundational to the tradition.[2] The movement of American Baptists away from this self-identifying feature has resulted in what some within the movement refer critically to as 'tradition-based rational biblicism.'[3] This characterization of the movement's present spiritual orientation defines 'rational biblicism' as a rigid *scriptura sola* capable of influencing the interpretation and application of Scripture. As a pejorative expression for the movement, 'tradition-based biblicism' functions as a denominational filter or pair of spectacles and results in narrow denominationally-specific interpretations of essential doctrines and praxis (e.g. water baptism, the Lord's Supper, polity, and the concept of church-state relations).[4] Cooperative Baptist Fellowship (CBF) scholar B. J. Leonard associates this spiritual orientation with literalistic interpretive tendencies that he likens to wearing hermeneutical spectacles with which to hold *sola scriptura* and *sola fide* in

---

[1] Edwin S. Gaustad, 'Baptists and Experimental Religion,' in *The Chronicle: Journal of the American Baptist Historical Society* (1952), 110.

[2] Ibid., 110-16.

[3] E. Glenn Hinson, 'In Search of Our Baptist Identity,' in James Leo Garrett, Jr., E. Glenn Hinson and James E. Tull, eds., *Are Southern Baptists Evangelicals?* (Macon: Mercer University Press, 1983), 139.

[4] Ibid.

tension.[5] His characterization correctly detects the inherent conflict these literalistic tendencies represent when, in the name of biblical authority, they oppose piety and praxis. Ensuing division is the result of an uncompromising biblicism which resists adaptations or modifications of belief.

The diminished foundational role of encounter-oriented spirituality helps to explain the reaction of some American Baptist leaders to P/C claims of profound spiritual experience attended by overt physical and emotional displays. In his self-described 1999 exposé of the charismatic renewal (*Spirit Works*), SBC pastor Jerry Vines defends his criticisms of renewalists using extreme examples of charismatic teaching and praxis (e.g. the questionable acceptance of Spirit-induced animal sounds during the revival at the Toronto Airport Vineyard Church and the association of tongues-speech with Shamanism, eastern religions, and demonic influence) to accommodate the prejudices of his (SBC) reader base.[6] To justify his denunciation of charismatic teaching and praxis, Vines cites the prevalence of P/C sponsored media presentations (radio, television, and books) which inform the rank and file Christian and the average American Baptist concept of P/C spirituality.[7] This is supported in part by the media-driven claims of P/C adherents to Spirit-inspired revelations from God granting equal status of their teachings to the Bible. The use of experience to validate praxis by some members of the P/C movement is considered in direct opposition to *sola scriptura* for many American Baptists. Vines is typical of this position when he concludes, 'if experience becomes the basic court of appeal, then the Bible is no longer our guide for determining truth.'[8] The primary difficulty with Vine's assessment is his use of extreme examples to generalize P/C spirituality which makes adopting his conclusions less than convincing.[9]

---

[5] Bill J. Leonard, *The Challenge of Being Baptist: Owning a Scandalous Past and an Uncertain Future* (Waco: Baylor University Press, 2010), 60.

[6] Jerry Vines, *Spirit Works: Charismatic Practices and the Bible* (Nashville: Broadman & Holman Publishers, 1999), 7-8.

[7] Ibid.

[8] Ibid. Carson similarly critiques the Emerging Church movement for its emphasis on 'feelings and affections over against linear thought and rationality.' See D. A. Carson, *Becoming Conversant with the Emerging Church: Understanding a Movement and its Implications* (Grand Rapids: Zondervan, 2005), 29.

[9] A similar denunciation of P/C teaching and praxis is John F. MacArthur, *Strange Fire: The Danger of Offending the Holy Spirit with Counterfeit Worship* (Nashville: Nelson Books, 2013). According to MacArthur, the modern Charismatic Movement attributes 'the work of the devil to the Holy Spirit.' He refers to movement as an army of 'Satan's false teachers, marching to the beat of their own illicit desires [in order to] gladly propagate his errors.' In sum, the charismatic movement comprises 'spiritual swindlers, con men, crooks, and charlatans.'

American Baptist criticism of experience-based P/C belief and praxis faces the further challenge of other evangelicals who similarly approve the validating role of experience. Evangelicals like Bloesch affirm the priority of Scripture over experience, but do not exclude the role of experience altogether.[10] Tradition-based rational Biblicism, on the other hand, favors the exclusive role of the Bible. Pressed too narrowly this position is inconsistent with the Reformer's understanding of *sola scriptura*[11] as 'the Bible being illuminated by the Spirit within the matrix of the church.'[12] This 'communal matrix' understanding allowed for the *sola scriptura* and *nuda scriptura* (the bare Scripture) distinction whereby 'the Bible is our primary authority, not our only authority.'[13] Bloesch effectively illustrates that the relation of spiritual experience to belief and praxis not only represents a significant impasse for American Baptists seeking to engage P/C adherents, but also a broader discontinuity within evangelicalism.

1.3   The Earliest American Baptists and the Encounter-Oriented Nature of Religion

American Baptist historian Gaustad considered divine encounter and BHS to be phenomena occurring logically prior to marks of identity often mentioned in American Baptist confessional statements of faith.[14] According to Gaustad, the 'rightful heritage' of American Baptist identity 'begins with the experience of God dealing directly with the sinner, of his love cleansing, his mercy granting full pardon and his power sustaining.'[15] The critical assessment of Gaustad offers valuable insight into the encounter-oriented nature of religion maintained historically by American Baptists to be their central identifying feature. It is crucial to note that according to the traditional Baptist view, religious expressions occurring prior to the divine encounter leading to the sinner's full pardon (e.g.

---

[10] Donald G. Bloesch, *A Theology of Word & Spirit: Authority & Method in Theology* (Downers Grove: InterVarsity Press, 1992), 191-93.

[11] According to Patterson, the reformers spoke of *sola scriptura* as *suprema scriptura*. In this sense, Scripture took priority over tradition, papal decrees, or any other human authority.' See James A. Patterson, 'Reflections on 400 Years of the Baptist Movement: Who we Are, What we Believe,' in David S. Dockery, ed. with Ray Van Neste and Jerry Tidwell, *Southern Baptists, Evangelicals, and the Future of Denominationalism* (Nashville: B & H Academic, 2011), 196-97.

[12] Bloesch, *A Theology of Word & Spirit,* 193.

[13] Ibid.

[14] Gaustad, 'Baptists and Experimental Religion,' 110. According to Leonard, there is 'surprising uniformity' among American Baptist confessions of faith. See Leonard, *The Challenge of Being Baptist*, 54-55.

[15] Gaustad, 'Baptists and Experimental Religion,' 110.

rites and rituals), though useful, do not constitute authentic religious (spiritual/Christian) experience. Gaustad links the earliest American Baptist spirituality to 'the baptism by the Holy Spirit...an event as objective and certain as the baptism by water.'[16] This description of an immediate and palpable divine encounter can be set in parallel to what Pentecostals and renewalists describe experientially as BHS. The historical witness to the encounter-oriented nature of American Baptist spirituality supports P/C scholar Edward Watson.[17] By an observer theologically committed to both traditions, Watson's assessment of SBC reactions to the charismatic renewal offers a perspective on American Baptist spirituality that is in harmony with the thesis of this study and the investigation of this chapter. According to Watson: 'It seems to me that when both of these colossal evangelical groups attain what they are seeking (true discipleship) they may find themselves looking more like one another than either one is presently willing to admit.'[18]

2. Encounter-Oriented Spirituality: Adducing American Baptist Identity

2.1 Voluntarism and the Supremacy of the Scriptures for Promoting Encounter-Oriented Religion among American Baptists

2.1.1 The Basic Baptist Witness

Many American Baptists consider compiling lists of distinctives and practices to be universally accepted an interminable dilemma.[19] For many outside the movement, the term 'Baptist' is an expression equivalent to division, dispute, and schism.[20] This is evident from the lack of uniformity which often characterizes the tradition.[21] Leonard considers the issue of Baptist identity to be critical to the movement's ability to respond meaningfully to twenty-first century

---

[16] Ibid.

[17] Watson possess a unique perspective as a licensed SBC minister serving in charismatic institutions. Edward Watson, 'A History of Influence: The Charismatic Movement and the SBC' in *CTR* (2006), 30.

[18] Watson, 'A History of Influence,' 30.

[19] Bill J. Leonard, *Baptist Ways: A History* (Valley Forge: Judson Press, 2003), 1; Patterson, 'Reflections on 400 Years of the Baptist Movement,' 193.

[20] Leonard, *The Challenge of Being Baptist*, 7. Leonard, *Baptist Ways*, 1-15.

[21] E. Glenn Hinson, 'Baptists and Evangelicals: What is the Difference?,' in James Leo Garrett, Jr., E. Glenn Hinson and James E. Tull, eds. *Are Southern Baptists Evangelicals?* (Macon: Mercer University Press, 1983), 173.

religion and culture.[22] Harrison is less optimistic and considers the identity-determining task 'freighted with ambiguity, and those who strive to establish the singularity of the [Baptist] tradition do so on a weak foundation.'[23] Of the two perspectives, Leonard's is the correct one. A schismatic movement presents the Baptist tradition in equivocal terms and minimizes the strength of its religious and cultural appeal. This does not serve the effective pursuit of doctrinal consensus. The aim of this section is to provide evidence to justify the claim that encounter-oriented spirituality is foundational to the American Baptist movement.

American Baptists critical of the process of determining 'the singularity of the [Baptist] tradition' (as per Harrison) are so because of a faulty historiography which assumes contemporary American Baptist principles and practices to have endured since the inception of the movement.[24] American Baptist history features theological debates which define the movement.[25] This section will argue that among the myriad of theological debates, encounter-oriented spirituality is foundational to the American Baptist movement. Encounter-oriented spirituality is often displaced, or even obfuscated at times, within a tradition cohered by a set of commonly held doctrinal affirmations (so-called 'Baptist Distinctives').[26] American Baptist denominations, local congregations, and ecclesiastical

---

[22] Leonard, *The Challenge of Being Baptist*, 7.

[23] Paul M. Harrison, *Authority and Power in the Free Church Tradition* (Carbondale: Southern Illinois University Press, 1959), 33.

[24] Patterson, 'Reflections on 400 Years of the Baptist Movement,' 193.

[25] Contemporary doctrinal struggles within the SBC have been well-documented by Ammerman. She attributes the documented SBC struggles to the denomination's insistence on 'a free conscience and independence from outside authority has made for a stormy history, full of conflicts inside and out.' See Nancy Tatom Ammerman, *Baptist Battles: Social Change and Religious Conflict in the Southern Baptist Convention* (New Brunswick: Rutgers University Press, 1990), 18. Dockery avers that three decades of embroiled controversy over theological issues and denominational polity has left the SBC 'asking important questions about the identity and future of Southern Baptists.' See David S. Dockery, *Southern Baptist Consensus and Renewal: A Biblical, Historical, and Theological Proposal* (Nashville: B & H Academic, 2008), 2. The need for a contemporary SBC identity is discussed by multiple contributors in David S. Dockery, ed., *Southern Baptist Identity: An Evangelical Denomination Faces the Future* (Wheaton: Crossway Books, 2011). Wills details the SBC controversies of the 1950s and 1960s. See Gregory A. Wills, 'Progressive Theology and Southern Baptist Controversies of the 1950s and 1960s,' in *SBJT* (2003), 12-31.

[26] For an online source dedicated to Baptist distinctives which includes research data from American Baptist leaders including McBeth and Pitts, see Baptist Distinctives, 2010. 'Baptist Distinctives Articles List,' n.p. Available from: http://www.baptist distinctives.org/articles_list.shtml. [Accessed 14 December 2011]. For a list of generally accepted Baptist distinctives from the ABCUSA's perspective, see Alvah Hovey, *Restatement of Denominational Principles* (Philadelphia: American Baptist Publication Society, 1982), 3. For a recent discussion on Baptist distinctives from an SBC point of view, see R. Stanton Norman, *The Baptist Way: Distinctives of a Baptist Church* (Nashville: B & H Publishers, 2005), 11-193.

institutions, are further identified by doctrinal statements[27] and confessions of faith[28] which generally reduce matters of belief and praxis to the *sola scriptura* principle (i.e. rooting belief and praxis in the Scriptures alone).[29]

Adducing American Baptist identity requires more than achieving consensus on denominationally-affirmed doctrinal distinctives composed in a unanimously acknowledged statement of faith. The matter of identity logically presupposes an experiential core for belief and praxis to have relevance. Encounter-oriented spirituality differs methodologically from investigating the evolution and content of Baptist belief, or the manner in which Baptists engage the divine, or the method by which praxis conforms to Scripture. For example, associating denominational identity with doctrinal distinctives fails when a definitive set of distinctives is presumed to uniformly represent the tradition.[30] Doctrinal distinctives are shared among traditions, leaving the identity issue unresolved unless a particular distinctive is deemed to be held exclusively by a tradition. More foundational to American Baptist identity is differentiating the substance of the movement from its formal confessional statements. Doctrinal statements and confessions of faith, while identifying critical affirmations, have the potential for serving as the catechetical means by which adherents become proficient in 'the Baptist way.' This is not to imply an American Baptist emphasis of form over substance. Rather, this observation highlights the weakness of establishing denominational identity based on formal (creedal) standards. Gaustad rightly concludes that doctrinal distinctives are symptomatic of the basic Baptist witness.[31] The spiritual foundation of the American Baptist movement has from its infancy been a free (voluntary) 'believers Church' comprised of members who profess a personal and

---

[27] Use of doctrinal statements by American Baptists to express key elements of the Christian faith serve as a general reference for instructing adherents and indicating points of differentiation from other Christian groups. The *Baptist Faith and Message* contains doctrinal affirmations for the Southern Baptist Confession. The doctrinal affirmations listed in the *BFM* are typical of most American Baptist denominations, churches, and institutions. The *BFM* is uniquely presented online in order for the reader to compare the revisions of the 1925, 1963, and 2000 editions.

[28] The classic reference for Baptist confessions of faith is William L. Lumpkin, *Baptist Confessions of Faith* (Philadelphia: The Judson Press, 1959). Full text editions of Baptist confession of faith have been compiled online. See The Reformed Reader, 1999. 'Historic Baptist Documents,' n.p. Available from: http://www.reformedreader.org/ccc/hbd.htm. [Accessed 14 December 2011].

[29] Baptist Distinctives, 2010. 'What Makes a Baptist a Baptist?,' n.p. Available from: http://baptistdistinctives .org/artpdf/article2_0105.pdf. [Accessed 14 December 2011].

[30] Norman writes, 'the theological tenets that comprise our distinctive identity, as defined and interpreted by Baptists, are true only of Baptists.' Norman, *The Baptist Way*, 186.

[31] Gaustad, 'Baptists and Experimental Religion,' 110.

regenerating encounter with God.[32] Alternative bases for identifying the tradition become correlative to the (logically presupposed) experiential core of American Baptist life and witness.[33]

2.1.2   Tracing the Historical Roots of a Free and Uncoerced Voluntarism

This section traces the foundational role of encounter-oriented spirituality to the historical roots of the earliest American Baptists. Theories of Baptist origins abound. While the 'successionist theory'[34] traces the Baptist movement to primitive Christianity, the 'English Separatist descent theory'[35] and the 'Anabaptist spiritual kinship theory' trace Baptist beliefs and praxis to sects and movements dating from the 16th and 17th centuries.[36] The 'successionist theory' is rightly rejected for the reasons advanced by American Baptist historian Robert Torbet, namely for its lack of scholarly rigor, reliance on secondary sources, and employment of *a priori* reasoning over critical scientific methodology.[37]

---

[32] Gaustad offers the early example of Obadiah Holmes (1606-82). As one of the founders of the early American Baptist movement, Holmes recognized the futility of his own merit to achieve salvation. The ordinance of baptism performed by immersion in water illustrated to Holmes the death, burial, and resurrection of Christ. Holmes experienced regeneration and soon after was baptized with 'the new baptism.' The 'new baptism' was for Holmes 'the irrevocable step toward separation or schism from New England's official way.' See Edwin S. Gaustad, *Baptist Piety: The Last Will and Testimony of Obadiah Holmes* (Washington: Christian College Consortium, 1978), 18.

[33] Leonard correctly cautions against what he terms 'the fallacy of origins.' To commit 'the fallacy of origins' is to root 'contemporary procedures' in the beliefs and praxis of the earliest Baptist communities. The 'fallacy of origins' involves selecting which Baptist tradition to regarded as normative. See Leonard, *Baptist Ways*, 15.

[34] Among the proponents of the successionist theory is W. M. Patterson, *Baptist Successionism: A Critical View* (Valley Forge: Judson Press, 1969).

[35] Robert G. Torbet, *A History of the Baptists* ([original work published 1950] Valley Forge: Judson Press, 1993), 18-19; Torbet, *A History of the Baptists*, 20-21; H. Leon McBeth, *The Baptist Heritage: Four Centuries of Baptist Witness* (Nashville: B & H Academic, 1987), 21.

[36] Advocates of Anabaptist influence on the teachings of the English Baptists are numerous. A representative selection would include Alfred Clair Underwood, *A History of the English Baptists* (London: Carey Kingsgate, 1947), 21-27, 35-55; James D. Mosteller, 'Baptists and Anabaptists,' in *The Chronicle* (1957), 3-27; '*The Anabaptist Story* (Nashville: Broadman Press, 1963), 200-22; Glen H. Stassen, 'Anabaptist Influence in the Origin of the Particular Baptists,' in *Mennonite Quarterly Review* (1962), 322-48. Those advocating the English Separatist origin of English Baptists apart from Anabaptist influence include Lonnie D. Kliever, 'General Baptist Origins: The Question of Anabaptist Influence,' in *Mennonite Quarterly Review* (1962), 291-321 and H. Leon McBeth, *The Baptist Heritage: Four Centuries of Baptist Witness* (Nashville: B & H Academic, 1987), 49-63.

[37] Torbet, *A History of the Baptists*, 19.

The 'English Separatist descent theory' traces the Baptist tradition to the Separatist wing of the 16th century Puritans and John Smyth.[38] In opposition to the established churches of the time, which recognized entry into the Church through the baptism of infants, Smyth rebaptized himself as an adult believer in 1609 as an indication of his own decision taken on the grounds of personal faith.[39] The rebaptism of Smyth is considered by historians to be instrumental to the formation of the first English Baptist church.[40] Vedder argues for origination after 1641[41] when the uniform existence of Baptist doctrine and practice became evident among a fellowship of churches sharing an understanding of NT belief and praxis.[42] The principal points of agreement can be summarized collectively by believer's baptism, a regenerate church membership, and the supremacy of the Scriptures.

The 'Anabaptist spiritual kinship' theory best identifies Baptists as the spiritual descendants of Anabaptists.[43] The theory traces cardinal Baptist doctrinal affirmations to Anabaptist influence (heritage).[44] Though the name 'Anabaptist' historically refers to numerous dissenting groups,[45] the rapid spread of Anabaptism in the Mennonite tradition is traced to Western Europe after 1525.[46] Patterson credits Anabaptists for influencing the early English Baptists.[47]

---

[38] Leonard, *Baptist Ways*, 12.

[39] According to Leonard, Smyth followed the Mennonite practice of affusion (pouring). See Leonard, *Baptist Ways*, 12.

[40] Ammerman, *Baptist Battles*, 19. Torbet, *A History of the Baptists*, 29. C. Douglas Weaver, *In Search of the New Testament Church: The Baptist Story* (Macon: Mercer University Press, 2008), 9.

[41] Henry C. Vedder, *A Short History of the Baptists* (Philadelphia: American Baptist Publication Society, 1907), 201. See also, Weaver, *In Search of the New Testament Church*, 20.

[42] Gregory A. Wills, 'Southern Baptist Identity: A Historical Perspective,' in David S. Dockery, ed., *Southern Baptist Identity: An Evangelical Denomination Faces the Future* (Wheaton: Crossway Books, 2009), 70.

[43] Early Baptist activity in the American Colonies was considered 'the increase of Anabaptistry.' The identification of Baptists with Anabaptists resulted in the arrest and expulsion of key Baptist leaders for sedition according to the 'law for the obstinate.' See Gaustad, *Baptist Piety*, 16-17, 19, 22-25. Yarnell cites Anabaptist theologian Balthasar Hübmaier, martyred in 1527, as an example for Southern Baptists seeking to rediscover their heritage as 'a believers-only Free Church people.' See Malcolm B. Yarnell, III., 'The Heart of a Baptist,' in *CTR* (2006), 80.

[44] Torbet, *A History of the Baptists*, 29.

[45] William R. Estep, Jr., *The Anabaptist Story: An Introduction to Sixteenth-Century Anabaptism, Third Edition* (Grand Rapids: William B. Eerdmans Publishing, 1996), 4.

[46] Lumpkin, *Baptist Confessions of Faith*, 13.

[47] Patterson, 'Reflections on 400 Years of the Baptist Movement,' 197.

Lumpkin considers the Anabaptist understanding of the NT Church to be the formative context for the 'basic witness' of contemporary American Baptists. He writes:

> The Anabaptists held that the New Testament Church is a voluntary community of individuals who have been transformed by the Spirit, in an experience of grace, and that baptism is the symbol and seal of the faith of the regenerated.[48]

This definition supports the position that Anabaptist influence is responsible for contemporary American Baptists being deliberate and determined followers of Christ, admitting members on the basis of personal confession and water baptism, existing as an autonomous body, and maintaining purity through discipline.[49] By this standard the locus of American Baptist belief and praxis is a free and uncoerced voluntarism indebted to Anabaptist roots.[50]

2.2 The Priority and Meaning of Voluntarism within the American Baptist Tradition

American Baptists citing the recovery of immersion as the NT mode of baptism believe that the water rite identifies the Baptist tradition. SBC theologian Yarnell is typical of those who consider the act of baptizing the believer by immersion in water, in contrast to the practice of infant baptism in the established churches, to be 'the heart of the Baptist movement.'[51] Contra Yarnell, SBC theologian Edgar Mullins advocated 'soul competency' as an experience occurring logically prior to the performance of the water rite. Soul competency, also known as 'voluntarism,' is the human capacity to respond to the initiative of God revealed in Christ.[52] This response is seen as taking place on several levels, intellectual, emotional, spiritual, and experiential. Voluntarism stipulates that people approach God in and through God's approach to them as recorded in the Scriptures.[53] Thus, accountability for an uncoerced response to God rests with the

---

[48] Lumpkin, *Baptist Confessions of Faith*, 13.

[49] Patterson, 'Learning from the Anabaptists,' 126.

[50] Lumpkin, *Baptist Confessions of Faith*, 13.

[51] Yarnell, 'The Heart of the Baptist,' 79-80.

[52] Edgar Y. Mullins, *The Axioms of Religion* ([original work published 1908] Macon: Mercer University Press, 2010), 73.

[53] Ibid.

individual.[54] On voluntarism, religious experience is the starting point of the Christian life and not the water baptism which serves as an external witness to an internal experience. Mullins referred to the soul's competency in religion as 'the distinguishing mark of the Baptists.'[55] However, the relevance of soul competency to American Baptist spirituality is challenged within the tradition. Albert Mohler charged soul competency with 'infecting' the SBC with an 'autonomous individualism' responsible for driving 20th century Southern Baptists from biblical authority.[56] This criticism of soul competency constitutes the principal reason for many American Baptists to reject encounter-oriented spirituality, which they consider treats experience as a rival to the authority of Scripture. E. Glenn Hinson counters those in dissent of the primacy of voluntarism within the American Baptist tradition. He rightly asserts that voluntarism was the distinguishing feature which set Baptists apart from the aforementioned groups from which they sprang.[57] Hinson demonstrates the relevance of voluntarism to the contemporary milieu of American Baptist spirituality. Citing Mullins as a prime exemplar, he shows how voluntarism drew positively from the Enlightenment's emphasis upon experience in religion.[58]

James Leo Garrett queries Mullins' continued influence among American Baptists.[59] In response to Garrett, Mullins did and does possess a formative role within the Southern Baptist Convention. He served the denomination as president of the SBC flagship Southern Baptist Theological Seminary (Louisville, KY) from 1989-1928.[60] Mullins was president of the Southern Baptist Convention from 1921-1924 and served as president of the Baptist World Alliance from 1923-1928.[61] He is also responsible for the report of the committee on the initial edition

---

[54] The Southern Baptist Convention, 2012. 'Soul Competency,' n.p. Available from: http:// www.sbc.net/aboutus/pssoul.asp. [Accessed 4 April 2012].

[55] Mullins, *The Axioms of Religion*, 53, 64, 68.

[56] Mark Wingfield, 'Mohler Criticizes Mullins' Influence and Doctrine of Soul Competency,' in *The Baptist Standard* (2000), 17-20.

[57] E. Glenn Hinson, 'Baptists and Evangelicals: What is the Difference?' unpublished transcribed address to the South Carolina Baptist Historical Society in Columbia on 10 November, 1980.

[58] Ibid., 15-23.

[59] James Leo Garrett, Jr., 'Are Southern Baptists Evangelicals?,' in James L. Garrett, Jr., E. Glenn Hinson, and James E. Tull, eds., *Are Southern Baptists Evangelicals?* (Macon: Mercer University Press, 1983), 123.

[60] Fisher Humphreys, 'Edgar Young Mullins,' in Timothy George and David S. Dockery, eds., *Theologians of the Baptist Tradition, Revised Ed.* (Nashville: B & H Publishing Group, 2001), 181.

[61] Ibid., 182.

(1925) of the SBC's official statement of faith, *The Baptist Faith and Message.*[62] Mullin's most enduring work, *The Axioms of Religion* (Philadelphia: Judson Press, 1908), featuring the central role of 'soul competency' to the movement's identity, was recently reprinted by Mercer University Press in a new edition edited by C. Douglas Weaver.[63] His well-articulated view of the role of experience in formulating doctrine systematically is represented in *The Christian Religion in it Doctrinal Expression* (Roger Williams Press, 1917).[64] These and other published works by Mullins will be discussed in the next section. Mullins has been central to topics debated within the SBC during the past 100 years. He has influenced the formation of the denomination and is an eminent American Baptist voice to inform this study.[65]

Centering Baptist identity on the practice of baptizing believers by immersion into water, as those such as Yarnell do, is not convincing for two reasons.

1) The practice necessitates a prior personal conversion experience.[66]

2) The occasion by which a person is able to profess conversional faith is logically prior to the water rite that symbolizes its experience.

Lumpkin rightly supports the voluntarism advocated by Mullins for determining the core of Baptist spirituality. He observes that compulsion is not the means by which Baptist adherents are made, but Baptists result from individual acts of uncoerced, voluntary choice.[67] American Baptists understand voluntarism (soul

---

[62] Edgar Y. Mullins, speech to the Southern Baptist Convention concerning the *Baptist Faith and Message* on 15 June 1925. Cited in Gregory A. Wills, *Southern Baptist Theological Seminary, 1859-2009* (Oxford: Oxford University Press, 2009), 289.

[63] C. Douglas Weaver, *The Axioms of Religion* ([original work published 1908] Macon: Mercer University Press, 2010).

[64] E. Y. Mullins, *The Christian Religion in its Doctrinal Expression* (Philadelphia: Roger Williams Press, 1917).

[65] See also, Curtis W. Freeman, 'Can Baptist Theology Be Revisioned?' in *Perspectives in Religious Studies 24* (1997), 288-92.

[66] Yarnell, 'The Heart of a Baptist,' 79.

[67] Renewal of persecution in 1673 brought dissenting groups in England together. In a conciliatory measure Particular Baptists sought to ratify acceptance of the Westminster Confession. By 1677, Elder William Collins of the Petty France Church in London modified the Confession for general acceptance of those who were 'baptized upon profession of their faith.' The result is the 1677 and 1689 Second London Confession of Faith. It is instructive that of the changes to the Westminster Confession, alterations with respect to the Baptist spirit of voluntarism are the most notable. A new chapter, Chapter 20, was inserted into the Second Confession which includes a final article (4) to emphasize conversion experience apart from any coercion other than the Holy Spirit. In addition, the third article of Chapter 21 is amended to bear witness to God as ultimate Judge rather than fellow humans. Article 4 of the same chapter is deleted as it cedes authority over the souls of

competency) in terms of the Holy Spirit working through an individual will to develop faith and life in believers. As such, voluntarism stands opposed to 'intentionalism' which considers the Spirit at work through 'composite structures' (e.g. clergy and sacraments) which give the church 'primary responsibility for the faith and life of believers.'[68] Defined more narrowly, voluntarism demonstrates the freedom to personally respond in faith to the claims of Jesus Christ, when disclosed by God the Father to his children.[69] This view is supported by Gaustad who rightly considers regenerated church membership[70] to be the direct result of the principle of voluntarism.[71]

2.3 Voluntarism and Encounter-Oriented Spirituality: The Affective Side of a Theological Abstraction

The purpose of this section is to describe the effects of voluntarism, previously defined in abstract theological terms. Developing the proper relation

---

men to the censures of the Church or to the civil magistrate. The Baptist preoccupation with voluntarism or liberty of conscience is notable. See Lumpkin, *Baptist Confessions of Faith*, 219-40.

[68] E. Glenn Hinson, 'The Future of the Baptist Tradition,' in James Leo Garrett, Jr., E. Glenn Hinson and James E. Tull, *Are Southern Baptists Evangelicals?* (Macon: Mercer University Press, 1983), 186.

[69] Hinson, 'In Search of Our Baptist Identity,' 137. American Baptist pastor Hallford considers 'soul competency' as 'a cardinal Baptist doctrine' whereby 'each soul is competent [without mediation] to approach his Creator for himself...and every genuine believer is a priest for himself in the New Testament sense of the word.' See R. F. Hallford, 'Distinctive Doctrines of Baptists,' in *CenQ* (1960), 40.

[70] The Baptist view of the 'visible church' is that 'the church must be composed of believers only.' John S. Hammett, *Biblical Foundations for Baptist Churches: A Contemporary Ecclesiology* (Grand Rapids: Kregel Publications, 2005), 81. The expression 'believers' church' initially described Anabaptists and Quakers. The expression became popular when Max Webber used it in *The Protestant Bible and the Spirit of Capitalism*, a series of essays composed in German (1904-1905). More recently, the revival of Anabaptist studies spawned a series of thirteen conferences around the phrase. Among the first conferences were the Mennonite 'Study Conference on the Believers' Church' (1955) and the conference sponsored by The Southern Baptist Theological Seminary (Louisville, KY) in 1967. The SBTS conference included seven denominational families. Papers from the 1967 conference are contained in James Leo Garrett, Jr., ed., *The Concept of the Believers' Church: Addresses from the 1967 Louisville Conference* (Scottdale: Herald Press, 1969); Donald Durnbaugh, *The Believers' Church: The History and Character of Radical Protestantism* (New York: Macmillan, 1968), ix.

[71] John Clarke's *Ill Newes from New England* tractates (1652-53) portrayed Baptists to Puritan detractors as more interested in limiting civil government than dissenting from the prevailing practice of infant baptism. Clarke's hiatus (with Roger Williams) to England on behalf of the Rhode Island and Providence Plantations enabled him to return with a charter authorizing 'a most flourishing civil state...with full liberty in religious concernments, and the true piety rightly grounded upon gospel principles will give the best and greatest security to sovereignty.' See Gaustad, *Baptist Piety*, 35, 37, 39, 42.

between Christian doctrine and experience, Mullins affirmed that 'all theology must be vitalized by experience before it can become a real force for the regeneration of men.'[72] In a brief treatise written for inclusion into *The Fundamentals*, Mullins intended to inform what he considered to be incomplete philosophical reflection with Christian experience. On his view, Christian experience is 'a distinct form [category] of human experience.'[73] Mullins describes that as 'the effect of God reaching down to man.'[74] This makes voluntarism an encounter-oriented experience that produces an existentially definitive effect upon the Christian. Herein is the link between voluntarism and personal conversion experience. Mullins describes the effects of these coterminous experiences in terms of moral (power) and intellectual transformation, intuitive knowledge and conviction. This is for Mullins a Christ-based encounter whereby 'the sinner turns to Christ' and is given a direct response from Christ. The convertive process involves the affective experience of Spirit-applied 'heat and pressure' whereby the subject experiences a sense of need due to sin prior to being intuitively assured of forgiveness and regeneration through the exercise of faith.[75] Intellectual difficulties die and a sense of moral power previously non-existent enters. This is an existential awakening to Christ that becomes 'final' (permanent) for the effected person. According to Mullins, this once-and-for-all 'finality' resolves previous reason-offending intellectual problems, removes obstructions to Godward volition and impediments to faith.[76] Soul competence, then, is the means to the end of the self-realization of Christ.[77] The soul's freedom must be directed (by the Holy Spirit) toward this end. Under the influence of the Spirit, the intellect is able to grasp the truth, the emotions arouse trust and affection, the volition yields control to a more commanding presence, and moral intuition consents to the deliberate act taken.[78] This is the encounter-oriented experiential dimension that is integral to the essential nature of the religion of Christ.[79]

---

[72] Mullins, *The Christian Religion in its Doctrinal Expression*, 3.

[73] E. Y. Mullins, 'The Testimony of Christian Experience,' in R. A. Torrey, A. C. Dixon, et al., eds., *The Fundamentals, Vol. 4* (Los Angeles: Bible Institute of Los Angeles, 1917), 314-23.

[74] Ibid.

[75] Mullins, *The Axioms of Religion*, 35-36.

[76] Mullins, 'The Testimony of Christian Experience,' 314-23.

[77] Mullins, *The Axioms of Religion*, 51.

[78] Ibid., 33.

[79] Ibid., 50.

Baptist theologian and contemporary of Mullins, Douglas Clyde Macintosh[80] formulated empirical proofs based on theological laws which, with the proper 'religious adjustment,' would produce divinely prompted or induced effects on the subject.[81] Macintosh's work offers an etiology for the experiences to which Mullins refers. He does so according to what he terms 'the laws of empirical theology.' By 'right religious adjustment' is meant the evidential out-working of the Christian life in terms of realizing in experience the values exemplified by Christ. Christianity is experienced in the sense of being realized volitionally. There are a variety of objects toward which the 'faith attitude' of the subject is directed. These include moral objectives, patience under affliction, or power for service to name a few. According to Macintosh, the intensity (psychological or intellectual) of the experience is dependent on the earnestness and persistence of the human will. This manifests itself in a 'sliding scale' of various degrees of growth in spiritual character under religious influence or the depths of emotional phases related to religious experience. His reference to 'laws' makes this model of spirituality praxis related. The subject seeking special enduement with power for service, or for overcoming temptation, is absent until total and absolute consecration or self-surrender exists. When consecration is present, the resulting intensity of experience will vary as the subject gives attention to prayer. Macintosh points out that there is an inexhaustible possibility to attain more of the divine. Every experience is inseparably linked to divine encounter.[82]

The conditions mentioned in association with the realization of encounter-oriented experience also exist among Pentecostal and renewalist expectations of the reception of BHS. Of greater interest to the present discussion is the nature of experience associated with voluntarism (soul competency). Macintosh describes experience in terms of the psychological effects of right religious adjustment regarding any given Christ-like objective. Since he is centering experience on volitional responses to God, the psychological effects depend wholly on desired moral states of the will whereby God the Holy Spirit produces the moral results desired. For example, in the case of regeneration (one of several 'composite experiences'), God the Holy Spirit works primarily in the will and ultimately in the nature to produce a new and specifically Christian life. On this view, there is a definite beginning to a life which is essentially Christian through the imminent

---

[80] Canadian born and educated at McMaster University in Toronto (Baptist Convention of Ontario and Quebec), Macintosh lived the majority of his life in the USA and was a professor at Yale University (New Haven, CT).

[81] Douglas Clyde Macintosh, *Theology as an Empirical Science* (New York: The Macmillan Company, 1919), 140-56.

[82] Ibid., 142-454.

operations of the Holy Spirit. The experiential dimension of this encounter-oriented phenomenon is the response of the Holy Spirit to the individual's right religious adjustment (repentance and faith), making it thoroughgoing and permanent.[83] While experience in this instance is focused on the human psyche, there is an emotional element as well. With regard to repentance, Macintosh applies a similar legal exercise in anticipation of profoundly experiential results. In the event of volitional repentance, the subject remains in a state of intense contemplation of the disparity between his/her past life and the ideal life expressed in the historic Jesus (what he terms 'self-measurement'). Contemporaneous with this concentrated focus, God the Holy Spirit produces the feeling of sorrow for sin. Experiences are catalogued by Macintosh as primary (volitional) and secondary theological laws, admitting a range of experience grounded and wholly dependent on divine encounter and the operations of the Holy Spirit.[84] Examples include the following:

1) Special providence in the form of answers to prayer.

2) Emotional experience in the form of conviction of sin and Christian peace, joy, and love.

3) Intellectual experience in the form of divine guidance and Christian assurance.

4) Physiological experience in the form of divine healing.

2.4 The Methodological Precedence of Authoritative Scripture: Is Voluntarism in Conflict with this Primary Baptist Doctrinal Tenet?

American Baptists rely on the nature and authority of Scripture to establish voluntarism and 'regenerated church membership' as the identifying (coterminous) elements of the tradition.[85] Scripture as the authoritative instrument for determining matters of belief and praxis is shared by other evangelical traditions.[86] American Baptist emphasis on the inspiration and authority of

---

[83] Ibid., 148.

[84] Ibid., 140-56.

[85] Hammett refers to Scripture as the 'sole normative source for theology.' See Hammett, *Biblical Foundations for Baptist Churches*, 16.

[86] Carnell describes evangelicalism as 'that branch of Christendom which limits the ground of religious authority to the Bible.' See Edward J. Carnell, *The Case for Biblical Christianity* ([original work published 1969] Eugene: Wipf & Stock Publishers, 2007), 14.

Scripture[87] has produced internal dissension in recent decades. A notable example is the biblical inerrancy debate among members of the SBC.[88] For many within the SBC, reliance upon the authority of Scripture is the identifying standard and formative principle of denominational life.[89] SBC scholar Nathan Finn refers to the authority of Scripture as being instrumental to the search for renewed identity in the wake of the SBC conservative resurgence.[90] He rightly attributes the resurgence to 'uncompromisingly *biblical* renewal.'[91] Post-resurgence Southern Baptists intend to avoid two extremes by upholding doctrinal assertions critical to the nature of Scripture (e.g. inspiration, interpretation, and authority):

1) The extreme liberal view which, in their view, diminishes scriptural authority by emphasizing moral experience as foundational to the church's message and theological understanding.

2) The extreme fundamentalist view which tends to equate scriptural truth with cultural norms and forms of philosophical rationalism.[92]

---

[87] A sample of American Baptist confessions of faith among conservative denominations reveal a substantial degree of unanimity on the issue of Scriptural authority. Conservative Baptists of America, 2011. 'Doctrinal Statement,' n.p. Available from: http://www. cbamerica.org/cba _Resources/Doctrinal_Statement.php. [Accessed 30 August 2011]; Baptist General Conference, 2011. 'Affirmations of Faith,' n.p. Available from: http://www.convergeworldwide.org/ about/values/ affirmation-faith. [Accessed 30 August 2011]; The General Association of Regular Baptist Churches, 2011. 'Articles of Faith,' n.p. Available from: http://www.garbc.org/about-us/our-beliefs/doctrinal-statement. [Accessed 16 December 2011].

[88] Ammerman, *Baptist Battles*, 80-87. Leonard, *The Challenge of Being Baptist*, 58-61. Harold Lindsell, *The Battle for the Bible* (Grand Rapids: Zondervan Publishing House, 1976). *The Bible in the Balance* (Grand Rapids: Zondervan Publishing House, 1979). In the wake of 'conservative-liberal' tension among North American Baptists, numerous scholars signed a manifesto issuing concerns relating to Baptist identity. Of concern to the signees was the internal threat posed by those 'who would shackle God's freedom to a narrow biblical interpretation and a coercive hierarchy of authority.' See Duke Divinity School, 1997. 'Re-envisioning Baptist Identity: A Manifesto for Baptist Communities in North America,' n.p. Available from: http://divinity. duke.edu/sites/default/files/documents/faculty-freeman/reenvisioning-baptist-identity.pdf [Accessed 30 August 2011]. Mercer University (Macon, GA) professor Walter B. Shurden offered a response to the manifesto. Shurden criticizes 'private interpretation,' the notion 'that each person in the church thereby is given the right to interpret the Scripture.' Walter B. Shurden, 'The Baptist Identity and the Baptist Manifesto,' in *Perspectives in Religious Studies* (1998), 321-40.

[89] David S. Dockery, *Southern Baptist Consensus and Renewal: A Biblical, Historical, and Theological Proposal* (Nashville: B & H Academic, 2008), 17-18.

[90] Nathan A. Finn, 'Priorities for a Post-Resurgence Convention,' in David S. Dockery, ed., *Southern Baptist Identity: An Evangelical Denomination Faces the Future* (Wheaton: Crossway Books, 2009), 259.

[91] Ibid.

[92] Dockery, *Southern Baptist Consensus and Renewal*, 19.

The polarization of these contrasting views has led Finn to isolate voluntarism as a historically crucial emphasis for the Baptist tradition.[93] He rightly tethers voluntarism to biblical authority.[94] Appearing universally within confessions of faith at the head of Baptist ideals, the freedom of conscience in matters of religion (voluntarism) is linked to a corresponding resolve to uphold the authority of Scripture.[95]

American Baptists consider the Bible to be the exclusive, external, objective, and independently authoritative means (legitimizing source) for validating religious truth and spiritual experience.[96] The necessity for a 'legitimizing source' is defended on two grounds:

1) Scripture meets the standard of revealed truth (e.g. intelligible, expressed in valid propositions, and universally communicable).

2) The discipline of theological inquiry requires a verifiability or controllability postulate understood to be the inspired Scriptures when used to verify truth about God (experienced or otherwise).[97]

This characterization of a legitimizing source does not make the authoritative role of Scripture dependent solely upon human reason, but combines in an interpretive process the intuitive and experiential Author-reader interaction.[98] The dependence upon the Scripture as a 'legitimizing source' and its use as 'a controlling postulate' reflects the 'simple biblicism' of the early American Baptists who separated from their Puritan colleagues on issues such as infant baptism and establishmentarian Protestantism.[99] This 'simple biblicism' is also linked to 'the sufficiency of the Scripture principle' present within the contemporary American Baptist movement. Attributing sufficiency to the Scriptures, American Baptists consider doctrines to be authoritative only when drawn exclusively from the Bible. In

---

[93] Finn, 'Priorities for a Post-Resurgence Convention,' 259.

[94] Ibid.

[95] Leonard, *The Challenge of Being Baptist*, 54-55.

[96] Dockery refers to Scripture as 'the central legitimizing source of Baptist belief. See Dockery, *Southern Baptist Consensus and Renewal*, 214. Ramm refers to this emphasis on Scripture as the 'Protestant principle of authority.' See Bernard Ramm, *The Pattern of Religious Authority* (Grand Rapids: William B. Eerdmans Publishing, 1959), 28.

[97] Carl F. H. Henry, *God, Revelation and Authority, Vol. 1* (Waco: Word Books, 1976), 229-30.

[98] Ramm writes, 'the proper principle of authority within the Christian church must be...the Holy Spirit speaking in the Scriptures, which are the product of the Spirit's revelatory and inspiring action.' See Ramm, *The Pattern of Religious Authority*, 28.

[99] Leonard, *The Challenge of Being Baptist*, 55.

practice, by implementing 'the sufficiency of Scripture principle' American Baptists intend to avoid two heretical trends:

1) Legalism, which places demands upon members beyond the mandates of Scripture.

2) Liberalism, which neglects the mandates expressed in Scripture.

Yarnell detects a favorable median between the heretical extremes which is suitable for framing Baptist identity: 'to be Baptist is to teach the Bible entirely and the Bible alone.'[100] This is a valid proposition, though its value to the movement depends on the hermeneutical principles being universally accepted. Furthermore, American Baptists generally consider the intuitive role of the Spirit to be essential to the Author-reader dynamic. This point must be underlined for the purposes of the current exploration of Baptist views of the Holy Spirit. Although Yarnell characterizes the Bible as an objective reference, he does not sufficiently represent the subjective role of the Spirit's interaction with the reader. American Baptists prioritize scriptural authority while holding dubious the experiential dimension involved in its interpretation. This tendency recalls Mohler's earlier criticism of Mullins' being responsible for the demise of biblical authority within the SBC.[101] It is worth noting that for Mullins, deducing all Christian doctrine from personal subjective experience is unwise. By taking an experiential approach to Scripture, Mullins believes he is no less biblical, systematic, or historical in the formulation of his doctrinal conclusions.[102] In *Axioms,* he clearly states that his findings are either directly or indirectly based on Scripture and that any break with Scripture (as the authoritative word of God) is incompatible with the interests of the kingdom of God.[103] Mullins' typology of spiritual experience may be summarized as follows:

1) Jesus Christ is the historical revelation of God to mankind.

2) The New Testament Scriptures are the indispensable source of knowledge concerning the historical Jesus and his saving work on our behalf.

---

[100] Yarnell, 'The Heart of a Baptist,' 81.

[101] Wingfield, 'Mohler Criticizes Mullins' Influence and Doctrine of Soul Competency,' 17-20.

[102] Mullins, *The Christian Religion in its Doctrinal Expression,* 3.

[103] Mullins, *The Axioms of Religion,* 26.

3) It is by means of the Holy Spirit that men and women are led (meaning of Christian facts is applied) to accept Christ.

4) Spiritual experiences are defined and understood in terms of the Spirit's operations of revealing Christ to mankind.[104]

Citing the two heretical extremes noted above, Gaustad attributes the decline of 'spiritual experiments' (i.e. encounter-oriented spiritual experiences) in his day (1952) to the extremes of 'rigid fundamentalism' (or legalism) and 'impotent, message-less liberalism.'[105] Rather than focusing on the rational and theological nature of these heretical threats to orthodoxy, he appropriately holds literalistic (rigid) 'fundamentalism' accountable for deprecating religious experience while it reacts to liberalism's (rationalistic) cold formalism.[106] The desirable mean position between the untenable extremes is the 'sufficiency of Scripture.' Contra Yarnell, Gaustad advocates approaching the Bible 'through the medium of private religious experience.'[107] This concurs with Mullins and rightly balances the mutual roles of the Author (Spirit) and the reader in a dynamic interpretive process. Historically for American Baptists, to replace an experienced faith with fundamentalist literalism or liberal rationalism is to abandon or to abuse the central role of Scripture to the movement. Gaustad and Ramm have demonstrated the fallacy of subordinating an experienced faith in order to avoid abdicating scriptural authority. The above analysis also demonstrates the difficulty of separating spiritual experience from the dynamic process of biblical interpretation.

It is necessary to link the present analysis with the broader issue of BHS and the American Baptist movement. Defining the movement in terms of voluntarism (soul competency) presupposes the necessary means by which the essential personal conversion-experience core exists. This reasoning is an appeal to prior personal-encounter experience as the basis for authentic spirituality. Classical Pentecostals and many renewalists consider BHS to be an intense personal-encounter experience and the ground for authentic spirituality. The foregoing analysis is meant to emphasize the historical role of personal experience (encounter-oriented spirituality) to the formative roots of the American Baptist

---

[104] Ibid., 4. See also, E. Y. Mullins, *Baptist Beliefs* ([original work published 1912] Valley Forge: Judson Press, 1925), 38.

[105] Gaustad, 'Baptists and Experimental Religion,' 114.

[106] Gaustad refers to 'cold formalism' as the sterile spirituality embodied in a 'heart unmoved by fellowship with God' and 'a head unimpressed by revelation.' See Gaustad, 'Baptists and Experimental Religion,' 114.

[107] Ibid., 115.

movement. Though having a different *locus* from which spiritual experience is generated, American Baptist voluntarism is encounter-oriented and thereby significantly lessens the perceived experiential gap between the two traditions. This opens the way for American Baptist spirituality to be informed by moving toward doctrinal BHS consensus with Pentecostals and many within the charismatic renewal.

2.5   Baptist Voluntarism and a Common Evangelical Piety

This section evaluates the contribution of American Baptist Pietistic roots to broader evangelical communion. It is relevant to consider them because the characteristics of Pietistic spirituality are clearly observable and emanating from experience rather than a set of intellectual teachings. Roger Williams is credited with founding the first Baptist church in the American colonies.[108] In 1652 Williams wrote, *Experiments of Spiritual Life & Health and their Preservatives in which the Weakest Child of God may get Assurance of his Spiritual Life and Blessedness and the Strong may find Proportionate Discoveries of his Christian Growth, and the Means of it.*[109] The treatise, originally written to promote the spiritual improvement of his ailing wife, displays evidence of piety and gives directions for its increase and maintenance.[110] Gaustad credits Williams for the Pietistic (encounter-oriented and voluntarist) roots of American Baptist approaches to validating religion.[111] The dynamic nature of the believer's communion with God (subjective/objective) expresses the encounter-oriented nature of Pietistic approaches to religion. Encounter-oriented spirituality (religion) necessitates the proper means of validation and begs the question of authority. Validating Baptist encounter-oriented spirituality is performed by evaluating subjective experience according to the objective and authoritative reference of Scripture.

---

[108] The present-day First Baptist Church in America was established in Providence (RI) by Roger Williams in 1638. The church is affiliated with the American Baptist Churches USA. First Baptist Church in America, 2011. 'History,' n.p. Available from: http://www.firstbaptistchurchin america.org/?page_id=60. [Accessed 19 December 2011].

[109] Roger Williams, *Experiments of Spiritual Life & Health and their Preservatives in which the Weakest Child of God may get Assurance of his Spiritual Life and Blessedness and the Strong may find Proportionate Discoveries of his Christian Growth, and the Means of it* ([original work published 1652] Providence: Sidney S. Rider, 1863); W. S. Hudson, *Experiments of Spiritual Life and Health* (Philadelphia: Westminster Press, 1950).

[110] Williams, *Experiments of Spiritual Life & Health*, i-ii.

[111] Gaustad, 'Baptists and Experimental Religion,' 119-20.

American Baptists have historically and universally embraced biblical authority as the movement's primary distinctive.[112] This distinctive is perceived to be in jeopardy by those who detect a 'methodological shift' from Scripture to the individual, placing personal experience logically prior to biblical authority.[113] The impetus behind this perceived methodological shift is Mullins[114] who argued that religious experience is the foundation for voluntarism (soul competency).[115] Mullin's thesis gained prominence among American Baptist leaders. Former BWA general secretary James Rushbrooke[116] argued that soul competency (voluntarism) is the 'unifying principle' for the distinctive elements of Baptist theology.[117] Jones considered soul competency (voluntarism) definitive to Baptist theological peculiarities.[118] Former SBC president Hays[119] identified the 'believer's church' as the theological concomitant of soul competency (voluntarism).[120] Kirtley argued that soul competency (voluntarism) necessitates biblical revelation and is the means by which Scripture is understood.[121] SBC scholar Ward[122] advanced the idea that soul competency (voluntarism) provides a

---

[112] R. Stanton Norman, 'Southern Baptist Identity: A Theological Perspective,' in David S. Dockery, ed., *Southern Baptist Identity: An Evangelical Denomination Faces the Future* (Wheaton: Crossway Books, 2011), 53.

[113] Ibid.

[114] Edgar Y. Mullins, *The Axioms of Religion* ([original work published 1908] Macon: Mercer University Press, 2010).

[115] Ibid.

[116] James H. Rushbrooke of England was General Secretary of the Baptist World Alliance (BWA) for the years 1928-39; McBeth, *The Baptist Heritage,* 524-25.

[117] James H. Rushbrooke, *Protestant of the Protestants: The Baptist Churches, Their Progress, and Their Spiritual Principle* (London: Kingsgate, 1926), 70.

[118] Philip L. Jones, *A Restatement of Baptist Principles* (Philadelphia: Griffith and Rowland, 1909), 16-17.

[119] U.S. Congressman and Arkansas native Lawrence Brooks Hays (1898-1981) was one of a few laymen to serve as president of the Southern Baptist Convention. The Encyclopedia of Arkansas History & Culture, 2011. 'Lawrence Brooks Hays,' n.p. Available from: http://encyclopediaofarkansas.net/encyclopedia/entry-detail.aspx?entryID=506. [Accessed 19 December 2011].

[120] Lawrence Brooks Hays, *The Baptist Way of Life* (Englewood Cliffs: Prentice hall, 1963), 38-47.

[121] James S. Kirtley, *The Baptist Distinctives and Objective* (Valley Forge: Judson Press, 1926), 7-8.

[122] Wayne E. Ward taught at The Southern Baptist Theological Seminary (Louisville, KY) during the years 1947-2000.

focal point for developing all other doctrines.[123] Modification to Mullin's thesis by the above SBC leaders is indicative of its broad appeal. Many contemporary Southern Baptists also embrace a voluntarist experience-based (piety-centric) understanding of evangelicalism.[124]

Encounter-oriented spirituality within contemporary evangelicalism and among American Baptists reflects Puritan and Pietist roots, marking a return to their pre-twentieth century evangelical heritage.[125] Puritan spirituality influenced contemporary evangelicalism by its emphasis on subjectivity in salvation and its focus on a prepared heart to receive the Word of God.[126] Pietism drew attention away from lethargy in the church.[127] Without eliminating interest in doctrinal inquiry,[128] Pietism identifies evangelicalism's essential character as 'convertive piety' and 'experimental [encounter-oriented] religion.'[129] Beginning with Philip Jacob Spener (1635-1705), Pietism contrasts Puritanism as an internal reform mechanism concerned with resolving the question of Christian authenticity.[130] The *ecclesiolae in ecclesia* ('churches within the church') expression of Pietism existed to promote the image of the early Christian community.[131] Early Pietism (as expressed by Spener) responded to the demise of Christian liberty at the hands

---

[123] Wayne E. Ward, 'What is a Baptist? Personal Religious Freedom,' in *Western Recorder* (4 April 1970), 2.

[124] According to Finn, this approach to evangelicalism is an attempt 'to rethink the nature of evangelical theology in a postmodern context.' See Nathan A. Finn, 'Southern Baptists and Evangelicals: Passing on the Faith to the Next Generation,' in David S. Dockery, ed. with Ray Van Neste and Jerry Tidwell (Nashville: B & H Academic, 2011), 236.

[125] Stanley J. Grenz, *Revisioning Evangelical Theology: A Fresh Agenda for the 21st Century* (Downers Grove: InterVarsity Press, 1993), 39.

[126] Ibid., 40.

[127] Roger E. Olson, *The Westminster Handbook to Evangelical Theology* (Louisville: Westminster John Knox Press, 2004), 4. Weborg describes 'a fruitful Christian life' as bearing evidence of the power and truthfulness of the gospel. In his view, the call to holy living is to positively demonstrate the triumph of the gospel rather than to negatively promote separatism. See C. John Weborg, 'Pietism: Theology in Search of Living Toward God,' in Donald W. Dayton and Robert K. Johnson, eds., *The Variety of American Evangelicalism* (Downers Grove: InterVarsity Press, 1991), 164, 174.

[128] Travis considers piety central to evangelicalism and views doctrine as 'the formal principle' (constitutive element) of the movement. See William G. Travis, 'Pietism and the History of American Evangelicalism,' in Millard J. Erickson, Paul Kjoss Helseth, and Justin Taylor, eds., *Reclaiming the Center: Confronting Evangelical Accommodation in Postmodern Times* (Wheaton: Crossway Books, 2004), 278.

[129] Stanley J. Grenz, *Renewing the Center: Evangelical Theology in a Post-Theological Era, 2nd Edition* (Grand Rapids: Baker Academic, 2006), 48.

[130] Ibid.

[131] F. Ernest Stoeffler, *Rise of Evangelical Pietism* (Leiden: E. J. Brill, 1965), 237.

of *assensus*-driven scholastic theology which compromised biblical authority.[132] Spener sought to reform a personal relationship with God that extended beyond the doctrinal concerns raised by Luther.[133] He emphasized Christian praxis as more than intellect-based faith accompanied by dogmatic allegiances.[134] Olson, a contemporary self-professed 'postconservative' evangelical, values the combination of 'experience and doxology' over 'second-order' reflection on theology.[135] This establishes Christian praxis and theological reflection on a narrative-shaped experience foundation rather than propositions enshrined in doctrines.[136] The Puritan and Pietist roots of the American Baptist movement do not impede evangelical communion and effectively demonstrate the interdependence of encounter-oriented religion with biblical authority.

3. Beyond Identity: The Case for Doctrinal Consensus

The issue of American Baptist identity has received recent critical attention by SBC leaders.[137] Since its 'conservative resurgence,' the SBC is admittedly in need of trans-denominational consensus to rally churches and members purposefully around a renewed sense of identity.[138] The research contained in this chapter has concluded that voluntarism, otherwise referred to as soul competency, is consistent with the basic Baptist witness and constitutes its primary identifying mark, or historical significance, as demonstrated by Mullins.[139] This point of view will not be accepted by all American Baptists, but it does demonstrate the strong encounter-oriented spirituality it shares with other evangelicals, including Pentecostals and many renewalists. Because of differing views concerning denominational identity, intra-denominational unity and consensus is a matter of contemporary American Baptist (SBC) debate. This section evaluates SBC

---

[132] Ibid., 184-85.

[133] Philip Jacob Spener, Trans. Theodore G. Tappert, *Pia Desideria* ([original work published 1675] Minneapolis: Fortress Press, 1964), 116.

[134] Grenz, *Renewing the Center*, 49-50.

[135] Roger E. Olson, 'Postconservative Evangelicals Greet the Postmodern Age,' in *The Christian Century* (3 May 1995), 480.

[136] Ibid., 481.

[137] Sixteen SBC scholars and leaders recently contributed to David S. Dockery, ed., *Southern Baptist Identity: An Evangelical Denomination Faces the Future* (Wheaton: Crossway Books, 2009).

[138] Dockery, *Southern Baptist Consensus and Renewal*, 12.

[139] Mullins, *The Axioms of Religion*, 57. See also E. Y. Mullins, 'The Contribution of Baptists to the Interpretation of Christianity' in *The Hibbert Journal 21:3* (1923), 534-44.

models for intra-denominational unity to consider the counter-productive results of non-consensus sectarian separatism, and their broader adaptation to intra-evangelical doctrinal consensus; specifically, it is concerned with the relevance of encounter-oriented P/C BHS experience to American Baptist spirituality.

3.1   Avoiding Evangelical Sectarian Separatism

Issues of evangelical identity and unity are traceable to Henry[140] who, in the mid-20th century, criticized fundamentalism for its denunciations of societal ills without offering substantive solutions.[141] Adapting his stance to challenge American Baptists' alignment with post-1925 fundamentalist separatism, Dockery employs Henry-like recrimination to denounce the 'infighting and discord' among SBC churches.[142] He calls upon the SBC to adopt what he terms 'a spirit of collaborative cooperation.'[143] Appealing to Henry (*The Uneasy Conscience*), Dockery advocates collaborative cooperation as a Baptist principle which roots 'convictional confessionalism' in 'the authority of Scripture.'[144] Interestingly, Henry premised evangelical unity on effective gospel propagation and called for 'a baptism of Pentecostal fire' to ignite 'a world missionary program and a divinely-empowered Christian community.'[145] This charge to evangelicals by a prominent American Baptist theologian presupposes an experiential encounter with God (BHS) which he believed would 'turn the uneasy conscience of modern evangelicalism into a new reformation.'[146] It is mentioned here as a support to an encounter-oriented rationale for American Baptist and P/C BHS doctrinal engagement.

---

[140] Carl F. H. Henry, *The Uneasy Conscience of Modern Fundamentalism* (Grand Rapids: William B. Eerdmans Publishing, 1947).

[141] Ibid., 16-23.

[142] Dockery, *Southern Baptist Consensus and Renewal*, 51. A similar pre-Henry critique s offered by Mullins. See Mullins, *The Axioms of Religion*, 13-16.

[143] David S. Dockery, 'Southern Baptists in the Twenty-First Century,' in *Southern Baptist Identity: An Evangelical Denomination Faces the Future* by David S. Dockery, ed. (Wheaton: Crossway Books, 2009), 17.

[144] Dockery, 'Southern Baptists in the Twenty-First Century,' 17-18.

[145] Henry, *The Uneasy Conscience of Modern Fundamentalism*, 84-89.

[146] Ibid.

3.2   American Baptist Intra-Denominational Consensus Models

3.2.1   The 'Center-Circumference' Model

An SBC model for intra-denominational doctrinal consensus involves what is termed a 'center-circumference' approach to unity.[147] At the center of the model is a 'full-orbed' irrevocable doctrine of Scripture.[148] According to the model, circumference matters are less definitive, but not less significant to unity. Doctrinal uniformity is rejected in deference to seekers desiring to reconcile circumference matters with Scripture. Parameters for consensus are established to eliminate the denaturing effects of rationalism, individualism, experientialism, and postmodernism. Thus conceived, SBC consensus is based on scriptural authority and aimed at reclaiming a dynamic orthodoxy (i.e. the *consensus fidei* of the Christian church).[149] The center-circumference model for unity incorporates peripheral issues nonessential to SBC orthodoxy without insisting on doctrinal uniformity. This model agrees with centered-set evangelicalism and is philosophically adaptable to achieving intra-evangelical consensus.

3.2.2   The Theological Triage Model

Another SBC model for achieving intra-denominational doctrinal consensus is a typology referred to as 'theological triage.' The model incorporates 'a robust confessionalism' for determining the bounds of SBC cooperation.[150] Theological triage prioritizes the central theological issues under debate to determine the nature of cooperation.[151] Prioritization includes 'first-order issues' which pertain to Christian orthodoxy and are not open to debate.[152] Things which prohibit believers joining the same covenant community are considered 'second-order

---

[147] R. Albert Mohler, Jr., 'Reformist Evangelicalism: A Center without a Circumference,' in Michael S. Horton, ed., *A Confessing Theology for Post-Modern Times* (Wheaton: Crossway Books, 2000), 131-53; Mohler, 'Confessional Evangelicalism,' 75-80.

[148] Dockery, 'Southern Baptists in the Twenty-First Century,' 18.

[149] Dockery, *Southern Baptist Consensus and Renewal*, 214.

[150] R. Albert Mohler, Jr., 'Southern Baptist Identity: Is There a Future?' in David S. Dockery, ed., *Southern Baptist Identity: An Evangelical Denomination Faces the Future* (Wheaton: Crossway Books, 2009), 30-31; R. Albert Mohler, Jr., 'Confessional Evangelicalism,' in Andrew David Naselli and Collin Hansen, eds., *Four Views on the Spectrum of Evangelicalism* (Grand Rapids: Zondervan, 2011), 75-80.

[151] Mohler, 'Southern Baptist Identity,' 31.

[152] Ibid. Mohler points to those who deny the bodily resurrection [of Jesus] as not [being] believers in the Lord Jesus Christ.

issues.'[153] Finally, 'third-order' issues represent differences which do not deprive believers from entering into a covenant communion.[154] Mohler describes 'the besetting sin of fundamentalism' as the representation of third-order issues as first-order issues.[155] The 'besetting sin of liberalism' is representing first-order issues as third order issues.[156] Theological triage bases unity on Christian orthodoxy. The model is useful for intra-evangelical unity and achieving doctrinal consensus, provided the 'besetting sins' are avoided and it is not denominationally self-serving.[157] By the expression, 'denominationally self-serving,' the intention is not to accuse Mohler of bias, but to appraise the value of the model according to his expressed concern that the SBC is a denomination 'adrift on uncertain evangelical waters.'[158] Of prime importance to Mohler is not the degree to which the SBC is evangelical, but the degree to which the denomination is authentically Baptist.[159] If the theological triage model is denominationally self-serving, it will trend towards demanding doctrinal uniformity and become an ineffective instrument for achieving intra-evangelical unity. Otherwise, the typology is suitable for advancing the cause of American Baptist and P/C BHS doctrinal engagement.

3.2.3   The Axioms of Religion Model

Mullins 1908 presentation (*The Axioms of Religion*) of the central role of soul competency, or voluntarism, to the Christian religion had implications that were intended to be broader than simply providing a basis for injecting an affective dimension into theological discourse. He offers a rationale for consensus that is

---

[153] Ibid. As examples of such communion dissolving issues, Mohler mentions differing views of baptismal subjects, or the role of women in the church, namely their ordination for ministerial service. This is not an assignment of spiritual relation to God, as both sides of the issues agree on first-order matters of orthodoxy and are Christian.

[154] Ibid., 32. Matters of cultural engagement and the issue of millennial timing are noted by Mohler, as not sufficient to rise to the level of division.

[155] Ibid.

[156] Ibid.

[157] A. H. Strong's use of 'regular' identified above approaches the 'besetting sin' of fundamentalism. In fact, one American Baptist denomination is identified by this orientation, The General Association of Regular Baptist Churches (Schaumburg, IL).

[158] R. Albert Mohler, Jr., 'Southern Baptists, Evangelicals, and the Future of Denominationalism,' in David S. Dockery, ed. with Ray Van Neste and Jerry Tidwell, *Southern Baptists, Evangelicals, and the Future of Denominationalism* (Nashville: B & H Academic, 2011), 283-84.

[159] Ibid.

beyond the SBC intra-denominational models outlined above. Mullins intended his work to be a contemporary restatement of the Baptist movement in terms of universal and self-evident truths (i.e. axioms) that represent the principia or essential nature of the religion of Christ.[160] In addition to Baptists, he interacted with Methodists, Presbyterians, and Episcopalians to set forth axioms that presupposed personal conversion experience as the experience that transcends sectarian denominational boundaries. According to Mullins, the Christian movement is founded on the common regenerative experience of its members regardless of denominational affiliation. Since soul competency is the basis for an encounter-oriented regenerative experience, it serves as the foundational means for achieving consensus among Christian groups considered sectarian or disparate.[161] Mullins provides both a model and a rationale for intra-evangelical consensus that is especially applicable to American Baptist and P/C communion, since both traditions recognize the central role of a personal conversion experience.

3.3   *Methodology for American Baptist Intra-denominational Consensus*

This section discusses the methodology of SBC intra-denominational doctrinal unity advanced by SBC theologian David Dockery. The methodology for unifying sectarian schisms begins with the factions renewing their commitment to Scripture (e.g. inspiration, truthfulness, and authority).[162] Consensus progresses when factions adopt a hermeneutical approach to Scripture which favors acceptance over suspicion. This 'hermeneutic of acceptance' is gospel-centered and demands that sectarian factions adhere to the scriptural priority for unity among the people of God (referring to, e.g., Ps 133:1; John 17:21; 1 Cor 12:4-13; Eph 4:1-6).[163] Building unity on scriptural authority eliminates endless debates centered on second and third-order matters, and contends that such nonessentials comprise an insufficient basis upon which to establish intra-denominational unity.[164] The rationale for consensus is premised on a scriptural principle whereby unity from diversity emerges along with the

---

[160] Mullins, *The Axioms of Religion,* 50, 72-75.

[161] Ibid., 94.

[162] Dockery, 'Southern Baptists in the Twenty-First Century,' 19.

[163] Dockery, *Southern Baptist Consensus and Renewal,'* 52.

[164] Dockery identifies first-order gospel issues as setting the parameters for unity. In his view, second and third-order matters are relegated to 'the imponderables of God.' See Dockery, 'Southern Baptists in the Twenty-First Century,' 20.

corresponding effects of Christian maturity and purity within the body of Christ (Eph 4:13-32). Unity occurs when the locus of denominational reflection is the love and unity for which Jesus petitioned (John 17:1-25) and about which the apostle Paul wrote (Eph 4:1-32).[165] The hermeneutic of acceptance is not a mere rational construct, but is effective when sins of sectarian disunity are confessed, God is sought for Spirit-led renewal, and 'a new spirit of mutual respect and humility' abounds toward those 'with whom we have differences of conviction and opinion.'[166] When unity is based on first-order issues (e.g. the exclusivity and uniqueness of the gospel), Dockery concludes that it is possible to build consensus with 'brothers and sisters who disagree on secondary and tertiary matters of theology' and to 'work together to extend the common good of Southern Baptists around the world.'[167]

The methodology offered by Dockery to achieve intra-denominational unity and doctrinal consensus is directly transferable to the broader scope and cause of intra-evangelical unity. In fact, Dockery calls attention to the need for broader intra-evangelical unity based on the rejection of early Pentecostals by the SBC and its member churches.[168] According to Dockery, the P/C movement is 'the fastest-growing movement in American Christianity,' but its relative lack of acceptance among SBC churches is attributed to an unbalanced emphasis on difference over commonality.[169] SBC scholar Daniel Akin affirms that first-order matters of Christian orthodoxy are beyond debate, but concedes that secondary and tertiary matters are open to dialogue 'in order to work together for the proclamation of the gospel of Jesus Christ and the building of his church.'[170] This rationale for SBC intra-denominational unity rejects sectarian separatism and engenders intra-evangelical cooperation in the spirit of personal conversion-based (that is, first-order) acceptance. When applied to intra-evangelical unity, it avoids the tenuous nature of one-dimensional approaches to consensus which reduce

---

[165] Dockery, *Southern Baptist Consensus and Renewal*,' 52, 212. See also Dockery, 'Southern Baptists in the Twenty-First Century,' 19-20.

[166] Dockery, 'Southern Baptists in the Twenty-First Century,' 20. Henry 'urged a more united evangelical witness' and drew criticism from 'separatist fundamentalists' and liberal evangelicals. See The Henry Center of Trinity Evangelical Divinity School, 2007. 'The Life of Carl F. H. Henry,' n.p. Available from: http://www.henry center.org/ about/carl-f-h-henry/life. [Accessed 29 June 2011].

[167] Ibid.

[168] Dockery, *Southern Baptist Consensus and Renewal*,' 9.

[169] Ibid.

[170] Daniel L. Akin, 'The Future of the Southern Baptist Convention' in David S. Dockery, ed. with Ray Van Neste and Jerry Tidwell, *Southern Baptists, Evangelicals, and the Future of Denominationalism* (Nashville: B & H Academic, 2011), 269.

cooperation to gospel-oriented evangelistic campaigns. SBC awareness of P/C numerical advances within evangelicalism makes imminent the need to address elements of difference on the basis of commonality. This rationale for seeking intra-evangelical consensus does not compromise American Baptist fidelity to the inspiration, truthfulness, and authority of Scripture.

4.   Neo-Pentecostalism and the American Baptist Odyssey

This section investigates the American Baptist response to evangelical diversity. The focus of the investigation is the response to the Pentecostal (1906) and charismatic renewal (neo-Pentecostalism) within American Baptist churches since its 1960 inception. The purpose of investigating this issue is to determine the response of American Baptists to P/C spirituality during the last century and to trace the course leading to its current position.

Baptists in America number in excess of 47 million adherents.[171] The SBC consists of 42,000 churches with 16 million members and is the largest Baptist denomination in the USA.[172] The American Baptist churches saw a Pentecostal renewal[173] that began with the formation of the Pentecostal Free-Will Baptist Church in 1908.[174] The renewal experienced by the Free Will Baptists occurred in close proximity to the 1906 Azusa Street revival and was rejected by local Baptist associations.[175] Disfellowshipped SBC leaders receiving the 'Pentecostal experience' were integral to the formation of Pentecostal denominations.[176] C. H.

---

[171] National and World Religion Statistics, 2004. 'Largest Religious Groups in the USA,' n.p. Available from: http://www.adherents.com/rel_USA.html. [Accessed 21 June 2011].

[172] Southern Baptist Convention, 2011. 'About the Southern Baptist Convention,' n.p. Available from: http://www.sbc.net/aboutus/default.asp. [Accessed 21 June 2011].

[173] The term 'Pentecostal renewal' is distinguished here from the term 'neo-Pentecostal' or 'charismatic renewal.' By 'Pentecostal renewal' is meant the historical roots and tangents of the Pentecostal movement.

[174] Vinson Synan, *The Century of the Holy Spirit: 100 Years of Pentecostal and Charismatic Renewal* (Nashville: Thomas Nelson Publishers, 2001), 186.

[175] Pentecostal Free Will Baptist Church, 2011. 'History of the Pentecostal Free-Will Baptist Church,' n.p. Available from: http://www.pfwb.org/ history.htm. [Accessed 27 June 2011]. The PFWBC had 150 churches with 28,000 members in 1998. Baylor University, 2001. 'Listing of Baptist Groups in North America,' n.p. Available from: http://www.baptistheritage.com/directory/NatBodies/BaptistBodies.pdf. [Accessed 27 June 2011].

[176] Synan, *The Century of the Holy Spirit*, 186.

Mason co-founded the Church of God in Christ (COGIC) in 1896.[177] E. N. Bell[178] became the first Chairman[179] of the Assemblies of God soon after its founding in 1914.[180] Independent Baptist evangelists, William Branham and Tommy Hicks, were instrumental in the healing-deliverance movement of the 1950s.[181] Notable Baptist leaders who did not resist the early Pentecostal renewal include C. H. Spurgeon (London),[182] F. B. Meyer (London), and A. J. Gordon (Boston).[183]

4.1   Southern Baptist Resistance to the Charismatic Renewal

4.1.1   Osteen, Simpson, and Conaster: 1960's –1970's

Among the first to seek and receive the Pentecostal experience[184] accompanied with tongues is John Osteen (1959), pastor of SBC affiliate Hibbard Memorial Baptist Church (Houston, TX).[185] Internal opposition by members of

---

[177] Sherry S. DuPree, 'Church of God in Christ,' in Stanley M. Burgess and Eduard M. Van Der Maas, eds., *NIDPCM* (Grand Rapids: Zondervan, 2002), 535-36.

[178] Former Baptist minister Arch P. Collins succeeded E. N. Bell as Chairman at the second General Council meeting held 15-29 November 1914. William W. Menzies, *Anointed to Serve: The Story of the Assemblies of God* (Springfield: Gospel Publishing House, 1971), 109.

[179] The term was later changed to 'Superintendent.' Menzies, *Anointed to Serve*, 97.

[180] Edith L. Blumhofer and Chris R. Armstrong, 'Assemblies of God,' in Stanley M. Burgess and Eduard Van Der Maas, eds., *NIDPCM*, (Grand Rapids: Zondervan, 2002), 333-40.

[181] Synan, *The Century of the Holy Spirit*, 186-87.

[182] Charles Haddon Spurgeon (1834-1892) is well known for his preaching ministry as pastor of London's New Park Street chapel and the Metropolitan Tabernacle. James E. Johnson, 'Spurgeon, Charles Haddon,' in Walter A. Elwell, ed., *Evangelical Dictionary of Theology* (Grand Rapids: Baker Book House, 1984), 1051. Spurgeon often spoke of a new outpouring of the Spirit in his day.

[183] According to Lederle, Meyer and Gordon were the leading proponents of Keswick spirituality promoted a two-stage work of the Spirit. This work of the Spirit achieved either a state of confirmed holiness, or it resulted in an enduement with power and an anointing for ministry. See Henry I. Lederle, *Treasures Old and New: Interpretations of Spirit-Baptism in the Charismatic Renewal Movement* (Peabody: Hendrickson Publishers, 1988), 14.

[184] The term 'Pentecostal experience' is a reference to the Pentecostal expression, 'the Baptism in the Holy Spirit.' While glossolalia ('speaking in tongues' or practicing 'private prayer language') has been the focus of recent SBC controversy, its relation to BHS among charismatic Baptists does not always follow the 'evidence of speaking in tongues' view of classic Pentecostalism. For example, charismatic Baptist Pastor Dwight McKissic claims to have received a distinct BHS experience, but he does not consider glossolalia necessary for confirming the reality of the experience. See William Dwight McKissic, 'The IMB Tongues Policy: Emotional Prejudice or Exegetical Precision?' 25 May 2007 [Retrieved 29 June 2011]. Online: http://dwightmckissic. wordpress.com/ 2007/05/25/the-imb-tongues-policy-emotional-prejudice-or-exegetical-precision.This is also true of many P/C adherents.

[185] Synan, *The Century of the Holy Spirit*, 184.

HMBC led Osteen to found Lakewood Baptist Church (Houston, TX) in 1961 which later evolved into the non-denominational Lakewood Church.[186] The reaction to Osteen's experience is typical of American Baptist reactions to the charismatic renewal. SBC resistance to the 'neo-Pentecostal' (charismatic) movement persisted into the 1960s. Many pastors and laymen receiving 'the baptism in the Holy Spirit' faced stern opposition from fellow pastors, though often solidly supported by their congregations.[187] By 1964, Pastor Charles Simpson of Bay View Heights Baptist Church (Mobile, AL) 'received a Pentecostal-style baptism in the Holy Spirit and spoke in tongues.'[188] Simpson won the confidence of the church which later became a charismatic center for the Southeast.[189] McBeth considers 1975 the peak year of neo-Pentecostal turbulence in the SBC.[190] As many as five SBC associations in four states excluded charismatic churches, while other churches drafted statements or warnings opposing the renewal.[191] Synan reports the select case of Pastor Howard Conaster of Beverly Hills Baptist Church (Dallas, TX).[192] BHBC was rejected by both the Dallas Baptist Association and the Texas Baptist State Convention[193] but claimed SBC membership on the national level.[194] This action prompted the 1976 National Southern Baptist Charismatic Conference which included BHBC and four other SBC churches.[195] A final notable mention occurring during this turbulent era is

---

[186] By 1990 Lakewood Church had grown to more than 5,000 families and 15,000 weekly attendees. Synan, *The Century of the Holy Spirit*, 185. Osteen's son Joel is currently Lakewood's pastor. According to the annual *Outreach Magazine* report of the 100 largest and fastest grouping in America, Lakewood Church heads the list with 43,500 in weekly attendance. Sermon Central, 2010. '2008 The Outreach 100,' n.p. Available from: http://www.sermoncentral.com/articleb.asp?article =top-100-largest-churches. [Accessed 27 June 2011].

[187] Synan, *The Century of the Holy Spirit*, 185-87.

[188] Albert Frederick Schenkel, 'New Wine and Baptist Wineskins: American and Southern Baptist Denominational Responses to the Charismatic Renewal, 1960-80,' in Edith L. Blumhofer, Russell P. Spittler, and Grant A. Wacker, eds. (Chicago: University of Illinois Press, 1999), 157.

[189] Ibid.

[190] McBeth, *The Baptist Heritage*, 697.

[191] Ibid.

[192] Synan, *The Century of the Holy Spirit*, 187.

[193] Pastor W. A. Criswell of the First Baptist Church (Dallas, TX), then the nation's largest Baptist congregation, was a significant voice of dissent. Synan, *The Century of the Holy Spirit*, 187. Weaver, *In Search of the New Testament Church*, 195.

[194] Synan, *The Century of the Holy Spirit*, 187. Upon Conaster's death in 1978, BHBC left the SBC to become an independent church.

[195] Robert J. O'Brien, 'Five Baptist Churches Plan National Charismatic Meet,' in *Baptist Press News Service* (3 November 1975), 1-6. This edition of the *Baptist Press* identifies several SBC associations that acted to 'disfellowship' churches for 'practicing charismatic gifts.' With regard to

M. G. 'Pat' Robertson who received the 'Pentecostal experience' as a student in 1957.[196] Robertson established the Christian Broadcasting Network (1960) and received an ordination to Christian ministry he would later decline (1987) from SBC affiliate Freemason Street Baptist Church (Norfolk, VA) in 1961.[197] Robertson founded Regent University (Virginia Beach, VA) in 1977.[198] His long-time Baptist association, like the other Christian leaders noted above, reflects the theological roots from which his Pentecostal experience contributed to a prolific ministry within the P/C movement.

4.1.2   Narrowing the Position on the Charismatic Renewal: 1980's –Present

The SBC position on the charismatic renewal narrowed in the 1980s.[199] A 1986 *Christianity Today* article estimated that 5% of SBC churches were charismatic.[200]   This period of SBC 'conservative resurgence' marked the burgeoning ministry of James Robison.[201] Robison experienced a 'series of life-altering changes' resulting in 'a new level of spiritual freedom' which prompted him to minister 'outside of his traditional [SBC] Baptist circles.'[202]   Robison is

---

the anticipated National Southern Baptist Charismatic Conference, a joint statement of the five pastors reveals the motivation behind and the purpose for the event: 'After receiving large number of letters from Southern Baptist pastors and laymen, we felt there was a need to bring spirit-filled Baptists together for fellowship, inspiration and encouragement...It is not our intention or purpose to start another denomination or be in conflict with... any association, state convention or the Southern Baptist Convention...Our coming together will not be to conduct business or promote any person or organization...Our sole purpose is to look into the Word of God and preach the simple gospel of Jesus Christ.' Three regional gatherings beginning in 1974 precipitated the planning of the national event. Attendance at the regional conferences grew from 500 to 850. Citing the *Baptist Faith and Message* (1963), the pastors did not feel their charismatic practices were 'un-Baptist' as claimed by the associations that took action to 'disfellowship' the churches. See also Garrett, *Baptist Theology*, 489-90.

[196] Synan, *The Century of the Holy Spirit*, 188.

[197] Robertson resigned his ordination credential during his campaign for the US presidency to avoid any conflict of interest charge. See John Dart, 'Questions Linger on Robertson's Dropping Status as Minister,' in *Los Angeles Times* (17 October 1987).

[198] Ibid.

[199] Weaver, *In Search of the New Testament Church*, 195.

[200] Robert Burrows, 'Americans Get Religion in the New Age: Anything is Permissible if Everything is God,' in *Christianity Today* (16 May 1986), 21. A *Christianity Today*-Gallup poll conducted in 1979 reported 20% of Baptists in America to be Pentecostal or charismatic Christians. This translated to approximately 5 million charismatic Baptists in the USA during 1979. See Kenneth Kantzer, 'The Charismatics Among Us,' in *Christianity Today* (22 Feb 1980), 25-29.

[201] Weaver, *In Search of the New Testament Church*, 272.

[202] Life Today, 2011. 'James and Betty Robison' n.p. Available from: http://lifetoday.org/about-life/james-and-betty-robison. [Accessed 31 August 2011].

indicative of the charismatic renewal's growing influence on the SBC.[203] SBC pastor and author Ron Phillips has organized the charismatically-oriented 'Fresh Oil and New Wine' conferences for more than a decade.[204] Approximately 600 SBC churches participate in the annual FONW conference.[205] Phillips' Central Baptist Church (Hixson, TN), referred to as 'Abba's House,' exists as '…a Spirit-filled Southern Baptist church' bringing balance 'to both evangelicals and charismatics as we operate in the gifts of the Spirit while firmly holding to the Word of God.'[206]

The growing influence of the charismatic renewal was not limited to local church life. In 1987 the SBC Home Mission Board[207] adopted a new policy on glossolalia.[208] The language of the new HMB policy went beyond provisions set forth in the *Baptist Faith and Message.*[209] SBC leader Caner[210] characterizes the HMB action as igniting 'the battle for the soul of the Southern Baptist Convention.'[211] In a correspondence dated 14 April 1987, newly elected HMB president Lewis acknowledged the intrusive nature of making policy which related to the practice of a 'private prayer language.'[212] In 2005 the International

---

[203] Synan, *The Century of the Holy Spirit*, 191. See also, Watson, 'A History of Influence,' 15-30.

[204] Phillips has written several books featuring neo-Pentecostal belief and praxis. Ron M. Phillips, *Awakened by the Spirit* (Nashville: Nelson Books, 1999); *Our Invisible Allies* (Lake Mary: Charisma House Publishers, 2009); *Everyone's Guide to Demons & Spiritual Warfare: Simple, Powerful Tools for Outmaneuvering Satan in Your Daily Life* (Lake Mary: Charisma House Publishers, 2010); *An Essential Guide to Baptism in the Holy Spirit* (Lake Mary: Charisma House Publishers, 2011); *An Essential Guide to Speaking in Tongues* (Lake Mary: Charisma House Publishers, 2011).

[205] Michael Spencer, 2011. 'Southern Baptists and Charismatics: What a Long, Strange Trip It's Been,' n.p. Available from: http://www.internetmonk.com/ archive/what-a-long-strange-trip-its-been. [Accessed 23 June 2011].

[206] Central Baptist Church, 2011. 'About Abba's House,' n.p. Available from: http://www.cbch.org. [Accessed 21 June 2011].

[207] The Home Mission Board is now known as the North American Mission Board (NAMB).

[208] James A. Hewett, 'Baptist Pentecostals and Charismatics,' in Stanley M. Burgess and Eduard M. Van Der Mass, eds., *NIDPCM* (Grand Rapids: Zondervan, 2002), 363-64.

[209] Ibid. The 1963 edition of the *BFM* was the most current at the time.

[210] Emir Caner is president of Truett-McConnell College (Cleveland, GA). The college is affiliated with the SBC.

[211] Emir Caner, 2006. 'Southern Baptists, Tongues, and Historical Policy,' in *The Center for Theological Research* (October 2006), 1-9.

[212] Dan Martin, 'Lewis Named President of the Home Mission Board,' in *Baptist Press* (14 April 1987), 1-10. Lewis commented on the pending action of the HMB: 'I don't think we should be part of employing or commissioning someone who is involved in speaking in tongues, but

Mission Board (IMB), desiring unanimity with the North American Mission Board (NAMB), moved to disqualify from missionary service candidates who practiced a private prayer language.[213] In 2007 IMB trustees revised the 2005 guidelines[214] being unconvinced 'that ecstatic utterance as a prayer language is a valid expression of the New Testament teaching on prayer.'[215] In the view of the IMB trustees, 'if an "ecstatic utterance as a prayer language" is part of the candidate's current practice, the candidate has eliminated himself or herself from being a representative of IMB or SBC.'[216] The action became more controversial when IMB president Rankin acknowledged practicing private prayer language for more than 30 years.[217] The official 2006 IMB position paper on glossolalia considers the phenomenon appearing in the book of Acts (Acts 2:8-11) and Paul's letter to the Corinthians (1 Cor 14:2, 19, 21, 26-27, 39) to be references to known languages (Acts 2:8) which were given as a sign to the Jewish people (1 Cor 1:22;

I am reluctant to see us invade the privacy of someone's prayer closet. How one prays in private should be private, and we should be very cautious in dealing with it.' Voting to forbid glossolalia in private prayer, the July 1987 HMB measure is reflected in the language of current NAMB policy: 'No person who is actively participating in or promoting glossolalia shall be appointed, approved or endorsed by NAMB. This includes having a private prayer language. A representative of NAMB shall counsel any mission personnel serving under NAMB appointment, approval or endorsement, who becomes involved in glossolalia. Continued participation will result in termination.' See North American Mission Board, 2011. 'Self-Assessment,' n.p. Available from: http://www.namb.net/self-assessment. [Accessed 28 June 2011].

[213] Weaver, *In Search of the New Testament Church*, 195. The 15 November 2005 IMB policy includes the following language concerning new candidates: 'In terms of general practice, the majority of Southern Baptists do not accept what is referred to as "private prayer language." Therefore, if "private prayer language" is an ongoing part of his or her conviction and practice, the candidate has eliminated himself or herself from being a representative of the IMB of the SBC.' See International Mission Board, 'Policy on Tongues and Prayer Language,' 03 June 2006 [Retrieved 28 June 2011]. Online: http://www.imb.org/main/news/details.asp?LanguageID=1709&StoryID=3834. See also, International Mission Board, 2011. 'Position Paper Concerning the IMB Policy on Glossolalia,' n.p. Available from: http://www.imb.org/main/news/details.asp?LanguageID=1709 &StoryID=3839. [Accessed 28 June 2011].

[214] International Mission Board, 2007. 'IMB Trustees Adopt Revised Baptism, Prayer Language Guidelines,' n.p. Available from: http://www.imb.org/main/news/details.asp?Language ID=1709&StoryID=5581. [Accessed 28 June 2011].

[215] International Mission Board, 2007. 'Guidelines on Tongues and Prayer Language,' n.p. Available from: http://www.gofbw.com/news.asp?ID=7358. [Accessed 28 June 2011].

[216] Ibid.

[217] Jerry Rankin served as the IMB president from 1993 until his retirement in 2010. Rankin's admission came in a 2006 *Associated Baptist Press News* interview. See Trennis Henderson, 2006. 'Rankin Talks Candidly about Private Prayer Language, Recent IMB Action,' n.p. Available from: http://www.abpnews.com/content/ view/951/119. [Accessed 28 June 2011].

14:22; see Isa 28:11).[218] The study likewise attributed the Corinthian abuses of glossolalia to envy, the desire for spiritual validation, and relics from their former mystery religion days. IMB leaders consider the charismatic practice of glossolalia to be a mark of spiritual pride (Corinth), or a fleshly imitation of the spiritual gift occurring on the Day of Pentecost.[219]

A 2007 poll conducted by SBC retailer Lifeway Christian Resources revealed that fully one-half of SBC senior pastors 'believe some people are granted a special, spiritual language for prayer.'[220] The poll provides contrast to the IMB policies and guidelines which deny appointment to personnel on the basis of glossolalia, whether exercised publicly or privately.[221] Further glossolalia controversy centered on Cornerstone Baptist Church (Arlington, TX) pastor and trustee of Southwestern Baptist Theological Seminary (Fort Worth, TX), William Dwight McKissic.[222] In 2007 McKissic contended with the IMB during a SWBTS chapel message by defending the practice of private prayer language. In his view, glossolalia 'is a valid [spiritual] gift for today' and accepted by a number of Baptist leaders and theologians. In rebuttal to McKissic, SWBTS trustees passed a resolution to clarify the school's position on private prayer language. The resolution invoked SWBTS's desire 'to remain faithful to the biblical witness and its emphases, taking into careful account the historic positions of Baptists in general and Southern Baptists in particular.'[223] SWBTS President Patterson concluded that McKissic's action was 'ill-timed, inappropriate, unhelpful, unnecessarily divisive, and contrary to the generally accepted understandings and practices of Southern Baptists.'[224] His comment was directed more at the motive behind McKissic's choice of venue to stage his critique than the substance of his remarks. McKissic considered the SWBTS resolution a message to

---

[218] International Mission Board, 2012. 'Position Paper Concerning the IMB Policy on Glossolalia,' n.p. Available from: http://www.imb.org/main/news/details.asp?LanguageID=1709 &StoryID=3839. [Accessed 6 April 2012].

[219] Ibid.

[220] Hannah Elliott, 'Study: Half of SBC Pastors Believe in Prayer Languages,' 04 June, 2007 [Retrieved 23 June 2011]. Online: http://www.abpnews.com/content/view/2556/120.

[221] Craig von Busek, 2007. 'Southern Baptists Struggle with the Holy Spirit,' n.p. Available from: http://www.cbn.com/spirituallife/churchandministry/vonbuseck_southernbaptist _holyspirit. aspx?mobile=false. [Accessed 28 June 2011].

[222] Weaver, *In Search of the New Testament Church*, 195.

[223] Craig von Busek, 2007. 'Southern Baptists Struggle with the Holy Spirit,' n.p. Available from: http://www.cbn.com/spirituallife/churchandministry/vonbuseck_southernbaptist _holyspirit. aspx?mobile=false. [Accessed 28 June 2011].

[224] Ibid.

potential faculty, administrators, students, donors, and the entire Southern Baptist family, that Southwestern Baptist Theological Seminary is not a place where a diversity of views about the work of the Holy Spirit within the history and theology of Baptists is tolerated.[225]

SBC scholar Howe attributes the IMB policy controversy to conflicting P/C post-conversion spiritual experience (second blessing) and SBC conversion experience (first blessing) emphases.[226] The SBC controversy manifests the root of American Baptist resistance to integrating P/C praxis; the perception that such praxis (e.g. BHS and glossolalia) results in the spiritual classification of its members (i.e. those who have experienced and those who have not). By wrongly creating a class of 'spiritually elite' and failing to recognize the equality of all believers, American Baptists deem P/C praxis an 'inward' (self-serving) and not 'outward' (others serving) exercise.[227] This evaluation of P/C praxis and spiritual orientation does not take into account the possible biblical justification for the enduring nature and universality of the controversial praxis for the contemporary church. Every tradition possesses a spiritual taxonomy. A given genus includes members whose spirituality exists in various stages of development. The apostle Paul classified fleshly and spiritual Christians (1 Cor 3:1-8). Therefore, prohibiting P/C praxis solely on the basis of the rhetorical 'spiritual classification' argument fails.

McKissic further roots SBC efforts to impede P/C praxis in 'emotional prejudice' which lacks 'exegetical precision.'[228] *Ad hominem* emotional prejudice results when beliefs or praxis are rejected on the basis of perceived Pentecostal origin.[229] McKissic also warns that 'Pentecostal elitism' can equally obstruct the American Baptist integration of P/C praxis.[230] He faults fellow Southern Baptists for exhibiting 'emotional prejudice' or 'charisphobia' that in reality is 'an elitist

---

[225] Ibid.

[226] Claude L. Howe, Jr., 'The Charismatic Movement in Southern Baptist Life,' in *BHH* (1978), 121-22.

[227] Ibid.

[228] William Dwight McKissic, 2007. 'The IMB Tongues Policy: Emotional Prejudice or Exegetical Precision?,' n.p. Available from: http://dwightmckissic.wordpress.com/ 2007/05. [Accessed 29 June 2011].

[229] Howe, Jr., 'The Charismatic Movement in Southern Baptist Life,' 122.

[230] Ibid. See also Frank D. Macchia, *Baptized in the Spirit: A Global Pentecostal Theology* (Grand Rapids: Zondervan, 2006), 27 and Warrington, *Pentecostal Theology*, 99.

and arrogant attitude.'[231] Another basis for SBC resistance to P/C praxis is the use of interpretive constraints on biblical texts offered in support of P/C praxis. During a 2006 interview, SBC scholar Alan Streett queried IMB chairman Hatley about the practice of narrowing doctrinal lines according to secondary issues (private prayer language). Specifically, he queried if this practice effectively moved the SBC from mainstream evangelicalism to become the new voice of fundamentalism.[232] Hatley denied any SBC movement from mainstream evangelicalism, but affirmed that mainstream evangelicalism had 'veered to the left of center.'[233] His denial openly contradicts the substantive IMB policy changes (movement) intended to bring (P/C) praxis into conformity with standards deemed definitional to the SBC. Hatley's characterization of the IMB action effectively makes the SBC the focal point of evangelical doctrinal fidelity. According to Hatley, 'I see Southern Baptists as the anchor for the evangelical community. If we drift to center stream we send the whole community even further left and weaken Christianity around the world.'[234] The IMB policy on glossolalia possesses the traits of separatist-fundamentalist 'bounded set' evangelicalism.[235] This is evident from Hatley's response during an interview with Richardson. He stated that 'the main intent of the new [IMB] policy regarding tongues is to be sure that our [SBC] churches and our church-planting movements across the land are solidly Baptist.'[236] Typical of SBC attempts to restrain the charismatic renewal is the 1975 resolution which targeted the exclusion of all churches who would not renounce their charismatic inclinations.[237] SBC leader Goatley avers in a manner typical of separatist-fundamentalist (bounded set) conviction, 'when congregations of individuals choose to move beyond the established bounds of the [Baptist] tradition, the "offenders" effectively remove themselves from fellowship with the

---

[231] McKissic, 2007. 'The IMB Tongues Policy.' McKissic uses the term 'charisphobia' coined by Lloyd Jack Gray, former SWBTS professor of missions.

[232] R. Alan Streett, 'An Interview with Tom Hatley,' in *CTR* (2006), 11.

[233] Ibid., 11-12.

[234] Ibid., 12.

[235] According to Alford: 'In terms of worship practices, the majority of Southern Baptist churches do not practice glossolalia. In terms of general practice, the majority of Southern Baptists do not accept what is referred to as a private prayer language.' See Dean Alford, 'Tongues Tied,' in *Christianity Today* (15 February 2006), 21.

[236] Suzy Richardson, 'Pastor Faces Removal for Tongues Challenge,' in *Charisma* (31 March 2006), 28.

[237] Watson, 'A History of Influence,' 19.

denomination.'[238] P/C scholar Hart correctly refers to this fundamentalist rigidity as 'entrenched traditionalism.'[239] This form of tradition occurs when a denomination requires its members to adhere to belief and praxis beyond[240] those stated in their Scripturally-derived articles of faith.[241] Hatley believes the IMB policy on practicing private prayer language avoids this charge and that it does not conflict with the spirit or letter of the *Baptist Faith and Message*.[242] Citing the preamble to its 2000 edition, Hatley claims that the *BFM* does not contain 'complete statements of [SBC] faith,' but instead refers questionable matters to the OT and NT in order to determine belief and praxis for Baptists.[243] In his view, the policy drafted by the IMB and its trustees followed this *BFM* principle.[244] However, the principle stated in the preamble can alternatively interpret *BFM* doctrinal ambiguity to intend a purpose of broader inclusion. The *BFM* can alternatively encourage inclusion when individuals or congregations interpret Scripture to determine the validity and application of nonessential doctrines not directly addressed by its articles. This interpretation provides SBC justification to engage P/C adherents to achieve a biblical BHS consensus.

4.2   American Baptist Openness

This brief section provides denomination contrast to the above SBC analysis. The American Baptist Churches USA (ABCUSA), while not as numerous as the

---

[238] David E. Goatley, 'The Charismatic Movement Among Baptists Today,' in *RevExp* (1997), 36.

[239] Larry Hart, 'Problems of Authority in Pentecostalism,' *RevExp* (1978), 261.

[240] Wade Burleson's 'Open Letter to the SBC' evinces disappointment and queries the slippery slope of the IMB policy. See Wade Burleson, 2005. 'Open Letter to the SBC,' n.p. Available from: http://www.puritan board.com/f24/southern-baptist-convention-new-ruling-10624. [Accessed 31 August 2011].

[241] Nothing in the *Baptist Faith and Message* (1963), including what is described under the heading 'God and the Holy Spirit,' precludes or excludes the spiritual gifts of speaking in tongues and healing. One might argue as well that nothing endorses or approves such practices either. Southern Baptist Convention, 2011. 'Comparison of 1925, 1963 and 2000 Baptist Faith and Message' Available from: http://www.sbc.net/bfm/bfmcomparison.asp. [Accessed 28 June 2011]. McKissic is right to ask 'a convention that is usually biblio-centric and exegetically accurate [can] reject plain, clear, scriptural, authoritive, inerrant and infallible biblical truth regarding the Spirit's gifting of some believers to pray in tongues in private according to the sovereign will of God (I Corinthians 12:7,10, 30; 14:2, 4, 5, 13-15)?' McKissic, 'The IMB Tongues Policy: Emotional Prejudice or Exegetical Precision?'

[242] Streett, 'An Interview with Tom Hatley,' 8-9.

[243] View the preamble at The Southern Baptist Convention, 2011. 'Baptist Faith and Message,' n.p. Available from: http://www.sbc.net/bfm/default.asp. [Accessed 30 August 2011].

[244] Streett, 'An Interview with Tom Hatley,' 8-9.

SBC,[245] is more favorable to charismatic belief and praxis among its members.[246] ABCUSA scholar Ervin served on the faculty of P/C Oral Roberts University (Tulsa, OK).[247] Ervin's scholarly contributions to the BHS debate place him within the P/C tradition.[248] ABCUSA churches influenced by the charismatic renewal in the 1970s formed the American Baptist Charismatic Fellowship (1971).[249] In 1982 the fellowship became Holy Spirit Renewal Ministries in American Baptist Churches.[250] By 2007 the ABCUSA renewal initiative (HSRM) broadened its scope to include members outside the ABCUSA denomination.[251] The ABCUSA represents a denomination which favors inclusivism toward the charismatic renewal within the American Baptist tradition. This openness contrasts the identified SBC trend toward excluding renewalists from denominational identity.

5. Conclusion

This chapter identified encounter-oriented spirituality in close relation to voluntarism (soul competency) as the formative root of American Baptist personal conversion-based spirituality. Voluntarism is conceived by American Baptists as spiritual experience expressed in terms of the human capacity to respond to the initiative of God revealed in Christ. In this sense, voluntarism fundamentally reflects an encounter-oriented spirituality. American Baptist emphasis on voluntarism includes nonnegotiable reliance on biblical authority. Expressed in

[245] There are 1.3 million members and 5,500 congregations in the American Baptist Churches USA. American Baptist Churches USA, 2011. '10 Facts You Should Know About American Baptists,' n.d. Available from: http://www.abc-usa.org/portals/0/ABC10Facts Brochure.pdf. [Accessed 23 June 2011].

[246] Schenkel, 'New Wine and Baptist Wineskins,' 153-57.

[247] Howard M. Ervin served as pastor of ABCUSA Emmanuel Baptist Church (Highlands, NJ). Ervin taught graduate theology at ORU for more than forty years. Danielle Parker, 2007. 'The Legacy of Howard M. Ervin,' n.p. Available from: http://www.oru.edu/news/alumni _news/20090923_legacy_howard_ervin.php. [Accessed 24 December 2011].

[248] Howard M. Ervin, *These Are Not Drunken As Ye Suppose* (Plainfield: Logos International, 1968). *Conversion-Initiation and the Baptism in the Holy Spirit* (Peabody: Hendrickson Publishers, 1984); *Spirit Baptism: A Biblical Investigation* (Peabody: Hendrickson Publishers, 1987).

[249] Holy Spirit Renewal Ministries, 2011. 'Roots,' Available from: http://www.hsrm.org/ index.php?option=com_content&view=article&id=50&Itemid=72. [Accessed 23 June 2011]; Leonard, *Baptist Ways*, 410; Weaver, *In Search of the New Testament Church*, 184.

[250] Holy Spirit Renewal Ministries, 2011. 'Roots,' Available from: http://www.hsrm.org/ index.php?option=com_content&view=article&id=50&Itemid=72. [Accessed 23 June 2011].

[251] Ibid.

these terms, encounter-oriented spirituality is in harmony with personal conversion-based 'centered set' evangelicalism. American Baptists aligned with their Puritan and Pietist roots oppose partisanship, separatism, and rigid fundamentalism in favor of sectarian Free Church nonconformism. The experiential locus of the American Baptist movement does not impede communion with other biblically-based evangelical traditions predisposed to encounter-oriented spirituality, including those within the P/C tradition. American Baptist voluntarism and the BHS experienced by Pentecostals and many renewalists differs categorically, but each tradition is encounter-orientated in its spirituality. This common orientation provides the enabling conditions for American Baptists to dialogue with Pentecostals and renewalists, even with those within their own denomination, with the aim of moving toward achieving a BHS doctrinal consensus.

The negative reaction of the SBC to the neo-Pentecostal charismatic renewal is indicative of the need for broader American Baptist doctrinal consensus. American Baptists who define themselves according to doctrines nonessential to unity become entrenched in separatist-fundamentalist tradition. This approach to American Baptist identity is contrary to the biblicism consistent with the theological, historical, and contemporary evangelicalism investigated in this work. The analysis of recent conciliatory responses to controversy within the SBC demonstrates the potential for denominational doctrinal consensus. Models proposed for SBC doctrinal consensus and denominational unity are essentially biblicist, appealing to scriptural authority, while adopting a hermeneutic of acceptance with humility toward those differing on theological nonessentials. The 'center-circumference' analogy grounds SBC unity on first-order issues (center) relating to the exclusivity and uniqueness of the gospel. At the same time, it dismisses secondary and tertiary theological matters (circumference) as nonessential to denominational communion. The model requires making a subtle distinction to be effective: Issues of circumference are not debated to determine the basis for unity; rather, issues of circumference are debated in light of scriptural authority and on the basis of first-order unity. This unity is not limited to common areas of doctrinal understanding, but recognizes the existing diversity present within the one body of Christ. Applied this way, the model is directly transferrable to broader evangelical doctrinal consensus.

Central to this chapter's findings is Mullins who represents a major influence on the American Baptist contribution to a biblically founded and philosophically cogent interpretation of religious experience. His restatement of the ideals of the Baptist movement with a view to the universal principia of the Christian faith firmly establishes a way for the advance of American Baptist and P/C BHS doctrinal consensus on common evangelical and experiential grounds.

-4-

AMERICAN BAPTIST PERSPECTIVES ON SPIRIT BAPTISM

1. Introduction

The purpose of this chapter is to provide exegetical analyses of the NT textual support commonly used by American Baptist scholars to interpret the BHS metaphor. The analyses are arranged according to the Synoptic Gospels (§2.1), the Gospel of John (§2.1) Luke-Acts (§2.3), and 1 Cor 12:13 (§2.4). This chapter investigates the mainstream positions exegetically defended by American Baptist BHS apologists. The chapter also investigates the historic BHS perspectives of two American Baptist theologians who informed Baptist orthodoxy during their respective eras (§3). The historic views add context to the BHS perspectives which dominate the contemporary American Baptist movement. The analyses demonstrate a lack of uniformity among American Baptist BHS views. While no uniform BHS view represents the entire tradition, a unified American Baptist BHS construct nevertheless emerges. This chapter contributes to the thesis of this study by delimiting features of a unified American Baptist BHS construct in order to determine the nature and extent of the existing BHS theological impasse with Pentecostals and many within the charismatic renewal.

2. Textual Evidence Supporting BHS Perspectives

American Baptists identify seven NT references to BHS (Matt 3:11; Mark 1:8; Luke 3:16; John 1:33; Acts 1:5; 11:16; 1 Cor 12:13). Four additional Pauline references to BHS are disputed (Rom 6:3-5; Gal 3:27; Eph 4:5; Col 2:12). In the discussion of this chapter, the undisputed texts are considered independently to adduce the relevant exegetical and theological issues presented by American Baptists according to the literary-authorial context of the BHS metaphor. Texts referring to BHS in Luke-Acts are combined due to the common authorship of the

110

books. The exegetical data reveals uniformity and divergence of BHS views within the American Baptist movement.

2.1   *The Synoptic Gospels*

John the Baptist (JTB) and Jesus are featured antithetically by the Gospel writers.[1] This is especially apparent in the Synoptic Gospels (Matt 3:1-17; Mark 1:4-8; Luke 3:1-18). Specifically, the antithesis concerns the nature of the baptizing ministries of JTB and Jesus. The Synoptists present BHS within the context of logia expressed by JTB. The logia demonstrate a perceived relationship between JTB's water rite and the future spiritual rite performed by the Coming One. American Baptist exegetes and theologians explore the life-situation of JTB to resolve textual issues relating to the various perspectives of the Synoptists. American Baptist scholars also demonstrate an interest in the respective theological orientation of the Synoptic writers. Methodologically, the American Baptist interpretation of BHS occurrences in the Gospels depends on these contextual author-related factors.

2.1.1   *Matthew 3:11*

This section provides comparative exegetical analysis of four prominent American Baptist theologians whose writings are influential in Baptist circles: John A. Broadus, Donald A. Carson, David L. Turner, and Craig L. Blomberg. The analyses together provide a representative and relatively comprehensive text-specific American Baptist perspective of BHS.

2.1.1.1   *Interpretive Foci*

Four interpretive foci indicate the unique textual emphases of American Baptist approaches to the text. John A. Broadus represents the first interpretive

---

[1] D. A. Carson, *Matthew,* in Frank E. Gaebelein, ed., *EBC, Vol. 8* (Grand Rapids: Zondervan Publishing House, 1984).

focus.[2] He interprets BHS according to this Matthean text in relation to the life-situation of JTB.[3] The following points demonstrate this approach:

1) The prophet Malachi contributed to the formation of JTB's self-consciousness and theological reflection. The appearance and lifestyle of JTB (Matt 3:4; 11:8) correspond to Elijah (2 Kgs 1:8) whose arrival Malachi predicted would precede that of the Messiah (Mal 3:1; 4:5). Whether emulating Elijah or not, the appearance and lifestyle of JTB were effective in making his message emphatic to the Jews.[4]

2) Though JTB demanded evidence (εἰς μετάνοιαν, 'for repentance,' Matt 3:11), he did not consider his water rite efficacious for producing repentance.[5]

3) JTB intended his water rite to be symbolic of the spiritual rite performed by 'the coming stronger one' (ἐρχόμενος ἰσχυρότερός).[6]

4) Broadus interprets the prepositional phrase ἐν πνεύματι ἁγίῳ καὶ πυρί locatively,[7] 'in Holy Spirit and fire.'[8]

[2] David S. Dockery, 'The Broadus-Robertson Tradition,' in Timothy George and David S. Dockery, eds., *Theologians of the Baptist Tradition, Revised Ed.* (Nashville: B & H Publishing Group, 2001), 181.

[3] John A. Broadus, *Commentary on the Gospel of Matthew,* in Alvah Hovey, ed., *An American Commentary on the New Testament* (Philadelphia: American Baptist Publication Society, 1886), 31-52. Broadus (1827-95) was an American Baptist pastor who also served as and professor president of The Southern Baptist Theological Seminary (Louisville, KY).

[4] Ibid., 37.

[5] Ibid., 37-39.

[6] A. T. Robertson, *Word Pictures in the New Testament, Vol. 1* (Nashville: Sunday School Board of the Southern Baptist Convention, 1930), 225.

[7] Broadus, *Commentary on the Gospel of Matthew,* 41.

[8] Ibid., 50.

5) JTB's use of the anarthrous πνεύματι ἁγίῳ refers to a proper name ('Holy Spirit')[9] that conceptually approaches NT hypostatization.[10]

6) Broadus supposes from JTB's use of other metaphorical references in the pericope (Matt 3:12) that his contemporaries did not understand BHS literally, but as a figurative immersion (in the Holy Spirit) akin to being '*immersed* in business,' '*plunged* in despair,' or '*bathed* in delight' (emphasis added).[11]

7) JTB portrays Jesus as 'the coming stronger one' who immerses in the Holy Spirit as the purifying medium.[12]

8) The expression καὶ πυρί ('and fire,' Matt 3:11) is understood by Broadus as a reference to the judgment of the wicked.[13] He bases this interpretation on the reference to consuming fire in the previous and following verses (Matt 3:10, 12), a pattern which he also observes from Luke's account (Luke 3:9, 16-17). In addition, Broadus notes that the absence of καὶ πυρί from the BHS references in Mark 1:8; John 1:33; Acts 1:5 and 11:16, demonstrates strong support for Matthew's association of consuming fire with the destruction of the wicked.

9) The single immersing act of the Coming One 'in Holy Spirit and fire' collectively scrutinizes the Jews (ὑμας, 'you all') to leave behind a purified nation by separating the repentant from the non-repentant.[14]

---

[9] Ibid. Hawthorne offers recent corroboration for Broadus, pointing out that the anarthrous πνεύματι ἁγίῳ in Matthew and Luke's infancy narratives warrants the translation 'the Holy Spirit.' See Gerald F. Hawthorne, *The Presence and the Power: The Significance of the Spirit in the Life and Ministry of Jesus* (Dallas: Word Publications, 1991), 66. The expressions used to refer to the Holy Spirit in the NT have been studied more recently by linguists, using objective criteria. See Jenny Read-Heimerdinger, *The Bezan Text of Acts: A Contribution of Discourse Analysis to Textual Criticism* (New York: Sheffield Academic Press, 2002), 145-72.

[10] Broadus does not claim absolute certainty on this point, but does not consider πνεύματι ἁγίῳ to mean JTB is referring to 'holy spirit' as an influence from God conceptualized in the OT.

[11] Broadus, *Commentary on the Gospel of Matthew*, 51.

[12] Ibid. See also, A. H. Strong, *Systematic Theology: A Compendium and Commonplace Book Designed for the Use of Theological Students*, Vol. 3 (Philadelphia: The Griffith & Rowland Press, 1909), 935.

[13] Broadus, *Commentary on the Gospel of Matthew*, 51.

[14] Ibid., 52.

Broadus concludes that the Holy Spirit produces 'new and pure life' in the repentant 'immersed' disciple.[15]

The second interpretive focus is offered by Donald A. Carson[16] who interprets the BHS occurrence in Matt 3:11 according to the author's eschatological 'fulfillment theme.'[17] The following points highlight the primary emphases of Carson's position:

1) Among the Gospel writers only Matthew has JTB including εἰς μετάνοιαν ('for repentance') with reference to his water rite. Matthew's variation of the logion may emphasize an eschatological connection between JTB and Jesus.[18]

2) Matthew's fulfillment theme (Matt 2:15; 5:17-20) encompasses the ministry of JTB (Matt 11:7-13).[19]

3) The purpose of JTB's water rite was preparatory: to prepare the way for the Lord by calling the people to repentance.[20] His water rite pointed symbolically to the eschatological 'spirit and fire' baptism to be performed by Jesus to inaugurate the Messianic age.[21]

4) 'Baptism in the Holy Spirit' is not a specialized term in the NT. Its conceptual background includes references in the OT and Qumran literature (Ezek 36:25-27; 39:29; Joel 2:28; 1QS 3:7-9; 4:21; 1QH 16:12) which support JTB's connecting 'the Holy Spirit' with cleansing

---

[15] Ibid.

[16] Carson's Baptist affiliation includes serving on the faculty of Northwest Baptist Theological Seminary (Vancouver, BC), receiving his M.Div. degree from Central Baptist Seminary (Toronto, ON), and serving as pastor of Richmond Baptist Church (Richmond, BC). The Renew Conference, 2011. 'D. A. Carson's Bio,' n.p. Available from: http://therenewconference.org/#/speakers/d-a-carsons-bio. [Accessed 26 December 2011].

[17] Carson, *Matthew*, 98-106.

[18] Ibid., 104.

[19] Ibid., 268.

[20] Carson follows British Methodist theologian James Dunn at this point. James D. G. Dunn, *Baptism in the Holy Spirit: A Re-examination of the New Testament Teaching on the Gift of the Spirit in relation to Pentecostalism Today*, 2nd ed. (Philadelphia: The Westminster Press, 2010), 14. Dunn's 'conversion-initiation' thesis articulated in *Baptism in the Holy Spirit* has become a seminal and enduring reference for those advocating single-stage (conversion experience-based) BHS systems, including American Baptist scholars.

[21] Carson, *Matthew*, 104-5.

and purification.[22] By this assertion, Carson intends to demonstrate that JTB had sufficient conceptual background to warrant a reference to the Holy Spirit in the logion.

5) The appearance of καὶ πυρί ('and fire') is for Carson combined with the Holy Spirit reference to suggest Spirit-fire purification. Purifying without destroying is an OT quality of fire (Isa 1:25; Zech 13:9; Mal 2:2-3).[23]

6) The water rite of JTB is performed exclusively on the penitent and implies that the eschatological Spirit and fire baptism is intended only for candidates with prepared hearts.[24]

7) The announcement of 'Spirit-fire' baptism' by JTB would be anticipated by Jews believing that the Holy Spirit had been withdrawn until the Messianic Age.[25]

Carson concludes that JTB's water rite related to repentance, preparing penitent hearts for purification (BHS) by means of an eschatological Spirit-fire baptizer.[26]

David L. Turner frames the third interpretive focus of Matt 3:11 in a manner similar to Carson,[27] emphasizing the eschatological nature of JTB's ministry but with an emphasis on Jesus as the Spirit-giver.[28] The following points represent his exegetical emphases:

1) JTB's water rite ('for repentance') prepares Israel for Jesus' more powerful Spirit-and-fire baptism. Matthew's 'power' motif is evident

---

[22] Ibid., 105. Carson appeals to Dunn who insists that JTB would have had at least some peripheral contact with the sect which spoke freely of 'God's holy spirit (or spirit of holiness) as a cleansing, purifying power.' See Dunn, *Baptism in the Holy Spirit,* 9.

[23] Ibid. Carson cites Dunn ('Spirit-and-fire'), *Baptism in the Holy Spirit,* 10-13 and Murray J. Harris, 'Appendix,' in Colin Brown, ed., *NIDNT, Vol. 3.* (ET Grand Rapids: Zondervan Publishing House, 1978), 1178 to support the unified 'Spirit-fire' baptism view.

[24] Carson, *Matthew,* 105.

[25] Ibid.

[26] Ibid.

[27] David L. Turner is an American Baptist pastor and professor. See Cornerstone University, 2012. 'David Turner,' n.p. Available from: http://assets1.mytrainsite.com/501431/turner_vitae.pdf?r=1536. [Accessed 20 April 2012].

[28] David L. Turner, *Matthew,* in Robert W. Yarbrough and Robert H. Stein, eds., *BECNT* (Grand Rapids: Baker Academic, 2008), 104-16.

from his connecting Jesus' conception with the miraculous agency of the Holy Spirit (Matt 1:18, 20).[29]

2) Jesus (the Spirit bearer) will dispense the eschatological Spirit to others (BHS), but his earthly ministry required the Spirit's empowerment to fulfill the messianic mission (Matt 4:1; 12:18, 28).[30]

Turner's observation on this point effectively raises the issue of determining the nature of BHS. American Baptists identify BHS as an event occurring contemporaneously with personal conversion experience. The relation of BHS to conversion is not merely one of occasion, but also of function. The necessity perceived by American Baptists of the Spirit's empowering presence to the fulfillment of Jesus' messianic mission is based upon the Spirit's reception at the moment of conversion. Correlative issues raised by the following questions are addressed below (see §2.3.1). These queries help to determine if the Spirit-bearer/Spirit-giver received the Spirit in the same sense as those upon whom he will perform BHS. If so, then Jesus' reception of the Spirit has paradigmatic value.

Several interpretative issues are raised:

- Is the Spirit's empowering limited to Jesus and the messianic mission, or is it paradigmatic for those who will later receive the Spirit?

- Does the Spirit function differently in relation to the Spirit-giver due his messianic status?

- Did Jesus perform the works associated with his unique messianic office by his own power or was he dependent on empowerment by the Spirit?

- Do the recipients of BHS receive the same capacity (empowerment) for mission as Jesus (the Spirit-giver)?

This interpretive line of questioning raises the lexical issue of defining πνεῦμα/רוּחַ ('Spirit/spirit, wind, breath') relative to BHS:

- Does the logion of JTB conceptually represent BHS as Spirit-reception in terms of inspired speech, soteriological cleansing, or some admixture of both (see §2.3.4)?

Turner relates charismatic empowering to Jesus and potentially to his disciples by his dispensing of the Spirit (BHS), but also, in a third exegetical emphasis, relates

---

[29] Ibid.

[30] Ibid., 114 n. 13.

'the outpouring of the Spirit' (BHS) through Jesus to divine purification and judgment:[31]

3) Turner, contra Carson, interprets ἐν πνεύματι ἁγίῳ καὶ πυρί ('in Holy Spirit and fire') as 'a single baptism with ostensibly two aspects.' He bases his interpretation on texts which associate the eschatological outpouring of the Spirit with both cleansing water (Isa 32:15; 44:3; Ezek 36:25-27; 37:14, 23; 39:29; Joel 2:28-29) and refining fire (Isa 1:25; 4:4; 30:27-30; Zech 13:9; Mal 3:1-3; 4:1; cf. 2 Esd [4 Ezra] 13:8-11; Acts 2:3).[32] BHS is a harvest (threshing/winnowing process, Matt 3:12)[33] which separates the wheat from the chaff (Ps 1:4; Prov 20:26; Isa 41:14-16; Jer 15:7; 51:33; Dan 2:35; Hos 6:11; 13:3; Joel 3:13; Mic 4:12-13; Rev 14:14-20).[34]

Turner's interpretive focus, therefore, conceives of a single eschatological outpouring of the Spirit administered by Jesus who purifies and judges (BHS).

Craig L. Blomberg[35] utilizes a fourth interpretive focus and understands BHS according to its coincidence with conversion and distinction from Spirit filling.[36] The following points make Blomberg's position clear:

---

[31] Ibid., 115-16. See also Craig S. Keener, *A Commentary on the Gospel According to Matthew* (Grand Rapids: William B. Eerdmans Publishing, 1999), 128.

[32] Turner notes that 1QS 3:7-9 (cf. 4:21; 1 QH 8:21) speak of 'the purifying work of the holy spirit in humbling members of the (Qumran) community so that they would obey the law of God.' This is preparatory for the sect's ceremonial ablutions practiced in view of the spirit's work. See Turner, *Matthew*, 115.

[33] Turner cites Webb to support BHS as a single purifying act. Webb relies on the work of Gustav Dalman on Palestinian agricultural practices, According to Dalman, the actual winnowing of the grain, separating the wheat from the straw was accomplished with the winnowing fork (θρῖναξ) and not the shovel (πτύον). See Gustav Dalman, *Arbeit und Sitte in Palästina, Vol. 3.* ([original work published 1928] Hilescheim: George Olms, 1964), 116. Webb concludes from Dalman that the use of 'shovel' (πτύον) in Matt 3:12 and Luke 3:17 indicates that the activity is not winnowing. According to Webb, the winnowing has already occurred and the wheat and chaff lie separated on the threshing floor. The owner brandishes the shovel (πτύον) to clean out the threshing floor (Matt 3:12; Luke 3:17). See Robert L. Webb, *John the Baptizer and Prophet: A Socio-historical Study* ([original work published in 1991] Eugene: Wipf & Stock Publishers, 2006), 297-98.

[34] Turner, *Matthew*, 115-16.

[35] Blomberg is professor of NT at Conservative Baptist affiliated Denver Seminary in Littleton, CO.

[36] Craig L. Blomberg, *Matthew*, in David S. Dockery, ed., *NAC, Vol. 22* (Nashville: Broadman Press, 1992), 71-80; Craig L. Blomberg, *Jesus and the Gospels: An Introduction and Survey, 2nd Ed.* (Nashville: B & H Academic, 2009), 169-70; 253-55.

1) JTB uses 'the Coming One' as a messianic title (Pss 40:7 and 118:26).[37]

2) The menial task of 'carrying' (βαστάζω) a master's dirty sandals confesses a status subordinate to a slave, and 'stronger' (ἰσχυρότερός) demonstrates JTB's intention to compare himself with the one coming 'after' him (ὀπίσω μου). JTB (or perhaps Matthew) links the 'more powerful' status of the 'coming one' to both messianic role and function (BHS).[38]

3) Both JTB and Jesus perform water baptism to illustrate externally inward transformation (John 4:1-2), but of the two water baptizers, only Jesus will 'baptize with the Holy Spirit and fire.'[39]

4) Blomberg interprets BHS according to its fulfillment, scope, and purpose. Considering the progression of events described in Acts chapters 1-2, the multiple NT references to the prediction of JTB (Mark 1:8; Matt 3:11; Luke 3:16; John 1:33; Acts 1:5; 11:16) refer to 'the outpouring of Spirit of God on the followers of Jesus at Pentecost, initiating the church age.'[40] Appealing to Paul, Blomberg sees 1 Cor 12:13 as the definitive NT BHS reference to an experience universally received by all Christians.[41] Matthew's focus is on two phases of a single BHS event by which the division of mankind occurs on the basis of their response to JTB and Jesus: conversion for believers and judgment (καὶ πυρί) for unbelievers (Matt 3:10, 12; 13:36-43).[42]

5) Blomberg insists that BHS is not a work of the Spirit subsequent to conversion ('second blessing')[43] or to be confused with the 'filling of the Spirit.'[44] On his view, BHS is a completed event which occurred on the

---

[37] Blomberg cites Davies and Allison on this point, *Matthew, Vol. 1*, 313-14. Among the six interpretive options for 'the coming one,' Davies and Allison see JTB's 'coming one' as pre-eminently 'a figure of eschatological judgment and there is more precedent for making the office of judgment belong to the Messiah.'

[38] Blomberg notes that Matthew records JTB using βαστάζω ('I carry') rather than λύω ('I loose/untie') appearing in the Markan (1:7) and Lukan (3:16) accounts. Blomberg, *Matthew*, 79. See also, Carson, *Matthew*, 104.

[39] Blomberg, *Matthew*, 79.

[40] Blomberg, *Jesus and the Gospels*, 253.

[41] Ibid., 169.

[42] Blomberg, *Matthew*, 80.

[43] Blomberg, *Jesus and the Gospels*, 169.

[44] Blomberg, *Matthew*, 80. Blomberg identifies interpreters (e.g. charismatics) who infer from the intermittent OT coming and going of the Spirit on the individual that his empowerment is a

Day of Pentecost[45] and the 'filling of the Spirit'[46] recurs repeatedly to empower believers for bold proclamation (Acts 2:4; 4:8, 31; 9:17; 13:9).'[47]

Blomberg concludes that the BHS metaphor is a reference to ritual (water baptism) which illustrates the believer's initiation (spiritual baptism) into the body of Christ by means of the indwelling (reception-gift) of the Holy Spirit.[48] However, he concludes more than is evident from Matt 3:11. Such conclusions are rightly criticized by P/C scholars, including Menzies who writes, 'It is often assumed that since the Holy Spirit inspired each of the various New Testament authors, they must all speak with one voice. That is to say, each biblical author must share the same theological perspective.'[49] Blomberg's use of Paul (1 Cor 12:13) to link BHS with conversion is beyond the immediate context of Matthew. To avoid BHS as a post-conversion blessing, Blomberg observes, 'But Luke, in agreement with the rest of the New Testament witness…makes it clear that every Christian is "baptized" in the Spirit from conversion on (Luke 3:16; Acts 1:5; 11:16; cf. esp. 1 Cor 12:13).'[50] This, however, is another instance where Blomberg interprets Luke by means of Paul. On the other hand, Menzies considers Luke to reconcile pneumatologically with Paul even though each has differing pneumatological perspectives.[51] This is not to exonerate Menzies' criticism, but rather to highlight a recurring American Baptist interpretive supposition.

---

subsequent post-conversion blessing for the NT Christian. See Blomberg, *Jesus and the Gospels,* 169. Blomberg refers to Menzies in Blomberg, *Jesus and the Gospels,* 169. See also Robert P. Menzies, *Empowered for Witness: The Spirit in Luke-Acts* (Sheffield: Sheffield Academic Press, 1994.

[45] Craig L. Blomberg, *From Pentecost to Patmos: An Introduction to Acts through Revelation* (Nashville: B & H Publishing Group. 2006), 27.

[46] Blomberg cites Max Turner to support his position contra Menzies. See Blomberg, *Jesus and the Gospels,* 169. See also Max Turner, *Power from on High: The Spirit in Israel's Restoration and Witness in Luke-Acts* ([original work published 1996] Sheffield: Sheffield Academic Press, 2000), 165-168 (168 n. 92).

[47] Blomberg, *Matthew,* 79-80. See also, SBC scholar James M. Hamilton, Jr., *God's Indwelling Presence: The Holy Spirit in the Old and New Testaments* (Nashville: B & H Academic, 2006), 95.

[48] Blomberg, *Matthew,* 79.

[49] Menzies refers to those holding an evangelical or conservative view of Scripture, namely the inspiration of Scripture. Menzies, *Empowered for Witness,* 240.

[50] Blomberg, *Jesus and the Gospels,* 169.

[51] Menzies, *Empowered for Witness,* 140.

2.1.1.2 Exegetical Challenges

2.1.1.2.1 εἰς μετάνοιαν, 'for repentance'

The anomalous Matthean addition of εἰς μετάνοιαν ('for repentance,' Matt 3:11) to the logion of JTB requires American Baptists to consider the relation of repentance to water baptism, and how it informs BHS conception. American Baptists agree that JTB is comparing his (water) rite with the rite of the Coming One. This comparison is the central interpretive issue for εἰς μετάνοιαν. While εἰς μετάνοιαν ('for repentance') indicates the relation between water baptism and repentance, βάπτισμα μετανοίας ('repentance-baptism,' Mark 1:4; Luke 3:3) is less definitive and only distinguishes JTB's water rite from other baptisms (Acts 13:24; 19:4).[52] American Baptists agree that JTB's water rite symbolizes the Coming One's spiritual rite[53] and that Christian water baptism is not the conveyance for BHS.[54] This interpretation is based in part on this Matthean anomaly. Among American Baptists, εἰς μετάνοιαν presents four interpretive options discussed briefly below.

1) The preposition εἰς is a reference to causative agency and εἰς μετάνοιαν is translated, 'in order that you may repent.'[55] This use of εἰς

---

[52] Broadus, *Commentary on the Gospel of Matthew*, 49.

[53] Moody identifies four views regarding the relationship between water baptism and Spirit baptism: (1) The first view is that of American dispensationalism which relegates to water baptism the role of 'ritual' and assigns to Spirit baptism the place of 'real' baptism. (2) Radical criticism reverses the previous order, claiming that the primitive church practiced only Spirit baptism and that water baptism entered when the spiritual fervor faded. (3) Some sacramental views regard the Spirit as being imparted by water baptism. (4) According to Moody, water baptism symbolizes Spirit baptism 'which is the spiritual substance that is normally expected with the symbol.' In his view, the ordering of the substance and symbol represented in the book of Acts cannot be pressed, but the controlling principle is repentance, apart from which there is no reception of the Spirit. See Dale Moody, *The Spirit of the Living God: What the Bible Says About the Spirit* ([original work published 1968] Nashville: Broadman Press, 1976), 64-65.

[54] Dunn's *Baptism in the Holy Spirit* has been cited thus far to link BHS with conversion (Carson). American Baptists doing so must reckon with Dunn's 'conversion-initiation' thesis. By the term 'conversion' Dunn is referring to 'that inner transformation' (corresponding to 'soul competency') which is distinct from ritual acts of 'initiation.' The idea that one is converted but not 'Christian' without the initiatory water rite, as Dunn claims, is foreign to American Baptist theology. Additionally, Dunn makes BHS integral to the event (process) of becoming a Christian. BHS coincides with the reception of the Spirit which he terms 'the decisive and climatic experience' in conversion-initiation. Dunn agrees with the P/C adherent's experiential assessment of BHS, but challenges separating BHS from conversion-initiation. Therefore, while Dunn supports American Baptists who associate BHS with conversion, there are points of discontinuity with his thesis. See Dunn, *Baptism in the Holy Spirit*, 4-7.

[55] Broadus, *Commentary on the Gospel of Matthew*, 49.

makes JTB's water rite the effective means which produces repentance in the candidate (sacerdotal).[56]

The 'causal agency' option is rejected on the basis of its unusual and difficult use in this context. This is demonstrated contextually since JTB's water rite presupposes repentance followed by evidence (Matt 3:2, 6, 8).[57] The water rite functioning as the agent of repentance is at odds with other NT texts (Acts 3:19: Rom 3:23-24; Eph 2:8-9).[58] Lastly, according to Josephus, JTB taught his disciples that baptism did not offer pardon for sins, but functioned to consecrate the body of a thoroughly cleansed soul.[59]

   2) The preposition εἰς is used in the causal sense. This use of εἰς is differentiated from the above interpretation by making repentance the cause ('because of') which occasions the water rite. A parallel text is Matt 12:41 where the preaching of Jonah occasioned ('because of') the repentance of the Ninevites.[60]

The causal sense of εἰς appears to fit the contextual fact that JTB required repentance of candidates presenting themselves for his water rite (Matt 3:7-9).[61] American Baptist grammarians Dana and Mantey endorsed the causal use of εἰς.[62] Those who criticize the causal εἰς interpretation believe Dana and Mantey based their conclusions on theological rather than linguistic grounds.[63]

---

[56] Turner, *Matthew*, 115.

[57] Broadus, *Commentary on the Gospel of Matthew*, 49.

[58] Turner, *Matthew*, 115.

[59] Josephus, 'The Antiquities of the Jews' (18.5.2), in William Whiston, Trans., *The Works of Josephus* (Peabody: Hendrickson Publishers, 1987), 484.

[60] Broadus, *Commentary on the Gospel of Matthew*, 49.

[61] Turner, *Matthew*, 115.

[62] H. E. Dana and Julius R. Mantey, *A Manual Grammar of the Greek New Testament* ([original work published 1927] New York: The Macmillan Company, 1957), 104. Mantey included Acts 2:38 with Matt 3:11 as occasions for the causal use of εἰς. See Julius R. Mantey, 'The Causal Use of *Eis* in the New Testament,' in *JBL 70* (1952), 45-58 and 'On Causal *Eis* Again,' in *JBL 70* (1952), 309-11. See also, Robertson, *A Grammar of New Testament Greek*, 389, 592 and *Word Pictures in the New Testament, Vol. 3*, 35.

[63] Turner believes that the arguments for causal εἰς are unpersuasive. Turner, *Matthew*, 115. Wallace believes Mantey insisted on a causal εἰς in Acts 2:38 to avoid violating salvation by grace. See Daniel B. Wallace, *Greek Grammar Beyond the Basics: An Exegetical Syntax of the New Testament* (Grand Rapids: Zondervan, 1996), 369-71. See also, Ralph Marcus, 'On Causal *Eis*,' in *JBL 70* (1952), 129-30 and 'The Elusive *Eis*,' in *JBL 71* (1953), 44 and Nigel James Hope Moulton and Nigel Turner, *A Grammar of New Testament Greek: Syntax, Vol. 3* (Edinburgh: T & T Clark, 1963), 266-67. For additional support of a causal εἰς in Matt 3:11, see Walter Bauer, William F. Arndt, F. Wilbur Gingrich, and Frederick W. Danker, *A Greek-English Lexicon of the New*

3) The preposition εἰς is understood in the telic (purpose) sense, 'in order to repent,'[64] 'for repentance,' or 'with a view to continued repentance.'[65] In this sense, εἰς plus the accusative frequently suggests purpose, 'I baptize in order that you will repent.'[66] This differs from option 1 in that it speaks of the intent associated with the rite's performance and not the ability of the rite in and of itself to produce repentance.

The context of Matt 3:7-8 calls attention to the dubious nature of the changed hearts by the Pharisees and Sadducees professing repentance and presenting themselves as candidates for JTB's water rite. According to the telic sense, the water rite is intended to reveal genuine repentance, though not having efficacious (causal) agency.[67] Broadus favors this view, though Carson considers the telic sense unlikely due to prior necessity (or simultaneity) of confession (Matt 3:6).[68]

4) The preposition εἰς is rendered 'in reference to,' 'as a token of,' or 'in connection with.'

More precisely, this rendering of εἰς μετάνοιαν distinguishes JTB's water rite from other religion's ritual washings which do not symbolize turning away from sin.[69] Blomberg and Harris favor this interpretation.[70]

While American Baptists embrace a variety of opinions for interpreting εἰς μετάνοιαν, they are unified concerning the non-efficacious nature of JTB's water rite. SBC scholar David S. Dockery additionally credits the Qumran community for influencing the nature and purpose of JTB's water rite,[71] though not

---

Testament and Other Early Christian Literature ([original work published 1957] Chicago: The University of Chicago Press, 1979), 230.

[64] Broadus, *Commentary on the Gospel of Matthew*, 49.

[65] Carson, *Matthew*, 104.

[66] Ibid.

[67] Broadus, *Commentary on the Gospel of Matthew*, 50.

[68] Ibid. Carson, *Matthew*, 104.

[69] Turner, *Matthew*, 115.

[70] Blomberg, *Matthew*, 80. Harris, 'Appendix,' 1208.

[71] David S. Dockery, 'Baptism,' in Joel B. Green and Scot McKnight, eds., *Dictionary of Jesus and the Gospels* (Downers Grove: InterVarsity Press, 1992), 55-58. Dockery cites Badia with reference to passages in the Qumran *Manual of Disciple* (1 QS 3:4-9; 4:18-22; 6:14-23) which contain similarities between the community's ritual washings and the water rite of JTB. The ritual washings were performed in the context of repentance and were preparatory to entrance in the future eschatological community. See Leonard F. Badia, *The Qumran Baptism and John the Baptist's Baptism* (Lanham: University Press of America, 1980), 49-51.

considering JTB a 'full-fledged' member of the community. On his view, the Essenic ritual baths, lustrations, and eschatological orientation as 'preparers of the way' (Isa 40:3) integrate with JTB's message (e.g. repentance, eschatological expectation, and preparation, Matt 3:2; Mark 1:4, 7-8; John 1:23).[72] It is possible to conclude from this that JTB's water rite and emphasis on repentance coincide with the Qumran community's belief that effective washings needed to be attended by genuine repentance (Matt 3:7-9). Beyond this similarity, Dockery points to the contrasting nature of JTB's unprecedented one-time initiation rite to the Qumran's self-administered daily (frequent) ritual lustrations.[73] He warns that although early Christian baptism was an initiatory rite into the church and emphasized moral purity and cleansing (Acts 2:38), one is mistaken to conclude that JTB's water rite is entirely analogous.[74] Rather, JTB's perspective on repentance centered on OT expectations of righteousness within the conceptual framework of a water rite analogous to the Qumran rite which functioned as both the means of cleansing and the sign of repentance.[75]

Dockery leaves open the question of the degree to which JTB's water rite is analogous with the lustrations of the Qumran community. American Baptists have typically held that JTB considered his water rite to be preparatory for repentance and symbolic of the real (spiritual) baptism of the Coming One.[76] SBC scholar Hobbs distinguishes βαπτισμός ('ceremonial lustration') from the βάπτισμα ('immersion, baptism')[77] performed by JTB (Mark 1:4; Luke 3:3). On his view, βάπτισμα ('immersion, baptism') does not connote the act, but the meaning of the act (e.g. 1 Pet 3:21). Hobbs concludes that the baptism performed by JTB 'was not a rite of ceremonial cleansing' (Qumran), but a symbol of the subject's

---

[72] Dockery, 'Baptism,' 57. SBC scholar Andreas Köstenberger believes JTB's water rite and Jewish proselyte baptism both harken back to Jewish ritual cleansing and bathing practices. See Andreas J. Köstenberger, 'Baptism in the Gospels,' in Thomas R. Schreiner and Shawn D. Wright, eds., *Believer's Baptism: Sign of the New Covenant in Christ* (Nashville: B & H Academic, 2006), 11-34. Dockery, however, argues that the Qumran community operated outside the Temple cult and that its only available rituals were the baths and lustrations described in the OT.

[73] Dockery, 'Baptism,' 57. This contrast is the basis for SBC scholar Stagg concluding that the daily and seemingly self-immersions of the Qumran community are note related to JTB's water rite. Stagg considers JTB's water rite an innovation or adaptation of Jewish proselyte baptism. See Frank Stagg, *Matthew*, in Clifton J. Allen, ed., *The Broadman Bible Commentary: General Articles, Matthew-Mark* (Nashville: Broadman Press, 1969), 92.

[74] Dockery, 'Baptism,' 57.

[75] Ibid.

[76] Broadus, *Commentary on the Gospel of Matthew*, 51; Carson, *Matthew*, 104-105; Turner, *Matthew*, 114; Blomberg, *Matthew*, 79.

[77] See Mark 7:4 and Heb 9:10. G. Abbott-Smith, *A Manual Greek Lexicon of the New Testament* ([original work published 1921] Edinburgh: T & T Clark, 1964), 75.

repentance demonstrated by confession of sins and a willingness to become part of the kingdom at hand.[78]

2.1.1.2.2   καὶ πυρί, 'and fire'

American Baptists differentiate themselves in part from post-conversion experience BHS models by the way they interpret the Matthean (3:11) and Lukan (3:16) καὶ πυρί ('and fire') additions to JTB's logion. This section will list and briefly treat five καὶ πυρί interpretations investigated by American Baptist exegetes.

1) The phrase καὶ πυρί ('and fire') is a reference to the Spirit's purifying work whereby an individual's faults are consumed.[79]

Gromacki characterizes this view as a separate 'baptism in fire' resulting in a post-conversion purifying experience.[80] This post-conversion experience is responsible for removing the desire to sin. According to the view, infused fire produces a wide range of spiritual experience (e.g. cleansing, freedom, filling, and revival). Gromacki rejects this view due to the lack of biblical precedent for such a mandated life experience.[81]

2) The phrase ἐν πνεύματι ἁγίῳ καὶ πυρί ('in-with-by the Holy Spirit and fire') is grammatically similar to the John 3:5 phrase γεννηθῇ ἐξ ὕδατος καὶ πνεύματος ('born of water and Spirit').[82]

Carson favors interpreting ἐν πνεύματι ἁγίῳ καὶ πυρί as a single Spirit-fire baptism which is entirely purifying. He defends his position on two grounds. The first is the need to avoid two baptisms, one for the repentant and another for the unrepentant. The second is to interpret ἐν ('in-with-by') as a preposition governing 'Holy Spirit' and 'fire' (i.e. hendiadys construction).[83] Gromacki,

---

[78] Herschel H. Hobbs, *An Exposition of the Four Gospels: The Gospel of Matthew and the Gospel of Mark, Vol. 1* (Grand Rapids: Baker Books, 1996), 32-42.

[79] Broadus, *Commentary on the Gospel of Matthew,* 51; Robert Gromacki, *The Holy Spirit* (Nashville: Word Publishing, 1999), 109.

[80] Gromacki, *The Holy Spirit,* 109.

[81] Ibid., 110.

[82] Broadus, *Commentary on the Gospel of Matthew,* 51.

[83] Carson, *Matthew,* 105. Idiomatically, the expression is ἐν διὰ δοῦσίν, 'one by means of two,' or hendiadys. See George Benedict Winer, *A Grammar of the Idiom of the New Testament: Prepared as a Solid Basis for the Interpretation of the New Testament* (Andover: Warren F. Draper, 1874), 630.

however, rejects equating 'fire' with purification due to JTB exclusively using 'fire' as a reference to eternal punishment.[84] He points out that Jesus' BHS reference (Acts 1:5) does not contain καὶ πυρί because he is informing the apostles of the Holy Spirit's coming.[85]

3) The phrase ἐν πνεύματι ἁγίῳ καὶ πυρί ('in-with-by the Holy Spirit and fire') refers to a single baptism consisting of two aspects ('Spirit-and-fire') with two possible effects on the recipient.[86]

Blomberg and Turner identify ἐν πνεύματι ἁγίῳ καὶ πυρί as a hendiadys construction, but without a unified purifying function (Carson). Instead, the phrase refers to a single baptism which has either cleansing or destructive effect.[87] The perceived strength of this and the previous view is that each takes into account ὑμᾶς ('you all') to represent the Jews collectively as subjects of the one baptism. Broadus (as Gromacki above) points to the use of καὶ πυρί in Matt 3:11 and Luke 3:16 where the expression has the same 'destructive' meaning as the other contextual references to 'fire' (Matt 3:10, 12; Luke 3:9, 17).[88] Hobbs locates three references to judgment 'fire' in the context, one implied (Matt 3:7) and two expressed (Matt 3:10, 12).[89] He considers the semantic range of רוּחַ and πνεῦμα ('wind, breath, spirit') as it relates to understanding the appearances of 'wind-spirit' and 'fire' in the context (Matt 3:10, 12). On his view, 'wind-spirit' and 'fire' constitute two basic elements of power and the end to which these elements serve depends on how one relates to them (e.g. re-creation, life, power, understanding of God's truth, or destruction). The appearance of רוּחַ ('wind, breath, spirit') in association with the original creation event (Gen 1:2) demonstrates the spiritual re-creation event occasioned by πνεῦμα. For Hobbs, BHS is virtually synonymous with conversion.[90]

---

[84] Gromacki, *The Holy Spirit,* 53.

[85] Ibid., 110.

[86] Habets, *The Anointed Son,* 131; Dunn, *Baptism in the Holy Spirit,* 13 and *Jesus and the Spirit,* 8-22; Turner, *Matthew,* 115; Blomberg, *Matthew,* 80.

[87] Blomberg, *Matthew,* 80 n. 68. According to Blomberg, 'the Greek employs one preposition to govern two nouns functioning as a compound object –*with the Holy Spirit and fire* – most naturally suggesting one baptism with two aspects to it.' See also, Thomas R. Schreiner, *New Testament Theology: Magnifying God in Christ* (Grand Rapids: Baker Academic, 2008), 439.

[88] Broadus, *Commentary on the Gospel of Matthew,* 51.

[89] Hobbs, *An Exposition of the Four Gospels: The Gospel of Matthew and the Gospel of Mark, Vol. 1,* 37.

[90] Ibid., 38.

4) The καὶ πυρί expression refers to the 'fire-like tongues' occurring on the Day of Pentecost (Acts 2:3).[91]

Gromacki denies associating the 'divided tongues' phenomenon occurring on the Day of Pentecost with καὶ πυρί (Matt 3:11; Luke 3:16) as a reference to actual fire-baptism.[92] He argues that the 'divided tongues' were analogous to fire (Acts 2:3) and not the actual fire indicated by καὶ πυρί. In addition, Jesus predicted BHS with no reference to fire-baptism (Acts 1:5).[93] Broadus believes that BHS and the 'flaming tongues' phenomenon coincide with the phenomena on the Day of Pentecost and symbolized the power to speak in other tongues. However, he rejects this interpretation as JTB's applied meaning due to the absence of καὶ πυρί in Acts 1:5 and Acts 11:16.[94]

5) The phrase ἐν πνεύματι ἁγίῳ καὶ πυρί ('in-with-by the Holy Spirit and fire') refers to two separate baptisms, the former ('Spirit') indicating salvation and the latter ('fire) indicating judgment.[95]

Stagg supports this view, applying the preposition ἐν ('in-with-by') to both nouns to render ἐν πνεύματι ἁγίῳ καὶ πυρί 'with Holy Spirit and with fire.'[96] He associates Jesus' 'gift of the Spirit' (BHS) with the universal reception of new life and not the limited application of 'second blessing' experience for some Christians. Stagg considers all Christians to be charismatic in the sense that each has received the baptism ('filling') of the Spirit. In so doing, he equates BHS ('gift of the Spirit') with personal conversion experience (Hobbs). Conversely, καὶ πυρί ('baptism with fire') is a necessary judgment that serves as a concomitant to salvation and is demonstrated contextually by the 'axe' and 'winnowing shovel' metaphors (Matt 3:10, 12).[97]

A definitive American Baptist interpretation of ἐν πνεύματι ἁγίῳ καὶ πυρί ('in-with-by the Holy Spirit and fire') does not emerge from the preceding survey. What does emerge is unanimity among the exegetes on the association of BHS with personal conversion experience.

---

[91] Broadus, *Commentary on the Gospel of Matthew*, 51.

[92] Gromacki, *The Holy Spirit*, 110.

[93] Ibid.

[94] Broadus, *Commentary on the Gospel of Matthew*, 51-52.

[95] Turner, *Matthew*, 115.

[96] Stagg, *Matthew*, 93.

[97] Ibid., 93.

2.1.2   Mark 1:8

This section considers American Baptist interaction with the unique presentation of the JTB tradition in the Markan prologue. The aim is to determine how the prologue's composition relates to BHS from an American Baptist point of view. Stein identifies the heavy concentration of 'christological materials' (1:1, 2-3, 7-8, 9-11, and 12-13), noting also that elements of the JTB tradition recorded by the other Synoptists (Matt 3:7-12; Luke 3:7-9, 15-18) are not recorded by Mark.[98] He notes the unique structure of Mark's prologue in that it (contra Matthew and Luke) functions to reveal that 'the good news of God' (1:14) is the 'good news about Jesus Christ, the Son of God' (Mark 1:1).[99] Garland focuses the investigation on Mark 1:1-8 as a pericope within the Markan prologue containing three interdependent parts (i.e. an introduction, 1:1; prophecy, 1:2-3; JTB tradition material, 1:4-8).[100] This narrative flow (editorial structuring) requires addressing the issues, though tangential to BHS (1:8), which frame the JTB tradition material (and BHS in particular) according to its perceived authorial intent.

In keeping with the above focus, Stein addresses the 1:1 introduction, noting that the appositional relation of υἱοῦ θεοῦ ('Son of God') and Ἰησοῦ Χριστοῦ ('Jesus Christ') with τοῦ εὐαγγελίον ('the gospel') is in the form of an objective genitive, 'the gospel about Jesus Christ the Son of God.'[101] The function of 1:1 within the 1:1-8 pericope is to introduce 1:2-8. Accordingly, the term Ἀρχὴ ('beginning,' 1:1) and the prophecy (1:2-3) directly relate to the JTB tradition (1:4-8) and not the remainder of the Gospel (1:4-16:8).[102] For Stein, Mark intends to place JTB at the forefront of 'gospel' origins.[103]

---

[98] Robert H. Stein, *Mark,* in Robert W. Yarbrough and Robert H. Stein, eds., *BECNT* (Grand Rapids: Baker Academic, 2008), 38.

[99] Ibid., 41.

[100] David E. Garland, *Mark,* in Terry Muck, ed., *The NIV Application Commentary* (Grand Rapids: Zondervan Publishing House, 1996), 42. According to Stein, Mark 1:1-8 stresses not only what Mark's Gospel is 'about,' but also that τοῦ εὐαγγελίον ('the gospel') is 'the fulfillment of the divine plan recorded in Scripture.' See Stein. *Mark,* 41.

[101] Stein does not comment on the disputed nature of υἱοῦ θεοῦ or its variant υἱοῦ τοῦ θεοῦ. Stein. *Mark,* 41.

[102] Stein. *Mark,* 41.

[103] Mark is not alone among the evangelists in describing 'gospel' origins in terms of the advent of JTB (see John 1:6ff.). Immediately after his prologue, Luke records the foretelling of JTB's birth (Luke 1:5ff.) and elsewhere indicates that the gospel message of the early church begins with JTB (Acts 1:22; 10:36-37; 13:24). Most likely, this view was shared by Jesus as well (Matt 11:11-15; Luke 7:24-35; 16:16). Stein, *Mark,* 42.

Next, Stein addresses the prophecy contained in 1:2-3. He detects the christological emphasis in the pericope which is enhanced when the prophecy is linked to the introduction (1:1) *rather than* the JTB tradition (1:4-8).[104] He justifies the 1:1 and 1:2-3 connection by citing Mark's repeated use of καθώς ('as') to support what has preceded (Mark 4:33; 11:6; 14:16; 15:8; 16:7; see also 9:13 and 14:21 where it introduces 'it is written').[105] He further considers the 'you' (σου) in 'your face' (1:2) to identify 'Jesus Christ, the Son of God' (1:1).[106] This leads Stein to understand 1:1 not as a title for the Gospel,[107] but as the means for introducing the key figure in the 1:2-3 OT quotations: Jesus, and not JTB.[108] Stein demonstrates this by the following points:

1) The 1:2-3 prophecy is a uniquely redacted conflation[109] of OT texts (Exod 23:20; Mal 3:1; and Isa 40:3) which have enduring value.[110]

2) The editorial work of Mark associating Isa 40:3 with the pairing of texts (Exod 23:30 and Mal 3:1) previously appearing in the pre-Markan JTB Q source (Matt 11:7-19/Luke 7:24-35; Luke 1:17) demonstrates that the

---

[104] Ibid. See also Robert A. Guelich, 'The Beginning of the Gospel,' in *Biblical Research* (1982), 6 and Marcus, *The Way of the Lord,* 17-18.

[105] Stein, *Mark,* 42.

[106] Ibid.

[107] France, *The Gospel of Mark,* 50-51. France considers the contents of 1:1 to point 'far beyond the first part of Chapter 1.' Hobbs believes the absence of the definite article with Ἀρχὴ ('beginning') in 1:1 supports the view that 'this is the beginning not of Mark's Gospel but of the facts of the gospel.' See also, Hobbs, *An Exposition of the Four Gospels: The Gospel of Matthew and the Gospel of Mark, Vol. 1,* 15.

[108] Stein, *Mark,* 42. See also, M. A. Tolbert, *Sowing the Gospel: Mark's World in Literary-Historical Perspective* (Philadelphia: Fortress Press, 1989), 239-48. France considers the function of 1:2-3 to indicate the significance of JTB whose story immediately follows in 1:4-8. See France, *The Gospel of Mark,* 50, 61. Marcus, however, notes that after 1:10 Mark refers to JTB only briefly (1:14; 9:13 and 11:30) with the exception of 6:14-29. For Marcus, this demonstrates Markan emphasis on Jesus in the prologue rather than JTB. See Joel Marcus, *The Anchor Bible: Mark 1-8* (New York: Doubleday, 2000), 137.

[109] Garland refers to Mark who follows postbiblical Judaism by blending originally unrelated texts. In this case, Mark follows the Jewish practice of identifying only the most important source, Isaiah. See Garland, *Mark,* 43. Marcus concurs, noting that Qumran exegesis is characterized by the juxtaposition of Scriptures. In addition, the rabbinic literature features the conflation of Exod 23:20 and Mal 3:1 (*Exod Rab* 32:9 and *Deut Rab* 11:9). There is a discernible pattern of Mark fusing Scripture in 1:11 (Isa 42:1/Ps 2:7); 11:17 (Isa 56:7/Jer 7:11); 13:24-26 (Isa 13:10/34:4/Joel 2:10/Ezek 32:7-8); and 14:62 (Dan 7:13/Ps 110:1). See Marcus, *The Way of the Lord,* 12-17.

[110] Stein, *Mark,* 42. According to Stein, Mark elsewhere cites various traditions (7:6; 9:12-13; 10:4-5; 11:17; 14:21, 27). The verb γέγραπται ('it is written') in 1:2 is a Greek intensive perfect indicating the durative value of the combined prophetic messages. See also Garland, *Mark,* 43.

mission of Jesus is a component part of the fulfillment of the divine plan for history.[111]

Specifically, Exod 23:20 uses 'your face' as a reference to the people of Israel, but Mark uses the expression as a reference to Jesus. Also, 'the way before me' appearing in Mal 3:1 (MT) is a reference to God, but Mark writes 'your way' as a reference to the ministry of Jesus.[112] Interpreting the prophecy by the introduction shifts the emphasis of 'my messenger' (1:2) from JTB to 'Jesus Christ, the Son of God' (1:1).[113] Mark's altering of Isa 40:3 (i.e. from 'highway for our God,' MT; 'the paths of our God,' LXX to 'his paths,' 1:3) is a reference to Jesus.[114]

Stein addresses the JTB tradition (1:4-8) as the final textual focus of the 1:1-8 pericope. He interprets the significance of 1:4-8 according to Mark's intention to focus his readers away from JTB's importance in first-century Judaism to his prophetic disclosure of Jesus, the central figure of the Gospel.[115] Stein demonstrates this authorial intention with the following points.

1) In OT prophet-like fashion (1:2-3), JTB initiates the Gospel by announcing the Coming One's arrival as a Scripture-fulfilling event (1:7).[116]

---

[111] Stein, *Mark,* 42-43. See also Robert Horton Gundry, *The Use of the Old Testament in St. Matthew's Gospel with Special Reference to the Messianic Hope* (Boston: E. J. Brill, 1967), 125. 'Q,' stands for the *Quelle* (source) Jesus sayings not found in Mark, but which are common to Matthew and Luke (though independently drawn). Kilian McDonnell and George T. Montague, *Christian Initiation and Baptism in the Holy Spirit: Evidence from the First Eight Centuries* ([original work published 1991] Collegeville: Liturgical Press, 1994), 4 n. 3.

[112] Stein, *Mark,* 43. The LXX reads, 'the way before my face.' The origin of Mark's quotation of Mal 3:1, also appearing in Matt 11:10; Luke 7:27; and Luke 1:17, is uncertain as it does not agree with either the MT of LXX readings. See also, Garland, *The Gospel of Mark,* 44-45.

[113] Stein, *Mark,* 43.

[114] The alteration of the reading is attributed to the pre-Markan tradition or to Mark himself. Stein, *Mark,* 43.

[115] Stein, *Mark,* 44.

[116] Ibid.

2) Mark understands the participles 'baptizing' and 'preaching' (1:4)[117] as references to the unique purpose of JTB's water rite.[118]

3) The phrase ἐν τῇ ἐρήμῳ ('in the wilderness,' 1:4) is not qualified by geographical location and follows the Isa 40:3 prophecy (1:3).[119]

This Markan adaptation of the tradition instructs his readers to associate the wilderness (1:4) with the Isa 40:3 prophecy (1:3) rather than the location of JTB.[120] JTB's association with 'the wilderness' is not due to its 'eschatological role for the prophets,'[121] nor is it to express an eschatological connection with Exodus typology[122] ('second exodus'),[123] or to identify 'the place where God

---

[117] In dispute is whether or not the substantival participle [ὁ] βαπτίζων ('the one who baptizes, the baptizer') functions as a title and is the original reading. Aware that Mark elsewhere uses the participle in this manner (6:14, 24-25; 8:28) and that some prominent MSS have the article before the participle (ℵ and B), Stein finds it highly unlikely that a scribe would omit the article and more likely that it would be added. He also considers the presence of καὶ ('and') to indicate that the participles 'baptizing' and 'preaching' are parallel and function as a periphrasis with the verb ἐγένετο (other examples of periphrastic construction are 1:6; 2:6; 5:5; 9:7; and 14:54). See Stein, *Mark,* 52. The *Holy Bible, English Standard Version* (Wheaton: Crossway, 2001) follows this reading as does The *Holy Bible: New International Version* (Grand Rapids: Zondervan, 1984). France, however, views ὁ βαπτίζων as the more natural reading. He reasons that that appearance of Ἰωάννης ὁ βαπτιστὴς elsewhere (Matt 3:1; 11:11-12; 14:2, 8; 16:14; 17:13; Mark 6:25; 8:28; Luke 7:20, 33; 9:19) indicates the likelihood that scribes would include the definite article rather than try to construe βαπτίζων and κηρύσσων as parallel participles. See France, *The Gospel of Mark,* 64-65. See also Garland, *Mark,* 45 and Turlington, *Mark,* 266. If Stein is correct, and Mark's emphasis is on Jesus in the pericope, the brevity of the JTB tradition material coupled with the redactional alterations of the OT texts are consistent with Mark's departure from the other gospel accounts which mention the arrival of JTB by title, Ἰωάννης ὁ βαπτιστὴς.

[118] According to Stein, the source of JTB's water rite was not the ceremonial lustrations of Judaism, the mystery religions, Jewish proselyte baptism, or the baptisms performed within the Qumran community. The water rite of JTB was unique, not as an initiatory rite, or in its form, or administration by someone else (1:5), or by its resultant forgiveness when accompanied by repentance. The uniqueness of JTB's water rite was in its purpose. See Stein, *Mark,* 44-45.

[119] Matthew and Luke each have Isa 40:3 appearing after the introduction of JTB (Matt 3:1-3 and Luke 3:2-6). Matthew identifies ἐν τῇ ἐρήμῳ as 'Judea' (Matt 3:1). Luke places JTB in the 'region around the Jordan' (Luke 3:3).

[120] Stein, *Mark,* 45.

[121] Robert A. Guelich, *Mark 1-8:26,* in Bruce M. Metzger, ed., *Word Biblical Commentary* (Dallas: Word, 1989), 18.

[122] Ulrich Mauser, *Christ in the Wilderness: The Wilderness Theme in the Second Gospel and Its Basis in the Biblical Tradition* (London: SCM Press, 1963), 46-52.

[123] Garland, *Mark,* 43. Schreiner details a number of indications in the Synoptics affirming that the new exodus has been fulfilled in Jesus' ministry. Schreiner, *New Testament Theology,* 26. See also, Rkki E. Watts, *Isaiah's New Exodus in Mark* ([original work published 1997] Grand Rapids: Baker Academic, 2000).

would once again act to deliver his people,'[124] or to recall OT themes of hope and new beginnings,[125] but as a means of identifying JTB with the Isa 40:3 prophecy.[126]

4) The βάπτισμα μετανοίας ('repentance-baptism') preaching of JTB (1:4; Luke 3:3) is christological in nature and provides eschatological impetus (i.e. the coming 'Stronger One') for repentance (1:7-8).[127]

5) Mark reports the enormous impact of JTB on the people of Israel (1:5) to contrast his relative greatness with the coming 'Stronger One' (1:7).[128] The description of JTB is symbolic (1:6) and, according to Stein, part of the pre-Markan tradition (Matt 11:8/Luke 7:25) which Mark adapts[129] to identify JTB with Elijah (see 9:11-13).[130]

6) Further evidence of the christological focus of the 1:1-8 pericope is Mark's limited references to JTB speaking (1:7-8; 6:13), recording only the portion of JTB's message directly pertaining to Jesus.[131]

---

[124] James R. Edwards, *The Gospel According to Mark,* in D. A. Carson, ed., *The Pillar New Testament Commentary* (Grand Rapids: William B. Eerdmans Publishing, 2002), 29.

[125] France, *The Gospel of Mark,* 57.

[126] Stein, *Mark,* 45. Stein follows Marxsen in this conclusion. See Willi Marxsen, *Mark the Evangelist: Studies on the Redaction History of the Gospel* (New York: Abington Press, 1969), 37.

[127] Stein follows Donahue and Harrington and understands this construction as a genitive of description, not as an objective genitive ('a baptism for repentance'), or genitive of source ('a baptism arising out of repentance'). See John R. Donahue and Daniel J. Harrington, *The Gospel According to Mark,* in Daniel J. Harrington, ed., *Sacra Pagina* (Collegeville: The Liturgical Press, 2002), 62; Stein, *Mark,* 45.

[128] Turlington, *Mark,* 268.

[129] According to Garland, 'the original auditors of Mark's Gospel were schooled to recognize symbolism.' Mark's readers may have been aware of the future return of Elijah as prophesied by Malachi (4:5). This is evident from Elijah's mention in Luke 1:17 and John 1:21, 25. Garland believes the large crowds drawn to JTB were convinced that he was Elijah 'reappearing for his second career, to prepare for the imminent coming of God.' See Garland, *Mark,* 48. See also Hobbs, *An Exposition of the Four Gospels: The Gospel of Matthew and the Gospel of Mark, Vol. 1,* 18.

[130] Stein, *Mark,* 49. Stein believes that Mark records JTB's eating habits to highlight his ministry in 'the wilderness' where his preaching fulfilled Isa 40:3. Garland believes Mark's rationale for including the minor details of the prophet's dress and diet while excluding major elements of his background is due to his desire to inform his readers that JTB is 'not mainstream' and that he is an 'Elijah-like prophet.' See Garland, *Mark,* 48.

[131] Garland, *Mark,* 48. According to Stein, it is uncertain as to whether Mark knew of the larger corpus of JTB's ethical teachings found in Luke 3:7-9 and Matt 3:7-10. Se Stein, *Mark,* 49. See also Turlington, *Mark,* 268.

7) Mark uses the definite article to identify the coming 'Stronger One' (ὁ ἰσχυρότερός), not as a technical term for Messiah, but for the person identified in the 1:1-8 pericope.[132] The identity of 'the Stronger One' is 'Jesus Christ, the Son of God' (1:1), the Lord (1:2) before whom JTB was preparing the way (1:3).[133]

8) The coming 'Stronger One' will have divine authority[134] and a greater role in God's plan of redemption for the world (Mark 10:45; 14:22-24).[135]

This is confirmed by JTB's confessed unworthiness to stoop down and to untie the sandal thongs of the coming 'Stronger One' (1:7).[136] Mark grammatically establishes the superior baptism of the 'Stronger One' using the pronouns ἐγώ ('I') and αὐτὸς ('he') to emphasize the comparison of the two baptisms.[137]

9) Since JTB, Jesus (John 3:22; 4:1-2), and the early church practiced water baptism, Mark intended his readers to interpret JTB's two 'baptize' (1:8) references literally and in light of their Christian baptism.[138]

Based on the 1:1-8 pericope of the Markan prologue, Stein identifies BHS as a phenomenon linked to water baptism, performed in response to repentance and faith, which results in the renewal of the Holy Spirit.[139] His complete Markan BHS

---

[132] Stein, *Mark*, 49; Hobbs, *An Exposition of the Four Gospels: The Gospel of Matthew and the Gospel of Mark, Vol. 1,* 19.

[133] Stein, *Mark*, 49.

[134] Divine authority is manifested internally in Mark in terms of Jesus' exorcisms (3:22-27; 9:14-29), healings (6:53-56), and miracles (4:35-5:43; 6:45-52).

[135] Stein, *Mark*, 50.

[136] France, *The Gospel According to Mark*, 70-71.

[137] Stein, *Mark*, 50-51. Stein writes, 'I, John, do this [a baptism of repentance] for all my disciples; he, the Stronger One, will do that [a baptism of the Holy Spirit] for all [not some] of his disciples' (1 Cor 12:13). The reference to 1 Cor 12:13 suggests reliance upon Paul to interpret Mark.

[138] Stein, *Mark*, 50. Vines favors interpreting 'baptize' figuratively with reference to the BHS that Jesus would perform. See Jerry Vines, *Spirit Works: Charismatic Practices and the Bible* (Nashville: B & H Publishers, 1999), 76.

[139] Robert H. Stein, *Luke,* in David S. Dockery, ed., *The New American Commentary: An Exegetical and Theological Exposition of Holy Scripture, Vol. 24* (Nashville: Broadman Press, 1992), 135. Contra Stein, Gromacki insists that the phrase 'one baptism' (Eph 4:5) is a reference to BHS. He advocates understanding 'baptism' figuratively in the case of BHS due to the diversity of modes and methods surrounding water baptism and concludes that each of the six spiritualties mentioned in Eph 4:4-6 mark every believer. This, he reasons, must be true of baptism. In his view, the only baptism which uniformly applies to all believers is the unity of the Spirit occasioned by BHS. See Gromacki, *The Holy Spirit,* 172-73. Schreiner, contra Gromacki, believes Paul did associate the reception of the Spirit with baptism (1 Cor 12:13; Tit 3:5) and never entertained the notion of people being baptized without a prior reception of the Spirit. However, he regards water

apologetic incorporates the use of additional biblical sources to fully interpret the role of the 'Stronger One' (1:7). Stein concludes that the baptism Jesus performs[140] (BHS) will function to inaugurate a new age by dispensing the Spirit as the Guarantor of the kingdom of God (2 Cor 1:22; 5:5; Eph 1:14).[141] In his view, Mark identified JTB with the old age and covenant, but the coming 'Stronger One' (1:7) will bring the kingdom of God (1:14-15) and the gift of the Spirit (Luke 24:49; Acts 1:4-5, 8; 2:1-4; John 7:39; 14:16-17, 25-26; 16:13-14). For Mark's readers, the coming (gift) of the Spirit was 'the mark' of being a Christian (Acts 11:15-18; 15:7-11; 19:2; Gal 3:2-5). The gift of the Spirit, promised by the prophets (Isa 32:15; 44:3; Ezek 11:19; 36:26-27; 37:14; 39:29; Joel 2:28-32 [MT 3:1-2]; Acts 2:17-21) as the mark of the new age will be dispensed by the coming 'Stronger One' (1:7) to all his followers.[142]

The question of the Markan fulfillment of JTB's BHS prophecy remains. Stein offers two possible resolutions.[143] First, if BHS occurs after the events recorded by Mark in his Gospel, it is coincident with the coming of the Spirit at Pentecost (Acts 2:1-4).[144] Second, if BHS is contemporaneous with the earthly ministry of Jesus, it is fulfilled in his use of the Spirit, not in his gift of the Spirit (i.e. to heal the sick, teach with authority, and to cast out demons, Mark 3:22-30).[145] The latter option is argued by Gundry, who affirms that Jesus is the 'Spirit-user' and not the 'Spirit-giver.'[146] Gundry does not deny the references to Spirit-reception by the disciples (Luke 24:49; Acts 1:4-5; 11:16; Luke 11:13; Acts 2:1-4), but he does not find evidence in Mark to support this interpretation of BHS.[147]

---

baptism being in the forefront of Paul's mind in Eph 4:5 and points to the book of Acts where water baptism functioned as the initiatory rite of the church. See Schreiner, *New Testament Theology*, 727.

[140] Garrett interprets all six NT references to BHS, whether spoken by JTB (Mark 1:8; Matt 3:11; Luke 3:16; and John 1:33) or Jesus (Acts 1:5 and 11:16) as identifying Jesus as the baptizer and the Spirit as the means or instrument. See James Leo Garrett, Jr., *Systematic Theology: Biblical, Historical, and Evangelical, Vol. 2* (Grand Rapids: William B. Eerdmans Publishing, 1990), 153.

[141] Stein, *Mark*, 51.

[142] Stein, *Mark*, 51. See also Turlington, *Mark*, 268; James A. Brooks, *Mark*, in David S. Dockery, ed., *The New American Commentary: An Exegetical and Theological Exposition of Holy Scripture, Vol. 23* (Nashville: Broadman Press, 1991), 41.

[143] Stein, *Mark*, 51.

[144] Hobbs, *An Exposition of the Four Gospels: The Gospel of Matthew and the Gospel of Mark, Vol. 1*, 20; Turlington, *Mark*, 268; Brooks, *Mark*, 42.

[145] Garland, *Mark*, 49.

[146] Robert H. Gundry, *A Commentary on His Apology for the Cross* (Grand Rapids: William B. Eerdmans Publishing, 1993), 38-39.

[147] Ibid.

American Baptists typically identify the Markan occasion of BHS (1:8) with conversion. For Stein, associating repentance with water baptism (human side) and regeneration with the work of the Spirit (divine side) links BHS with conversion. Turlington views the arrival of the Spirit and the new covenant as simultaneously occurring eschatological events resulting in the spiritual transformation of the repentant encountering the power of God.[148] Hobbs contrasts the water rite of JTB (on his view the water rite is an outward symbol of inward change) and BHS, the inner cleansing and transformation performed by Jesus and effected by the Spirit on the human heart.[149] This is the language of conversion.

Though Stein carefully noted the editorial work in the Markan pericope (1:1-8), he did not comment on the absence of καὶ πυρί ('and fire') from the JTB tradition (1:4-8). Turlington understands the absence of καὶ πυρί ('and fire'), appearing in Matt 3:11-12 and Luke 3:16-17 in connection with judgment, in terms of Mark's emphasis on the victorious nature of divine deliverance, rather than the severity of divine judgment.[150]

2.2 John 1:33

This section breaks the canonical sequence so that Luke-Acts may be treated as a unit. Under consideration is the American Baptist BHS view of William E. Hull[151] who contextually frames the Johannine BHS logion of JTB within the 1:29-34 (1:33) pericope. Significant for Hull are the affirmations of Jesus[152] in

---

[148] Turlington, *Mark*, 269.

[149] Hobbs, *An Exposition of the Four Gospels: The Gospel of Matthew and the Gospel of Mark, Vol. 1,* 20. See also Charles R. Eerdman, *The Gospel of Mark* (Philadelphia: The Westminster Press, 1956), 27.

[150] Turlington, *Mark,* 269. See also Gundry, *A Commentary on His Apology for the Cross,* 39.

[151] SBC pastor for more than thirty years, Hull is research professor in residence at Samford University (Birmingham, AL) where he also served as provost and professor from 1987-96. He is the recipient of the Charles D. Johnson Outstanding Educator Award presented by the Association of Southern Baptist Colleges and Schools (ASBCS). Hull served previously as provost and professor at The Southern Baptist Theological Seminary (Louisville, KY) from 1954-75. Mercer University, 2012. 'William E. Hull,' n.p. Available from: http://www.mupress.org/contributorinfo.cfm?Contrib ID =641. [Accessed 20 April 2012].

[152] Blomberg, *Jesus and the Gospels,* 254. See also Herman Ridderbos, *The Gospel of John: A Theological Commentary* (Grand Rapids: William B. Eerdmans Publishing, 1997), 62.

this pericope which balance the personal denials[153] made by JTB in 1:9-28.[154] A third and climactic JTB confession (1:31-33) concerns the relation of Jesus to the Spirit.[155] It is this relation that informs his BHS view according to the following points:

1. JTB based his ministry on the Messiah's revelation to Israel by a combination of his water rite (1:31) together with the Spirit's dove-like descent and abiding presence (ἐπί, 'upon,' 1:33).[156]

2. The revelation of 'the Son [Chosen] of God'[157] specified messianic function, ὁ βαπτίζων ἐν πνεύματι ἁγίῳ ('the one who baptizes in-with-by the Holy Spirit,' 1:33-34).[158]

3. Hull considers this messianic baptizing function as a dispensing of the Holy Spirit and not in literal association with JTB's water rite.[159]

---

[153] Though there is noted overlapping of JTB treatments in the Synoptics (1:23, 26-27, 30, 32), the Fourth Gospel emphasizes who JTB is not (1:20-21). Blomberg attributes this to a 'Baptist-worshipping' sect. Contra Synoptic figurative associations of JTB with Elijah (Matt 11:14; Luke 1:17), the Fourth Gospel explicitly denies this identification (1:21) stressing JTB's desire to decrease in relative importance to Jesus (3:30). Evidence of overzealous JTB followers includes the mid-first century Ephesian group having an incomplete understanding of the gospel (Acts 19:1-7) and a second-century group of followers who attributed messianic status to him. Blomberg, *Jesus and the Gospels*, 192, 254.

[154] William E. Hull, *John*, in Clifton J. Allen, ed., *The Broadman Bible Commentary: Luke-John* (Nashville: Broadman Press, 1970), 223.

[155] Ibid.

[156] American Baptist views differ on the significance of the event. Schreiner views the Spirit's dove-like descent as Jesus being anointed for messianic ministry (an allusion to Gen 1:2). Once anointed, Jesus remains in this state throughout his ministry. In the Fourth Gospel the anointing of Jesus serves the christological interest of designating him as 'the Son of God' (1:34). See Schreiner, *New Testament Theology*, 461. Yarnell, believes the dove may allude to 'the Spirit's finding a place to rest.' The descent of the dove-like Spirit resting upon Jesus is a fulfillment of Isa 11:2. According to Yarnell, Jesus is not only one who receives the Spirit fully, but also gives the Spirit fully. See Malcolm B. Yarnell, III, 'The Person and Work of the Holy Spirit,' in Daniel L. Akin, ed., *A Theology for the Church* (Nashville: B & H Academic, 2007), 613. See also, Gerald L. Borchert, *John 1-11*, in E. Ray Clendenon, ed., *The New American Commentary: An Exegetical and Theological Exposition of Holy Scripture, Vol. 25a* (Nashville: Broadman Press, 1996), 138.

[157] The reading ὁ υἱός ('the Son') is well-attested by the majority of the witnesses, but the editors of the *NET Bible* prefer the reading ὁ ἐλεκτός ('the Chosen') based on one of the earliest MSS for the verse, p⁵. See Biblical Studies Press, *The NET Bible* (Dallas: Biblical Studies Press, 2007), 2022 n. 7.

[158] Hull, *John*, 223.

[159] Ibid.

4. This dispensing ('gift') of the Spirit marks the arrival of a new age inaugurated by Jesus' (3:5-8, 34; 4:23-24; 6:63; 7:37-39).[160]

The "fire motif" (Mark 1:7-8; Matt 3:11; Luke 3:16) is absent in the Johannine account of the BHS logion of JTB. A possible explanation for this is the author's intention to focus on the Spirit. Specifically, the author may envision a parallel between the experience of the Spirit expressed by the BHS logion of JTB and the sending of the Spirit by Jesus (cf. John 14:15-17; 20:21-22).[161] This focus on the relation of Jesus to the Spirit, one that was arguably demonstrated through the water rite of JTB, may explain why the Gospel writers described BHS in terms of a baptism. JTB personally identified with the fulfillment of Isaiah's prophecy (John 1:23; Isa 40:3) and the Gospel writers understood the ministry of JTB within the context of fulfilled OT prophecy (Mark 1:2-3; Matt 3:3; Luke 3:4). Therefore, the contrasting nature of messianic Spirit baptism to JTB's water rite may be attributed in the Jewish writings that anticipate the expected rejuvenation of Israel through the Spirit (Isa 32:15-17; 44:3; Ezek 36:26-27; 37:14; 1 QS 4:20-21; *Jub.* 1:23) by the one on whom the Spirit rested (Isa 11:2; 42:1; *T. Jud.* 24:1-3).[162]

2.3 Luke-Acts

This section explores the BHS views of American Baptist exegetes in relation to the unique theological perspective represented in the Luke-Acts corpus. Concretizing the American Baptist view of Lukan pneumatology is helpful when comparing and contrasting the findings with those of classical Pentecostals and many within the charismatic renewal. This comparison/contrast is substantive to the consensus BHS construct offered in Chapter Six. It is not the purpose of this section to investigate the extensive scholarly debate surrounding Luke's unique pneumatological perspective. This section focuses only on that portion of the debate engaged by American Baptist exegetes in the formulation of their BHS views.

Blomberg, Stein, and Schreiner note the higher frequency of Spirit-references by Luke (Luke-Acts) than the other Synoptists.[163] The prevalence of

---

[160] Ibid. See also Cook who considers BHS part of the Johannine witness to the deity of Christ. W. Robert Cook, *The Theology of John* (Chicago: Moody Press, 1979), 54. Schreiner, *New Testament Theology*, 455.

[161] Borchert, *John 1-11*, 138-39.

[162] Ibid., 138.

[163] Blomberg, *Jesus and the Gospels*, 169. Robert H. Stein, *Luke*, in David S. Dockery, ed., *The New American Commentary: An Exegetical and Theological Exposition of Holy Scripture, Vol. 24* (Nashville: Broadman Press, 1992), 47; Schreiner, *New Testament Theology*, 440. Hur

pneumatological references in Luke-Acts is suggestive of authorial intent. Stein insists that the wealth of diverse material found in Luke-Acts militates against the existence of a single theme which explains why Luke wrote his entire two-volume work.[164] At the same time, Stein advocates treating the Gospel of Luke and the book of Acts as a unified work (Luke-Acts) in order to understand the purpose behind Luke's composition.[165] There is some debate among American Baptists concerning the combined versus independent treatment of Luke's Gospel and the book of Acts to best consider the author's theological perspective. Due to differences in historical settings and genres, Polhill removes the hyphen in Luke-Acts and treats each book independently.[166] Stein favors considering Luke's pneumatological perspective according to his unified corpus[167] and notes several theological emphases, including the Holy Spirit, whose references are evenly dispersed throughout Luke-Acts.[168] Polhill considers the Spirit's presence in the book of Acts to be ubiquitous (though unmentioned in eleven chapters) and the

---

compares the frequency of the term 'Holy Spirit' in Luke (13), Matthew (5), and Mark (4) with its 41 occurrences in the book of Acts. His analysis includes direct definition, indirect presentation (speech, action, external appearance, and environment), repetition and similarity (repeated effects of Spirit-endowment, similar expressions for Spirit-endowment), and comparison and contrast. See Ju Hur, *A Dynamic Reading of the Holy Spirit in Luke-Acts* (London: T & T Clark International, 2001), 295-301.

[164] Stein, *Luke,* 36. See also Hans Conzelmann, Trans. Geoffrey Buswell, *The Theology of St. Luke* (ET New York: Harper & Row, 1961), I. Howard Marshall, *Luke: Historian and Theologian* (Grand Rapids: Zondervan Publishing House, 1971), A. T. Robertson, *Luke the Historian in Light of Research* ([original work published 1920] Grand Rapids: Baker Book House, 1977), Joseph A. Fitzmyer, *Luke the Theologian: Aspects of His Teaching* (New York: Paulist Press, 1989), and François Bovon, *Luke the Theologian, Revised 2nd Ed.* (Waco: Baylor University Press, 2006).

[165] Stein, *Luke,* 36.

[166] John B. Polhill, *Acts,* in David S. Dockery, ed., *The New American Commentary: An Exegetical and Theological Exposition of Holy Scripture, Vol. 26* (Nashville: Broadman Press, 1992), 54.

[167] This is not to suggest that Luke's pneumatology represents his total purpose for Luke-Acts. Stein refers to Wilson who considers as unsatisfactory the isolation of any one theme to represent Luke's entire purpose for writing. See S. G. Wilson, *The Gentiles and the Gentile Mission in Luke-Acts* (Cambridge: University Press, 1973), 265-66.

[168] Stein notes that the Holy Spirit is active in the birth of JTB (Luke 1:15, 17) and in Jesus' conception (Luke 1:35) and birth (Luke 2:25-27). The Holy Spirit anointed and empowered Jesus for ministry at his baptism (Luke 3:22). The Holy Spirit was present at the temptation of Jesus (Luke 4:1) and during his earliest ministry (Luke 4:14; 5:17). Jesus referred to the Holy Spirit in his first sermon (Luke 4:18). JTB prophesied the Holy Spirit's coming upon Jesus's disciples (Luke 3:16), whose coming was also promised by Jesus to his disciples (Luke 24:49; Acts 1:4-5, 8). BHS comes upon every believer at Pentecost in fulfillment of Joel 2:28-32 (Acts 2) and is promised to future Christians (Acts 2:38-39). The Holy Spirit is the distinctive mark of the Christian as evidenced in Cornelius whose possession of the Spirit was proof of God's acceptance of Gentile believers into the full membership of the church (Acts 10-11). The question of Christian identity was premised on the reception of the Spirit at the point of belief (Acts 19:2). Stein, *Luke,* 47-48.

Spirit's role in Christian mission to be the primary characteristic of the book.[169] Included in his appraisal is the Spirit's role in legitimizing new groups (e.g. the Samaritans, 8:17-25; Cornelius and his fellow Gentiles, 10:44-48; and the disciples of JTB, 19:6-7).[170] Among American Baptist exegetes, Schreiner provides the most extensive analysis of the pneumatological focus of Luke-Acts. His analysis differentiates Luke from the other Synoptists and provides interpretive context for the Lukan BHS references (Luke 3:16; Acts 1:5; 11:16).[171] Since Schreiner presents the most thorough American Baptist perspective of Luke's pneumatology and soteriology relative to BHS, his analysis will inform the following sections.[172]

2.3.1   The Spirit in Relation to Jesus

Schreiner and Polhill note the general Synoptic interest in the Spirit-bearing role of Jesus. Each of the Synoptists records the anointing of Jesus by the Spirit at his baptism (Matt 3:16; Mark 1:10; Luke 3:22).[173] By recording the birth narratives of JTB and Jesus (1:15 and 1:35), Schreiner and Stein adduce Luke's intent to emphasize the superior pneumatic experience of Jesus, conceived by the Spirit and the unique bearer of the Spirit.[174] Also distinctive is Luke's relation between the Spirit's anointing of Jesus and his ministry being conducted in the power of the Spirit to fulfill the will of God (Luke 4:1, 14, 18-21; Acts 4:26-27; 10:37-38).[175] Stein further identifies the relation of the Spirit to power and contends that the empowering of Jesus by the Spirit is paradigmatic of the future empowerment of the disciples (Luke 24:49; Acts 1:4-8).[176] In relation to Jesus,

---

[169] Polhill, *Acts*, 64-65.

[170] Ibid.

[171] Schreiner, *New Testament Theology*, 440-60.

[172] Ibid., 440. Schreiner mentions the works of Menzies and Turner as excellent surveys of scholarship relative to Holy Spirit studies with a Luke-Acts focus. See Menzies, *Empowered for Witness*, 17-45; Turner, *Power from on High*, 20-79.

[173] Schreiner, *New Testament Theology*, 441; Polhill, *Acts*, 262.

[174] Schreiner, *New Testament Theology*, 441; Stein, *Luke*, 85.

[175] Schreiner, *New Testament Theology*, 442. Luke's description of the anointing of Jesus by the Spirit is reminiscent of the Spirit coming upon the servant of the Lord (Luke 4:18-19; Acts 10:38; Isa 42:1; 61:1), the prophets (Luke 1:15; 2:25-38; 2 Chr 15:1; 20:14; Neh 9:30), judges (Judg 3:10; 6:34; 11:29), and the Messiah (Isa 11:2). Stein, *Luke*, 139.

[176] Luke favors referring to the Holy Spirit's influence as 'power.' This is evidenced by the synonymous parallelism of the phrases 'the Holy Spirit will come on you' and 'the power of the Most High will overshadow you' (Luke 1:35). For the Lukan relation of 'spirit' and 'power,' see

Schreiner considers that Jesus' performance of miracles and healings depends on the Spirit's empowering presence and is not evidence of his native power.[177] This theme concerning the source of Jesus' empowerment is given prominence by the first recorded event of his ministry (Luke 4:16-30) which Schreiner considers thematic for Luke and programmatic for the Luke-Acts corpus.[178] Specifically, as one uniquely strengthened by the Spirit, Jesus' ministry (i.e. opening blind eyes, liberating the oppressed and proclaiming good news to the poor) directly relates to the flow of power from the Spirit's anointing (Isa 61:1-2; Luke 4:18).[179] Stein draws the added conclusion that the church's later ministry, like that of Jesus', follows the same pattern of Spirit empowerment (Luke 4:36; 5:17; 8:46; 10:13; Acts 10:38; see also, Luke 9:1; 10:19; 24:49; Acts 1:8; 4:7, 33; 6:8; 19:11).[180]

2.3.2   The 'Prophetic Spirit'

Schreiner's mention of the 'prophetic Spirit' refers to the Spirit coming upon people to reveal the Scriptures and induce inspired speech.[181] The mention of the 'prophetic Spirit' (or 'Spirit of prophecy') here is not intended to engage fully the contemporary robust theological debate relating to this descriptive category of the Spirit in Luke-Acts, but is intended to address the relevant points which have influenced the American Baptist BHS apologetic. According to Schreiner's

---

Luke 1:17, 35; 4:14; Acts 1:8; 10:38. When 'power' is mentioned (Luke 5:17; 24:49), it is likely the Spirit is doing the empowering. Stein, *Luke,* 76, 140.

[177] Schreiner, *New Testament Theology,* 442. For a contrasting P/C view, see Warrington who notes the plethora of scholars who identify the role of the Spirit in the achievement of Jesus' messianic task. This corresponds both to the confession of Jesus (Luke 4:18-19) and the observation of Peter (Acts 10:37-38). At issue is the purpose of the Spirit's power. Warrington contends that the Gospels (Luke in particular) do not present significant evidence to conclude Jesus' dependence upon the Spirit, especially where his healing ministry is concerned. In fact, the opposite is maintained in Luke-Acts where 'the Spirit is prominent when Jesus is absent and functions in his own authority' (Luke 4:36; 5:12, 17; 6:19; 8:46; 9:1; 10:19; 21:27). The implication is that the intention of the Gospel writers is to present Jesus as the unique Christ, the one who will confer the Spirit (Matt 3:11; Mark 1:8; Luke 3:16) in a manner previously reserved for Yahweh in the OT (Gen 6:3; Num 11:29; Isa 42:1; 63:11; Joel 2:28-32). According to Warrington, the Spirit does not support Jesus, but it is Jesus who is the Lord of the Spirit. Pentecost validates the promise of Jesus regarding the coming of the Spirit (Luke 24:49; Acts 1:4). See Keith Warrington, *Jesus the Healer: Paradigm or Unique Phenomenon* (Carlisle: Paternoster Press, 2000), 152-53; 'The Message of the Holy Spirit: The Spirit of Encounter,' in Derek Tidball, ed., *The Bible Speaks Today* (Downers Grove: InterVarsity Press, 2009), 63.

[178] Schreiner, *New Testament Theology,* 442.

[179] Ibid. *Acts,* 262.

[180] Stein, *Luke,* 148-49.

[181] Schreiner, *New Testament Theology,* 442.

analysis, Luke links the prophetic word to the fulfillment of salvation history.[182] He cites as evidence those numerous occasions in Luke-Acts where Luke connects the 'filling' of the Spirit (πίμπλημι) with prophecy and where the Spirit influences mission-specific tasks among the people of God. Contributing to Schreiner's assessment of the Lukan prophetic Spirit is a Spirit-word alliance which involves the Spirit speaking through Scripture and the human authors who wrote under the influence of the prophetic Spirit. Lastly, the prophetic Spirit is associated with the ongoing mission of the church in fulfillment of redemptive history whereby Spirit-guided messengers advance the gospel beyond its initial (Jewish) recipients (Acts 1:8).[183] In summation, Schreiner does not go so far as to associate the Lukan prophetic Spirit with soteriological function, though he does view the Spirit as integral to empowering witnesses for gospel proclamation.[184]

2.3.3   Life in the Spirit

Schreiner evaluates Luke's depiction of the Spirit's influence in Luke-Acts by using terms which denote the state of being 'full' of the Spirit or the experience of being 'filled' with the Spirit.[185] Specifically, he notes Luke's use of the adjective 'full' (πλήρης) and the verb 'to fill' (πληρόω)[186] to characterize life in the Spirit (Acts 6:3, 5, 8; 7:55; 9:36; 11:24; see also conversely of Elymas, Acts

---

[182] Ibid., 443.

[183] In the case of the Ethiopian eunuch, the gospel is proclaimed by Philip to a God-fearer. According to Schreiner, Cornelius and his friends hear the gospel as uncircumcised persons (Acts 11:3). Paul and Barnabas undertook the first international gospel mission to the Gentiles. Ibid., 446.

[184] Schreiner acknowledges the 'Spirit of Prophecy' theme in Acts and refers to its development by Turner, Menzies, and Shelton, though he does not engage them at length. He notes that Turner (contra Menzies and Shelton) argues that the Lukan prophetic Spirit both empowers and imparts the soteriological gift. See Turner, *Power from on High,* 107-10. See also Max Turner, 'The Spirit of Prophecy as the Power of Israel's Restoration and Witness, in I. Howard Marshall and David Peterson, eds., *Witness to the Gospel: The Theology of Acts* (Grand rapids: William B. Eerdmans Publishing, 1998), 333-37 and Max Turner, 'Luke and the Spirit: Renewing Theological Interpretation of Biblical Pneumatology,' in Craig G. Bartholomew, Joel B. Green, and Anthony C. Thiselton, eds., *Reading Luke: Interpretation, Reflection, Formation* (Grand Rapids: Zondervan, 2005), 267-93. See also, Robert P. Menzies, *The Development of Early Christian Pneumatology with Special Reference to Luke-Acts* (Sheffield: Sheffield Academic Press, 1991), 107-10 and James B. Shelton, *Mighty in Word and Deed: The Role of the Holy Spirit in Luke-Acts* ([previous work published 1991] Eugene: Wipf & Stock Publishers, 1999), 15-32.

[185] Schreiner, *New Testament Theology,* 448-49.

[186] Schreiner emphasizes Paul's similar use of 'fill' (πληρόω) in Rom 1:29; 15:13-14; 2 Cor 7:4; Phil 1:11; Col 1:9; and 2 Tim 1:4. Ibid., 449.

13:10).[187] The term is indicative of the transformational (ethical) influence that accompanies Spirit-induced inspired utterance or empowering to speak forth God's word, according to Schreiner's analysis.[188] In so doing, he identifies a soteriological dimension to Luke's depiction of the prophetic Spirit (i.e. the Spirit not only empowers for witness, but also plays a role in ethical transformation).[189] As previously noted, the verb 'to fill' (πίμπλημι) is linked to the Spirit being the impetus for speaking out God's word.[190] Conversely, Luke describes living contrary to the Spirit's influence as resisting or blaspheming the Spirit (Luke 12:10; Acts 5:1-11; 6:10; and 7:51).[191]

2.3.4 *Jesus as the Dispenser of the Spirit*

Schreiner considers Luke 24:46-49 to be programmatic for Luke, with the gift of the Spirit appearing to demonstrate its vital connection with the suffering of Jesus (Luke 24:46-49).[192] He relates the programmatic significance of this connection to Luke's understanding of Jesus, the one who dispenses the Spirit. Specifically, the Father (Luke 11:13) gives the Spirit to the exalted Jesus (Acts

---

[187] Schreiner supports his analysis citing Turner who considers Luke's use of 'full' (πλήρης) a metaphor which expresses a state of being full used of the Spirit on five occasions (Luke 4:1; Acts 6:3, 5; 7:55; 11:24). With reference to 'full' (πλήρης) plus the subjunctive genitive of quality, Turner identifies the construction (though not used of the divine Spirit) as a relatively standard idiom with reference to persons in the LXX (Job 10:15; 14:1; 32:18; 36:17; Isa 51:20; Sir 1:30; 19:26; 3 Macc 6:31). The construction 'full' (πλήρης) plus the defining genitive (of persons) is used as a spatial metaphor indicating that the quality is a visible expression of the activity that marks the person's life (Tabitha's life characterized by or abounding in goods works and charitable acts, Acts 8:36). See Turner, *Power from on High,* 166-67.

[188] Schreiner, *New Testament Theology,* 449.

[189] Schreiner supports his conclusion citing Turner who interacts with the works of Gunkel and Haya-Prats. Turner notes that the terms 'filled with' or 'full of' when coupled with a second quality (Acts 6:3, 5; 11:24; 13:52) denote that the quality in question is a derivative (either clearly or implied) of the Spirit's working. See Hermann Gunkel, Trans. Roy A. Harrisville and Philip A. Quanbeck II, *The Influence of the Holy Spirit: The Popular View of the Apostolic Age and the Teaching of the Apostle Paul* (ET Philadelphia: Fortress Press, 1979), 16-21 and Gonzalo Haya-Prats, Paul Elbert, ed., Trans. Scott A. Ellington, *Empowered Believers: The Holy Spirit in the Book of Acts* (ET Eugene: Cascade Books, 2011), 157-67. Specifically, Turner argues that Christianity, growing out of Judaism, would relate the life-transforming 'spirit of understanding' (or 'insight,' or 'wisdom') to the 'Spirit of prophecy' as activities readily expected in anyone who had received the fulfillment of Joel's promise. See Turner, *Power from on High,* 408-12.

[190] In his analysis of the verb 'fill' (πίμπλημι), Turner believes its use is to denote relatively short events or immediate effects. In his view, Luke tends to use the aorist indicative or participle with the genitive of divine Spirit for inspirations of short duration (Luke 1:41, 67; Acts 2:4; 4:8, 31; and possibly 13:9). See Turner, *Power from on High,* 167-68.

[191] Schreiner, *New Testament Theology,* 449.

[192] Ibid.

1:9-11; 2:30, 34-36) who once-for-all pours out 'the promise of the Father' to 'clothe' waiting disciples with 'power from on high' (Acts 2:33) to proclaim the gospel to the ends of the earth (Acts 1:8).[193] Schreiner's analysis further considers the verbal expressions used by Luke to represent the dispensing of the Spirit ('receive,' 1:8; 2:33, 38[194]; 8:15, 17; 10:47; 19:2; 'pour out,' Acts 2:17-18 [Joel 2:28-32]; Acts 2:33; 10:45-46; 'give,' Luke 11:13; Acts 8:18-19; 11:17; 15:7-11; 'come upon,' Luke 1:35; Acts 1:8; 19:6; 'fall upon,' Acts 10:44; 11:15; and 'baptize,' Luke 3:16; Acts1:4-5; 11:16).[195] He concludes that the verbal expressions occur in association with four main events: (1) the giving of the Spirit at Pentecost (Luke 3:16; Acts 1:5, 8; 2:17-18, 33; 11:15-16), (2) to the Samaritans (Acts 8:15-19),[196] (3) to Cornelius and his friends (Acts 10:44-45, 47; 11:15-17; 15:8), and (4) to the Ephesian Twelve (Acts 19:1-7).[197]

Schreiner and Hamilton believe that these verbal expressions which represent a common experience occurring in each of the four events form a useful semantic domain for adducing BHS according to Luke's pneumatological perspective.[198] According to Schreiner, this sematic relationship indicates that a rigid separation between the empowering and regenerating ministry of the Spirit cannot be textually sustained.[199] In his view, the Pentecostal gift of the Spirit describes the

---

[193] Schreiner disagrees with Menzies who interprets 'the promise of the Father' as a reference to the prophetic Spirit who empowers for witness as per Joel's prophecy (Joel 2:28). See Schreiner, *New Testament Theology,* 450 n. 43. See Menzies, *Empowered for Witness,* 168-72.

[194] Schreiner criticizes Menzies' assertion that Acts 2:38 refers to the prophetic Spirit and not the soteriological gift of the Spirit. He further contends that Menzies' interpretation (according to Joel 3:1 MT) wrongly assumes that use of 'the Spirit' by Luke is always intended to be a reference to the prophetic role of the Spirit. See Schreiner, *New Testament Theology,* 451. See also Menzies, *Empowered for Witness,* 203-4. Schreiner agrees with Turner who interprets Acts 2:38 as programmatic for receiving the Spirit at conversion. Turner understands the 'Spirit of prophecy' to be more than an empowering presence, having the functional role of developing the spiritual life of the believer and in the community of Christians. See Schreiner, *New Testament Theology,* 451. See also Turner, *Power from on High,* 358-59.

[195] Schreiner, *New Testament Theology,* 451.

[196] According to Schreiner, the Samaritans who received the Spirit subsequent to believing in Jesus are the only examples of NT believers failing to receive the Spirit contemporaneously with conversion. Ibid.

[197] Ibid.

[198] Ibid., 454; James M. Hamilton, Jr., *God's Indwelling Presence: The Holy Spirit in the Old and New Testaments,* in E. Ray Clendenen, ed., *NAC Studies in Bible & Theology* (Nashville: B & H Academic, 2006), 183-203.

[199] Schreiner agrees with Menzies' claim that the Pentecostal gift of the Spirit empowers for witness, but rejects Menzies' elimination of soteriological function of the Pentecostal gift. Schreiner, *New Testament Theology,* 454. See Menzies, *Empowered for Witness,* 173-201. Schreiner

reception of charismatic power by a Spirit-endowed people of God.[200] Since baptism is the language of initiation, Schreiner interprets references to BHS performed by Jesus (e.g. Acts 1:5) to indicate the commencement of the new age of the Spirit (Acts 2:17-18, 33 [Joel 2:28]).[201] Carson supports this position, but is critical of P/C praxis which, he claims, wrongly bases personal Pentecost tarrying experiences on the corresponding injunction of Jesus to wait for the gift of the Father (Acts 1:4).[202] Of the more than two dozen conversion experiences recorded in Acts after the Day of Pentecost, Carson finds no injunctions to wait for the gift of the Spirit.[203] He attributes this phenomenon to Luke's salvation-historical focus which emphasizes Joel's prophecy (Acts 2:16-21) as eschatological fulfillment and not paradigmatic of personal experience.[204] Schreiner points to Luke's intention in the Cornelius account to reveal the inclusion of uncircumcised Gentiles into the people of God (Acts 11:15; 15:8).[205] Polhill refers to the Spirit-reception experienced by the Samaritans (variously interpreted) being an exceptional incident recounted merely because it is unique.[206] Schreiner does not detect a pattern in Luke's description of the 'Ephesian Twelve' (Acts 19:1-7) who, as old covenant believers, had not received the gift of the Spirit as the accompanying mark of life in the new age of redemption.[207]

---

further believes that Luke's Acts 8:14-17 accounting of the Samaritans' secondary experience of the Spirit is anomalous. See Schreiner, *New Testament Theology*, 456-57. American Baptists are typically critical of BHS as a post-conversion experience due to the perceived lack of any biblical mandate for believers to seek its reception. Henry and Criswell represent this criticism. See Henry, *God, Authority and Revelation, Vol. 6*, 385-86. See also Criswell, *The Holy Spirit in Today's World*, 101-2.

[200] Schreiner, *New Testament Theology*, 454.

[201] Ibid.

[202] D. A. Carson, *Showing the Spirit: A Theological Exposition of 1 Corinthians 12-14* ([original work published 1987] Grand Rapids: Baker Books, 2003), 139-40.

[203] Ibid.

[204] Ibid. Carson refers to J. I. Packer, *Keep in Step with the Spirit* ([original work published 1984] Grand Rapids: Fleming H. Revell, 2002), 205. Packer critiques what he terms 'the common Pentecostal-charismatic handling of Acts 2' (also that of holiness teachers such a Torrey). Contra P/C and holiness conceptions, Packer believes Luke recorded the particular experiences of the Spirit in Acts to detail the progress of the gospel, not to provide paradigms for how God always functions.

[205] Schreiner, *New Testament Theology*, 455.

[206] Polhill, *Acts*, 217-18. According to Polhill, Acts presents no set pattern and 'the Spirit cannot be tied down to any manipulative human schema.'

[207] Schreiner cites Dunn and Turner who deny that these JTB disciples, having not received the Spirit, were believers in Jesus. See Dunn, *Baptism in the Holy Spirit*, 83-89. See also Turner, *Power from on High*, 388-97. Menzies and Barrett regard the Ephesian Twelve as true

Schreiner's analysis deviates from the usual American Baptist practice of linking BHS with conversion. While not denying ministry function to the Spirit, he suggests that Luke's primary purpose for Spirit-reception in the four stated occasions is to certify the people of God.[208] Hamilton concurs, adding that the BHS occurrences in Acts 2, 8, 10, and 19 do not illustrate what happens at conversion.[209] Instead, Hamilton believes that Luke's BHS references indicate unique occurrences in the history of the church. Of the fifteen personal conversion experience accounts described in the book of Acts, Hamilton finds no BHS language (2:41, 47; 4:4; 5:14; 6:7; 8:12-13, 36-37; 9:35, 42; 13:48; 16:5, 14, 31-34; 17:11-12; 18:8).[210] This leads him to conclude that BHS initiates the age of the eschatological gift of the Spirit and that the recipients were believers when the Spirit fell upon them.[211] By this observation, Hamilton does not affirm a two-stage pneumatology, but rather the uniqueness of events detailed by Luke to present Spirit-reception (BHS) as God's means of approving his people.[212] Blomberg addresses the potential for adducing post-conversion (second blessing) experiences of God patterned after the Samaritans (Acts 8:15-19) and the Ephesian Twelve (Acts 19:1-7). He concludes that Luke is describing the initial (personal) reception of the Spirit which is consistent with Paul's pattern for becoming a Christian (e.g. Rom 8:9).[213] Blomberg differs from Hamilton and Schreiner who equate Luke's pneumatological perspective of BHS with a once-for-all non-repeatable eschatological certification of the people of God.

---

disciples; they had received forgiveness of sins, but were unaware of any additional endowment. See Menzies, *Empowered for Witness,* 218-25. See also C. K. Barrett, *Acts 15-28* ([originally published 1998] London: T & T Clark, 2006), 894.

[208] Schreiner, *New Testament Theology,* 459.

[209] Hamilton, *God's Indwelling Presence,* 191. Hamilton rejects Ladd on this point for offering the standard explanation; that BHS occurs at the moment of saving faith, an NT event occurring simultaneously with water baptism and incorporating believers into the church. See George Eldon Ladd, *A Theology of the New Testament, Revised* ([original work published 1973] Grand Rapids: William B. Eerdmans Publishing, 1993), 384.

[210] Ibid.

[211] Ibid., 192.

[212] Ibid., 193.

[213] Craig L. Blomberg, *1 Corinthians,* in Terry Muck, ed., *The NIV Application Commentary* (Grand Rapids: Zondervan Publishing House, 1994), 253.

2.4   1 Corinthians 12:13

BHS references in the NT epistles are confined to Pauline passages[214] and include one clear reference (1 Cor 12:13) and four other references that are disputed (Rom 6:3-5; Gal 3:27; Eph 4:5; Col 2:12).[215] This section demonstrates the importance of 1 Cor 12:13 to American Baptist BHS perspectives. Specifically, the section will investigate these perspectives in relation to the agent, result and occasion, and occurrence of BHS.

2.4.1   Agency

Determining the agent of BHS depends upon resolving a few interpretive questions regarding the meaning of ἐν ἑνὶ πνεύματι...ἐβαπτίσθημεν ('in-with-by one Spirit...we were baptized').

1) Is Paul's description of the phenomenon univocally associated with the prior references found in the Gospels and Luke-Acts?

If Paul is referring to an identical phenomenon, then the agent of BHS described in the Gospels and Luke-Acts necessarily follows, Jesus.

2) Is Paul's description of the phenomenon equivocally associated with the prior references found in the Gospels and Luke-Acts? For example, is Paul referring to the Christian's conversion experience?

At issue here is the relationship between the verbs ἐβαπτίσθημεν ('we were baptized') and ἐποτίσθημεν ('we were given to drink'). In this case, the baptism to which Paul refers is synonymous with regeneration and the agent is the Spirit.

3) Is Paul referring to the gift of Spirit (i.e., reception of the Spirit) via water baptism?

If so, then BHS is a distinctive operation of the Spirit not mentioned in the text. Another possibility is that Paul is representing the close relation between Spirit-reception and water baptism. In such a case Jesus is regarded as dispensing (giving) the Spirit and simultaneously incorporating believers into his body via water baptism.

---

[214] For a discussion on 1 Pet 3:21, see Thomas R. Schreiner, 'Baptism in the Epistles: An Initiation Rite for Believers,' in E. Ray Clendenen, *Believers Baptism: Sign of the New Covenant in Christ* (Nashville: B & H Academic, 2006), 67-96.

[215] Gromacki, The Holy Spirit, 167.

4) Another possibility is that Paul refers to the mediate (indirect) agency of the Spirit, but with reference to the same phenomenon detailed in the Gospels and Luke-Acts.

In this case, Jesus remains the primary agent, who performs BHS by means of the Spirit.

Of the four interpretive options, American Baptists predominately favor either (1) or (4). Option (2) is typically a P/C interpretation and generally denied by American Baptists who interpret the text as a reference to BHS.[216] Option (3) is appealing to some American Baptists,[217] but it does not reflect the primary position held by those who believe Paul is referring to a baptism distinct from water baptism.[218] For example, Gromacki notes Paul's mention of water baptism (1 Cor 1:13-17) but argues that his mention of baptism elsewhere (1 Cor 12:13; Rom 6:3-5; Gal 3:27; Eph 4:5; Col 2:12) refers to BHS. He bases this conclusion on contexts which discuss spiritual realities.[219] Schreiner supports the contention that in 1 Cor 12:13 (also Titus 3:5) Paul associates the reception of the Spirit with (water) baptism and does not conceive of people being baptized who have not also

---

[216] Wayne Grudem, *Systematic Theology: An Introduction to Biblical Doctrine* (Grand Rapids: Zondervan Publishing, 1994), 767; Garrett, *Systematic Theology, Vol. 2*, 166-67. See Gordon D. Fee, *The First Epistle to the Corinthians* (Grand Rapids: William B. Eerdmans Publishing, 1987), 604-5. See also Howard M. Ervin, *Spirit Baptism: A Biblical Investigation* (Peabody: Hendrickson Publishers, 1987), 28-37.

[217] Garrett provides bibliographic evidence for the widely accepted view among commentators (Baptist and non-Baptist) that 1 Cor 12:13 refers to water baptism. See Garrett, *Systematic Theology: Biblical, Historical, and Evangelical, Vol. 2*, 166-67 n. 14. See also Hamilton, *God's Indwelling Presence*, 187 n. 14. Garland is non-committal on whether Paul refers to water or Spirit baptism in 1 Cor 12:13a. He considers the construction ἐν ἑνὶ πνεύματι either instrumental ('by one Spirit') and a reference to the Spirit's work of placing new believers into the body of Christ at conversion, or locative ('in one Spirit') in the sense of the new convert being placed (by Jesus) into the sphere of the Spirit and incorporated into one body. For Garland, these are not mutually exclusive views, but together represent all Christians in terms of one body immersed in (or by) the Spirit. See David E. Garland, *1 Corinthians*, in Robert W. Yarbrough and Robert H. Stein, eds., *BECNT* ([original work published 2003] Grand Rapids: Baker Academic, 2007), 591.

[218] Garrett, *Systematic Theology, Vol. 2*, 166.

[219] Gromacki, *The Holy Spirit*, 167. According to Walvoord, there are eleven 'specific references to spiritual baptism in the NT (Matt 3:11; Mark 1:8; Luke 3:16; John 1:33; Acts 1:5; 11:16; Rom 6:1-4; 1 Cor 12:13; Gal 3:27; Eph 4:5; Col 2:12). See John F. Walvoord, *The Holy Spirit: A Comprehensive Study of the Person and Work of the Holy Spirit, 3rd Ed.* ([original work published 1943] Findlay: Dunham Publishing Company, 1958), 139. MacArthur believes that the Pauline texts (1 Cor 12:13; Gal 3:27; Rom 6:3-5) refer to 'spiritual' and not water baptism. See John F. MacArthur, Jr., *The MacArthur New Testament Commentary: 1 Corinthians* (Chicago: The Moody Bible Institute, 1984), 312; *The MacArthur New Testament Commentary: Galatians* (Chicago: The Moody Bible Institute, 1987), 98-99. Unger argues that Paul's theme in Eph 4:5; Rom 6:3-4; Gal 3:27; and Col 2:12 is not ritual baptism, but spiritual baptism. See Merrill F. Unger, 'The Baptism with the Holy Spirit, Part 1' in *BSac* (1944), 232-47. Unger's writings are known and generally esteemed among American Baptists.

received the Spirit.[220] He interprets Paul's 'one baptism' (Eph 4:5) as the church's initiatory water rite, the mark of unity given upon conversion.[221] According to Schreiner, Paul is referring to the common experience of water baptism in 1 Cor 12:13, a tradition stemming from JTB.[222] On his view, the grammar attributes BHS agency to Jesus. The preposition ἐν should be translated 'in' as a reference to the element and not the agent of BHS.[223] He concludes that the water baptism rite mentioned in 1 Cor 12:13 is linked with incorporation into the body of Christ.[224] Following fellow Baptist Beasley-Murray,[225] Schreiner believes 1 Cor 12:13 to demonstrate that water baptism and Spirit-reception are simultaneously experienced events.[226]

American Baptists favoring option (1) examine the Greek text and conclude that ἐν ἑνὶ πνεύματι...ἐβαπτίσθημεν ('in-with-by one Spirit...we were baptized') is virtually identical to the six expressions found in the Gospels and Luke-Acts (Matt 3:11; Mark 1:8; Luke 3:16; John 1:33; Acts 1:5; 11:16). American Baptist theologian Grudem argues that the only difference between Paul's reference to BHS and the six occurrences in the Gospels and Luke-Acts is his mention of 'one Spirit' rather than 'the Holy Spirit.'[227] All other elements in the text are identical, including the verb βαπτίζω ('I baptize') and the prepositional phrase ἐν plus the dative noun πνεύματι.[228] He reasons that if the Greek text is translated 'baptize in/with the Holy Spirit' in the Gospels and Luke-Acts, then consistency requires the same translation in 1 Cor 12:13.[229] By uniformly translating the Greek text, this view finds concurrence between Paul,

---

[220] Schreiner, *New Testament Theology,* 727.

[221] Ibid.

[222] Ibid.

[223] Ibid., 727-28. Schreiner notes that the preposition ὑπό regularly designates the agent of baptism (Matt 3:6, 13-14; Mark 1:5; Luke 3:7; 7:30) with ἐν identifying the element (Matt 3:6, 11; Mark 1:8; Luke 3:16; John 1:26, 31, 33; Acts 1:5; 11:16).

[224] Ibid., 728.

[225] G. R. Beasley-Murray, *Baptism in the New Testament* (New York: Macmillan & Co., Ltd., 1962), 167-71. See also British scholar G. W. H. Lampe, *The Seal of the Spirit: A Study in the Doctrine of Baptism and Confirmation in the New Testament and the Fathers* (London: Longmans, Green and Co., 1951), 57.

[226] Schreiner, *New Testament Theology,* 728.

[227] Wayne Grudem, 'A Baptist Because of the Bible,' in Tom J. Nettles and Russell D. Moore, eds., *Why I Am A Baptist* (Nashville: Broadman & Holman Publishers, 2001), 201-8; Grudem, *Systematic Theology,* 767.

[228] Ibid.

[229] Ibid., 764 n. 3.

the Gospels, and Luke-Acts: that Jesus is the agent who baptizes in/with the Spirit. MacArthur, noting ἐν ἑνὶ πνεύματι can mean 'by' or 'with' one Spirit, favors the rendering 'with one Spirit' to identify that it is Christ's baptism.[230]

Option (4) translates ἐν ἑνὶ πνεύματι 'by one Spirit.'[231] American Baptist pastor/theologian W. A. Criswell considered this rendering open to the charge of placing Paul at odds with the Gospels and Luke-Acts, which attribute BHS agency to Jesus.[232] He answered the charge of apparent Pauline discontinuity by distinguishing an initial (ascension) giving of the Spirit by Jesus, occurring once-for-all on the Day of Pentecost (described in the Gospels and Luke-Acts) from the post-Pentecost work of the Spirit who performs baptizes and thereby joins believers to the body of Christ.[233] On this view, Jesus is the originator of the baptizing act and the Holy Spirit assumes the subsequent baptizing role. Accordingly, all believers via the agency of the Spirit are placed εἰς ἓν σῶμα

---

[230] MacArthur, *The MacArthur New Testament Commentary: 1 Corinthians,* 312. See Gromacki, *The Holy Spirit,* 169. Gromacki favors 'in one Spirit,' but identifies BHS as a work performed by Christ on behalf of believers.

[231] P/C scholar Ray Hughes dismisses this rendering as a BHS reference. According to Hughes, this is a reference to conversion. Ray H. Hughes, *What is Pentecost?* (Cleveland: Pathway Press, 1963), 23. Hughes refers to the P/C distinction between a prior baptism (*of* or *by* the Spirit) in which the Spirit is the agent (conversion and initiation into the body) and a subsequent baptism (*in* the Spirit) in which Christ is the agent (empowerment for service). P/C theologian Williams holds a similar view. See Ernest S. Williams, *Systematic Theology, Vol. 3* ([original work published 1953] Springfield: Gospel Publishing House, 1991), 47. Bruner rejects this P/C distinction of two (spiritual) baptisms for lack of NT grammatical support. According to Bruner, the NT texts (Matt 3:11; Mark 1:8; Luke 3:16; Acts 1:4; 11:16) uniformly refer to disciples being baptized ἐν ('in/with/by') the Spirit and in 1 Cor 12:13 'the Greek text is both the agent *and* gift of the *one* baptism.' See Frederick Dale Bruner, *A Theology of the Holy Spirit: The Pentecostal Experience and the New Testament Witness* (London: Hodder & Stoughton, 1970), 60, 291-95.

[232] Criswell refers to this as a 'dualist' rendering of the Greek expression. The preposition ἐν as it appears in the Gospels and Luke-Acts is understood in the location sense while Paul's reference in 1 Cor 12:13 is understood in an instrumental sense. See W. A. Criswell, *The Holy Spirit in Today's World* (Grand Rapids: Zondervan Publishing House, 1966), 94.

[233] Criswell, *The Holy Spirit,* 95. The writings of Lewis Sperry Chafer receive varying degrees of acceptance among American Baptists. Chafer resolved the issue of apparent discontinuity by positing two baptisms. The first is a baptism (identified in the Gospels and Luke-Acts) performed by Christ at conversion. The second baptism (identified by Paul in 1 Cor 12:12-13; Gal 3:27; Rom 6:1-4; Col 2:9-13; Eph 4:4-6) is performed by the Spirit with the body of Christ as the receiving element. The former baptism is ritual and the latter is real. Chafer relies heavily on the writings of James W. Dale to define 'baptism' in terms of 'controlling influence' and the ritual versus real dichotomy. See Lewis Sperry Chafer, *Systematic Theology, Vol. 6* ([original work published 1948] Dallas: Dallas Seminary Press, 1980), 138-51. See also James W. Dale, *Classic Baptism: An Inquiry into the Meaning of the Word ΒΑΠΤΙΖΩ, as Determined by the Usage of Classical Greek Writers* ([original work published 1867] Philadelphia: Presbyterian Board of Publication and Sabbath School Work, 1912), 354.

('into one body'), the baptizing medium, the body of Christ.[234] This interpretation attempts to avoid the problem of two media, 'in one Spirit/into one body.'[235] Criswell's explanation avoids the charge of anachronistically interpreting the BHS references in the Gospels and Luke-Acts according to Paul's 'incorporation into the body of Christ' description.[236]

2.4.2   Result and Occasion

Regardless of the varying positions on the agency of BHS, contemporary American Baptist scholars are nearly uniform on its result and occasion according to 1 Cor 12:13.[237] While it is common for American Baptists to characterize BHS as the non-affective and positional uniting of the believer with Christ, Grenz and

---

[234] Jerry Vines, *Spirit Works,* 77-79. MacArthur, *The MacArthur New Testament Commentary: 1 Corinthians,* 312.

[235] The 'problem' for American Baptist interpreters is that the translation 'in one Spirit we were all baptized into one body' parallels the P/C position, if the metaphors refers to distinct pneumatic events; conversion and initiation into the body of Christ (1 Cor 12:13a) followed by a secondary reception of the fullness of Spirit, 'and were all given one Spirit to drink' (1 Cor 12:13b). Ervin, *Spirit Baptism,* 32-33. Gromacki translates 'in one Spirit,' but contra P/C scholar Ervin believes it is a reference to BHS and not conversion (initiation). See Gromacki, *The Holy Spirit,* 169. Carson favors translating the preposition ἐν according to the locative ('in one Spirit') and though the added 'into one body' is awkward in English, it is not apparent to him that this is a problem in the Greek. If the preposition ἐν is used instrumentally in 1 Cor 12:13, it is the only occasion in the NT. Carson emphasizes the repeated 'one' and not the preposition. He follows MacGorman who identifies Paul's emphasis, 'that there are no one-member churches, nor are there any every-member gifts.' Carson, *Showing of the Spirit,* 46-47. See Jack W. MacGorman, *The Gifts of the Spirit: An Exposition of 1 Corinthians 12-14* (Nashville: Broadman Press, 1974), 394. For a similar discussion on Paul's emphasis on 'one' see Moody, *Spirit of the Living God,* 97.

[236] This is Ervin's criticism of those who employ a faulty methodology which suggests that Luke understood the BHS metaphor in a manner identical with Paul. See Ervin, *Spirit Baptism,* 34-35.

[237] Carl F. H. Henry, *God, Revelation and Authority, Vol. 6* (Waco: Word Books, 1983), 385. Criswell, *The Holy Spirit in Today's World,* 99-100. Vines, *Spirit Works,* 78-9; Gromacki, *The Holy Spirit,* 169; Schreiner, *New Testament Theology,* 727-30; Carson, *Showing the Spirit,* 47; Grudem, *Systematic Theology,* 768-69; Erickson, *Christian Theology,* 1037; MacArthur, *The MacArthur New Testament Commentary: 1 Corinthians,* 312. Though Hamilton associates 1 Cor 12:13 with water baptism, he identifies Paul's emphasis 'on the Spirit's work in unifying the church.' Regarding BHS and conversion, Hamilton disagrees with the theological inferences of Dunn and Turner regarding Luke's intention to represent Spirit-baptism occurring at every conversion. See Hamilton, *God's Indwelling Presence,* 187, 193. See also Dunn, *Baptism in the Holy Spirit,* 90 and Max Turner, *The Holy Spirit and Spiritual Gifts, Revised Ed.* (Peabody: Hendrickson Publishers, 1998), 45. Garrett does not see BHS in 1 Cor 12:13. Instead, he interprets the baptism reference as 'spiritual rebirth, or Christian conversion, by the Spirit, apart from any subsequent baptism in or with the Spirit as evidenced by speaking in tongues.' Garrett offers an extensive bibliography of other non-Pentecostal Protestant commentators holding this view. See Garrett, *Systematic Theology, Vol. 2,* 167-68.

Grudem add an affective dimension to the phenomenon.[238] Grenz considers the expression 'in the Spirit' to be a reference to a radical encounter with the Holy Spirit expressed in Pauline terms as 'immersion in the Spirit.'[239] The Pentecostal 'filling of the Spirit' (Acts 2:4) produced a new corporate reality of fellowship due to everyone being given 'the one Spirit to drink' (1 Cor 12:13).[240] For Grenz, BHS and 'the filling of the Spirit' occurring on the Day of Pentecost are identical phenomena. The 'filling of the Spirit' occurring at Pentecost was an inward experience of communal obligation whereby all participated in the same spiritual reality.[241] By being joined to the community of Christ (1 Cor 12:13), Grenz infers that all believers participate in the Pentecost experience and receive the empowering endowment of the Spirit.[242] The contemporary coming of the Spirit

---

[238] Vines is typical of this position. In his view, BHS described in 1 Cor 12:13 does not include any mention of tongues or any other physical manifestation to give evidence of having received BHS. See Vines, *Spirit Works,* 79. The non-affective nature of BHS is indicated by Gromacki who notes that the positional oneness of the believer in Christ is a universal reality among believers, though many believers are experientially unaware of its occurrence. See Gromacki, *The Holy Spirit,* 167-68.

[239] Grenz, *Theology for the Community of God,* 550.

[240] Ibid., 479. Moody contextually establishes a type and antitype relationship between the exodus from Egypt (1 Cor 10:2-4) and BHS (1 Cor 12:13a). He distinguishes BHS from the filling with the Spirit described in 1 Cor 13b, 'all were given one Spirit to drink.' According to Moody, BHS is not repeated, but filling with the Spirit is. See Moody, *Spirit of the Living God,* 96.

[241] Grenz, *Theology for the Community of God,* 550. The affective nature of BHS is supported also by Criswell who attributes the lack of unity in the body of Christ to a corresponding failure to appropriate BHS. See Criswell, *The Holy Spirit in Today's World,* 97-102. Among contemporary American Baptist scholars, Piper uniquely holds that BHS is a distinct post-conversion enduement with power for Christ-exalting ministry. He bases this primarily on Luke and notes that the work of the Spirit described by Paul in 1 Cor 12:13 refers not to the Acts 2 baptism with the Spirit, but to baptism by the Spirit (conversion) and union with Christ. For Piper, Paul's reference is to a non-affective phenomenon, but Luke's reference to BHS is a gift that is knowingly received. See John Piper, 1990. 'You will be Baptized with the Holy Spirit,' n.p. Available from: http://www.desiringgod.org/resource-library/sermons/you-will-be-baptized-with-the-holy-spirit. [Accessed 20 March 2012]. Piper's view is in the tradition of fellow Gordon. See A. J. Gordon, *The Ministry of the Spirit* ([original work published 1894] Philadelphia: The Judson Press, 1950), 67-96. Schreiner agrees with Piper (and Menzies, *Empowered for Witness*) that BHS involves empowerment for ministry, but rejects the notion that the enduement occurs as a secondary spiritual experience. Schreiner, *New Testament Theology,* 454 n. 55.

[242] Ibid., 483. Grenz raises the issue of the occurrence of BHS. Specifically, is the occurrence of BHS a matter of personal reception at the moment of conversion, or corporate reception occurring historically, definitively, and completely at Pentecost? American Baptists are somewhat divided on this issue. For Grenz, BHS occurred at Pentecost and is a finished and unrepeatable reality. At the moment of conversion, all believers participate in the once-for-all occurrence of BHS at Pentecost. See Grenz, *Theology for the Community of God,* 551. See A. J. Gordon, *The Ministry of the Spirit* ([original work published 1894] Philadelphia: The Judson Press, 1950), 66-67. According to Schreiner, BHS occurred at Pentecost and post-Pentecost converts participate in the prior initiated 'new age of the Spirit.' See Schreiner, *New Testament Theology,* 454-55. Vines, contra Grenz, Gordon, and Schreiner, characterizes BHS as a personal event occurring on the occasion of one's conversion. According to Vines, 'at the moment of salvation, all

is foundational to belonging to Christ (Rom 8:9) and is the dynamic for life in the post-Pentecost era.[243] On this view, BHS is a dimension of conversion. It is a bestowment of the Spirit whereby all believers share in the new age and the blessings of the new covenant.[244] According to Grenz, there is no need to wait for or to expect any subsequent experience that mediates a greater relationship to the Spirit or a deeper experience of his power.[245]

Grudem portrays the ministry of the Spirit in terms of an old and new covenant duality. The experience of the Spirit under the old covenant was less powerful and extensive than what is anticipated under the terms of the new covenant (Num 11:29; Jer 31:31-33; Ezek 36:26-27; Joel 2:28-29).[246] JTB possessed an old covenant experience of the Spirit when he prophesied that Jesus would baptize with the Holy Spirit (Luke 3:16). Jesus received and demonstrated the new covenant power of the Spirit in his life and work (Luke 3:21-22; 4:14). Grudem associates the working of the Spirit in the life and work of Jesus as paradigmatic of those who would later receive the Spirit in new covenant power.[247] He characterizes BHS in terms of the new covenant power for ministry received by the disciples on the Day of Pentecost.[248] This Pentecostal reception of the Spirit resulted in those with a less powerful experience of the Spirit receiving a more powerful experience of the Spirit. Grudem identifies a two-fold function of BHS: power for living the Christian life and power for carrying out Christian ministry (Acts 1:8).[249]

3. Historic American Baptist Perspectives on BHS

The BHS analyses of this chapter conclude with two early and notable SBC theologians, namely Edgar Y. Mullins and Benajah H. Carroll. Due to their early and scholarly prominence in the SBC, these theologians are cited to demonstrate

---

believers are placed into the universal, invisible church, the body of Christ.' See Vines, *Spirit Works,* 78-79. See Criswell, *The Holy Spirit in Today's World,* 100.

[243] Grenz, *Theology for the Community of God,* 550.

[244] Ibid.

[245] Ibid.

[246] Grudem, *Systematic Theology,* 770.

[247] Ibid., 771.

[248] Ibid.

[249] Ibid. Grudem follows Ladd's eschatological construct. See Ladd, *A Theology of the New Testament,* 68-69.

the primary historic American Baptist BHS perspectives. John A. Broadus also represents an early American Baptist BHS perspective, but his exegesis of Matt 3:11 was relevant for inclusion above (see §2.1.1). A. H. Strong[250] is also a notable and early American Baptist theologian, but his limited treatment of BHS in his encyclopedic *Systematic Theology (1886)* is too brief for analysis in this section. Thus, Mullins and Carroll are sufficient witnesses to an early and scholarly representation of American Baptist BHS perspectives. Each becomes foundational (in varying degrees) to the later BHS doctrinal formulations detailed in the previous sections.

3.1 Edgar Y. Mullins (1860-1928)

Mullins took issue with the rhetoric and confrontational style of what he termed 'big F' fundamentalists.[251] Against what he perceived to be fundamentalist reliance on scholastic logic and syllogistic deduction as a theological method,[252] Mullins stressed an inductive approach which emphasized the major contribution of Christian experience (soul competency).[253] The 1915 edition of the *International Standard Bible Encyclopedia (ISBE)* contains an article by Mullins detailing his BHS position.[254] This article informs the presentation of Mullins' BHS position below.

Mullins frames his argument by noting BHS predictions in the four Gospels, its fulfillment described in the book of Acts and significance according to a variety of viewpoints. The BHS predictions recorded in the four Gospels (Matt 3:11; Mark 1:8; Luke 3:16; John 1:33 [7:37-39]) anticipate Luke's description of its coinciding with the events recorded in the early chapters of Acts. Luke mentions the promised BHS (Acts 1:5) in relation to the reception of the Spirit that results in power to witness for Jesus (Acts 1:8). This, coupled with Jesus' prior (partial) bestowal of the Spirit (John 20:22), suggests to Mullins that Luke is describing

---

[250] Augustus Hopkins Strong (1836-1921) was an American Baptist pastor and theologian. Strong was president of Rochester Theological Seminary (Rochester, NY).

[251] Nettles, 'E. Y. Mullins: Reluctant Evangelical,' 24.

[252] Mullins wrote an article on Christian experience in *The Fundamentals*. See E. Y. Mullins, 'The Testimony of Christian Experience,' in R. A. Torrey, A. C. Dixon, et al., eds., *The Fundamentals, Vol. 4* (Los Angeles: Bible Institute of Los Angeles, 1917), 314-23.

[253] Nettles, 'E. Y. Mullins: Reluctant Evangelical,' 24.

[254] E. Y. Mullins, 'Baptism of the Holy Spirit,' in James Orr, ed., *ISBE* (Chicago: The Howard-Severance Company, 1915), 399-401.

the fulfillment of the promised BHS.[255] Evidence of the fulfillment of BHS on the Day of Pentecost is both physical (Acts 2:2-3) and spiritual (Acts 2:4; Peter's declaration, Acts 2:16-21 [Joel 2:28-32]).[256] The significance of BHS is related by Luke who offers a variety of viewpoints. From an OT point-of-view Peter's citation of Joel suggests that the prophesied extraordinary and new manifestations of the Spirit would be accompanied by new demonstrations of power and enjoy universal diffusion among the people of God.[257] From the point-of-view of the ascended Christ, the Gospels reveal Christ as the giver of the Spirit (Luke 24:49; John 15:26; 16:13).[258] The Day of Pentecost represents an historic occasion when the Spirit takes the place of the ascended Christ and reveals the things of Christ to the disciples (John 14:16; 16:14). Mullins considers the historical importance of the Day of Pentecost to be its signaling of the arrival of the kingdom of God and formally initiating the task of global evangelization.[259] From the point-of-view of the disciples, BHS occurring at Pentecost established the church by strengthening the existing spiritual relation of Christ to his disciples.[260] According to Mullins, this was accomplished in the following ways:

1) BHS provided an internal spiritual bond for the church.

2) BHS made the church conscious of its spiritual mission.

3) BHS endued the church with power to accomplish its mission (e.g. prophecy to speak for God, the gift of tongues to speak foreign languages, power to witness for Christ, power to work miracles, and, according to the Pauline epistles, the gift of the Spirit as the sanctifying agent in the hearts of believers).[261]

Mullins considers Luke's portrayal of the arrival of the Spirit to have messianic implications. In the book of Acts the Spirit's activities are related to the extension of the messianic kingdom. The phenomena associated with the occurrence of BHS

---

[255] Ibid., 399-400.

[256] Ibid.

[257] Ibid. This is similar to Grudem's characterization of BHS. See Grudem, *Systematic Theology*, 771-72.

[258] Mullins, 'Baptism of the Holy Spirit,' 400.

[259] Ibid. This is effectively Grenz's position of corporate BHS whereby all believers participate in the experience of Pentecost. See Grenz, *Theology for the Community of God,* 550. See also A. J. Gordon, *The Ministry of the Spirit* ([original work published 1894] Philadelphia: The Judson Press, 1950), 66-67.

[260] Mullins, 'Baptism of the Holy Spirit,' 400.

[261] Ibid.

on the Day of Pentecost relate the task of world-wide evangelization to bringing in the kingdom of God.[262]

Mullins presents BHS as a once-for-all event occurring on the Day of Pentecost.[263] The Pentecost occurrence of BHS extends to the outpourings described by Luke in the early chapters of the book of Acts. Mullins limits BHS fulfillment to the initial events associated with the progress of the gospel recorded by Luke in the book of Acts. He offers the following evidence to prove that BHS is a historically fulfilled event:

1) Jesus gave a definitive prediction that BHS was a specific event and not a continuing process (Acts 1:5).

2) Peter's citation in Acts 2:17-21 is evidence that he thought the prophecy of Joel was fulfilled by the events which occurred on the Day of Pentecost.

3) The passage of Acts 10:1-11:18 is the only other NT description of the BHS event.

Mullins links the phenomena occurring among the household of Cornelius (Acts 10:1-11:18) to the initial outpouring at Pentecost. These events represent to Mullins a critical turning point in the progress of the gospel, having missionary significance and designed 'to complete the Pentecostal gift of the Spirit by showing that gentiles as well as Jews are to be embraced in all the privileges of the new dispensation.'[264]

4) The epistles do not repeat the baptism of the Spirit.

Multiple references would be expected if BHS was intended to be a repeated phenomenon among the people of God. Mullins denies that evidence exists outside the book of Acts for the occurrence of BHS in later NT times. On his view, Paul's reference to baptism in 1 Cor 12:13 refers to the water rite which initiates the candidate into the church.[265]

Mullins concludes that BHS occurring at the home of Cornelius completes its NT teaching, and all subsequent NT writings assume the presence and availability

---

[262] Ibid.

[263] Ibid., 400-401.

[264] Ibid., 401.

[265] Ibid.

of the Spirit for all believers.[266] On his view, there is one definitive, historic, and unrepeatable BHS occurring on the Day of Pentecost for the church. Post-Pentecost believers appropriate the gifts and the blessings of the Spirit which attended the once-for-all Day of Pentecost BHS event. Though not adhering to a post-conversion endowment of the Spirit, Mullins does consider the gifts and manifestations of the Spirit exhibited in the book of Acts apropos to contemporary kingdom-related activity, including the propagation of the gospel. His view makes BHS a reality for all believers and central to the mission of the church. By regarding Paul's mention of baptism in 1 Cor 12:13 as functionally distinct from the 'spiritual' baptism predicted by JTB and fulfilled in the book of Acts, Mullins interprets the text as an allusion to water baptism (Hamilton, Schreiner) which occasions the placing of believers into the body of Christ.[267] According to Mullins, the text is not a reference to a second spiritual baptism performed via the Spirit's agency, because all the texts where Paul mentions baptism are, on his view, references to water baptism (Rom 6:3; 1 Cor 1:14-17; 10:2; 12:13; 15:29; Gal 3:27; Eph 4:5; Col 2:12).[268]

3.2   Benajah H. Carroll (1843-1914)

B. H. Carroll aided in the founding of Southwestern Baptist Theological Seminary (1908) and served as its president until his death (1914).[269] A portion of a 1939 compilation of Carroll's writings, *The Holy Spirit: Comprising a Discussion of the Paraclete, the Other Self of Jesus, and Other Phases of the Work of the Spirit of God*, expresses the substance of his view on BHS.[270]

The textual focus for Carroll is Acts 2:1-4. Carroll dismisses several misapprehensions about the Pentecost event and BHS. He insists that no church or kingdom was 'established' on the Day of Pentecost. This point is central to his concept of BHS. Carroll does not mean that no church existed on the Day of Pentecost. Rather, he insists that Jesus had already established his church and

---

[266] Ibid.

[267] This is Schreiner's position. See Schreiner, *New Testament Theology*, 727.

[268] Mullins, 'Baptism of the Holy Spirit,' 402.

[269] James Spivey, 'Benajah Harvey Carroll,' in Timothy George and David S. Dockery, eds., *Theologians of the Baptist Tradition, Revised Ed.* (Nashville: B & H Publishing Group, 2001), 163-80.

[270] B. H. Carroll, *The Holy Spirit: Comprising a Discussion of the Paraclete, the Other Self of Jesus, and Other Phases of the Work of the Spirit of God* (Nashville: Broadman Press, 1939), 30-50.

completed it in his lifetime. Carroll opposes the ritual (water) baptism versus real (Spirit) baptism dichotomy; the former being external and symbolic, and the latter spiritual and antitypical. The assertion that BHS is synonymous with regeneration or conversion is a perversion of the truth, according to Carroll. He reasons that if conversion existed prior to Pentecost and BHS occurred at Pentecost, then conversion and BHS do not represent the same phenomenon. For the believer to ponder whether or not he or she has received or merits BHS is a meaningless exercise in Carroll's view. Important to Carroll is the proper understanding of NT references to the 'church' which, on his view, refer to particular local congregations. The local church is not to be confused with the completed body of Christ in heaven described in Rev 21-22. This completed body will not exist until after the final judgment.[271]

Carroll identifies Jesus as the administrator of BHS. He stipulates, however, that Jesus never baptized an 'individual' in water or in Spirit. Accordingly, BHS does not pertain to the individual, but corporately to the church occurring as an immediate event. This view describes Jesus performing BHS without means, intervention, or instrumentality on the Day of Pentecost to dispense the Spirit to occupy and authenticate the existing church as God's organization. Those not present on the Day of Pentecost receive the benefits of BHS mediately through an apostle as detailed by Luke in the book of Acts. Carroll interprets the events of Pentecost as an appointed day (e.g. the new Sabbath) when the Holy Spirit descended to occupy the established church which was built and completed previously by Jesus during his lifetime. This is the corporate and immediate nature of BHS, according to Carroll. On his view, the occurrence of BHS on the Day of Pentecost provided a replacement for Jesus (i.e. the Spirit), the One who previously occupied the church. This permits Carroll to interpret Jesus' compelling the disciples to wait (Luke 24:49) in view of the One who would come, occupy the church, and empower its mission.

The subsequent miraculous multi-lingual witness of those present on the Day of Pentecost represents a once-for-all authentication and commissioning of the church to disseminate the gospel to all nations. Carroll supports this interpretation from Paul's assessment of tongues and prophecy as limited functioning gifts (1 Cor 13:8) by which he implies the further cessation of miraculous deeds. According to Carroll, the cessation of the so-called 'miraculous gifts' eliminate the need for an on-going process of authentication for the church. He interprets 1 Cor 12:13 as a reference to a BHS that is not experienced by the individual, but corporately ('in one Spirit') as the baptism performed by Jesus on the Day of

---

[271] Ibid., 31-39.

Pentecost ('we were' not 'we are') 'for/with reference to' the church. Beyond the occurrence of BHS on the Day of Pentecost, Carroll envisions separate and further baptisms performed by Jesus; a fire-baptism occurring at the final judgment (Matt 3:11; Luke 3:16) to be followed by the baptism of the complete heavenly body (Rev 21). On his view, post-Pentecost believers participate in the effects of BHS as constituent parts of the church, though the effects of BHS differ due to the once-for-all commissioning of the church (Acts 2:1-4) and the subsequent cessation of phenomena mentioned by Paul in his definitive teaching on BHS (1 Cor 12-14).[272]

Carroll's reduction of BHS to an epochal (Day of Pentecost) event involving the exchanged places of Jesus and the Spirit leaves the baptism metaphor without interpretation unless it is understood as the means for commencing the mission of the church. The view that an already existing church is present on the Day of Pentecost is unique to Carroll's BHS apologetic. The language of conversion which normally informs American Baptist BHS constructs is noticeably absent from Carroll.

4. Conclusion

This chapter examined the NT data relating to the BHS metaphor according to the analyses of American Baptist scholars. Key BHS issues cited by American Baptists occasioned interaction with scholars outside their tradition (e.g. Turner and Menzies). This demonstrates a breadth of theological inquiry that is limited in this case to a given exegetical context (e.g. the empowerment and/or soteriological function of 'the gift of the Spirit' in Luke-Acts). The analysis provided in this chapter focused on American Baptist conceptualizations of the BHS metaphor and was not intended to be a comprehensive exegetical engagement of BHS in light of rival theological constructs. The analysis does demonstrate that a BHS theological construct which uniformly represents the American Baptist tradition has not emerged from this study. A unified view may nevertheless be adduced from the diverse American Baptist BHS perspectives presented in this chapter and may be stated as follows:

---

[272] Carroll's repeated emphasis on the role of Pentecost and BHS as an authenticating event/experience for the church recalls similar emphases by Schreiner and Hamilton. Ibid., 32-45. See Schreiner, *New Testament Theology,* 459 and Hamilton, *God's Indwelling Presence,* 191.

BHS is the eschatological work of Jesus initiated on the Day of Pentecost and completed at the home of Cornelius; whereby the gift of the Spirit unified and authenticated the body of Christ to be empowered witnesses that disseminate the gospel message to the ends of the earth.

American Baptists largely conceive of BHS in personal conversion experience terms. As such, BHS is neither a secondary post-conversion work of the Spirit, nor is it associated with the limited function of charismatic (miraculous) gifts depicted in the book of Acts and described by Paul. These delimiting features of BHS contribute to a theological impasse between American Baptists and P/C adherents. The Luke-Acts analyses of Schreiner and Hamilton, however, demonstrate that although American Baptists normally identify 'the gift of the Spirit' (BHS) theologically and in accordance with Pauline soteriological non-affective incorporation into the body of Christ function, this perspective is less dominant due to their acknowledgment of a Lukan 'empowering for service' motif. It follows that American Baptist BHS constructs are not derived out of a theological vacuum and that the burgeoning influence of various forms of P/C spirituality have served to create a constructive theological tension (dialectic) which has resulted in a moderation of American Baptist BHS views. With its emphasis on a once-for-all completed and corporate BHS event occurring on the Day of Pentecost, American Baptists are confronted with the extent to which the gift of the Spirit is evidentially expressed in post-Pentecost believers who participate in a purportedly non-repeatable event.

-5-

SPIRIT BAPTISM DOCTRINAL CONSTRUCTS WITHIN THE P/C MOVEMENT

1. Introduction

The task of this chapter is to describe the BHS doctrinal constructs which best represent the differentiated spiritual traditions of the P/C movement. The analyses consider the hermeneutical, theological, and exegetical basis for P/C doctrinal BHS formulations. BHS is universally regarded by P/C adherents as instrumental (or foundational) to spiritual experience. This investigation reveals the range of discontinuity between P/C and American Baptist perceptions of the BHS metaphor. The conclusions derived from the investigation complement the analyses of the previous chapter to further concretize the nature and extent of the theological impasse between American Baptist and P/C BHS doctrinal constructs. The overall thesis of this study is advanced by focusing consensus on doctrinal areas most critical to American Baptists.

2. Classical Pentecostalism: Two-stage Pneumatology Accompanied by Initial Evidence

2.1 Statement of the Position

Three spiritual traditions combine to represent North American classical Pentecostalism.[1] Though variously identified and individually differentiated, Keswick, Holiness, and Oneness Pentecostals represent a departure from the

---

[1] Harold D. Hunter, *Spirit-Baptism: A Pentecostal Alternative* (Lanham: University Press of America, 1983), 3-4.

unified pattern of Christian experience.[2] The unitary model of the Christian life is an all-encompassing framework which links BHS with conversion and regeneration,[3] either with or without experiential significance.[4] By contrast, classical Pentecostals make the Christian life divisible by two stages.[5] Though other groups have historically advocated pneumatological experiences subsequent to conversion and regeneration,[6] classical Pentecostals describe this experience in BHS terms[7] as a distinct work of the Spirit usually subsequent (logically or temporally/chronologically) to his prior work of regeneration, adoption, and justification.[8] In addition to its timing, the nature, purpose, and evidence of BHS represent key components for articulating the classical Pentecostal position.

2.1.1   Nature

It is important to preface this section by explaining the classical Pentecostal understanding of 'experience' according to the two-stage model of the Christian life. Christian initiation, the first stage of the Christian life, is not dependent upon experience to validate its reception.[9] The adequacy of personal experience or

---

[2] Henry I. Lederle, *Treasures Old and New: Interpretations of "Spirit-Baptism" in the Charismatic Renewal Movement* (Peabody: Hendrickson Publishers, 1988), 2.

[3] For a brief accounting of this position see Iain H. Murray, *Pentecost Today? The Biblical Basis for Understanding Revival* (Edinburgh: The Banner of Truth Trust, 1998), 112-17.

[4] Dunn refers to BHS as a definite and often dramatic experience that is decisive and climactic in conversion-initiation. See D. G. Dunn, *Baptism in the Holy Spirit: A Reexamination of the New Testament Teaching on the Gift of the Spirit in Relation to Pentecost Today* (Philadelphia: The Westminster Press, 1970), 4. Gaffin describes BHS as the 'all-comprehensive reality of the application of redemption.' BHS as the gift of the Spirit is to be distinguished from the one-time manifestation of the Pentecostal phenomena. Gaffin's use of the term 'experience' to describe BHS refers more to its objective reality than to its subjective realization. See Richard B. Gaffin, Jr., *Perspectives on Pentecost: New Testament Teaching on the Gifts of the Holy Spirit* (Phillipsburgh: Presbyterian and Reformed, 1979), 27-31.

[5] Lederle, *Treasures Old and New*, 15. Michael Green, *I Believe in the Holy Spirit* ([original work published 1975] Grand Rapids: William B. Eerdmans Publishing Company, 1977), 125-26.

[6] Lederle gives an historical excursus of four groups advocating a two-stage approach to the Christian life. Lederle, *Treasures Old and New*, 5-15.

[7] Stronstad notes the gift of the Spirit occurring on the Day of Pentecost is a complex phenomenon which 'no single term adequately denotes the meaning.' See Roger Stronstad, *The Charismatic Theology of St. Luke* ([original work published 1984] Peabody: Hendrickson Publishers, 2002), 61.

[8] Hunter, *Spirit-Baptism*, 4.

[9] Frank D. Macchia, *Baptized in the Spirit: A Global Pentecostal Theology* (Grand Rapids: Zondervan Publishing House, 2006), 153.

response of faith is not the divine standard for Christian initiation.[10] Classical Pentecostals consider BHS to be an experience-dependent threshold to the second stage of the Christian life.[11] Fee refers to classical Pentecostals as a body often charged with the practice of seeking biblical support to validate personal experience.[12] He attributes this practice to an understanding of BHS being a God-given and thoroughly life-changing experience which must reconcile with the God-given text of Scripture.[13] Atkinson rejects as a false dichotomy the 'Scripture interprets experience and not experience the Scripture' criticism of an experience-based hermeneutic.[14] Stronstad supports Atkinson's appraisal of critics by representing the Spirit as an existential and presuppositional source of both the written text of Scripture and personal spiritual experience.[15] Arrington attributes classical Pentecostal experience-based validation of truth to a relational understating of knowledge where God, rather than cognitive recognition, is the impetus behind adherence to the life-governing precepts he has given.[16] Ervin supports an experience-based hermeneutic with a pneumatic epistemology which identifies the Holy Spirit as the functional mediator between Scripture and its human reader/interpreter.[17] For some classical Pentecostals, Arrington and Ervin appear esoteric and elitist on this point.[18]

Classical Pentecostals agree that as a personally experienced reality BHS is more than the result of reasoned doctrinal affirmation; it is traceable to an identifiable, conscious and definitive moment.[19] Chan describes BHS explicitly

---

[10] Ibid.

[11] Hurst refers to BHS as a 'point of entrance into a life of Spirit-empowered witnesses for Christ.' Randy Hurst, 'Power for Purpose,' in *TPE* (June 2003), 13.

[12] Gordon D. Fee, *Gospel and Spirit: Issues in New Testament Hermeneutics* (Peabody: Hendrickson Publishers, 1991), 107. Stronstad writes, 'it is precisely here — Pentecostal experience and theology — that … Pentecostals run afoul of their critics.' Roger Stronstad, 'Pentecostal Experience and Hermeneutics,' in *Paraclete* (1992), 15.

[13] Fee, *Gospel and Spirit,* 107.

[14] William P. Atkinson, 'Worth a Second Look? Pentecostal Hermeneutics,' in *Evangel* (2003), 52.

[15] Roger Stronstad, 'Trends in Pentecostal Hermeneutics,' in *Paraclete* (1988), 6.

[16] French L. Arrington, 'Hermeneutics, Historical Perspective on Pentecostal and Charismatic,' in Stanley M. Burgess and Gary McGee, eds., *DPCM* (Grand Rapids: Zondervan Publishing House, 1988), 382.

[17] Howard M. Ervin, 'Hermeneutics: A Pentecostal Option,' in *Pneuma* (1981), 16.

[18] Gordon L. Anderson, 'Pentecostal Hermeneutics, Part 1,' in *Paraclete* (1994), 9.

[19] Keith Warrington, *Pentecostal Theology: A Theology of Encounter* (London: T & T Clark, 2008), 22; Dale Coulter, 'What Meaneth this? Pentecostals and Theological Inquiry,' in *JPT* (2001), 43; Stanley M. Horton, 'Spirit Baptism: A Pentecostal Perspective,' in Chad Owen Brand,

in terms of an overwhelmingly intense Christ-centering spiritual experience.[20] MacDonald roots classical Pentecostal theology in the perceived availability of God's preternatural power and presence.[21] He associates 'Pentecostal experience'[22] with other synonymous phenomena recorded by Luke in the book of Acts ('filled,' 'poured out,' 'received,' and 'came upon,' 2:4, 33; 10:45; 2:38; 8:17; 10:44; 11:15; 19:16).[23] Stronstad also identifies BHS in terms of an experience which restores the immediacy of God's presence by means of the outpoured Spirit of Prophecy to grant dynamism and vitality to worship.[24] Many classical Pentecostals hold that the BHS phenomena occurring on the Day of Pentecost represent the personally repeatable experience of receiving the same power possessed by Jesus during his earthly ministry.[25] The General Council of the Assemblies of God (Springfield, MO) associates the following biblical phenomena with the BHS experience:

1)   An overflowing fullness of the Spirit (John 7:37-39; Acts 4:8).

Perspectives on Spirit Baptism (Nashville: Broadman & Holman Publishers, 2004), 47-56; Koo Dong Yun, *Baptism in the Holy Spirit: An Ecumenical Theology of Spirit Baptism* (Lanham: University Press of America, 2003), 40-41.

[20] Simon Chan, 'Evidential Glossolalia and the Doctrine of Subsequence,' in *AJPS* (1999), 198. See also P. S. Brewster, *Pentecostal Doctrine* (Cheltenham: Grenehurst Press, 1976), 35 and L. Thomas Holdcroft, *The Holy Spirit: A Pentecostal Interpretation* ([original work published 1962] Springfield: Gospel Publishing House, 1992), 124.

[21] William G. MacDonald, 'Pentecostal Theology: A Classical Perspective,' in Russell P. Spittler, ed., *Perspectives on the New Pentecostalism* (Grand Rapids: Baker Book House, 1976), 62.

[22] By 'Pentecostal experience' MacDonald means the definitive experience of being Spirit-filled by the Lord which results in the Spirit articulating the praise and glory of God in another (unlearned) language. See William G. MacDonald, 'Pentecostal Theology: A Classical Perspective,' in Russell P. Spittler, ed., *Perspectives on the New Pentecostalism* (Grand Rapids: Baker Book House, 1976), 65; Howard M. Ervin, *Spirit Baptism: A Biblical Investigation* (Peabody: Hendrickson Publishers, 1987), 35.

[23] William W. Menzies and Stanley M. Horton, *Bible Doctrines: A Pentecostal Perspective* ([original work published 1993] Springfield: Logion Press, 2000), 125; Stanley M. Horton, *What the Bible Says About the Holy Spirit* ([original work published 1976] Springfield: Gospel Publishing House, 1977), 138-39; John W. Wyckoff, 'The Baptism in the Holy Spirit,' in Stanley M. Horton, ed., *Systematic Theology: A Pentecostal Perspective* (Springfield: Logion Press, 1994), 426.

[24] Roger Stronstad, 'The Prophethood of all Believers: A Study in Luke's Charismatic Theology,' in Wonsuk Ma and Robert P. Menzies, eds. *Pentecostalism in Context: Essays in Honor of William W. Menzies* ([original work published 1997] Eugene: Wipf & Stock Publishers, 2008), 75.

[25] It is not repeatable in the sense of some aspects of Pentecost unique to that day, but in the sense of being paradigmatic for the experience future believers. Carl Brumback, *What Meaneth This?* (Springfield: The Gospel Publishing House, 1947), 196; Donald Gee, *Wind and Flame* (Croydon: Heath Press, Ltd., 1967), 7; MacDonald, 'Pentecostal Theology: A Classical Perspective,' 59. Brumback, *What Meaneth This?*, 197.

2) A deepened reverence for God (Acts 2:43; Heb 12:28).

3) An intensified consecration to God and dedication to his work (Acts 2:42).

4) A more active love for Christ, for his Word and for the lost (Mark 16:20).[26]

Classical Pentecostals also emphasize the individuality of the 'Pentecostal experience.'[27] The water rite of JTB from which the BHS metaphor derives its meaning (Matt 3:11; Mark 1:8; Luke 3:16; John 1:33) demonstrates baptism as administered to individuals.[28] When the verb βαπτίζω is translated as 'to dip, or immerse,'[29] the corresponding mode connotes being enveloped by (or saturated with) the Spirit who, being the medium, subjects the yielded believer to his influence.[30] The emphasis on individual experience does not preclude consideration for the corporate implications of BHS. Faupel identifies Pentecostalism with the latter day outpouring of the Spirit and the corporate missional enterprise of the end-time movement.[31] Macchia agrees[32] but centers BHS on personal realization.[33] In summary, BHS is a definitive personal experience traceable to a precise moment which parallels the disciples' experience on the Day of Pentecost.[34]

---

[26] Assemblies of God USA, 2010, 'Our 16 Fundamental Truths,' n.p. Available from: http://ag. org/top/Beliefs/Statement_of_Fundamental_Truths/sft_full.cfm#8. (Accessed: 17 April 2012). MacDonald provides a similar listing of internal and external BHS results. See MacDonald, 'Pentecostal Theology: A Classical Perspective,' 66. See also Holdcroft, *The Holy Spirit*, 114-15.

[27] J. J. McNamee, *The Role of the Spirit in Pentecostalism: A Comparative Study* (PhD diss., Eberhard Karls University, 1974), 46.

[28] Horton, *What the Bible Says About the Holy Spirit*, 139.

[29] G. Abbott-Smith, *A Manual Greek Lexicon of the New Testament* ([original work published 1921] Edinburgh: T & T Clark, 1964), 74.

[30] Holdcroft, *The Holy Spirit*, 107; Frank Holder, *The Holy Spirit* (Kisumu: Evangel Publishing House, 1966), 9.

[31] D. William Faupel, 'The Everlasting Gospel: The Significance of Eschatology in the Development of Pentecostal Thought' (PhD diss., University of Birmingham, 1989), 62-70.

[32] Brewster, *Pentecostal Doctrine*, 28.

[33] Macchia, *Baptized in the Spirit*, 40-41.

[34] Yun, *Baptism in the Holy Spirit*, 30; Ernest S. Williams, *Systematic Theology, Vol. 3* ([original work published 1953] Springfield: Gospel Publishing House, 1991), 42.

2.1.2   Purpose

A brief explanation of classical Pentecostal spirituality relative to BHS is necessary in order to summarize elements mentioned previously in this work. Classical Pentecostals derive the purpose for BHS from interpreting Luke's Pentecost narrative as the charismatic Christ dispensing the gift of the Spirit (BHS) to launch the mission of the disciples.[35] Reliance on Luke includes the 'Spirit of prophecy/inspired witnesses' motif.[36] BHS results in the formation of a prophetic community of witnesses who become powerful in words and works (Acts 1:5, 8; 2:4).[37] Gee, alluding to the Holiness roots of Pentecostal origins, cautions that spiritual gifts are not a sign of holiness and that BHS does not guarantee sinless perfection.[38] It follows then, that classical Pentecostals regard BHS to be more about power than purity. The prophetic vocation of the disciples is patterned after the 'Spirit-anointed, Spirit-full (-filled), Spirit-led and Spirit-empowered ministry of Jesus' who performed miracles, signs, and wonders (Luke 24:19; Acts 2:22, 43; 3:1-10; 5:12; 6:8; 8:6, 13; 14:3, 8-12; 15:12; 19:11).[39] As stated by Jesus (Luke 24:49; Acts 1:8), BHS is primarily an endowment with power for service that consists of a release of the Spirit in life to enable the disciples to accomplish their global evangelistic mission.[40] BHS is also co-extensive in that it permits Spirit-full/filled agents to spread the gospel and to dispense the gift of the prophetic Spirit to new followers of Christ (Acts 8:15-17; 10:44-48; 11:15-17; 19:6).[41] Another purpose of BHS is evident from its role in the communal life of the believer. That is, BHS produces a mode of worship which permits the exercise of the *charismata* in order to bless the larger assembly while

---

[35] Stronstad, *The Charismatic Theology of St. Luke*, 62.

[36] Macchia, *Baptized in the Spirit*, 153; Wyckoff, 'The Baptism in the Holy Spirit,' 447. Stronstad, 'The Prophethood of all Believers,' 121; James B. Shelton, *Mighty in Word and Deed: The Role of the Holy Spirit in Luke-Acts* ([previous work published 1991] Eugene: Wipf & Stock Publishers, 1999), 144-48.

[37] Stronstad, 'The Prophethood of all Believers,' 121; Horton, 'Spirit Baptism,' 78-83.

[38] McNamee, *The Role of the Spirit in Pentecostalism*, 71.

[39] Stronstad, 'The Prophethood of all Believers,' 118; Roger Stronstad, 'The Holy Spirit in Luke-Acts,' in *Paraclete* (1989), 26.

[40] Brumback notes that enduement for power is the primary, and not the only, purpose for BHS. See Brumback, *What Meaneth This?*, 197. See also Myer Pearlman, *Knowing the Doctrines of the Bible* (Springfield: Gospel Publishing House, 1937), 309; Robert P. Menzies, 'The Distinctive Character of Luke's Pneumatology,' in *Paraclete* (1991), 18; Macchia, *Baptized in the Spirit*, 153; Brewster, *Pentecostal Doctrine*, 30-32; Holdcroft, *The Holy Spirit*, 124; Fee, *Gospel and Spirit*, 107; Wyckoff, 'The Baptism in the Holy Spirit,' 448. Ervin notes the progress of the gospel is outlined in Acts 1:8 and is indicative of world evangelization. See Ervin, *Spirit Baptism*, 38.

[41] Stronstad, 'The Prophethood of all Believers,' 119-120.

engendering a deepened sense of love for God, his Word, one another, and for non-Christians (Acts 2:42, 46-47).[42]

2.1.3   Initial Evidence

The doctrine of 'initial evidence'[43] emphasizes the need for an immediate indication of BHS reception and represents the primary doctrinal distinctive of classical Pentecostalism.[44] Classical Pentecostals maintain that the gift of the Spirit (BHS) received by the earliest disciples was marked by observable physical manifestations (Acts 2:33).[45] Reliance upon the book of Acts not only gives the doctrine historical precedent, but also theologically and hermeneutically justifies the normativity of the evidence for the church of all ages.[46] The most common and persistent evidence associated with BHS reception in the book of Acts (implicitly or explicitly) is 'speaking in tongues' (Acts 2:4; 10:44; 19:6).[47] This observation has led classical Pentecostals to conclude that the phenomenon of

---

[42] Menzies and Horton, *Bible Doctrines*, 126.

[43] The doctrine of 'initial evidence' is predominately an American Pentecostal teaching. Lederle, *Treasures Old and New*, 15-32.

[44] Holdcroft, *The Holy Spirit*, 122. Tracing the classical Pentecostal doctrine of initial evidence to Charles F. Parham, McGee observes that the doctrine accomplished more than providing a theological foundation for the movement; it differentiated Pentecostalism from Wesleyan and Keswick rival groups which also accentuated the Spirit-filled life. See McGee, 'Initial Evidence,' 790. See also Frederick Dale Bruner, *A Theology of the Holy Spirit: The Pentecostal Experience and the New Testament Witness* (London: Hodder and Stoughton, 1970), 76. Use of the term 'evidence' is debated among classical Pentecostals with some opting for 'provision' or 'sign' as a means of avoiding modernistic (positivistic) formalistic proofs. See Jack W. Hayford, *The Beauty of Spiritual Language: Unveiling the Mystery of Speaking in Tongues* (Nashville: Thomas Nelson Publishers, 1996), 95-98; Frank D. Macchia, 'Groans too Deep for Words: Toward a Theology of Tongues as Initial Evidence,' in *AJPS* (1998), 3; Gary B. McGee, 'Initial Evidence,' in Stanley M. Burgess and Eduard M. Van Der Maas, eds., *NIDPCM* (Grand Rapids: Zondervan, 2002), 784; See also Yun, *Baptism in the Holy Spirit*, 34-37.

[45] Gee, *Wind and Flame*, 7.

[46] Menzies and Horton, *Bible Doctrines*, 135; Yun, *Baptism in the Holy Spirit*, 32-33. MacDonald, 'Pentecostal Theology,' 65; Wyckoff, 'The Baptism in the Spirit,' 441.

[47] Classical Pentecostals believe 'tongues' is implied by Luke elsewhere in the book of Acts where it is not directly stated in cases of initial evidence for BHS (see Acts 8:4-24). See Wyckoff, 'The Baptism in the Spirit,' 441; Ervin, *Spirit Baptism*, 74; Yun, *Baptism in the Holy Spirit*, 33; Menzies and Horton, *Bible Doctrines*, 137. Petts provides a useful table which summarizes the biblical data supporting the classical Pentecostal BHS view and its corresponding doctrine of initial (physical) evidence. See David Petts, 'The Baptism in the Holy Spirit: The Theological Distinctive,' in Keith Warrington, ed., *Pentecostal Perspectives* (Carlisle: Paternoster Press, 1998), 118; Gee, *Wind and Flame*, 7; Wyckoff, 'The Baptism in the Spirit,' 440. Ervin, *Spirit Baptism*, 79; Ralph M. Riggs, *The Spirit Himself* (Springfield: Gospel Publishing House, 1949), 87; Horton, *What the Bible Says About the Holy Spirit*, 157.

'speaking with tongues' is the scriptural evidence of BHS.[48] This conclusion is formally acknowledged by the AG denomination in its *16 Fundamental Truths*.[49] This is not to suggest that classical Pentecostals uniformly agree on which evidence constitutes BHS reception. It merely demonstrates that the 'tongues as initial evidence' position is adopted by the majority of classical Pentecostals in the USA.[50]

The expression 'speaking in tongues' (glossolalia) identifies the biblical phenomenon believed by classical Pentecostals to constitute the initial evidence of BHS. The nature of the phenomenon is determined according to its initial occurrence on the Day of Pentecost (Acts 2:4).[51] Most classical Pentecostals agree that glossolalia in this context refers to the Spirit-aided ability to speak a foreign language previously unknown to the tongues-speaker.[52] Strictly speaking, use of the term 'glossolalia' does not have biblical support. Rather, the expression has become the technical equivalent for the Pentecostal phenomenon. Classical Pentecostals consider glossolalia to be intelligible and communicative speech that is capable of interpretation, whether of earthly or extraterrestrial origin (Acts 2:8, 11; 10:46; 1 Cor 14:15; 13:1).[53] The phenomenon of tongues-speech occurring on

---

[48] McNamee, *The Role of the Spirit in Pentecostalism*, 50-51.

[49] The eighth fundamental truth, 'The Initial Physical Evidence of the Baptism in the Holy Spirit,' states: 'The baptism of believers in the Holy Spirit is witnessed by the initial physical sign of speaking in tongues as the Spirit of God gives them utterance (Acts 2:4).' See Assemblies of God USA, 2010, 'Our 16 Fundamental Truths,' n.p. Available from: http://ag. org/top/Beliefs/Statement _of_ Fundamental_Truths/sft_full.cfm#8. (Accessed: 24 April 2012).

[50] Tongues as evidence of initial BHS reception is a predominately USA-based Pentecostal doctrinal affirmation. See Alan Anderson, *An Introduction to Pentecostalism* (Cambridge: Cambridge University Press, 2004), 10. See also Petts, 'The Baptism in the Holy Spirit,' 99. For a contrasting viewpoint, see Larry W. Hurtado, 'Normal, but not the Norm: "Initial Evidence" and the New Testament,' in Gary B. McGee, ed., *Initial Evidence: Historical and Biblical Perspectives on the Pentecostal Doctrine of Spirit Baptism* (Peabody: Hendrickson Publishers, 1991), 199-200. For a brief summary of Pentecostal Statements of Faith see Walter J. Hollenweger, *The Pentecostals: The Charismatic Movement in the Churches* (Minneapolis: Augsburg Publishing House, 1972), 513-22.

[51] Holdcroft, *The Holy Spirit*, 121.

[52] Menzies and Horton, *Bible Doctrines*, 136; Brumback, *What Meaneth This?*, 198; Holdcroft, *The Holy Spirit*, 121. Though no longer conceived as such, early American Pentecostalism considered the speaking in tongues phenomenon as 'divinely granted xenoglossic tongues to facilitate the transmission of the gospel.' On the basis of reports from missionary activities, Charles Parham concluded that this language gift was dispensed by God as part of a worldwide revival. See James R. Goff, Jr., 'Initial Tongues in the Theology of Charles Fox Parham,' in Gary B. McGee, ed., *Initial Evidence: Historical and Biblical Perspectives on the Pentecostal Doctrine of Spirit Baptism* (Peabody: Hendrickson Publishers, 1991), 64; Warrington, *Pentecostal Theology*, 92.

[53] Holdcroft, *The Holy Spirit*, 121. William G. MacDonald, *Glossolalia in the New Testament* (Springfield: Gospel Publishing House, 1964), 4. Menzies refers to 'inspired speech' as both intelligible and unintelligible. The appearance of 'speaking in tongues' (ἐλάλουν τε

the Day of Pentecost involved fifteen distinct foreign language dialects and is likely to be an incidence of xenolalia.[54] Classical Pentecostals further distinguish the Spirit-induced glossolalia/xenolalia occurring on the Day of Pentecost from the Pauline 'gift of tongues' charism imparted permanently to the believer and subject to his/her control.[55] On this view, the former phenomenon (glossolalia) is intended for the universal and evidential experience of every BHS recipient, while the latter charism is given to some Christians for personal benefit in order to serve the communal function of building up the body of Christ (1 Cor 12:4-10, 28).[56] Another classical Pentecostal perspective is that all who experience BHS receive the gift of tongues for personal use (1 Cor 14:5, 28), but only some have the capacity to exercise the gift publicly (1 Cor 12:30).[57]

The analysis of this section permits the succinct statement of the classical Pentecostal BHS position: BHS is the personal realization of an intense experience of the Spirit of God, whereby the Christian is specially empowered for prophetic vocation (inspired words and supernatural deeds)[58] that is consistent with the ministry of Jesus and marked by speaking in tongues to validate its reception.

2.2 *The Classical Pentecostal BHS Apologetic*

The classical Pentecostal BHS apologetic attempts to validate biblically a distinct experience of the Spirit separate from regeneration. In order to establish

---

γλώσσαις) in Acts 19:6 denotes unintelligible inspired speech whereas the attending verb ἐπροφήτευον ('prophesying') 'may imply that forms of inspired speech (intelligible) accompanied the manifestation of tongues-speech.' See Robert P. Menzies, *The Development of Early Christian Pneumatology with Special Reference to Luke-Acts* (Sheffield: Sheffield Academic Press, 1991), 276 n. 2. See also William W. Menzies and Robert P. Menzies, *Spirit and Power: Foundations of Pentecostal Experience* (Grand Rapids: Zondervan, 2000), 126.

[54] The mention of the crowd 'hearing' their native dialects in Acts 2:6, 8, 11 is not understood as the miracle, but rather the ones speaking under the influence of the Spirit. Anthony D. Palma, *The Holy Spirit: A Pentecostal Perspective* (Springfield: Gospel Publishing House, 2001), 143. Spittler defines 'xenolalia' as an incidence of glossolalia 'when the language spoken is identifiable as one among the over 3,000 known to occur on the globe.' See Spittler, 'Glossolalia,' 670.

[55] Williams, *Systematic Theology, Vol. 3,* 48; D. W. Kerr, 'Not Ashamed,' in *Pentecostal Evangel* (April 1921), 5.

[56] Yun, *Baptism in the Holy Spirit,* 32; Warrington, *Pentecostal Theology,* 89.

[57] Menzies and Menzies, *Spirit and Power,* 133-44; Warrington, *Pentecostal Theology,* 123.

[58] See §2.2.1.2.1 where Menzies includes 'special insight.' Menzies, *The Development of Early Christian Pneumatology with Special Reference to Luke-Acts,* 122.

a two-stage pneumatology[59] classical Pentecostals rely on Luke to demonstrate the following phenomena: that BHS is a missiologically necessary enduement of the Spirit for Christians and that a delay exists between the regenerating work of the Spirit and the reception/gift of the Spirit (BHS).[60] Classical Pentecostals are divided over the exegetical and hermeneutical model to construct the BHS apologetic. Contributing to the division is a BHS apologetic which historically evolved from the simple (unscientific/pragmatic) 'Pentecost as Pattern' hermeneutic to more complex exegetical models advanced in recent decades.[61] The division queries whether or not the five historical accounts recorded by Luke in the book of Acts were intended to function normatively as a biblical precedent for future Christians. Those answering in the affirmative adduce that a programmatic pattern exists as evidenced by these passages which substantiate a chronological-temporal delay between regeneration and BHS reception (i.e. a doctrine of subsequence).[62] Classical Pentecostals favoring this position defend BHS as a separate missiological function of the Spirit in the life of the Christian that occurs logically subsequent to regeneration.[63] Others, unconvinced that attesting a doctrine of subsequence and separability on the sole basis of biblical precedent is sufficient, argue that the aforementioned Acts passages focus theologically on Luke's pneumatological intention (e.g. Menzies, Shelton, and Stronstad). This theological focus conccives BHS to be a work of the Spirit definitively separate from regeneration. A further divisive issue concerns the normative value of historical portions of Scripture, including the book of Acts. Menzies considers the crucial center of the evolving classical Pentecostal BHS apologetic to be exegesis-oriented. It aims at discerning Luke's unique pneumatological perspective, rather than invoking the historical precedent hermeneutic.[64]

---

[59] Menzies does present Lukan pneumatology in a way that attributes conversion to the work of the Spirit, though he acknowledges that BHS occurs subsequent to and separate from conversion. With this qualification, Menzies identifies Luke's pneumatology as single-stage. See Menzies and Menzies, *Spirit and Power*, 125. See also Menzies, *The Development of Early Christian Pneumatology with Special Reference to Luke-Acts*, 114-34.

[60] Petts, 'The Baptism in the Holy Spirit,' 100.

[61] The applied label is used by Stronstad to designate the earliest hermeneutic for BHS adopted by classical Pentecostals. It assumes a self-evident and self-authenticating transferability of Acts events to contemporary experience. Stronstad, 'Trends in Pentecostal Hermeneutics,' 3.This pragmatic hermeneutic was later advanced by Brumback. See Carl Brumback, *What Meaneth This? A Pentecostal Answer to a Pentecostal Question* (Springfield: Gospel Publishing House, 1947).

[62] Holdcroft, *The Holy Spirit*, 110-12.

[63] Yun, *Baptism in the Holy Spirit*, 39.

[64] Menzies and Menzies, *Spirit and Power*, 118.

2.2.1 Subsequence and Separability

2.2.1.1 The Evolving Classical Pentecostal Hermeneutic

As intimated above, the classical Pentecostal BHS apologetic centers on five historical events recorded by Luke in the book of Acts (2:1-13; 8:14-19; 9:17-18; 10:44-46; 19:1-7).[65] Critics of a narrative-based hermeneutical method argue that didactically intended Scripture is preferred over the historical portions of Scripture in order to determine normative experience.[66] In reply, classical Pentecostal apologists state that Luke's historical discernment represents clear didactic and pastoral purpose.[67] This hermeneutical challenge is posed even by those within the classical Pentecostal camp[68] and has given rise to more robust exegetical interpretations of relevant Acts texts in the light of a developed Lukan pneumatological perspective.[69] Succinctly stated, classical Pentecostals minimize

[65] Stronstad, *The Charismatic Theology of Luke,* 5.

[66] While not denying value to the narrative and descriptive passages in the Bible, Stott assigns normative value to didactic Scripture. See John R. W. Stott, *Baptism & Fullness: The Word of the Holy Spirit Today, 2nd Ed.* (Downers Grove: InterVarsity Press, 1975), 15.

[67] Atkinson, 'Worth a Second Look? Pentecostal Hermeneutics,' 51. Atkinson is supported by numerous works detailing the theological character of Luke's writings. Hans Conzelmann, Trans. Geoffrey Buswell, *The Theology of St. Luke* (ET New York: Harper & Row, 1961); J. C. O'Neill, *The Theology of Acts in its Historical Settings* (London: S.P.C.K., 1961); I. Howard Marshall, *Luke: Historian and Theologian* (Grand Rapids: Zondervan Publishing House, 1971); Joseph A. Fitzmyer, *Luke the Theologian: Aspects of His Teaching* (New York: Paulist Press, 1989); Joel B. Green, *The Theology of the Gospel of Luke* (Cambridge: Cambridge University Press, 1995); Jacob Jervell, *The Theology of the Acts of the Apostles* (Cambridge: Cambridge University Press, 1996); I. Howard Marshall and David Peterson, eds., *Witness to the Gospel: The Theology of Acts* (Grand Rapids: William B. Eerdmans Publishing, 1998); François Bovon, *Luke the Theologian, Revised 2nd Ed.* (Waco: Baylor University Press, 2006).

[68] Dayton refers to the traditional classical Pentecostal insistence on general patterns observed from the book of Acts as a 'subjectivizing hermeneutic.' See Donald W. Dayton, *The Theological Roots of Pentecostalism* ([original work published 1987] Peabody: Hendrickson Publishers, 2000), 23. Fee has opposed this hermeneutic which in his view derives normative experience from narrative and historical biblical genre. See Gordon D. Fee, 'Hermeneutics and Historical Precedent: A Major Problem in Pentecostal Hermeneutics,' in Russell P. Spittler, *Perspectives on the New Pentecostalism* (Grand Rapids: Baker Book House, 1976), 118-32. Stronstad rejects the 'didactic' versus 'descriptive' (narrative) dichotomy in favor of a developed Lukan historiography. The episodes recorded by Luke have historical-theological intent. See Stronstad, *The Charismatic Theology of St. Luke,* 9. William W. and Robert P. Menzies engage Fee's thesis in *Spirit and Power,* 109-19.

[69] William P. Atkinson, *Baptism in the Spirit: Luke-Acts and the Dunn Debate* (Eugene: Pickwick Publications, 2011); Frank D. Macchia, *Baptized in the Spirit: A Global Pentecostal Theology* (Grand Rapids: Zondervan Publishing House, 2006), 153; Roger Stronstad, *The Prophethood of All Believers: A Study in Luke's Charismatic Theology* ([original work published 1999] Sheffield: Sheffield Academic Press, 2003) and *The Charismatic Theology of St. Luke* ([original work published 1984] Peabody: Hendrickson Publishers, 2002); James B. Shelton, *Mighty in Word and Deed: The Role of the Holy Spirit in Luke-Acts* ([previous work published 1991]

the historical uniqueness of the Acts narratives while maximizing their theological character.[70] Since the locus of the hermeneutical landscape has shifted from biblical precedent to Luke's pneumatological perspective as historian-theologian, the following investigation of the Luke-Acts data will focus on the classical Pentecostal 'subsequence and separability apologetic' accordingly.[71]

2.2.1.2   The Paradigmatic Value of Jesus' Jordan Experience

As a precursor to conclusions drawn from specific events detailed by Luke in the book of Acts, some classical Pentecostals connect the pneumatic experiences of Jesus (i.e. infancy and inauguration)[72] with the gift of the Spirit occurring on the Day of Pentecost.[73] The case for the doctrine of subsequence and separability

---

Eugene: Wipf & Stock Publishers, 1999); Robert P. Menzies, *The Development of Early Christian Pneumatology with Special Reference to Luke-Acts* (Sheffield: Sheffield Academic Press, 1991) and *Empowered for Witness: The Holy Spirit in Luke-Acts* (Sheffield: Sheffield Academic Press, 1994); William W. Menzies and Robert P. Menzies, *Spirit and Power: Foundations of Pentecostal Experience* (Grand Rapids: Zondervan, 2000); Howard M. Ervin, *Conversion-Initiation and the Baptism in the Holy Spirit* (Peabody: Hendrickson Publishers, 1984) and *Spirit Baptism: A Biblical Investigation* ([originally published as *These Are Not Drunken As Ye Suppose* (Plainfield: Logos International, 1968)] Peabody: Hendrickson Publishers, 1987).

[70] Stronstad, *The Charismatic Theology of Luke*, 5. Holdcroft considers the entire NT relevant for establishing the Christian church theologically and experientially. See Holdcroft, *The Holy Spirit*, 110.

[71] The issue of 'subsequence' initially taken up by P/C scholars such as Stronstad and Menzies intended to provide an exegetical defense to Dunn and Bruner. See James D. G. Dunn, *Baptism in the Holy Spirit: A Reexamination of the New Testament Teaching on the Gift of the Spirit in Relation to Pentecost Today* (Philadelphia: The Westminster Press, 1970) and Frederick Dale Bruner, *A Theology of the Holy Spirit: The Pentecostal Experience and the New Testament Witness* (London: Hodder and Stoughton, 1970). For a discussion of Pentecostal alternatives to Dunn, see William P. Atkinson, *Baptism in the Spirit: Luke-Acts and the Dunn Debate* (Eugene: Pickwick Publications, 2011), 66-91. Common to Stronstad and Menzies is their shift from 'subsequence' to a theological and exegetical distinction between the Pauline pre-faith 'salvific' (soteriological) Spirit-reception and the Lukan post-faith empowering of the (prophetic) Spirit. Stronstad proposes adding Lukan charismatic theology to [e.g. Reformed and Wesleyan] initiation-conversion and holiness experiences of the Spirit. See Roger Stronstad, *The Charismatic Theology of St. Luke* ([original work published 1984] Peabody: Hendrickson Publishers, 2002), 75-83. On the 'prophetic' character of Spirit-reception, see Roger Stronstad, *The Prophethood of all Believers: A Study of Luke's Charismatic Theology* ([original work published in 1999] Sheffield: Sheffield Academic Press, 2003), 114-24. See also Robert P. Menzies, *The Development of Early Christian Pneumatology with Special Reference to Luke-Acts* (Sheffield: Sheffield Academic Press, 1991), 316-18 and Robert P. Menzies, *Empowered for Witness: The Spirit in Luke-Acts* ([original work published in 1991] Sheffield: Sheffield Academic Press, 1994), 256-57.

[72] These terms are used to differentiate the pneumatic significance of two events occurring in the life of Jesus. See Stronstad, *The Charismatic Theology of St. Luke*, 33-46.

[73] French L. Arrington, *The Acts of the Apostles: Introduction, Translation, and Commentary* (Peabody: Hendrickson Publishers, 1988), 19; Shelton, *Mighty in Word and Deed*, 53.

is made theologically prior to the Day of Pentecost event. That is, Luke's pneumatological perspective of the Spirit is adduced primarily from the infancy and inauguration narratives and then inserted into the relevant BHS events in the book of Acts. Therefore, the case for subsequence is not one of establishing biblical precedent but one of determining Luke's unique pneumatology.

The gospel writers uniformly identify Jesus as the agent of BHS (Matt 3:11; Mark 1:8; Luke 3:16; John 1:33). Whatever JTB intended by the added καὶ πυρί ('and fire') in Matt 3:11 and Luke 3:16, the BHS logion is interpreted by Jesus as a reference to Pentecost (Luke 3:16; Acts 1:5; 11:16). Identifying Jesus as the agent of BHS is closely associated with his personal pneumatic experience (John 1:33). Luke used the phrase 'Spirit of Jesus' (Acts 16:7) to indicate that the Spirit who anointed Jesus (Luke 3:22; Acts 10:38) is the same Spirit poured out by Jesus upon his disciples (Acts 2:33).[74] This raises the issue of how the pneumatic experiences of Jesus connect to the pneumatic experience of the disciples, specifically as Jesus' personal anointing relates to the BHS experience. Classical Pentecostals argue that the correspondence of the pneumatic experiences of Jesus (infancy and inauguration) to those of his disciples is both analogous and paradigmatic.[75] This makes understanding Luke's depiction of Jesus' anointing (Luke 3:22; Acts 10:38) the chief exegetical task in determining how his pneumatic experience supports the classical Pentecostal doctrine of subsequence and separability.[76] Two facets of this investigation are significant for understanding the classical Pentecostal position. The first facet involves the chronology of Jesus' Spirit-reception[77] and the epochal nature of pneumatic activity recorded by Luke in the infancy narrative (Luke 1:5-2:52). The second facet concerns the role of the Spirit in Jesus' anointing at his inauguration (baptism) and its paradigmatic relevance to the Christian experience of BHS.

---

[74] Hunter, *Spirit-Baptism*, 72.

[75] Shelton, *Mighty in Word and Deed*, 53; Stronstad, *The Charismatic Theology of St. Luke*, 79.

[76] Hunter, *Spirit-Baptism*, 72.

[77] Use of the term 'reception' is not to obscure the ontological relationship of Christ and the Spirit, but to identify in a temporal sense the occasion of pneumatic activity experienced by Jesus.

2.2.1.2.1   *The Significance of Epochal Pneumatic Activity in the Infancy Narrative (Luke 1:5-2:52)*

Classical Pentecostals deriving their BHS model from Luke-Acts and consider the dual pneumatic experiences of Jesus (i.e. his conception and empowerment for ministry) to correspond normatively to the two-stage pneumatic experience of the believer. The theological implication is that by temporally separating the pneumatic experiences of Jesus, a pattern is established to justify the separation of regeneration and later charismatic experience (BHS).[78] Classical Pentecostals are aware of pressing the analogy to the point of improperly deducing a faulty Christology.[79] The misapplied parallel of the birth of Christ to the rebirth of Christians is resolved by attributing Christ's birth and Christian rebirth to a common work of the Spirit.[80]

Other classical Pentecostals, emphasizing the unique nature of Jesus' ontological and Messianic role, point to Mary's conception of Jesus by 'the overshadowing of the divine presence' (Luke 1:35). The phenomenon is understood in new creation terms and is reminiscent of the hovering Spirit at creation (Gen 1:2).[81] This initial experience of the Spirit by Jesus is recorded by Luke (and Matthew [1:19-20])[82] in the infancy narrative (Luke 1:5-2:52 [1:35]). At his baptism, Jesus is anointed for ministry and experiences a new and distinct

---

[78] Hunter, *Spirit-Baptism,* 74. Not all classical Pentecostals consider the role of the Spirit 'necessary' to the performance of miraculous works by Jesus. Warrington argues for the affirming role of the Spirit 'to formalize the role of Jesus, not to facilitate his supernatural ministry.' See Keith Warrington, *Jesus the Healer: Paradigm of Unique Phenomenon?* (Carlisle: Paternoster Press, 2000), 158. Menzies thesis on Lukan pneumatology does not include attributing miraculous power or soteriological function to the Spirit. See Menzies, *The Development of Early Christian Pneumatology with Special Reference to Luke-Acts,* 114-34.

[79] Bruner is critical of classical Pentecostals who associate personal conversion with the virgin birth of Jesus in order to justify subsequence on the basis of Jesus' Jordan experience of the Spirit. See Bruner, *A Theology of the Holy Spirit,* 221-22.

[80] Hunter, *Spirit-Baptism,* 74. Smail identifies Reformed sources advocating a similar position. See Thomas A. Smail, *Reflected Glory: The Spirit in Christ and Christians* (London: Hodder and Stoughton, 1975), 82. See also Edwyn Clement Hoskyns and Francis Noel Davey, *The Fourth Gospel, 2nd Ed.* (London: Faber & Faber, 1956), 164-65; Karl Barth, Trans. Gabriel Vahanian, *The Faith of the Church: A Commentary on the Apostle's Creed According to Calvin's Catechism* (ET London: Fontana Books, 1960), 107-8.

[81] Stronstad, *The Charismatic Theology of St. Luke,* 37.

[82] Luke modified the Matthean tradition which described the role of the Spirit in more graphic and biological terms in order to downplay the contrast of 'creative' versus 'prophetic' understanding of the Spirit. See Menzies, *The Development of Early Christian Pneumatology with Special Reference to Luke-Acts,* 127.

relationship with the Spirit (Luke 3:22; 4:18; Acts 10:38).[83] This uniquely experienced pneumatic activity differs from other charismatic experiences recorded by Luke in the infancy narrative (e.g. JTB, Elizabeth, and Zacharias are filled with the Spirit [prophetic inspiration], 1:15; 1:42-45; 1:67-79).[84] Stronstad identifies typological, programmatic, and paradigmatic elements in the infancy narrative, especially as it relates to JTB and Jesus (1:15, 76; 1:32, 35).[85] He considers the manifestation of the creative power of the Spirit evident in Mary's conception of Jesus a unique creative event but having broad epochal significance.[86] According to Luke, this unique creative event occurs distinctly within an epoch containing a programmatic 'nexus of pneumatic activity,'[87] beginning with the gift of the Spirit received by the disciples on the Day of Pentecost (Acts 2:4).[88] In this case, subsequence and separability are maintained on the basis of the Spirit's epochal function and not according to Jesus' unique pneumatic experience. Warrington points out that Luke 1:35 is a motif of 'presence' (intended affirmation) rather than 'power.'[89] This distinction is supported on two grounds. The first is articulated by Atkinson who argues, contra Turner, that the term 'reception' is an inaccurate depiction of the pneumatic activity resulting in the conception of Jesus.[90] The pre-Jordan references to Jesus as 'the Christ' (Luke 2:11, 26) are proleptic of his later 'reception' of the Spirit (Luke 3:22).[91] This present action of the Spirit (Luke 1:35) is upon Mary and not Jesus.[92] The second is presented by Menzies who (with Stronstad) is less

---

[83] Roger Stronstad, *The Prophethood of All Believers: A Study in Luke's Charismatic Theology* ([original work published 1999] Sheffield: Sheffield Academic Press, 2003), 41.

[84] Stronstad, *The Charismatic Theology of St. Luke,* 37-38.

[85] Ibid., 38. Menzies raises the JTB-Jesus typological connection to explain the structure of Luke's narrative and his inclusion of 'the tradition concerning the Spirit's creative role in Jesus' conception. See Menzies, *The Development of Early Christian Pneumatology with Special Reference to Luke-Acts*, 123. Atkinson considers the JTB-Jesus typology indicative of Jesus' superiority to JTB. See Atkinson, *Baptism in the Spirit*, 81 n. 71.

[86] Stronstad, *The Charismatic Theology of St. Luke,* 37-38.

[87] Stronstad attributes the expression to Turner. See Max Turner, *Power from on High: The Spirit in Israel's Restoration and Witness in Luke-Acts* ([original work published 1996] Sheffield: Sheffield Academic Press, 2000), 199.

[88] Stronstad, *The Charismatic Theology of St. Luke*, 39.

[89] Warrington, *Jesus the Healer,* 154.

[90] Turner writes, 'Jesus had already received the Spirit in some fundamental way in Luke 1:35'; Turner, *Power from on High,* 434. See also Max Turner, *The Holy Spirit and Spiritual Gifts* ([original work published 1996] Peabody: Hendrickson Publishers, 1998), 154.

[91] Atkinson, *Baptism in the Spirit,* 81.

[92] Atkinson understands Luke to be avoiding *pneuma* (S/spirit) terminology in the case of Jesus in the infancy narrative. He speculates that this is due to Luke's intention not to confuse this

concerned with the paradigmatic value of the pneumatic activity in relation to Jesus and is more concerned with how the Spirit is characterized by Luke in the narrative.[93] Menzies provides a highly nuanced analysis of πνεῦμα (S/spirit) and δύναμις (power) to attach Lukan pneumatology to the 'special insight and inspired speech' represented in intertestamental Judaism.[94] Luke's 'prophetic' pneumatology is differentiated from the miraculous perspective of the primitive church and the inner soteriological (ethical) renewal advocated in the Pauline literature.[95] By narrowing the field of pneumatic activity to prophetic insight and inspired speech, Luke provides a basis for interpreting the events in the book of Acts as non-soteriological pneumatic experiences occurring subsequent to conversion.[96]

2.2.1.2.2 The Anointing of Jesus with the Spirit as Paradigmatic to Christian BHS

The principle feature of Luke's inauguration narrative (Luke 3:1-4:44) is the anointing of Jesus with the Holy Spirit on the occasion of his water baptism by JTB (Luke 3:21-22).[97] Classical Pentecostals textually establish the water rite prior to Jesus' Spirit-reception.[98] This Lukan redaction separates water baptism from Spirit-reception and classical Pentecostalism from sacramental

---

narrative with his account of Jesus' Jordan anointing. The nexus of pneumatic activity specific to Jesus would occur at the Jordan. See Atkinson, *Baptism in the Spirit,* 82 n. 73, 83.

[93] Menzies, *The Development of Early Christian Pneumatology with Special Reference to Luke-Acts*, 122.

[94] Ibid., 122-28.

[95] Ibid., 48.

[96] This is not to say that classical Pentecostals do not integrate Paul's soteriological pneumatology into their understanding of the Spirit's role in conversion. Atkinson presents a range of classical Pentecostal opinions on the nature of Spirit-reception relative to conversion and BHS. These he admits are inconsistent, but reveal that the bulk of classical Pentecostal literature traces the indwelling presence of the Spirit to conversion. See Atkinson, *Baptism in the Spirit,* 106-8.

[97] Stronstad, *The Charismatic Theology of St. Luke,* 39.

[98] Menzies contra Turner follows Dunn (also Blass and Debrunner) to argue for Luke's alteration of the Markan account (Mark 1:9-11) to include the present participle προσευχομένου ('praying') with the aorist participle βαπτισθέντος ('being baptized') in order to indicate a probable and temporal separation of events. See Menzies, *The Development of Early Christian Pneumatology with Special Reference to Luke-Acts*, 148-49. See also Max Turner, 'Luke and the Spirit: Studies in the Significance of Receiving the Spirit in Luke-Acts' (PhD diss., University of Cambridge, 1980), 211 n. 77; *Power from on High,* 195 n. 24. Dunn, *Baptism in the Holy Spirit,* 33; F. Blass and A. Debrunner, *A Greek Grammar of the New Testament and Other Early Christian Literature* (Chicago: The University of Chicago Press, 1961), §401; Shelton, *Mighty in Word and Deed,* 129.

pneumatological constructs.[99] Luke places emphasis upon Jesus' reception of the Spirit (occasioned by prayer)[100] rather than on his water baptism.[101] Divergent views of this event exist among classical Pentecostals who emphasize the pneumatological implications of this event on the role of the Spirit in the ministry of Jesus. The views stem in part from the interpretation given to the phenomena of the 'dove' and 'voice' detailed by Luke in the account (Luke 3:22). Menzies considers the enigmatic nature of the dove's identity as inconclusive for determining the Spirit's role in relation to Jesus' ministry.[102] This focuses attention on the heavenly voice that also appears in Josephus and the rabbinic literature.[103] The two strophes conflate two biblical texts (Ps 2:7 and Isa 42:1) in order to identify Jesus as the Servant-Messiah.[104] Classical Pentecostals, resisting adoptionistic interpretations of Jesus' anointing with the Spirit, regard Jesus' Jordan experience as initiating Spirit-empowered ministry and signaling the beginning of his messianic task, not his messiahship.[105] Stronstad explains that Jesus, having become 'the Christ' by virtue of his anointing by the Spirit, and having received the Spirit, is subject to the Spirit's leading and is dependent on

---

[99] Horton, *What the Bible Says About the Holy Spirit,* 153-54.

[100] Prayer is a motif emphasized in Luke-Acts (Luke 5:16; 6:12; 9:18, 28-29; 11:1; 22:41; 23:46) and includes occasions of Spirit-reception associated with prayer (Luke 11:13; Acts 1:14; 4:31; 8:15). Menzies, *The Development of Early Christian Pneumatology with Special Reference to Luke-Acts,* 149 ns. 2-3. See also Shelton, *Mighty in Word and Deed,* 51.

[101] Shelton sees the role of JTB minimized by Luke (and Q) in preference for the Spirit's descent on Jesus. See Shelton, *Mighty in Word and Deed,* 48, 54 n. 2. See also Stronstad, *The Charismatic Theology of St. Luke,* 40; Dunn, *Baptism in the Holy Spirit,* 33. E. Earle Ellis, ed., *New Century Bible: The Gospel of Luke* ([original work published 1966] London: Thomas Nelson & Sons Ltd., 1977), 91; Joachim Jeremias, *New Testament Theology: The Proclamation of Jesus* (New York: Charles Scribner's Sons, 1971), 55.

[102] Menzies provides the primary interpretations regarding the significance of the dove in the narrative, but finds none of them sufficient for determining the nature of the Spirit's role at the Jordan. See Menzies, *The Development of Early Christian Pneumatology with Special Reference to Luke-Acts,* 149. See also Leander E. Keck, 'The Spirit and the Dove,' in *NTS* (1970), 41-57. Stronstad sees Luke emphasizing the experience of the dove's by his objective 'bodily' reference to the event. See Stronstad, *The Charismatic Theology of St. Luke,* 40.

[103] Josephus (*Ant* XIII X.3) records John Hyrcanus hearing a voice while offering a sacrifice in the temple. See William Whiston, Trans., *The Works of Josephus* (Peabody: Hendrickson Publishers, 1987), 354. Judaism held that God communicated rarely and only by the 'echo' (*bat kol*) of his voice following the death of the last prophets (Tosefta: Sotah 13.2).

[104] Stronstad, *The Charismatic Theology of St. Luke,* 40. Stronstad follows C. K. Barrett, *The Holy Spirit and the Gospel Tradition* ([original work published 1947] London: S.P.C.K., 1975), 41-43.

[105] Shelton, *Mighty in Word and Deed,* 52-53; Menzies, *The Development of Early Christian Pneumatology with Special Reference to Luke-Acts,* 152.

the Spirit's power (Luke 4:1, 14).[106] Warrington concludes that the baptism of Jesus with the attending phenomena does not confer 'a new dignity' to Jesus. Rather, it affirms an already existing status as he commences his mission.[107] Similar to Schweizer, Warrington does not attribute pneumatic empowerment to Jesus at the Jordan, but with Bock concludes that the Spirit's leading of Jesus is due to his being the Messiah and not for messianic function.[108] These nuances of the classical Pentecostal position present, on the one hand, the Spirit serving as an affirming presence whose anointing designates Jesus as the Davidic Messiah-King and Servant of the Lord who dispenses the Spirit on the eschatological community.[109] On the other hand, Jesus' Spirit-reception represents the arrival of a new nexus of pneumatic activity whereby he is empowered for ministry to be the anointed prophet and charismatic Christ, the unique bearer of the Spirit.[110] The gift of the Spirit on the Day of Pentecost involves Jesus transferring charismatic power to his disciples as successors to his ministry.[111]

Variously stated by classical Pentecostals, the role of the Spirit in the ministry of Jesus has implications for the paradigmatic value of the Jordan experience of Jesus to the reception of the Spirit (BHS) by his disciples beginning on the Day of Pentecost. Shelton holds that though important to the early church's understanding of its experience of the Spirit, the anointing of Jesus at the Jordan is an example for believers.[112] Jesus was empowered by the Spirit at the Jordan,

---

[106] Stronstad, *The Charismatic Theology of St. Luke,* 39.

[107] Warrington references I. Howard Marshall, *The Gospel of Luke: A Commentary on the Greek Text* (Grand Rapids: William B. Eerdmans Publishing, 1978), 155; Warrington, *Jesus the Healer,* 155.

[108] Warrington, *Jesus the Healer,* 156; Darrell L. Bock, *Luke 1:1-9:50* in Moisés Silva, ed., *BECNT* ([original work published 1994] Grand Rapids: Baker Academic, 2006), 104-16.

[109] Turner is cited by Warrington in favor of 'Lord of the Spirit' terminology originating with Schweizer. This makes Jesus the subject of an action performed by the Spirit (Luke 4:1), but not functioning in ministry as a pneumatic. Warrington does not rule out all possibility of Jesus' empowerment at the Jordan, but is more comfortable narrowing the Spirit's role to legitimization. Schweizer does not connect the Spirit with miraculous deeds in Luke-Acts, only inspired speech. Menzies seems to follow Schweizer at this point, though attributing divine empowering to the anointing of the Spirit. See Max Turner, 'Jesus and the Spirit in Lucan Perspective,' in Max Turner, 'Jesus and the Spirit in Lucan Perspective,' in *TynBul* (1981), 40. See also Warrington, *Jesus the Healer,* 154; Eduard Schweizer, Trans. Geoffrey Bromiley, 'πνεῦμα, πνευματικός,' in Gerhard Kittel and Gerhard Friedrich, eds. *TDNT, Vol. 6* ([original work published 1968] Grand Rapids: William B. Eerdmans Publishing, 1988), 405-7; Menzies, *The Development of Early Christian Pneumatology with Special Reference to Luke-Acts,* 153.

[110] Stronstad, 'The Prophethood of all Believers,' 43, 53.

[111] Stronstad, *The Charismatic Theology of St. Luke,* 49.

[112] Shelton, *Mighty in Word and Deed,* 53.

and he will pour out the same Spirit on all who believe and empower them for witness.[113] Warrington also accepts this analogical understanding of the anointing of Jesus but denies to disciples the universal Spirit-aided ability to emulate Jesus' miraculous works.[114] Menzies argues that Luke elsewhere (Luke 4:1) portrays Jesus as subordinate to the Spirit.[115] On his view, the anointing of Jesus consisted of the Spirit of prophecy whereby he received special revelation and guidance. He uses Luke's redactional insertion of Ἰησοῦς δὲ πλήρης πνεύματος ἁγίου ('And/Then/But Jesus full of the Spirit') in Luke 4:1 to link the Jordan experience of Jesus to that of the early church. Menzies views the redaction (see Matt 4:1 and Mark 1:12) as a conscious Lukan intention to depict Jesus' experience at the Jordan as the occasion of his filling with the Spirit. In this way, Luke draws continuity between the Jordan experience of Jesus and the disciples' filling with the Spirit on the Day of Pentecost (Acts 2:4). Specifically, the phrase Ἰησοῦς δὲ πλήρης πνεύματος ἁγίου ('And-Then-But Jesus full of the Spirit') is Luke's way of establishing the pneumatic experience of Jesus at the Jordan as the moment when he was 'filled with the Spirit' to carry out his divinely appointed task.[116] Menzies describes Luke's unique pneumatological understanding of the gift of the Spirit in terms of prophetic enabling in order to participate in the mission of God. Three conceptual emphases represent Menzies' depiction of Luke's pneumatology on this point: that the gift of the Spirit is (1) non-soteriological, (2) prophetic, and (3) missiological.[117]

Classical Pentecostals are divided as to whether or not the disciples on the Day of Pentecost are anointed with the same capacity to function as Jesus in the performance of ministry. Stronstad and Arrington favor this characterization, while Warrington represents an alternate position. On Warrington's view, the Spirit functions in the disciples according to the power given to them by Jesus as 'Lord of the Spirit' (Acts 1:8).[118] These differing views among classical Pentecostals do not jeopardize the doctrine of subsequence and separability. Much of this discussion is subordinate to conclusions drawn from the unique character

[113] Ibid., 54.

[114] Warrington, *Jesus the Healer,* 154-58.

[115] Menzies, *The Development of Early Christian Pneumatology with Special Reference to Luke-Acts,* 156.

[116] Ibid., 157.

[117] Robert P. Menzies, 'The Spirit of Prophecy, Luke-Acts and Pentecostal Theology: A Response to Max Turner,' in *JPT* (1999), 49-74.

[118] Stronstad, 'The Prophethood of all Believers,' 53; Arrington, *The Acts of the Apostles,* 19; Warrington, *Jesus the Healer,* 155.

of Lukan pneumatology. Atkinson demonstrates this point insightfully in his exegesis of the commissioning of the Twelve in Luke 9:1. The passage appears to be an early pre-Pentecost model for the Spirit's operations in the lives of the disciples under the authority of Jesus. Following Menzies, Atkinson references the πνεῦμα (S/spirit) and δύναμις (power) dichotomy in Luke-Acts to differentiate the operations of Jesus and the Spirit. The Spirit granted Jesus power to perform miraculously (Luke 4:14, 18, 36; 7:14-16; 24:19). The miraculous power given to the commissioned disciples by Jesus (Luke 9:1) forms the conceptual basis for their expecting further power in accordance with his promise (Luke 24:49). Luke is clear that this promised power refers to the future arrival of the Spirit (Acts 1:4-8). This permits Atkinson to conclude that Luke conceived of Jesus' empowering with the same Spirit with which he was anointed (Luke 24:45; Acts 1:2; Acts 6:3; 15:28; 20:23; 21:11). Atkinson is correct to question the substantive difference between the disciples' pre-Pentecost subjective experience of power (Luke 9:1), by which they performed the miraculous and were empowered to preach effectively, and the promised power necessary for Christian service (Luke 24:49; Acts 2:4). The reception of the Spirit on the Day of Pentecost would not be 'Luke 9 all over again,' but an inner sense of the life of Jesus within his disciples by virtue of the Spirit's coming upon them.[119] On this view, Pentecost begins a new dimension of the Spirit's role in the lives of the disciples whereby Jesus becomes a living reality in them. Prior to Pentecost, a geographical separation existed between Jesus and his commissioned disciples (Luke 9:1). The Pentecost and post-Pentecost reception of the Spirit by will grant to the disciples the immediate and experienced presence of Jesus.[120] Space does not permit a thorough discussion on Menzies' exegesis of Luke's redaction of Luke 11:13b (see Matt 7:11b).[121] This is another example of Luke encouraging post-Pentecost disciples to request the gift of the Spirit to become effective witnesses for Christ (Luke 12:12; Acts 1:8).[122] Having demonstrated the case for subsequence and separability from the unique perspective of Lukan pneumatology, the concept of

---

[119] Atkinson, *Baptism in the Spirit,* 83-85.

[120] Hunter, *Spirit-Baptism,* 74 and Herbert Schneider, 'Baptism in the Holy Spirit in the New Testament,' in Kilian McDonnell, ed., *The Holy Spirit and Power* (Garden City: Doubleday, 1975), 49.

[121] Menzies and Menzies, *Spirit and Power,* 115-18. Stronstad finds additional evidence for subsequence and separability in Luke's 'silence' concerning the imprisonment of JTB, an account appearing between Jesus' baptism and the initiation of his Galilean ministry in Matthew 4:12 and Mark 1:14. Luke places the account before Jesus' baptism (Luke 3:19-20) to connect his Jordan experience of the Spirit with his pneumatic (charismatic) empowering (Luke 4:1). See Stronstad, *The Charismatic Theology of St. Luke,* 41-42.

[122] Ibid., 117.

the non-soteriological role of the Spirit may be inserted into the BHS case studies identified in the book of Acts.

2.2.1.3   The Book of Acts as Normative and Programmatic

The normative and programmatic value of the case studies in the book of Acts is based upon the disciples experiencing regeneration prior to the Day of Pentecost.[123] Hunter argues unequivocally that before the Day of Pentecost Jesus' followers were genuine believers in every sense of the word (Luke 9:20; 10:20).[124] Horton also emphasizes that the disciples that Jesus left behind constituted the church as a new covenant body (Luke 22:20; Heb 9:11-29; 10:10).[125] Petts applies a unique set of criteria to acknowledge the regenerate status of the disciples prior to the Pentecost.[126]

The use of details in selected BHS narratives in the book of Acts to infer a doctrine of subsequence and separability presents two interpretive issues for classical Pentecostals. The first interpretive issue concerns Luke's intention to record the details in the narratives as programmatic accounts of Spirit reception (BHS). The second interpretive issue is related to the first and concerns Luke's intention to present the programmatic BHS accounts as normative (to be repeated experientially) for all believers of all time. Of central importance to the issue of normativity is the classical Pentecostal understanding that as a historian-theologian, Luke has presented in his narratives a unique pneumatology with intended theological implications (see §2.2.1.1).[127] Lukan intent roots the mission of Jesus and the Christian mission (the book of Acts) in a resurrection-based apologetic. This apologetic links OT references (e.g. Joel 2:28-29) with the continuing mission of Jesus accomplished through outpourings of the Spirit on

---

[123] The term 'converted' is preferred here over 'Christian' due to arguments that consider Acts 2:38 programmatic for determining what constitutes being 'fully' Christian. Horton refers to Dunn agreeing with his assessment that the disciples were not 'Christians' in the full sense of the word on the Day of Pentecost. Dunn attributes this to the church's lack of existence until the Day of Pentecost. Without the church existing prior to Pentecost, no Christians in the proper sense of the word could exist. See Dunn, *Baptism in the Holy Spirit*, 51.

[124] Hunter, *Spirit-Baptism*, 82.

[125] Horton, 'Spirit Baptism,' 57

[126] The disciples had confessed Jesus as Lord (Matt 16:16), were pronounced clean (John 15:3), were told that their names were written in heaven (Luke 10:20) and had forsaken all to follow Jesus (Matt 19:27). Petts, 'The Baptism in the Holy Spirit,' 99.

[127] Menzies writes of Luke that he is 'both a historian who utilizes traditional material and a theologian who skillfully shapes and interprets it.' See Menzies, *The Development of Early Christian Pneumatology with Special Reference to Luke-Acts*, 208.

those who receive the salvation message (Acts 1:8; 2:38-39; 8:1, 4). The progression of the church's mission in the book of Acts depicts a body of believers receiving the leading and the power of the Spirit from the risen Lord. Luke's use of ἐπί ('upon') is traceable to LXX occurrences which commonly express Spirit manifestation in terms of inspired utterance and power.[128] The overt manifestations of the Spirit in the book of Acts reflect Luke's intention to link the mission of the church with the ongoing and unfolding nature of salvation-history.[129] Referring to the ἐπί ('upon') passages in the book of Acts (1:8; 2:17; 8:16; 10:44; 19:6), Petts identifies a programmatic and repeatable pattern intended by Luke to describe BHS as the normative experience for every Christian since Pentecost.[130] Luke's intention is not to consider the coincidence of Spirit-reception with personal conversion experience.[131] Shelton is less certain regarding Luke's understanding of the Spirit's role, but stresses that Lukan pneumatology is dominated by the Spirit-inspired witness of believers.[132]

To summarize, classical Pentecostals place the burden of proof for the doctrine of subsequence and separability on differentiating BHS from regeneration as a distinct pneumatic experience for the believer. The timing of BHS becomes irrelevant to the issue of subsequence. Petts refers to the issue of timing as 'immediate subsequence' with BHS occurring ideally as soon as possible after regeneration. BHS may appear to be a constituent part of the conversion process, but remains logically (if not temporally) distinct from regeneration.[133]

2.2.1.3.1   *Determining a Normative Pattern from the Programmatic Texts*

Classical Pentecostals base expectations for personal pneumatic experience on several passages in the books of Acts which reflect Luke's unique theological perspective. The narratives describe the reception of the Spirit in Jerusalem by Jews on the Day of Pentecost (Acts 2:1-13), by a crowd in Samaria (Acts 8:14-17), by Saul of Tarsus in Damascus (Acts 9:17-18), by the Gentile household of

---

[128] Charles L. Holman, 'Spirit-Reception: Luke Vis A Vis Paul' (paper presented at the November 1998 meeting of the Evangelical Theological Society in Orlando, FL), 3-4.

[129] Stronstad, *The Charismatic Theology of St. Luke*, 49.

[130] Petts, 'The Baptism in the Holy Spirit,' 101.

[131] Holman, 'Spirit-Reception,' 4.

[132] Shelton, *Mighty in Word and Deed*, 135-36.

[133] Petts, 'The Baptism in the Holy Spirit,' 101.

Cornelius in Caesarea (Acts 10:44-48; 11:15-17), and by twelve disciples of JTB in Ephesus (Acts 19:1-7). Attributing normative intention to Luke from these narrative accounts requires an interpretive key. Once understood according to the interpretive key, the narrative accounts are deemed programmatic for the anticipated pneumatic experience (BHS) of all believers of all time. Two passages are offered as possible interpretive keys for the narrative counts. The first passage suggests that the collocation (repentance, baptism, and the gift of the Holy Spirit) appearing in Acts 2:38 is evidence of a temporal gap between regeneration and a second empowering work of the Spirit (BHS) upheld by Luke in the other narrative accounts.[134] The classical Pentecostal view hinges on associating 'the gift of the Spirit' with 'prophetic enabling granted to the repentant.'[135] Menzies believes that the case for this association is justified by Joel 3:1 (LXX) when it is used as the interpretive key for explaining 'the promise of the father' and 'clothed with power from on high' as contemporaneous experiences of the disciples (Luke 24:49; Acts 1:4; 2:33). The reception of the Spirit in this manner transformed the disciples into effective witnesses of Jesus (Acts 1:8).[136] The normative features of Acts 2:38 are reduced to the potential universality of BHS[137] and the identification of the church, as 'a prophetic community with a missionary task.'[138] Problematic for this programmatic use of Acts 2:38 by classical Pentecostals linking evidential

---

[134] Menzies, *The Development of Early Christian Pneumatology with Special Reference to Luke-Acts,* 247. Shelton interprets the rebaptizing of the Ephesian Twelve on the basis of the relation between Christian water baptism to Spirit reception. See Shelton, *Mighty in Word and Deed,* 135. Shelton notes the opposing viewpoint of Marshall who closes the temporal gap represented in the two gifts of forgiveness and the Holy Spirit. Marshall argues that the Spirit represents the close association between inner cleansing [regeneration] and outward symbol [water baptism]. See Shelton, *Mighty in Word and Deed,* 129. See also I. Howard Marshall, *The Acts of the Apostles: An Introduction and Commentary* ([original work published 1980] Leicester: InterVarsity Press, 1986), 81.

[135] Menzies apologetic is in conversation with Dunn who considers Acts 2:38 Luke's portrayal of Spirit-reception the climatic element in Christian initiation and therefore of soteriological necessity. See Menzies, *The Development of Early Christian Pneumatology with Special Reference to Luke-Acts,* 246-48. See also Dun, *The Baptism in the Holy Spirit,* 90-92. Shelton notes that Luke's concern is not with a precise definition of conversion experience, but 'that the Spirit confirmed through Spirit-witness that it had occurred.' See Shelton, *Mighty in Word and Deed,* 133.

[136] Menzies, *The Development of Early Christian Pneumatology with Special Reference to Luke-Acts,* 200-4.

[137] Stronstad, *The Charismatic Theology of St. Luke,* 57.

[138] Menzies, *The Development of Early Christian Pneumatology with Special Reference to Luke-Acts,* 248. See also Arrington, *The Acts of the Apostles,* 32.

tongues to BHS is the need to infer glossolalia where it is unmentioned (see also Acts 4:31a).[139]

The second passage considered to be a possible interpretive key is Acts 2:1-13. This passage contains the narrative account of the reception of the Spirit on the Day of Pentecost. Menzies sees a striking parallel between the unfolding of events occurring on the Day of Pentecost and Jesus' pneumatic anointing with the Spirit at the Jordan (Luke 3:22; 4:18). The parallel is indicative of Luke interpreting the latter event in light of the former. Luke's literary method presents the historical narrative in a manner which yields theological implications.[140] The passage portrays the gift of the Spirit as the source of prophetic inspiration (Acts 2:9-11) with the significant missiological implication (Acts 2:5) of coming upon everyone present to empower them to carry out their divinely appointed tasks (Acts 2:4). Menzies concludes that the disciples' pneumatic anointing at Pentecost followed the pattern of Jesus' experience at the Jordan and similarly equipped them with power for prophetic ministry (Luke 24:49; Acts 1:8).[141] The normative value of this programmatic text is reinforced by the events depicted in the succeeding narratives. In Acts 8:4-25, there is a distinct separation of Spirit reception (vv. 15-17) from water baptism (v. 12) that can only be explained in terms of Luke's prophetic pneumatology.[142] According to Menzies, Luke understood the Spirit-reception of the Samaritans (Acts 8:17) to have the same character as the Pentecost gift: prophetic enabling for the converted to effectively

---

[139] Shelton attributes this criticism to the absence of speaking in tongues in Acts 2:41 noted by Haenchen. See Shelton, *Mighty in Word and Deed,* 129. See also Haenchen, *The Acts of the Apostles,* 184 n. 4. Ervin also identifies lack of uniformity in the narrative accounts to demonstrate the occurrence of evidential glossolalia. See Ervin, *Spirit-Baptism,* 71.

[140] Menzies, *The Development of Early Christian Pneumatology with Special Reference to Luke-Acts,* 205-10.

[141] Menzies observes three points of emphasis regarding Luke's redaction of Joel 3:1-5 (LXX) which make it the hermeneutical key for interpreting the Pentecost narrative and subsequent narratives in Acts. See Ibid., 210-12, 224-92.

[142] Shelton, *Mighty in Word and Deed,* 130; Hunter, *Spirit-Baptism,* 83-84. Menzies discusses possible theories offered to explain the delay in Spirit-reception for the Samaritans from Luke modifying his source material to a unique exception involving the withholding of the giving of the Spirit to demonstrate Jewish-Samaritan solidarity in the one church. See Menzies, *The Development of Early Christian Pneumatology with Special Reference to Luke-Acts,* 246-58. The former position is described by Haenchen as Luke incorporating a conflation of events, including a Christianized Simon tradition, into his narrative. See Haenchen, *The Acts of the Apostles,* 308. The latter position is endorsed by Lampe, Green, Bruner, and Marshall. See G. W. H. Lampe, *The Seal of the Spirit: A Study in the Doctrine of Baptism and Confession in the New Testament and the Fathers* (London: Longmans, Green and Co., 1951), 70. See also Michael Green, *I Believe in the Holy Spirit* (Grand Rapids: William B. Eerdmans Publishing, 1975), 138-39; Bruner, *A Theology of the Holy Spirit,* 175-76; Marshall, *The Acts of the Apostles,* 153-57.

perform the mission of the church.[143] The commission formula contained in Acts 9:15-16 is linked to the reception of the Spirit and considered to be an endowment which enables Saul to 'fulfill his missionary call' (v. 20).[144] Though considered to be problematic for the doctrine of subsequence and separability by non-Pentecostals, the narrative account and subsequent summaries of the regeneration and BHS of Cornelius' household (Acts 10:44-38; 11:15-17; 15:8-10) support the premise of Luke's distinctive pneumatology.[145]

Menzies believes the account is programmatic due to the presence of inspired speech in relation to the Gentile's reception of the Spirit (Acts 10:46).[146] Based on this premise, Menzies associates the presence of inspired speech due to the gift of the Spirit granted to Cornelius' household with Pentecostal prophetic inspiration and not with cleansing and forgiveness.[147] The repetition by Luke concerning the Gentiles receiving the same gift as the Jewish disciples at Pentecost (Acts 10:47; 11:15, 17; 15:8) both initiates and validates the prospective Gentile mission (Acts 18:22; 21:8).[148] The final case study involves the disciples at Ephesus (Acts 19:1-7). The preeminent issue of the text involves whether or not τινας μαθητὰς ('some disciples,' v. 1) is a Lukan reference to disciples of Jesus.[149] Luke's use of the indefinite pronoun (τὶς) is used elsewhere to describe

---

[143] Menzies, *The Development of Early Christian Pneumatology with Special Reference to Luke-Acts,* 258.

[144] Hunter, *Spirit-Baptism,* 85; Menzies, *The Development of Early Christian Pneumatology with Special Reference to Luke-Acts,* 263.

[145] Dunn, *The Baptism in the Holy Spirit,* 79-82; Bruner, *A Theology of the Holy Spirit,* 192; Menzies, *The Development of Early Christian Pneumatology with Special Reference to Luke-Acts,* 264.

[146] Ibid., 265 n. 4. Menzies alludes to Luke describing eight occurrences of initial reception of the Spirit by an individual or group. Of the eight, five describe a form of inspired speech as an immediate result (Luke 1:41, 67; Acts 2:4; 10:46; 19:6), one is implied (Acts 8:15, 18), and the remaining two (Luke 3:22; Acts 9:17) where inspired speech is absent, it is found in the pericopes which follow (Luke 4:14, 18; Acts 9:20).

[147] Ibid., 267. Stronstad notes that Luke directs his readers to the Pentecost narrative in order to interpret the gift of the Spirit to the household of Cornelius. Similar terminology is used with reference to tongues-speaking (Acts 2:4; 10:46) and exalting God (Acts 2:11; 10:46). See Stronstad, *The Charismatic Theology of St. Luke,* 67. See also, David Hill, *New Testament Prophecy* (London: Marshall, Morgan, and Scott, 1979), 96-97.

[148] Hunter points to the fact that the Jewish disciples at Pentecost differed from other Spirit-reception cases which were preceded by 'confrontation' with the message of Jesus Christ.' This proclamation was absent at Pentecost because the disciples were already converted. The outpouring of the charismatic Spirit is confirmation. The same confirmation is evident in the household of Cornelius. See Hunter, *Spirit-Baptism,* 87. See also Stronstad, *The Charismatic Theology of St. Luke,* 67. Menzies, *The Development of Early Christian Pneumatology with Special Reference to Luke-Acts,* 267.

[149] Shelton, *Mighty in Word and Deed,* 135.

Ananias (Acts 9:10) and Timothy (Acts 16:1) as disciples of Jesus.[150] When unqualified, as in this occurrence, the term μαθητής or μαθηταί (disciple/s) is always employed by Luke as a reference to disciples of Jesus.[151] Menzies attributes the regeneration of the twelve disciples to the work of the 'inspired preacher active in the same city' (see Apollos, Acts 18:24-28).[152] The negative reply by the Ephesian disciples to Paul's query regarding Spirit-reception (vv. 2-3) is interpreted by Menzies according to Luke's unique pneumatological perspective as an inquiry[153] into whether or not they had received the prophetic gift of the Spirit.[154] Luke's mention of the Holy Spirit (v. 2) refers to empowerment and not to conversion.[155] Absent from the pericope is Luke's conversional 'believed and were baptized' language (Acts 2:41; 8:12-13; 16:14-15, 33-34) and his systemic 'faith-repentance' prerequisite for receiving the forgiveness of God (Luke 5:20; 24:47; Acts 3:19; 5:31; 10:43; 13:38; 26:18).[156] The rebaptism of the Ephesian Twelve was not linked to conversion, but to a further explanation of the faith and the necessity for being baptized in the name of Jesus in order to receive the Holy Spirit.[157] By identifying the Ephesians as μαθηταί (disciples), Luke constructs the narrative to separate their regeneration from their Spirit-reception. The manifestation of glossolalia attending the reception of the Spirit is identified by Luke with the term 'prophesying' (v. 6). Menzies attributes the familiar allusion to the imposition of hands (Acts 8:17; 9:17; 19:6) to Luke's equating the reception of the prophetic gift of the Spirit with effective participation in the mission of the church. He sees continuity between

---

[150] Stronstad, *The Charismatic Theology of St. Luke,* 90 n. 4.

[151] See Luke 9:16, 18, 54; 10:23; 16:1; 17:22; 18:15; 19:29, 37; 20:45; 22:39, 45; Acts 6:1, 2, 7; 9:10, 19, 26, 38; 11:26, 29; 13:52; 14:20, 22, 28; 15:10; 16:1; 18:23, 27; 19:1, 9, 30; 20:1, 30; 21:4, 16. Menzies, *The Development of Early Christian Pneumatology with Special Reference to Luke-Acts,* 272.

[152] Ibid.

[153] Menzies explains that the ensuing dialogue between Paul and the Ephesian disciples is 'a Lukan composition' highlighting the need for Spirit-enablement and 'its normal prerequisite, Christian baptism.' See Menzies, *The Development of Early Christian Pneumatology with Special Reference to Luke-Acts,* 274 n. 4. See also, Atkinson, *Baptism in the Spirit,* 110.

[154] Stronstad, *The Charismatic Theology of St. Luke,* 68; Shelton, *Mighty in Word and Deed,* 134.

[155] Shelton, *Mighty in Word and Deed,* 134.

[156] Menzies, *The Development of Early Christian Pneumatology with Special Reference to Luke-Acts,* 275.

[157] Hunter explains that classical Pentecostals refer to the Ephesian disciples as 'saved' and knowing the 'indwelling of the Holy Spirit,' but not yet knowing the power of 'the (possibly) subsequent experience of Spirit-baptism.' See Hunter, *Spirit-Baptism,* 89. See also Shelton, *Mighty in Word and Deed,* 135.

the pneumatic experience of the Ephesian disciples, the Samaritans, Saul, the household of Cornelius, and the disciples in Jerusalem on the Day of Pentecost. This continuity is an established pattern consisting of Spirit-reception and prophetic endowment for the prophetic people of God to participate effectively in mission.[158] Stronstad is in general agreement with Menzies on the programmatic value of Pentecost. He attaches two purposes to Luke's writing of the Acts narratives: (1) to indicate that the commission Jesus gave to the disciples, to extend the gospel throughout the empire (Acts 1:8), had been fulfilled; and (2) to demonstrate the universality of the vocational gift of the Spirit.[159]

2.2.1.3.2   BHS as a Pneumatic Experience Distinct from Regeneration

A unique feature of Lukan pneumatology informs the classical Pentecostal apologetic for the doctrine of subsequence and separability. The phrase ἐπλήσθη/σαν πνεύματος ἁγίου ('filled with the Holy Spirit') is uniquely Lukan and appears nine times in Luke-Acts.[160] The phrase is related to (though not identical with) another expression, πλήρης πνεύματος ἁγίου ('full of the Holy Spirit'), which is used by Luke to describe the pneumatic experience of Jesus (Luke 4:1), the seven chosen servants (Acts 6:3), Stephen (Acts 6:5; 7:55) and Barnabas (Acts 11:24).[161] The close relation of the two phrases is described by Shelton who considers the former to be a reference to the empowering of an individual and the latter being used by Luke to express the character of a disciple.[162] Stronstad further distinguishes the two phrases; the former refers to prophetic inspiration and the latter describes the Spirit's enabling.[163] Both Shelton and Stronstad note ancillary associations with the Spirit's fullness: wisdom (Acts 6:3), faith (Acts 6:5; 11:24), and power (Luke 4:1; Acts 6:8).[164] Menzies, however, describes the two phrases in terms of a causal relation: πλήρης πνεύματος ἁγίου ('full of the Holy Spirit') implies the prior experience

---

[158] Menzies, *The Development of Early Christian Pneumatology with Special Reference to Luke-Acts*, 275-77.

[159] Stronstad, *The Charismatic Theology of St. Luke*, 68-69.

[160] Luke 1:15, 41, 67; Acts 2:4; 4:8, 31; 9:17; 13:9, 52. Stronstad, *The Charismatic Theology of St. Luke*, 53.

[161] Ibid., 55.

[162] Shelton, *Mighty in Word and Deed*, 137.

[163] Stronstad, *The Charismatic Theology of St. Luke*, 55.

[164] Shelton, *Mighty in Word and Deed*, 137; Stronstad, *The Charismatic Theology of St. Luke*, 55.

designated by the phrase ἐπλήσθη/σαν πνεύματος ἁγίου ('filled with the Holy Spirit').[165] Of the two Lukan expressions, ἐπλήσθη/σαν πνεύματος ἁγίου ('filled with the Holy Spirit') is significant to Luke's characterization of BHS. One important area of significance is Luke's use of the phrase to indivisibly blend the pneumatic experiences occurring during the events portrayed in the infancy narrative, in the life of Jesus, and in the post-Pentecost church.[166] The same expression is used to identify the pneumatic experiences of the disciples at Pentecost, JTB, Elizabeth, Zechariah, and Jesus with the same effect: inspired speech (prophetic inspiration) and empowerment to carry out their divinely appointed tasks.[167] Classical Pentecostals understand the Pentecostal Spirit-filling of the disciples as the initial (infilling) Spirit-reception constituting BHS,[168] one that indicates that the authoritative speaking of believers is the result of a special dispensation of the Spirit (Acts 2:4; 4:8, 31; 9:17; 13:9).[169] Though Spirit-filling generally produces a short-lived and repetitive inspired state, a more permanent dimension is evident in the cases of JTB (Luke 1:15), Jesus (Luke 3:22) and Paul (Acts 9:17).[170] The contextual evidence from these uniquely Lukan expressions for pneumatic experience leads to the conclusion that where ἐπλήσθη/σαν πνεύματος ἁγίου ('filled with the Holy Spirit') indicates the initial reception of the Spirit, it is associated with inspired speaking, the proclaiming of the gospel message, and/or witnessing to Jesus as Messiah.[171]

2.2.2. Tongues as the Initial Evidence of Spirit Reception

Having previously mentioned the doctrine of initial evidence (§2.1.3), this section details its apologetic use by many classical Pentecostals.[172] Tan is critical of her classical Pentecostal denomination (AG) for being complacent regarding

---

[165] Menzies, *The Development of Early Christian Pneumatology with Special Reference to Luke-Acts*, 156.

[166] Shelton, *Mighty in Word and Deed,* 136.

[167] Ibid., 137; Stronstad, *The Charismatic Theology of St. Luke,* 55; Menzies, *The Development of Early Christian Pneumatology with Special Reference to Luke-Acts*, 212.

[168] Horton, 'Spirit Baptism,' 59.

[169] Shelton, *Mighty in Word and Deed,* 137.

[170] Menzies, *The Development of Early Christian Pneumatology with Special Reference to Luke-Acts*, 212.

[171] Paul's reference in Eph 5:18 to being filled with the Spirit is the lone exception. Stronstad, *The Charismatic Theology of St. Luke,* 53; Shelton, *Mighty in Word and Deed,* 137.

[172] Holdcroft, *The Holy Spirit,* 120-23.

what Macchia terms 'critical theological reflection.'[173] She attributes this complacency to the classical Pentecostal preference for validating spiritual realities by experience rather than fruitful theologizing.[174] Tan calls for the development of conceptual tools (theologizing) and integrating them with the experiential dimensions of classical Pentecostal practitioners.[175] This balance frames the 'initial evidence' apologetic.[176] Chan is similarly critical of an apologetic which defends the doctrine of initial evidence according to historical or biblical evidence.[177] He prefers to establish the doctrine by a logical relationship between BHS and glossolalia.[178] This methodology avoids the hermeneutical/exegetical difficulties raised by Fee, Hurtado, and Menzies who, while not opposing tongues-speech, challenge the doctrine of initial evidence as indicative of normative experience.[179] Macchia is similarly critical and bases his dissent on tongues functioning as a law which governs BHS.[180] On his view, tongues compensate for the limitations of human speech to describe the mystery of God's redemptive presence and function less as rationalistic evidence or a visible 'sacramental sign.'[181] Chan, Menzies, and Macchia respond to classical Pentecostal apologetic challenges by presenting theological 'initial evidence'

---

[173] Tan May Ling, 'A Response to Frank Macchia's "Groans too Deep for Words: Towards a Theology of Tongues as Initial Evidence,' in *AJPS* (1998), 2; Frank D. Macchia, 'Sighs too Deep for Words: Toward a Theology of Glossolalia,' in *JPS* (1992), 49.

[174] Ling, 'A Response to Frank Macchia's "Groans too Deep for Words: Towards a Theology of Tongues as Initial Evidence,' 2.

[175] Ibid. Pentecostal David Lim writes: 'Tongues is spiritual experience, not just doctrine to be analyzed.' See David Lim, 'A Reflection on the "Initial Evidence" Discussion from a Pentecostal Pastor's Perspective,' in *AJPS* (1999), 226.

[176] Macchia refers to this balance as bridging the 'gap between charismatic experience and academic theology.' See Macchia, 'Sighs too Deep for Words,' 50.

[177] Simon K. H. Chan, 'Evidential Glossolalia and the Doctrine of Subsequence,' in *AJPS* (1999), 196. *Pentecostal Theology and the Christian Spiritual Tradition* ([original work published 2000] Sheffield: Sheffield Academic Press, 2003), 41. See also Warrington, *Pentecostal Theology,* 119-20; A. Reuben Hartwick, 'Speaking in Tongues: The Initial Physical Evidence of the Baptism in the Holy Spirit,' in *Paraclete* (1995), 9-15. For the biblical/historical approach see Horton, 'Spirit Baptism,' 78 and Palma, *The Holy Spirit,* 156-57.

[178] Chan, 'Evidential Glossolalia and the Doctrine of Subsequence,' 196.

[179] Fee, *Gospel and Spirit,* 83-119; Hurtado, 'Normal, but not the Norm,' 189-210; Menzies and Menzies, *Spirit and Power,* 123.

[180] Macchia, *Baptized in the Spirit,* 281. See also Frank D. Macchia, 'The Question of Tongues as Initial Evidence: A Review of *Initial Evidence,* Edited by Gary B. McGee,' in *JPT* (1993), 117-27.

[181] Macchia, 'Sighs too Deep for Words,' 47-73; Macchia, 'The Question of Tongues as Initial Evidence,' 122.

constructs that are based largely on inferences drawn from the biblical text.[182] The following three sections are brief summations of their positions.

2.2.2.1   Robert P. Menzies

Menzies, a former missionary to the Philippines and adjunct faculty at (AG) Asia Pacific Theological Seminary (Baguio City, Philippines) is Director of Synergy, a rural service organization in Kunming, China.[183] He bases his 'initial physical-evidence' apologetic on conclusions drawn from his assessment of Lukan pneumatology which associates the Pentecostal gift (BHS) with prophetic inspiration. Menzies acknowledges that the 'tongues as initial physical-evidence' view is not an explicit NT teaching, but represents an appropriate inference due to the prophetic function of BHS and the evidential (sign) character of tongues-speech (Acts 2:4-5, 17-20; 10:45-48). The normativity of evidential tongues is implied from the combined prophetic pneumatology of Luke and the complementary perspective of Paul. The edifying nature and universal availability of tongues-speech suggests that it is integral to BHS. Therefore, it is reasonable to expect the manifestation of tongues-speech upon receiving the Pentecostal gift (BHS).[184]

2.2.2.2   Frank D. Macchia

Macchia is editor of *Pneuma: The Journal for the Society of Pentecostal Studies* and professor of theology at (AG) Vanguard University (Costa Mesa, CA).[185] He considers the classical Pentecostal apologetic more sacramental than evidential.[186] The term 'sacramental' applied to initial tongues-speech refers to a

---

[182] The term 'inference' used here applies to occasions where the doctrine is implicitly referenced and not explicitly expressed. Vinson Synan, 'The Role of Tongues as Initial Evidence,' in Mark W. Wilson, ed., *Spirit and Renewal: Essays in Honor of J. Rodman Williams* (Sheffield: Sheffield Academic Press, 1994), 69. Menzies justifies this hermeneutical method according to Hurtado who validates the Trinity by the same method. See Menzies and Menzies, *Spirit and Power,* 123-24. See Hurtado, 'Normal, but not a Norm,' 191.

[183] Zondervan, 2012. 'Robert P. Menzies,' n.p. Available from: http://zondervan.com/ menziesr. [Accessed 21 May 2012].

[184] Menzies and Menzies, *Spirit and Power,* 125-29.

[185] Vanguard University, 2012. 'Frank Macchia,' n.p. Available from: http://religion. vanguard.edu/faculty/frank-macchia. [Accessed 21 May 2012].

[186] Frank D. Macchia, 'Tongues as a Sign: Towards a Sacramental Understanding of Pentecostal Experience,' in *Pneuma* (1993), 69.

visible/audible phenomenon integral to the experience of the Spirit.[187] Specifically, there is an integral (sacramental) relationship between the sign and the divine action signified.[188] Macchia lists a range of individually distinct integral relations used by classical Pentecostal scholars to connect tongues with BHS. However, he emphasizes that the connection is ultimately made theologically with tongues as an integral aspect of the BHS experience.[189] Macchia then defines tongues-speech as a response to the free and transcendent move of the Spirit[190] occasioned by a physical dimension of worship where the freedom of the Spirit functions in a unique kind of sacramental (theophanic) spirituality.[191] The term 'theophanic' refers to a divine self-disclosure such as occurred in the phenomena associated with the descent of the Spirit on the Day of Pentecost. Theophanic theological perspective fuels classical Pentecostal expectations for Spirit-induced signs and wonders into the church where the pneumatic Christ is actively establishing the kingdom of God. Macchia cautions against an inordinate desire for divine theophany that reduces spirituality to the sensationalistic pursuit of literal signs and wonders. Tongues-speech is a free and unpredictable theophanic divine self-disclosure that is both experiential and evidential.[192]

2.2.2.3   Simon K. H. Chan

Chan is Earnest Lau Professor of Systematic Theology at (AG) Trinity Theological College (Singapore).[193] He is critical of Menzies for his definitional narrowing of BHS to the parameters of Lukan pneumatology.[194] Chan posits the necessary glossolalia and BHS relation based on 'broader canonical meaning' which identifies BHS experientially in terms of a special kind of relationship with

---

[187] Ibid., 68.

[188] Ibid. 71. Macchia uses the term 'sacrament' admittedly in a 'broad or analogical sense' as opposed to what he refers to as 'principal sacraments' such as the Eucharist and water baptism .

[189] Ibid., 68.

[190] Macchia, 'Sighs too Deep for Words,' 49.

[191] Macchia, 'Tongues as a Sign,' 71-73.

[192] Macchia, 'Sighs too Deep for Words,' 72-73.

[193] Trinity Theological College, 2012. 'Faculty,' n.p. Available from: http://www.ttc.edu.sg/ index.php?option=com_content&task=view&id=22&Itemid=30. [Accessed 21 May 2012].

[194] Simon Chan, *Pentecostal Theology and the Christian Spiritual Tradition* ([original work published 2000] Sheffield: Sheffield Academic Press, 2003), 45. See also Chan, 'Evidential Glossolalia and the Doctrine of Subsequence,' 201.

God. The relational element of the Spirit's work represents a more fundamental category than mission (Menzies). In his view, 'canonical meaning' proposes evidential tongues by integrating various strands of NT pneumatology. This approach corresponds with the early Pentecostals whose BHS experience was more than infused power for witness; it was an experienced sense of God's nearness to which tongues-speech bore witness.[195] Chan's apologetic identifies glossolalia as a theological marker validated by specific (mystical) experiences that Pentecostals share with the broader Christian community.[196] On his view, the integration of NT pneumatologies results in a theologically coherent relationship between BHS and glossolalia.[197] BHS becomes a soteriologically-centered concept (Paul) with power (Matthew, Mark and Luke) resulting from a revelational encounter (John) with God. The doctrine of initial evidence is logically inferred from the experiential distinctiveness (encounter and intimacy-related) of BHS. Chan alludes to forming a doctrine to specify this distinctiveness and commends Macchia's sacramental view for grounding BHS in conversion-initiation while preserving the Pentecostal experience.[198]

3. Charismatic Renewal

3.1   Early Stages: Adopting the Classical Pentecostal Interpretive Framework

As previously demonstrated in this work, the charismatic renewal has made significant inroads into the American Baptist movement. This is a growing trend that deserves mention in this work due to the impact of BHS on charismatic spirituality. The two-stage or 'second blessing' pneumatological model of BHS promoted by classical Pentecostals is also embraced by many within the charismatic renewal. Therefore, a brief section evaluating its importance within the renewal movement will promote:

1) A general understanding of BHS within the charismatic renewal.

2) A means for distinguishing renewalists from classical Pentecostals where BHS is concerned.

---

[195] Chan, *Pentecostal Theology and the Christian Spiritual Tradition,* 45-46.

[196] Chan, 'Evidential Glossolalia and the Doctrine of Subsequence,' 201.

[197] Chan, *Pentecostal Theology and the Christian Spiritual Tradition,* 46-50.

[198] Chan, 'Evidential Glossolalia and the Doctrine of Subsequence,' 205-10.

3) An increased awareness of P/C spirituality by American Baptists in order to find fresh ground on which there is significant convergence if not total consensus.

The broad ecumenical appeal of the charismatic renewal (otherwise referred to as neo-Pentecostalism) is considered within the movement to be an antidote to the onset of separatist-oriented Pentecostal denominationalism.[199] Cardinal Leo Joseph Suenens personally encountered the renewal in 1972. From 1974-86 he composed a series of six 'Malines Documents' as a guide to the renewal for Catholic Christians.[200] Central to the neo-Pentecostal appeal is the transcendent character of BHS which demonstrates no preference for creed, denominations, liturgies, traditions, or theological/doctrinal and geo-political bounds. Pentecostal theologian Yong identifies the Pentecostal experience as the agency by which the charismatic renewal comprised a unity of eclectic spiritual traditions.[201] The advent of the charismatic renewal within the churches did not initially inspire interest in a rational, biblical, and theological apologetic to justify an intensely personal experience of the Spirit. Christenson in fact, representing the Lutheran viewpoint, commended humble obedience and faith over attempts to understand a personal experience within the single-stage pneumatological categories of his Lutheran tradition.[202] Noting the incomprehensibility of deeply existential experience, J. Rodman Williams, a prolific Reformed theologian of the renewal, implies the setting aside of pneumatological systems and biblical teaching in favor of accepting the reality of the personal experience.[203] Fellow Reformed theologian, D. Martyn Lloyd-Jones, delivered a series of sermons describing BHS as a post-conversion experience. The 1964 sermons were published in 1984 as *Joy*

---

[199] See the published papers from the 1991 Brighton Conference in Harold D. Hunter and Peter D. Hocken, eds., *All Together in One Place: Theological Papers from the Brighton Conference on World Evangelization* (Sheffield: Sheffield Academic Press, 1993).The theme of the international symposium, attracting participants from many ecumenical and academic bodies, was planned by the International Charismatic Consultation on World Evangelization (ICCOWE). For a short overview of scholarly works by mainline publishers emerging from the charismatic renewal and representing the Anglican, Episcopal, Catholic, and Lutheran traditions, see John Koenig, 'Documenting the Charismatics,' in *Word & World* (1981), 287-90.

[200] Killian McDonnell, *Presence, Power, Praise: Documents on the Charismatic Renewal* (Collegeville: Liturgical Press, 1980).

[201] Amos Yong, *The Spirit Poured Out on All Flesh: Pentecostalism and the Possibility of Global Theology* (Grand Rapids: Baker Academic, 2005), 181. See also Margaret M. Poloma, *Main Stream Mystics: The Toronto Blessing & Reviving Pentecostalism* (New York: AltaMira Press, 2003), 15-35.

[202] Larry Christenson, *Speaking in Tongues and its Significance for the Church* (Minneapolis: Bethany House, 1968), 37.

[203] J. Rodman Williams, *The Pentecostal Reality* (Plainfield: Logos, 1972), 17.

Unspeakable.[204] Spiritual (charismatic) experiences identical to those of classical Pentecostals occurred in non-Pentecostal assemblies and left many Christians in the early stages of the renewal looking to classical Pentecostalism for an interpretive framework.[205] Bashan (Pentecostal), Bennett (Episcopal), Christenson (Lutheran), Ervin (Baptist), and Williams (Reformed)[206] represent early neo-Pentecostal attempts to define BHS theologically.[207] Since their views approximate those articulated by the classical Pentecostal apologetic, they are not detailed in this section.[208] One distinction does bear mention. With the exception of Ervin,[209] early charismatic apologists were guarded[210] in their defense of the role of tongues-speech as initial evidence of BHS. This minimized role of glossolalia as evidence for BHS, while not clearing the way for consensus, does remove a critical barrier to substantive dialogue for American Baptists.

---

[204] D. M. Lloyd-Jones, *Joy Unspeakable: Power & Renewal in the Holy Spirit* (Wheaton: Harold Shaw Publishers, 1984).

[205] Lederle, *Treasures Old and New,* 38. See also Carter Lindberg, *The Third Reformation? Charismatic Movements and the Lutheran Tradition* (Macon: Mercer University Press, 1983), 223.

[206] The following is a bibliographic summary of relevant works: Don Basham, *A Handbook on Holy Spirit Baptism* (New Kensington: Whitaker House, 1969); Dennis Bennett, *Nine O'Clock in the Morning* (Plainfield: Logos, 1970); Dennis Bennett and Rita Bennett, *The Holy Spirit and You: A Study Guide to the Spirit-Filled Life* (Plainfield: Logos, 1971); Larry Christenson, *Speaking in Tongues and its Significance for the Church* (Minneapolis: Bethany House, 1968); Howard M. Ervin, *Conversion-Initiation and the Baptism in the Holy Spirit* (Peabody: Hendrickson Publishers, 1984); *Spirit Baptism: A Biblical Investigation* ([originally published as *These Are Not Drunken As Ye Suppose* (Plainfield: Logos International, 1968)] Peabody: Hendrickson Publishers, 1987); J. Rodman Williams, *The Era of the Spirit* (Plainfield: Logos International, 1971); 'Pentecostal Theology: A Neo-Pentecostal Viewpoint' in Russell P. Spittler, ed., *Perspectives on the New Pentecostalism* by (Grand Rapids: Baker Book House, 1976). *The Pentecostal Reality* (Plainfield: Logos, 1972); *The Gift of the Holy Spirit Today* (Plainfield: Logos, 1980). *Renewal Theology: Systematic Theology from a Charismatic Perspective, 3 Vols.* (Grand Rapids: Zondervan, 1996).

[207] Larry Christenson, *The Charismatic Renewal Among Lutherans* (Minneapolis: Lutheran Charismatic Renewal Services, 1976), 37.

[208] Synan, 'The Role of Tongues as Initial Evidence,' 75.

[209] While other early neo-Pentecostal apologists opted for 'normal' or 'necessary' in referring to the association of tongues speech with BHS, Ervin unequivocally upheld the traditional initial evidence view of classical Pentecostal in the USA. Ervin, *Spirit Baptism,* 83-84. See also Lederle, *Treasures Old and New,* 78.

[210] Lederle, *Treasures Old and New,* 74.

3.2   The Organic-Sacramental View of the Spirit's Work in BHS

The charismatic renewal transitioned from its early roots in classical Pentecostal theological categories to discover interpretive schemes for BHS among non-Pentecostal theological traditions.[211] The result is the predominance of the 'organic' or 'sacramental' BHS[212] view which exists among members of the renewal.[213] Catholic renewal theologians McDonnell and Bittlinger describe the BHS experience in terms of a 'release' or 'actualization' which is ultimately tied to Spirit-reception obtained via ritual baptism.[214] Modifying his earlier Lutheran view, Christenson combines BHS with the water rite, though its 'release' occurs at a later time being 'actualized' via tongues-speech.[215] The language of 'release' was not entirely absent from earlier BHS formulations in the renewal, but it was used at that point in association with two-stage pneumatological constructs.[216] The 'organic-sacramental' view is theologically a one-stage

---

[211] Synan, 'The Role of Tongues as Initial Evidence,' 78.

[212] See Lederle (*Treasures Old and New*) for a catalogue of charismatic BHS positions. See also Larry Hart, 'Spirit-Baptism: A Dimensional Charismatic Perspective,' in Chad Owen Brand, *Perspectives on Spirit Baptism* (Nashville: Broadman & Holman Publishers, 2004), 105-80. Hart presents what he terms a 'dimensional' approach to BHS. He bases his view on BHS as a metaphor that is contextually understood according to its NT use by a variety of authors.

[213] Veli-Matti Kärkkäinen, *Pneumatology: The Holy Spirit in Ecumenical, International, and Contextual Perspective* (Grand Rapids: Baker Academic, 2002), 95. Catholic theologians Francis Sullivan and George Montague take a non-sacramental position on BHS. Citing Acts 4:31, Spirit filling (Acts 2:4) occurs in non-sacramental contexts and is attributed to prayer. See Francis Sullivan, *Charisms and Charismatic Renewal: A Biblical Theological Study* (Ann Arbor: Servant Publications, 1982), 62. See also Kilian McDonnell and George T. Montague, *Christian Initiation and Baptism in the Holy Spirit: Evidence from the First Eight Centuries*, 2nd Ed. (Collegeville: Liturgical Press, 1994), 40. The views of Sullivan and Montague address concerns raised by Lederle that 'the renewal experience cannot be seen as something new or something that God is doing in people's lives at the time at which they experience it.' See Lederle, *treasures Old and New,* 109. Lederle categorizes non-sacramental charismatic BHS views as 'integrative' and offers a variety of examples (144-212). Joy refers to Sullivan's position as 'innovation.' See John Joy, 'The Outpouring of the Holy Spirit in the Catholic Charismatic Renewal: Theological Interpretation of Experience,' in *Antiphon* (2005), 165.

[214] Kilian McDonnell and Arnold Bittlinger, *The Baptism in the Holy Spirit as an Ecumenical Problem* (Notre Dame: Charismatic Renewal Services, 1972), 29-53.

[215] Christenson, *The Charismatic Renewal Among Lutherans*, 37, 52. Christenson did not accept the classical Pentecostal doctrine of initial evidence, though he seems to fall within the ranks of those who consider tongues-speech expected and normal. See Christenson, *Speaking in Tongues and its Significance for the Church* , 8-10.

[216] Bennett, *Nine O'Clock in the Morning*, 136; Williams, *Era of the Spirit*, 55. Macchia reports that the tendency among contemporary classical Pentecostals is to view BHS 'as empowerment for witness' in terms of releasing of an already-indwelling Spirit in life. See Macchia, *Baptized in the Spirit*, 77. Palma refers to the various NT images referring to BHS as 'figurative and graphic ways of portraying an overwhelming experience of the already-indwelling Spirit.' See Anthony Palma, 'Spirit Baptism: Before and After,' in *Enrichment Journal* (2005), 94.

Spirit Baptism Doctrinal Constructs within the P/C Movement

pneumatological construct. On this view, Spirit-reception (BHS) occurs at conversion-initiation.[217] Due to the experience of the Spirit being deferred, the view functions in a manner similar to the two-stage classical Pentecostal construct.[218] The primary attraction of the 'organic-sacramental' view for charismatics is the ability to avoid collateral BHS issues such as initial evidence, the appearance of two baptisms, and the inherent hierarchical division of Christians into stages of spiritual experience (e.g. the charge of promoting elitism).[219] For American Baptists, the presence of an alternative one-stage pneumatological BHS construct, while not clearing the way for consensus, does move the debate closer to a common ground for substantive dialogue.

3.3 BHS-Related Challenges for the Renewal

Charismatics rejecting the classical Pentecostal doctrine of initial evidence do so without eliminating the viable role of glossolalia in Christian experience.[220] Most renewalists associate tongues-speech with general manifestations of the *charismata* and do not consider glossolalia the '*sine qua non*' for validating BHS experience.[221] Integrating charismatic praxis into the mainline traditions poses an additional challenge for renewalists.[222] The issue of integration centers on the inability of charismatics to express BHS according to tradition-specific theological categories.[223] Lacking denominational theological categories to

---

[217] Killian McDonnell, 'Five Defining Issues: The International Classical Pentecostal/Roman Catholic Dialogue,' in *Pneuma* (1995), 180; Kilian McDonnell and George T. Montague, *Fanning the Flame: What Does Baptism in the Holy Spirit Have to Do with Christian Initiation?* (Collegeville: The Order of St. Benedict, 1991), 9.

[218] Synan, 'The Role of Tongues as Initial Evidence,' 77.

[219] Kärkkäinen, *Pneumatology*, 95.

[220] Frank D. Macchia, 'God Present in a Confused Situation: The Mixed Influence of the Charismatic Movement on Classical Pentecostalism in the United States' in *Pneuma* (1996), 40. See also, Thomas A. Smail, *Reflected Glory: The Spirit in Christ and Christians* (London: Hodder and Stoughton, 1975), 40.

[221] Henry I. Lederle, 'Initial Evidence and the Charismatic Movement,' in Gary B. McGee, ed., *Initial Evidence: Historical and Biblical Perspectives on the Pentecostal Doctrine of Spirit Baptism* (Peabody: Hendrickson Publishers, 1991), 132. According to Lederle, charismatics have more in common international and not American Pentecostals. See Larry Vern Newman, *The Ultimate Evidence: Rethinking the Evidence Issues for Spirit Baptism* (Eugene: Wipf & Stock, 2009), 42-48. See also Hollenweger, *The Pentecostals*, 335. Gee is an exception to this rule. See Gee, *Wind and Flame*, 7-8.

[222] Lederle, *Treasures Old and New*, 37.

[223] Richard A. Jensen, *Touched by the Spirit: One Man's Struggle to Understand His Experience of the Holy Spirit* (Minneapolis: Augsburg Press, 1975), 87.

interpret their new spiritual experiences, charismatics adopted the available interpretive framework of classical Pentecostalism.[224] The practice of importing classical Pentecostal theological categories poses a threat to traditions that desire to maintain their native denominational identity.[225] The challenge of integrating charismatic praxis into mainline denominational churches encompasses traditions as diverse as Catholic, Lutheran, Anglican-Episcopal, Presbyterian, Reformed, Baptist, Methodist, non-denominational, and independent. The task of integration is intensified when charismatic praxis and theological systems native to the mainline denominations overlap (e.g. Reformed doctrine).[226] The difficulty presented by associating BHS with specific denominational doctrinal categories is apparent when renewalists must concretize their BHS views in a context that requires them to adapt previously held (classical Pentecostal) theological categories.[227]

4.   The Third Wave

The third wave BHS apologetic combines the phenomenon with conversion-initiation.[228] The BHS metaphor is understood in terms of what happens when one becomes a Christian.[229] Storms equates BHS experience with being immersed as in water baptism. This experience results in a sense of being overwhelmed, engulfed, and drenched by the Holy Spirit.[230] These concurrent pneumatological events (i.e. regeneration and BHS) are followed by a range of subsequent

---

[224] Lederle, *Treasures Old and New,* 38.

[225] Lutheran pastor Arnold Bittlinger is cited by Hollenweger in dissent of this American practice. Bittlinger wrote, 'I am disturbed at the development in the USA, where the Pentecostal vocabulary is simply transferred to the new charismatic revival.' See Hollenweger, *The Pentecostals,* 245.

[226] Lederle, *Treasures Old and New,* 38.

[227] Grossman refers to the product of this process as a 'church-integrated theology.' See Siegfried Grossmann, *Stewards of God's Grace* (Exeter: Paternoster Press, 1981), 50.

[228] John Wimber, *Power Points* (San Francisco: Harper Collins, 1991), 136; C. Peter Wagner, *The Book of Acts: A Commentary* ([original work published in 1994] Ventura: Regal Books, 2008), 426.

[229] C. Samuel Storms, 'A Third Wave View,' in Wayne A. Grudem, ed., *Are Miraculous Gifts for Today? Four Views* (Grand Rapids: Zondervan, 1996), 176.

[230] John Piper, 2008. 'This is He Who Baptizes with the Holy Spirit,' n.p. Available from: http://www.desiringgod.org/resource-library/sermons/this-is-he-who-baptizes-with-the-holy-spirit. [Accessed 18 August 2013].

experiences of the Spirit subsumed under the NT reference to the term 'filling.'[231] BHS does not preclude intense post-conversion pneumatological experiences which display the presence of the Spirit.[232] Wagner considers these experiences to be necessary for effectively engaging in ministry-specific tasks via the operation of the *charismata*.[233] Third wave adherents, in contrast to classical Pentecostals, do not consider tongues-speech to be the initial physical evidence of BHS, but a gift used by some recipients for ministry or for prayer language.[234] Conceptually and semantically differentiating the pneumatological experiences recorded in the NT is important to many Christians. The third wave emphasizes unity and conciliation, not potentially divisive labels.[235]

The third wave BHS apologetic adduces a single-stage pneumatological construct from 1 Cor 12:13 (ἡμεῖς πάντες, 'we all') that is applicable to every believer.[236] This is supported by contextual references to the 'many' existing as 'one body' (1 Cor 10:17; 11:29; 12:4-11).[237] The unity of the body of Christ demonstrated in 1 Cor 12:13 concerns the Corinthians' common experience of the Spirit. This is implied stylistically by Paul's use of 'we' to personally identify with the common experience of the Corinthian believers (1 Cor 2:7; 5:7-8; 6:3; 8:8; 10:16; 11:31).[238] The disputed initial clause of 1 Cor 12:13 (ἐν ἑνὶ πνεύματι...εἰς ἓν σῶμα, 'in one Spirit...into one body') provides the exegetical basis used by third wavers to adduce the common experience of the Spirit.[239] The awkwardness of rendering this Greek expression into English prompts interpreters

---

[231] C. Peter Wagner, 'Third Wave,' in Stanley M. Burgess and Eduard M. Van Der Mass, eds., *NIDPCM* (Grand Rapids: Zondervan, 2002), 1141. Alvin J. Vander Griend, *Discover Your Gifts and Learn How to Use Them* (Grand Rapids: CRC Publications, 1996), 45.

[232] Storms, 'A Third Wave View,' 176.

[233] Wagner, 'Third Wave,' 1141.

[234] J. Lee Grady, *The Holy Spirit is Not for Sale* (Grand Rapids: Chosen Books, 2010), 181-186.

[235] J. P. Moreland, *Kingdom Triangle* (Grand Rapids: Zondervan, 2007), 180. See also, David Pawson, *Fourth Wave: Charismatics and Evangelicals –are we ready to come together?* (London: Hodder & Stoughton, 1993), 58-59.

[236] Charles H. Kraft and Marguerite G. Kraft, 'Communicating and Ministering the Power of the Gospel Cross-Culturally,' in Gary S. Greig and Kevin N. Springer, eds., *The Kingdom and the Power: Are Healing and the Spiritual Gifts Used by Jesus and the Early Church Meant for the Church Today?* (Ventura: Regal Books, 1993), 355.

[237] Gordon D. Fee, *NICNT: The First Epistle to the Corinthians* (Grand Rapids: William B. Eerdmans Publishing, 1987), 602.

[238] Ibid., 603.

[239] Murray J. Harris, 'Appendix,' in Colin Brown, ed., *NIDNTT, Vol. 3.* (ET Grand Rapids: Zondervan Publishing House, 1978), 1207-11.

such as Carson to translate the preposition ἐν as 'by' to indicate that the Spirit is the agent of the corresponding baptism.[240] In so doing, the English paronomasia is dismissed, rendering Paul's intended meaning, 'all Christians have been baptized in one Spirit; all Christians have been baptized into one body.'[241] For third wavers, this interpretation agrees contextually (1 Cor 10:2) with a similar Pauline grammatical construction ('into Moses in the cloud and in the sea') describing participation in the Mosaic covenant and the fellowship of the people of God led by Moses.[242] Third wavers also point to other NT references that attribute BHS agency to Jesus' locative use of the preposition ἐν to describe the element into which one is immersed (Matt 3:11; Mark 1:8; Luke 3:16; John 1:33; Acts 1:5; 11:16).[243] Based on the perceived NT lack of evidence to support the Spirit's agency in baptism, Storms identifies Jesus as the baptizer places Spirit-immersed disciples in union with the spiritual organism of the church (the body of Christ).[244] The additional metaphor in the parallel expression found in 1 Cor 12:13b is indicative of Semitic parallelism[245] and raises the issue of whether it (ποτίζω, 'I make to drink, flood, irrigate') refers to the same reality conveyed by βαπτίζω ('I baptize, immerse') in the first clause.[246] Storms interprets the co-extensive or synonymously parallel metaphors,[247] 'immersion into' and 'drinking one's fill of,' as references to the same reality: a 'common, lavish experience of the Spirit' occurring 'almost certainly' at conversion.[248]

---

[240] Storms, 'A Third Wave View,' 177-78.

[241] D. A. Carson, *Showing the Spirit: A Theological Exposition of 1 Corinthians 12-14* ([original work published 1987] Grand Rapids: Baker Books, 2003), 47.

[242] Wayne Grudem, *Systematic Theology: An Introduction to Biblical Doctrine* (Grand Rapids: Zondervan Publishing, 1994), 768.

[243] Storms notes the NT grammatical construction of the preposition ὑπό ('by') plus the genitive to express agency in the act of baptizing. Examples include JTB baptizing people in the Jordan (Matt 3:6; Mark 1:5; Luke 3:7) and Jesus' baptism by JTB (Matt 3:13; Mark 1:9). Paul could have used this construction if he meant to attribute instrumentality to the Spirit. Instead, Paul opted to use ἐν plus the dative. See Storms, 'A Third Wave View,' 178 n. 8.

[244] Storms, 'A Third Wave View,' 178.

[245] Ervin interprets the two clauses as an example of synthetic parallelism. He considers the second clause to express an added feature to the phenomenon identified by the first clause. 'Conversion and initiation are followed by a Pentecostal fullness of the Holy Spirit.' See Ervin, *Spirit Baptism*, 33.

[246] Storms, 'A Third Wave View,' 178.

[247] See also Gordon D. Fee, *God's Empowering Presence: The Holy Spirit in the Letters of Paul* ([original work published 1994] Peabody: Hendrickson Publishers, 1995), 181, 861.

[248] Ibid., 181.

Tangential to the third wave BHS construct is the nature and role of post-conversion experiences of the Spirit. Though single-stage in its pneumatological approach to the contemporaneous timing of conversion and BHS, the Spirit's role of providing discrete post-conversion and ministry-essential experiences makes the third wave construct function as a two-stage pneumatological model.[249] The absence of any NT imperative to seek BHS has led third wavers to treat the command 'to be Spirit filled' (πληροῦσθε –Eph 5:18) as normative for contemporary believers. This translates into a post-conversion, relationship-intensifying (with Christ), and ministry-empowering experiences of the Spirit.[250] No single post-conversion experience of the Spirit is considered to be BHS. Key to interpreting Eph 5:18 is its portrayal of the Spirit's ongoing appropriation by the disciple, rather than the occurrence of a one-time dramatic or definitive experience.[251] Citing evangelical scholar Gaffin, Storms refers to the possible reception of BHS accompanied by the permanent indwelling of the Spirit at conversion. According to Storms, Gaffin's view does not include the experience of the Spirit's infilling which would make irrelevant the Eph 5:18 imperative.[252] Two senses of the Spirit's filling are identified by Storms. First, there is the condition/character (moral disposition) of being 'full' of the Spirit (Luke 4:1; Acts 6:3, 5; 7:55; 11:24; 13:52). Second, there is the lasting or task-specific momentary 'filling' of the Spirit (Luke 1:15-17; Acts 9:17).[253] Repeated experiences of the Spirit manifest multiple re-issues of the Spirit (e.g. anointings, infillings, or fresh waves of the Spirit's presence and power). These phenomena are not to be confused with the Spirit-empowering already received.[254] This leads third wavers

---

[249] Gary S. Greig, 'The Purpose of Signs and Wonders in the New Testament,' in Gary S. Greig and Kevin N. Springer, eds., *The Kingdom and the Power: Are Healing and the Spiritual Gifts Used by Jesus and the Early Church Meant for the Church Today?* (Ventura: Regal Books, 1993), 133-174.

[250] James I. Packer, 'The Empowered Christian Life,' in Gary S. Greig and Kevin N. Springer, eds., *The Kingdom and the Power: Are Healing and the Spiritual Gifts Used by Jesus and the Early Church Meant for the Church Today?* (Ventura: Regal Books, 1993), 207-15. See, Rich Nathan and Ken Wilson, *Empowered Evangelicals: Bringing Together the Best of the Evangelical and Charismatic Worlds* (Ann Arbor: Servant Publications, 1995), 207-28. See also, Jack Deere, *Surprised by the Voice of God: How God Speaks Today Through Prophecies, Dreams, and Visions* (Grand Rapids: Zondervan, 1996), 51-52.

[251] Spirit filling is an expressive metaphor describing the believer's 'continuous, ongoing experience and appropriation of the Holy Spirit...to come under progressively more intense and intimate influence of the Spirit.' Storms, 'A Third Wave View,' 179-80.

[252] Gaffin, *Perspectives on Pentecost*, 33.

[253] Storms, 'A Third Wave View,' 180.

[254] John Nolland, *Luke 9:21-18:34,* in Bruce M. Metzger, ed., *Word Biblical Commentary* (Dallas: Word, 1993), 632.

to apply 'in' and 'on' terminology to describe contemporaneous works of the Spirit performed 'on' the believer 'in' whom the Spirit already resides.[255] Related to and not identical with Spirit-filling is a range of other post-conversion 'encounters' which function to 'experientially enlarge' known theological truth.[256] These experiences include revelatory impartations and illumination (Eph 1:15-23; Isa 11:2), anointing with power for the performance of miracles (Gal 3:1-5),[257] the provision of the Spirit to face hardship with hope (Phil 1:19), strength from the Spirit for purity (1 Thess 4:8), and a raised awareness of confidence and assurance of salvation (John 14:15-23; Rom 5:5; 8:15-17; Eph 3:16-19; 1 Pet 1:8).[258] Third wave emphasis on visible and unmistakable evidence of the Spirit's initial reception[259] contributes to the acceptance of a range of 'unusual physical and emotional phenomena' (e.g. trembling, awestruck reverence, inability to stand, or overwhelming joy) considered appropriate to occasions when the extraordinary outpouring of God's Spirit issues revival and renewal.[260]

5. Conclusion

This chapter presented BHS doctrinal constructs for the differentiated spiritual traditions within the P/C movement. There is general agreement among P/C Christians that, subsequent to personal conversion experience, intense Spirit-induced experiences occur largely for the performance of mission-related tasks. The use of differing terminology to label these experiences represents the conceptual variance that exists within the movement. Third wave 'filling' is deemed to be 'BHS' by classical Pentecostals and 'release' (i.e. a profusion of the previously received gift of the Spirit) by sacramentally-oriented charismatics.

---

[255] John White, *When the Spirit Comes with Power: Signs & Wonders Among God's People* (Downers Grove: InterVarsity Press, 1988), 230.

[256] Rodney M. Howard-Browne, *Flowing in the Holy Ghost: A Practical Handbook on the Gifts of the Spirit* (Louisville: RHBEA Publications, 1991), 21-109.

[257] Third wave emphasis on miracles relates to the movement's conviction that the book of Acts is normative for the contemporary church. See Jack Deere, *Surprised by the Power of the Spirit: A Former Dallas Seminary Professor Discovers that God Speaks and Heals Today* (Grand Rapids: Zondervan Publishing, 1993), 114.

[258] Storms, 'A Third Wave View,' 181-85

[259] Fee, *God's Empowering Presence*, 384.

[260] Philip J. Richter, 'God is Not a Gentleman!,' in Michael J. McClymond, ed., *Embodying the Spirit: New Perspectives on North American Revivalism* (Baltimore: Johns Hopkins University Press, 2004), 153-72. Storms, 'A Third Wave View,' 181-82 n. 12. Storms gives an extensive bibliography of works evaluating the extraordinary phenomena accompanying the acclaimed outpouring of the Spirit in times of revival and renewal (e.g. the 'Toronto Blessing'). See also Fee, *God's Empowering Presence*, 388-89.

Theologically associating BHS with personal conversion experience by third wave and sacramental charismatics approximates non-Pentecostal evangelical one-stage pneumatological models. This is especially true of third wavers who defend the co-extensive nature of conversion and BHS on the basis of 1 Cor 12:13. American Baptists and third wave proponents largely agree on this point. However, they contend with classical Pentecostalism's Lukan identification of BHS as a definitive post-conversion experience of the Spirit. Regardless of the label or the nature of its evidential phenomena (*charismata*), the classical Pentecostal expectation of a definitive and secondary experience of the Spirit has unified and even galvanized the P/C movement. The two-stage classical Pentecostal pneumatological model may appear abrogated by one-stage third wave/sacramental BHS constructs, but this is functionally not the case. The doctrine of subsequence which requires a second definitive work of the Spirit has survived in sacramental and third wave BHS constructs. These constructs anticipate profound Spirit-induced endowments which are subsequent to personal conversion experience. When conceived as a secondary endowment of Spirit, BHS unifies P/C Christianity by either being instrumental or foundational to the disciple's life and witness. Though not all P/C adherents subscribe to BHS confirmed by evidential glossolalia, the movement as a whole is unified by the expectation of physical and visible signs which indicate the presence and power of the Spirit in the life of the recipient.

The conclusions of this chapter further support the contention that the primary BHS-related impasse between American Baptists and P/C adherents is not attributed to the ongoing role of the Spirit subsequent to conversion, or the expected evidence of the Spirit's presence in the believer's life, but to the repeatable and definitively experienced Pentecostal BHS experience. The American Baptist point of contention is the association of this experience with miraculous *charismata* deemed by P/C adherents to be necessary for effective Christian living and ministry.

-6-

STEMMING THE HERMENEUTICAL DIVIDE: LUKE-ACTS AS THE DOCTRINAL FOUNDATION FOR SPIRIT BAPTISM

1. Introduction

The purpose of this chapter is to explore the hermeneutical basis for the doctrinal impasse between American Baptist and P/C BHS constructs. The doctrinal impasse is rooted in the classical Pentecostal doctrine of subsequence (also embraced by many renewalists) which affirms repeated personal Pentecostal BHS experiences associated with the miraculous *charismata* deemed necessary for effective Christian living and ministry performance.[1] The doctrine of BHS, when conceived as a work of the Spirit separate from and subsequent to conversion-initiation, is articulated by classical Pentecostals who employ a variety of hermeneutical models. Reliance on Luke-Acts is uniform among presentations of the classical Pentecostal BHS apologetic. Redaction-critical hermeneutical methods have given classical Pentecostal scholars the means for articulating and defending narrative analysis as a means for formulating a distinct Lukan theology (pneumatology). Because of the relative acceptance of redaction-criticism among American Baptist scholars[2] mentioned in this work (e.g. Stein, Blomberg, and Polhill)[3] and the highly regarded redaction-critical BHS apologetic

---

[1] Classical Pentecostals emphasize the vocational necessity of BHS, but do not exclude spiritual benefit from the experience.

[2] This is not an admission that redaction-critical methods are uniformly accepted among American Baptists. It also does not suggest that classical Pentecostals uniformly accept the redaction-critical hermeneutic.

[3] Hamilton also exegetically establishes a distinct Lukan pneumatology from the book of Acts. See James M. Hamilton, Jr., *God's Indwelling Presence: The Holy Spirit in the Old and New Testaments* (Nashville: B & H Academic, 2006), 183-203.

put forth by classical Pentecostal Robert Menzies, the model provides a common hermeneutical basis for dialogically approaching consensus.

By differentiating distinct Lukan and Pauline pneumatologies, classical Pentecostals avoid interpreting Paul through the lens of Luke and thereby present Luke-Acts as a unique message about Christian initiation.[4] Theological conclusions drawn from a narrative-based[5] analysis of Luke-Acts permit classical Pentecostals to present BHS as a distinct personal spiritual experience in the life of the believer. The conclusions are considered to reconcile ultimately with Paul's distinct pneumatology which associates BHS with soteriological function (conversion-initiation). American Baptists can find common hermeneutical ground with classical Pentecostals who incorporate redaction-critical methods while upholding a high view of Scripture and the reliability of the biblical narrative. This hermeneutical consensus is foundational to moving toward BHS doctrinal consensus. The following investigation focuses on Luke-Acts since the classical Pentecostal BHS apologetic relies on conclusions drawn from Lukan pneumatology. At issue is the hermeneutical soundness and implications of deriving a BHS doctrinal construct exclusively from Luke-Acts. The narrative-based redaction-critical approach to Luke-Acts informs American Baptist perceptions of the function of BHS. Though differing from classical Pentecostals on the timing of BHS, American Baptists may access a Lukan pneumatological rationale for enlarging their expectation of spiritual experience via BHS. The chapter will demonstrate that by moving toward doctrinal BHS consensus with classical Pentecostals and many within the charismatic renewal, American Baptists inform their encounter-oriented spirituality.

2. The Evangelicalization of the Classical Pentecostal Hermeneutic: Toward a Common Ground for Doctrinal Consensus

This section is intended to demonstrate how the incorporation of evangelical hermeneutical methods relates to the classical Pentecostal BHS apologetic. It is not, however, intended to be a comprehensive analysis of classical Pentecostal

---

[4] William P. Atkinson, 'Worth a Second Look? Pentecostal Hermeneutics,' in *Evangel* (2003), 53-54.

[5] Use of the term 'narrative-based' is not meant to exclude the didactic portions of the narrative from classical Pentecostal consideration.

hermeneutical trends.[6] The premise is that commonly accepted hermeneutical methods occasion the opportunity for doctrinal consensus.

2.1 The Redaction-Critical Hermeneutic as a Basis for American Baptist/Classical Pentecostal Dialogical Engagement

The application of mutually accepted hermeneutical methods does not always result in common interpretations and systematically arranged texts which unite divergent sides of a doctrinal issue. The BHS debate is indicative of the scholarly sophistication utilized by classical Pentecostalism to defend its doctrinal distinction.[7] This ability is attributed to what has been termed the 'evangelicalization' of North American classical Pentecostal hermeneutics.[8] The expression is used primarily to identify classical Pentecostals within the academy, such as notable P/C scholar Gordon Fee, who aligns with evangelicals[9] that adopt the methods of historical criticism while remaining committed to the reliability of the biblical narrative.[10] William Menzies is an advocate of the redaction-critical method to derive a Pentecostal theology ('Spirit-baptism initiation accompanied by tongues') from narrative texts.[11] Robert Menzies and Roger Stronstad are among classical Pentecostal scholars who utilize the redaction-critical method to ascertain Lukan authorial intent and an independent pneumatological

---

[6] For a helpful overview of hermeneutical developments within classical Pentecostalism, see Roger Stronstad, 'Trends in Pentecostal Hermeneutics,' in *Paraclete* (1988), 1-12. Other scholarly treatments of the historical development of classical Pentecostal hermeneutics include: Richard D. Israel, Daniel E. Albrecht and Randal G. McNally, 'Pentecostals and Hermeneutics: Texts, Rituals and Community,' in *Pneuma* (1993), 137-61; Timothy B. Cargal, 'Beyond the Fundamentalist-Modernist Controversy: Pentecostals and Hermeneutics in a Post-Modern Age,' in *Pneuma* (1993), 163-87; Jean-Daniel Plüss, 'Azusa and Other Myths: The Long and Winding Road from Experience to Stated Belief and Back Again,' in *Pneuma* (1993), 189-201; Joseph Byrd, 'Paul Ricoeur's Hermeneutical Theory and Pentecostal Proclamation,' in *Pneuma* (1993), 203-14. For a thorough analysis, see Kenneth J. Archer, *Hermeneutics for the Twenty-First Century: Spirit, Scripture and Community* (London: T & T Clark, 2004).

[7] Kenneth J. Archer, 'Pentecostal Hermeneutics: Retrospect and Prospect,' in *JPT* (1996), 73.

[8] French L. Arrington, 'The Use of the Bible by Pentecostals,' in *Pneuma* (1994), 101.

[9] Gordon D. Fee, *New Testament Exegesis: A Handbook for Students and Pastors, 3rd Ed.* (Westminster: John Knox Press, 2002).

[10] Cargal, 'Beyond the Fundamentalist-Modernist Controversy,' 163.

[11] William W. Menzies, 'The Methodology of Pentecostal Theology: An Essay in Hermeneutics,' in Paul Elbert, ed., *Essays on Apostolic Themes: Studies in Honor of Howard M. Ervin* (Peabody: Hendrickson Publishers, 1985), 8.

perspective.[12] These scholars turn to the 'evangelical wing of the church' in order to find 'particular hermeneutical assistance.'[13] The appropriation of evangelical hermeneutical methods by some classical Pentecostals does not suggest its acceptance by others within the tradition,[14] or for that matter other evangelicals, including American Baptists. Archer, for example, critiques fellow classical Pentecostal Robert Menzies for focusing his hermeneutic exclusively on authorial intent and the understanding of the text for the original readers.[15] Cargal is similarly critical of William Menzies for emphasizing authorial intent and the historical context of biblical narratives to derive textual meaning.[16] He warns that hermeneutical strategies based on historical concerns emerge from a philosophical paradigm that ignores the influence of postmodernism in Western society.[17] These criticisms reveal classical Pentecostalism's desire for a 'holistic' hermeneutic which is less an accommodation to modernism and more a dialogical interaction between levels of understanding (e.g. critical-historical literary, pneumatic, experience-community).[18]

Adopting some elements of 'evangelical methodology' (e.g. historical/source and redaction criticism) creates tension with some evangelicals and American Baptist scholars who oppose higher critical methods in favor of the grammatical-historical hermeneutic.[19] Evangelical scholar Thomas is critical of classical

---

[12] Robert P. Menzies, *The Development of Early Christian Pneumatology with Special Reference to Luke-Acts* (Sheffield: Sheffield Academic Press, 1991). See also Robert P. Menzies, *Empowered for Witness: The Holy Spirit in Luke-Acts* (Sheffield: Sheffield Academic Press, 1994); Roger Stronstad, *The Charismatic Theology of St. Luke* ([original work published 1984] Peabody: Hendrickson Publishers, 2002).

[13] Robert K. Johnston, 'Pentecostalism and Theological Hermeneutics: Evangelical Options,' in *Pneuma* (1984), 55.

[14] Cargal notes the further discontinuity between the academy and the 'preachers within parish communities' who have retained 'traditional modes of Pentecostal interpretation' and emphasize 'the immediacy of the text and multiple dimensions of meaning.' See Cargal, 'Beyond the Fundamentalist-Modernist Controversy,' 164. This approximates a reader-centered, or reader-response hermeneutical method, which subjects the text to the reader's preunderstanding (bias) and results in textual distortion or contradiction with the author's intent. See Robert H. Stein, *The Basic Guide to Interpreting the Bible: Playing by the Rules, 2nd Ed.* ([original work published 1994] Grand Rapids: Baker Academic, 2011), 18-20.

[15] Archer, 'Pentecostal Hermeneutics,' 75.

[16] Menzies, 'The Methodology of Pentecostal Theology,' 8.

[17] Cargal, 'Beyond the Fundamentalist-Modernist Controversy,' 164.

[18] Arrington, 'The Use of the Bible by Pentecostals,' 101-7. See also French L. Arrington, 'Hermeneutics,' in Stanley Burgess and Gary B. McGee, eds. *DPCM* (Grand Rapids: Zondervan Publishing, 1988), 384.

[19] See Robert L. Thomas and F. David Farnell, eds., *The Jesus Crisis: The Inroads of Historical Criticism into Evangelical Scholarship* (Grand Rapids: Kregel Publications, 1998). See

Pentecostal scholars William and Robert Menzies for their admitted reliance on redaction criticism.[20] He opposes their attributing to Marshall[21] the bringing about of a revolution in evangelical attitudes 'toward the theological significance of biblical narrative.'[22] Conversely, Robert Menzies commends the work of American Baptist scholars Stein and Blomberg for their 'impressive array of scholarly studies' which judiciously discriminate the positive insights of the redaction-critical method from the more radical presuppositions.[23] Though embattled over the issue of inerrancy,[24] American Baptists have historically maintained a high view of Scripture in their doctrinal confessions.[25] This high view of Scripture is shared by classical Pentecostals. Arrington writes:

> At the heart of classical Pentecostalism is the conviction that the whole Bible is the inspired Word of God. This conviction affirms that the Bible is a reliable revelation of God, and that it states the exact truths the Holy Spirit intends to convey. The writing of Scripture by the prophets and apostles does not detract from the divine origin and authority of Scripture. God joined his Word with the words of men and women in the Scriptures. The starting point and very foundation for Pentecostal faith and praxis has been the biblical text.[26]

There is no discernible difference between the stated classical Pentecostal regard for the Scriptures and the American Baptist confessional positions.[27] At issue, however, is the hermeneutical approach to the Scriptures.

---

also Robert L. Thomas, *Evangelical Hermeneutics: The New Versus the Old* (Grand Rapids: Kregel Publications, 2002).

[20] Robert L. Thomas, 'The Hermeneutics of Noncessationism,' in *TMSJ* (2003), 291. See William W. and Robert P. Menzies. *Spirit and Power: Foundations of Pentecostal Experience* (Grand Rapids: Zondervan, 2000), 40-41.

[21] I. Howard Marshall, *Luke: Historian and Theologian* (Grand Rapids: Zondervan Publishing House, 1971).

[22] Thomas, 'The Hermeneutics of Noncessationism,' 40-41.

[23] Menzies and Menzies, *Spirit and Power,* 41.

[24] See Nancy Tatom Ammerman, *Baptist Battles: Social Change and Religious Conflict in the Southern Baptist Convention* (New Brunswick: Rutgers University Press, 1990). See also L. Russ Bush and Tom J. Nettles, *Baptists and the Bible* ([original work published 1980] Nashville: B & H Academic, 1995) and Harold Lindsell, *The Battle for the Bible: The Book that Rocked the Evangelical World* (Grand Rapids: Zondervan, 1976).

[25] See William L. Lumpkin, *Baptist Confessions of Faith* (Philadelphia: The Judson Press, 1959).

[26] Arrington, 'The Use of the Bible by Pentecostals,' 101.

[27] Classical Pentecostals regard the human authors of Scripture as passive instruments in the process of transmission. This position amounts to a dictation theory of the Bible's inspiration. See Arrington, 'Hermeneutics,' 380. Wacker describes the early (classical) Pentecostals as holding

In addition to the evangelicalization of North American classical Pentecostal biblical scholarship is the move toward a 'holistic' hermeneutical model. Such a model considers the distinctive nature and function of Scripture and its interpretive process in terms of the corresponding roles of the Holy Spirit, the Christian community, grammatical-historical research, and personal experience.[28] The community-centered 'holistic' hermeneutic advocated among classical Pentecostals is a perceived corrective to hermeneutical systems that emphasize rationalism and downplay the contributions of personal experience and the Holy Spirit.[29] To the degree that some classical Pentecostals oppose the exclusive use of rational grammatical-historical and redaction-critical hermeneutical models,[30] many American Baptists disdain what Dayton terms a 'subjectivizing hermeneutic.'[31] Thomas expresses an American Baptist perspective when he refers to the classical Pentecostal 'doctrine-based-on-narrative' rationale as the 'new hermeneutical subjectivism.'[32] The redaction-critical hermeneutic integral to narrative analysis and literary criticism does not satisfy every constituent of the American Baptist and classical Pentecostal traditions, but it does offer the advantage of a common hermeneutical ground approved by many scholars within the respective movements. Among hermeneutical alternatives, the redaction-critical approach to Luke-Acts combined with a corresponding BHS apologetic methodologically offer the best point of departure for American Baptist/classical Pentecostal dialogical engagement.

---

to a rigid dictation theory that viewed the Bible as a 'sacred meteor.' This contributed to its regard as being 'preserved from errors of any sort –historical, scientific, or theological.' See Grant Wacker, *Heaven Below: Early Pentecostals and American Culture* ([original work published 2001] Cambridge: Harvard University Press, 2003), 73.

[28] Arrington, 'The Use of the Bible by Pentecostals,' 101.

[29] John C. Thomas, 'Women, Pentecostals and the Bible: An Experiment in Pentecostal Hermeneutics,' *JPT* (1994), 41.

[30] McDonnell refers to the former trend among classical Pentecostal scholars who refrained from what was considered 'a sterile evangelical rationalism in hermeneutics.' See Kilian McDonnell, 'Five Defining Issues: The International Classical Pentecostal/Roman Catholic Dialogue,' in *Pneuma* (1995), 176.

[31] Donald W. Dayton, *The Theological Roots of Pentecostalism* ([original work published 1987] Peabody: Hendrickson Publishers, 2000), 23.

[32] Thomas, 'The Hermeneutics of Noncessationism,' 287.

2.2 Experience-Based Preunderstanding and the Subjectivizing Hermeneutic

The restorationist orientation[33] of classical Pentecostalism achieved a type of 'present-tenseness' to biblical interpretation, a kind of pre-critical 'biblicism.'[34] The phenomenon occurs when a Spirit-aided interpreter enters the world of the Bible[35] without the perceived need to engage the hermeneutical difficulties that are associated with reading an ancient text within a modern context.[36] In addition, a 'praxis-driven'[37] application orientation[38] forges a near exclusive dependence on Luke-Acts as the model of Christian living and ministry.[39] The result is the classical Pentecostal assertion[40] that the manner of the Spirit's reception on the Day of Pentecost is the normative experience for each individual believer.[41] The movement's self-analysis includes the recognition and unapologetic defense of its 'subjectivizing hermeneutic.'[42]

---

[33] Macchia describes the restorationist orientation as 'the goal of recovering the full life of the Spirit experienced by the churches of the apostles and depicted for us in the NT.' See Frank D. Macchia, 'Theology, Pentecostal,' in Stanley M. Burgess and Eduard M. Van Der Mass, eds., *NIDPCM* (Grand Rapids: Zondervan, 2002), 1121. Wacker refers to this principle as the 'plenary relevance' of the Bible. See Wacker, *Heaven Below*, 70-72. See also Cargal, 'Beyond the Fundamentalist-Modernist Controversy,' 168 and Archer, *A Pentecostal Hermeneutic for the Twenty-First Century*, 3 and Dayton, *Theological Roots of Pentecostalism*, 25.

[34] Cargal, 'Beyond the Fundamentalist-Modernist Controversy,' 171.

[35] Arrington writes: 'The personal experience of Pentecost informs their [classical Pentecostals] interpretation of Scripture.' See French L. Arrington, *Christian Doctrine: A Pentecostal Perspective, Vol. 1* (Cleveland: Pathway Press, 1992), 77. Pearlman maintained a distinction between experiencing the Spirit in text origination (inspiration) and interpretation (illumination). See Myer Pearlman, *Knowing the Doctrines of the Bible* (Springfield: Gospel Publishing House, 1937), 21-22. Cargal notes the increasing classical Pentecostal trend to gloss this distinction and to claim 'that modern interpreters share the same phenomenological encounter with the Spirit as the ancient authors…this experience informs and supports their interpretations.' See Cargal, 'Beyond the Fundamentalist-Modernist Controversy,' 176.

[36] Macchia, 'Theology, Pentecostal,' 1122.

[37] Kenneth J. Archer, 'Early Pentecostal Biblical Interpretation,' in *JPT* (2001), 43.

[38] Archer, *A Pentecostal Hermeneutic for the Twenty-First Century*, 157; Arden C. Autry, 'Dimensions of Hermeneutics in Pentecostal Focus,' in *JPT* (1993), 31.

[39] Dayton, *Theological Roots of Pentecostalism*, 23; Walter J. Hollenweger, *The Pentecostals: The Charismatic Movement in the Churches* (Minneapolis: Augsburg Publishing House, 1972), 336.

[40] See the definition of the movement offered by William Menzies in, *Anointed to Serve: The Story of the Assemblies of God* (Springfield: Gospel Publishing House, 1971), 9.

[41] Dayton, *Theological Roots of Pentecostalism*, 23.

[42] Ibid.

Opposition to the subjectivizing hermeneutic, on the charge that classical Pentecostals exegete their experience,[43] is answered by Stronstad who opines that non-Pentecostals perform the same experience-based exegesis based on non-charismatic experience.[44] It is useful to recall that American Baptists base their doctrinal teachings and interpretation of Scripture on experience as well as intellectual reasoning. As previously demonstrated (see Chapter 3), spiritual experience is foundational to American Baptist Christian living. Such experience relates not only to conversion but also to an ongoing awareness of the presence of God in worship, prayer, preaching and Bible study. This includes the intervention of God in daily living, especially in times of crisis (e.g. sickness, difficult relationships, financial need). It would not, however, include the more dramatic manifestations of being overwhelmed by the Spirit or speaking in tongues, as professed by many adherents in the P/C movement.

The specific charge of subjectivity concerns the classical Pentecostal practice of precluding biblical exegesis to arrive at an experience-based understanding of BHS.[45] The charge makes experience presuppositional to the classical Pentecostal hermeneutic. This preunderstanding, however, does not occur without qualification.[46] MacDonald considers the aim of the classical Pentecostal hermeneutic to be a fully realized theology, or what he terms, 'Christ-centered, experience-certified theology.'[47] Stronstad readily defends the presuppositional (or 'preunderstanding'[48]) role of experience in hermeneutics by emphasizing the inviolate objective reality of the Bible.[49] The subjective stimuli of saving faith and charismatic experience, considered to be insufficient bases for sound interpretation by classical Pentecostals, do provide an important pre-

---

[43] Gordon D. Fee, *Gospel and Spirit: Issues in New Testament Hermeneutics* (Peabody: Hendrickson Publishers, 1991), 86. Carson expresses the typical non-Pentecostal caricature of classical Pentecostals as having succumbed 'to the modern love of experience... [and] thought to be profoundly unbiblical.' See also D. A. Carson, *Showing the Spirit: A Theological Exposition of 1 Corinthians 12-14* ([original work published 1987] Grand Rapids: Baker Books, 2003), 12.

[44] Stronstad, 'Pentecostal Experience and Hermeneutics,' 20.

[45] Peter Hocken, *The Glory and the Shame: Reflections on the 20th Century Outpouring of the Holy Spirit* (Wheaton: Harold Shaw Publishers, 1994), 46. See also Fee, *Gospel and Spirit*, 86. See also, Leon Morris, *Spirit of the Living God: The Bible's Teaching on the Holy Spirit* (London: InterVarsity Press, 1960), 64-65.

[46] Keith Warrington, *Pentecostal Theology: A Theology of Encounter* (London: T & T Clark, 2008), 193.

[47] William G. MacDonald, 'Pentecostal Theology: A Classical Perspective,' in Russell P. Spittler, ed., *Perspectives on the New Pentecostalism* (Grand Rapids: Baker Book House, 1976), 64.

[48] Thomas, 'The Hermeneutics of Noncessationism,' 294.

[49] Roger Stronstad, 'Pentecostal Experience and Hermeneutics,' in *Paraclete* (1992), 26.

understanding of the text. This is especially true regarding the role of charismatic experience to the preunderstanding of Luke-Acts on the part of the interpreter.

As previously indicated, American Baptists also emphasize experiential criteria as being necessary for effective biblical interpretation. Blomberg, Klein and Hubbard describe the hermeneutical process as not only giving attention to the ancient text and the conditions which produced it, but also its modern context and circumstances experienced by contemporary interpreters.[50] On their view, all interpreters have presuppositions and preunderstandings, making biblical interpretation inclusive of these phenomena but not limited to them.[51] Stein refers positively to the interpretive act of discerning the author's conscious meaning of the text and its present implications on the reader.[52] He warns, however, that this process must be performed without the interpreter unknowingly reading bias and prejudice into the text.[53] Citing 1 Cor 2:14, Stein acknowledges the illuminating role of the Spirit to aid the believer's cognitive grasp of the text and to induce conviction where the personal implications of the text are concerned.[54] Ramm, though not using the word 'experience,' emphasizes the role of the interpreter's 'spiritual qualifications.'[55] Alluding to Rom 8:7 and 1 Cor 2:14, he cites Dods in defense of the modern interpreter of Scripture being under the similar influence of the Spirit, who, through the inspired text, continues to encounter modern man.[56] Dods assertion is strikingly similar to P/C scholar Howard Ervin who views the Spirit's guidance of the human author of Scripture to be equally essential to the

---

[50] William W. Klein, Craig L. Blomberg, and Robert L. Hubbard, Jr., *Introduction to Biblical Interpretation* ([original work published 1993] Nashville: Thomas Nelson Publishers, 2004), 7.

[51] Ibid. See Fee, *Gospel and Spirit*, 50. See also Rudolf Bultmann, 'Is Exegesis without Presupposition Possible?,' in S. M. Ogden, ed., *Existence and Faith: Shorter Writings of Rudolf Bultmann* (London: Collins, 1964), 342-52 and Graham N. Stanton, 'Presuppositions in New Testament Criticism,' in I. Howard Marshall, ed., *New testament Interpretation: Essays on Principles and Methods* ([original work published 1977] Grand Rapids: William B. Eerdmans Publishing, 1992), 60-71. Stanton directly states that 'a completely detached stance,' what he refers to as 'spectator exegesis,' is not even possible in textual criticism [because] whenever the textual evidence is ambiguous the scholar's decision will be influenced, however indirectly, by his own presuppositions' (65).

[52] Stein, *The Basic Guide to Interpreting the Bible*, 10.

[53] Ibid., 12.

[54] Ibid., 20-27.

[55] Bernard Ramm, *Protestant Biblical Interpretation, 3rd Ed.* ([original work published 1970] Grand Rapids: Baker Book House, 1984), 12-16.

[56] Marcus Dods, *The Bible: Its Origin and Nature* ([original work published 1905] New York: Charles Scribner's Sons, 1912), 102.

process of human interpretation.[57] Ramm refers to additional spiritual qualifications (e.g. 'born again,' 'a passion to know God's word,' and 'an utter dependence on the Holy Spirit') which combine with the 'intellectual requirements' for an effective interpretive process.[58] In many instances, it is evident that the difference between American Baptist and Pentecostal interpreters is one of semantics, not experience.

Stronstad largely agrees, emphasizing 'the pneumatic' experience (i.e. charismatic experience and illumination of the Spirit) which, when combined with sensitivity to the literary genre and Protestant biblical exegesis, constitutes the experiential and rational dimensions of the hermeneutical process.[59] The classical Pentecostal hermeneutic is incomplete without verification. The aim of its holistic approach is to integrate sound exegesis and theology into contemporary experience. For the classical Pentecostal, experience-certified theology is a matter of Christian experience.[60] It is evident within the academy that classical Pentecostals and American Baptists share general conceptual agreement on the elements of effective biblical interpretation. The terminology used to describe the hermeneutical process may vary ('experience' versus 'spiritual' and 'conviction'), but the reality is the same; the interpreter or reader subjectively engages with the text to ascertain its author-intended meaning.[61]

2.3   Authorial Intent and the Development of a Narrative-Based Lukan Pneumatology

This focus of this section is authorial intent, a distinct feature of redaction criticism. The section will consider the contribution of Luke's writings and their significance to advancing the objective of American Baptist and P/C consensus on matters concerning the role of the Spirit in the Christian life.

---

[57] Howard M. Ervin, 'Hermeneutics: A Pentecostal Option,' in *Pneuma* (1981), 22.

[58] Ramm, *Protestant Biblical Interpretation,* 13-15.

[59] Stronstad, 'Pentecostal Experience and Hermeneutics,' 27.

[60] Ibid., 28.

[61] Stein is correct to qualify the public and private factors of interpretation. Authorial intention is not a matter for the interpreter to reproduce the emotional or psychological experience of the author, but to determine what the author meant by the written text. The public factor is the text from which the interpreter ascertains meaning. The author's mental faculties are private and inaccessible to the interpreter. See Stein, *The Basic Guide to Interpreting the Bible,* 22.

2.3.1 *Evangelical Influence and the Classical Pentecostal Thesis*

The fact that Robert Menzies commended Marshall for shifting the focus of evangelical thought in Lukan studies is significant for classical Pentecostal theologizing. It is also significant to the task of building broader consensus on the basis of adopting mutually accepted hermeneutical principles.[62] As early as 1927 Cadbury focused on Luke's deliberate literary purpose.[63] Conzelmann later contributed to Lukan studies with his 1960 seminal work that argues for Luke as a theologian.[64] These works are succeeded thematically by Marshall's 1970 *Luke: Historian and Theologian*. This work gave rise to classical Pentecostal scholarship's elevation of the book of Acts from mere historical narrative to historical-theological narrative.[65] This expansion of the field of hermeneutical inquiry argues for a distinct Lukan pneumatology[66] which complements the Pauline corpus and/or the rest of the NT.[67] Marshall concretized this understanding of Luke-Acts which served as a corrective influence upon classical Pentecostal exegesis. Previously, classical Pentecostal scholarship read Paul in light of Acts, thereby making no distinction between Lukan and Pauline pneumatology.[68] Luke's unique theological perspective is critical to the BHS debate given the fact that classical Pentecostalism admits dependence on Luke-Acts to trace the biblical roots of BHS.[69] Robert Menzies' redaction-critical

---

[62] Robert P. Menzies, 'The Essence of Pentecostalism: Forum Conducted at the Asia Pacific Theological Seminary Chapel,' in *Paraclete* (1992), 4.

[63] Henry J. Cadbury, *The Making of Luke-Acts* (New York: Macmillan, 1927), 133-5.

[64] Hans Conzelmann, Trans. Geoffrey Buswell, *The Theology of St. Luke* (ET New York: Harper & Row Publishers, 1960). Bovon's second revised edition is exemplary of the scholarly work devoted to Lukan studies. See François Bovon, *Luke the Theologian, Revised 2ⁿᵈ Ed.* (Waco: Baylor University Press, 2006).

[65] Archer, 'Pentecostal Hermeneutics,' 73. See Roger Stronstad, *The Charismatic Theology of St. Luke* ([original work published 1984] Peabody: Hendrickson Publishers, 2002).

[66] Menzies, 'The Essence of Pentecostalism,' 1.

[67] Archer, 'Pentecostal Hermeneutics,' 73.

[68] Menzies and Menzies, *Spirit and Power,* 40. Archer, 'Pentecostal Hermeneutics,' 74.

[69] See Hollenweger's 1972 appraisal of classical Pentecostalism and the charismatic movement. Walter J. Hollenweger, *The Pentecostals: The Charismatic Movement in the Churches* (Minneapolis: Augsburg Publishing House, 1972), 336-7. Hollenweger's later assessment of classical Pentecostalism's 'more scholarly' and critical hermeneutical approach considers not its move away from the book of Acts, but from old-school subjectivity to 'a more objective, reasoned, rational and historically sensitive hermeneutic.' See Walter J. Hollenweger, 'The Critical Tradition of Pentecostalism,' in *JPT* (1992), 17.

approach to Luke-Acts[70] is a classical Pentecostal BHS apologetic which not only identifies a distinct Lukan pneumatology,[71] but corresponds with accepted evangelical hermeneutical methods.[72] Stronstad's case for Lukan authorial intent is based on the literary and theological homogeneity of Luke-Acts.[73] On this view, Luke-Acts is historical narrative that required historiographical methodology to compose.[74] Further, Luke's intent is didactic, or at least instructional, rather than a mere transmission of information.[75] This makes Luke a theologian in his own right and sets him apart from the other evangelists. Also, his purpose of recording history (whether that be a primary or secondary purpose is not important for the current discussion) sets him apart from the writers of the epistles. When interpreted according to Stronstad's historiographical method, Luke presents a charismatic rather than soteriological pneumatology.[76] Key to the Menzies' and Stronstad's theses is the role of Luke as an independent theologian.

American Baptist Polhill agrees with Stronstad's form-critical assessment of Luke's literary method being indicative of Hellenistic historiography. He attributes authorial intention to Luke's interest in world events as they intersected with the incipient Christian movement. Thus, the tension of this interaction produced the witness of the Savior 'of the world *with* the world.' Polhill insists (as do Menzies and Stronstad) that Luke is a theologian who was writing from the perspective of faith. Though not advocating a charismatic theology, he inclines toward the classical Pentecostal view of non-soteriological Luke-Acts authorial intent (though he prefers independent theological constructs for the Gospel and for Acts). Polhill also considers 'the power of the Spirit' to be an integral theme of the book of Acts and a functionally necessary element for Christian mission.[77]

---

[70] Robert P. Menzies, *The Development of Early Christian Pneumatology with Special Reference to Luke-Acts* (Sheffield: Sheffield Academic Press, 1991). See also Robert P. Menzies, *Empowered for Witness: The Holy Spirit in Luke-Acts* (Sheffield: Sheffield Academic Press, 1994).

[71] Atkinson, 'Worth a Second Look? Pentecostal Hermeneutics,' 54.

[72] Robert P. Menzies, 'The Spirit of Prophecy, Luke-Acts and Pentecostal Theology: A Response to Max Turner,' in *JPT* (1999), 51-54.

[73] Polhill agrees when he writes: 'For Luke the Gospel and Acts represent two stages of the same story.' See John B. Polhill, *Acts,* in David S. Dockery, ed., *The New American Commentary: An Exegetical and Theological Exposition of Holy Scripture, Vol. 26* (Nashville: Broadman Press, 1992), 42-43.

[74] Roger Stronstad, 'The Hermeneutics of Lucan Historiography,' in *Paraclete* (1988), 15.

[75] Ibid.

[76] Stronstad, *The Charismatic Theology of St. Luke,* 11-12.

[77] Polhill, *Acts,* 51-65.

Stronstad and Polhill represent respectively the general classical Pentecostal and American Baptist consensus that Luke composed the homogeneous narrative of Luke-Acts as a historian with theological intent. There is additional 'qualified' consensus on the non-soteriological theological orientation of Luke-Acts. The nature of this qualified consensus is that where Stronstad speaks of 'charismatic' theology in the classical Pentecostal non-cessationist 'present-tenseness,' Polhill speaks with cessationist 'past-tenseness.'

2.3.2   *American Baptists: Redaction-Criticism, the Genre of Luke-Acts and the Prospect of Narrative Theology*

American Baptists, mindful of the abuses associated with redaction-criticism,[78] believe these to be a reflection on the interpreters and not on the method.[79] Soulen's definition for redaction criticism is adopted by Blomberg, Klein, and Hubbard to reveal the biblical writer's theological perspectives. This is accomplished by analyzing editorial or compositional techniques and interpretations used by the author to shape the available written and/or oral traditions (e.g. Luke 1:1-4).[80] Following American fellow Baptist scholar Guelich, Blomberg, Klein, and Hubbard adhere to the formal/material dichotomy of gospel genre. According to Guelich, the Gospels have formal parallels with other literature being narrative accounts of the public life and teaching of a significant person.[81] Materially, the Gospels are literarily distinct and are uniquely Christian.[82] Blomberg, Klein, and Hubbard conclude with Marshall that the Gospels are best referred to as 'theological biographies.'[83] On their view, the

---

[78] Carson warns that the method is 'often pursued in such a way that the historical trustworthiness of the gospel is called into question.' He does not fault the redaction-critical method, but the redaction critic who, after the manner of radical form criticism, asserts the gospel writers disinterest in historical accuracy. Carson rightly attributes the redaction critic's 'anti-historical biases' to the method's 'reputation of being a method that attacks the historical reliability of the gospels.' See D. A. Carson and Douglas J. Moo, *An Introduction to the New Testament, 2nd Ed.* (Grand Rapids: Zondervan, 2005), 109. See also D. A. Carson, 'Redaction Criticism: On the Legitimacy and Illegitimacy of a Literary Tool,' in D. A. Carson and J. D. Woodbridge, eds., *Scripture and Truth* (Grand Rapids: Zondervan, 1983), 119-42, 376-81.

[79] Klein, Blomberg, and Hubbard, *Introduction to Biblical Interpretation*, 406.

[80] Richard N. Soulen and R. Kendall Soulen, *Handbook of Biblical Criticism, 3rd Ed.* (Louisville: Westminster John Knox Press, 2001), 158.

[81] Robert A. Guelich, 'The Gospel Genre,' in Peter Stuhlmacher, ed., *The Gospel and the Gospels* (Grand Rapids: William B. Eerdmans Publishing, 1991), 206.

[82] Klein, Blomberg, and Hubbard, *Introduction to Biblical Interpretation*, 406.

[83] I. Howard Marshall, 'Luke and His Gospel,' in Peter Stuhlmacher, ed., *The Gospel and the Gospels* (Grand Rapids: William B. Eerdmans Publishing, 1991), 273-82.

genre of Luke's Gospel and the book of Acts (e.g. Luke 1:1-4; Acts 1:1) is 'theological history' composed into a narrative of selected and interrelated events that conveys theological truth.[84] The interpretive ethos of this genre attributes didactic authorial intent to Luke who compiles history in such a way that he communicates to readers: (1) what he considers God to be doing in the world, and (2) what God commands believers to perform in and through the narrated events.[85] Though indirect in its didactic function, narrative is equally normative once the author's intention is discerned.[86] In his endorsement of narrative theology, Hamilton acknowledges its merits contra attempts to deduce a concrete pneumatology from the book of Acts (e.g. Barrett).[87] Following Marshall, he analyzes phrases used by Luke to record Spirit manifestations as evidence for a developed theme in the book of Acts.[88] Schreiner also regards the frequent mention of the Spirit in Luke-Acts to be grounds for attributing theologian status to Luke.[89] Polhill adduces Lukan authorial intent for Luke-Acts from the prologue-like function of Luke 1:1-4. In Luke 1:4 he sees evidence not only for an historian's interest (e.g. literary procedures, eyewitnesses, and careful investigation), but also a theologian's interest in the confessed well-ordered arrangement of the content.[90] The theology of Acts is evident from its narration of episodic themes and story line motifs. Polhill identifies numerous themes within the book of Acts which collectively reveal authorial intent.[91] Stein also methodologically favors interpreting historical narrative to deduce authorial intent.[92] He considers the focus of the biblical exegete to be the author's

---

[84] Klein, Blomberg, and Hubbard, Introduction to Biblical Interpretation, 418.

[85] Ibid., 419.

[86] Ibid., 423. See Leland Ryken, *The Literature of the Bible* (Grand Rapids: Zondervan Publishing House, 1974), 45-106. See also Walter L. Liefeld, *Interpreting the Book of Acts* (Grand Rapids: Baker Book House, 1996), 113-28.

[87] C. K. Barrett, *A Critical and Exegetical Commentary on the Acts of the Apostles, Vol. 1* (Edinburgh: T & T Clark, 1994), 115. See also Gordon D. Fee, 'Hermeneutics and Historical Precedent: A Major Problem in Pentecostal Hermeneutics,' in Russell P. Spittler, *Perspectives on the New Pentecostalism* (Grand Rapids: Baker Book House, 1976), 118-32.

[88] I. Howard Marshall, 'The Significance of Pentecost,' in *SJT* (1977), 355.

[89] Thomas R. Schreiner, *New Testament Theology: Magnifying God in Christ* (Grand Rapids: Baker Academic, 2008), 440.

[90] Polhill, *Acts,* 54-56.

[91] Ibid., 57-72. According to Polhill, no single purpose should be attributed to Luke for writing the book of Acts. Instead, the variety of themes 'interweaves and overlaps with one another to furnish the rich tapestry that is the story of Acts' (57).

[92] Stein, *The Basic Guide to Interpreting the Bible,* 38.

interpretation of the reported event and not the divine revelation contained therein.[93]

Blomberg is in substantial agreement with the above endorsement of narrative theology via the discovery of authorial intent. He emphasizes that such discovery includes a dialogical component which is critical to textual analysis and is significant to American Baptist engagement with classical Pentecostals to achieve some level of doctrinal consensus. Blomberg identifies what he terms a 'globalizing' hermeneutic which transcends parochialism within and the historical and social conditioning created by the interpreting community. Dialogical interaction occurs when questions and answers posed to the interpreter exceed the bounds of personal experience. According to Blomberg, the potential for an interpretive paradigm shift exists for a given text when representative voices from different nationalities, ethnic groups, gender, socio-economic strata, or even religions other than those that have normally dominated the guild of biblical interpretation reveal new questions or suggest new answers to old questions. This insightful proposal opens the door for American Baptists to dialogically engage classical Pentecostals whose experience, in Blomberg's terms, may more closely approximate that of the text(s) under consideration. More important to the dialogical process is being mutually committed to the text's actual meaning and/or significance. Each participant in the dialogical process has historically and grammatically researched the text and is convinced that their interpretations are accordingly defensible. Though not referencing classical Pentecostals, Blomberg positively acknowledges the interpretive process of those who consider their personal experience to relate closely to the setting of the texts under investigation, thus making these modern analogies close approximations to those experienced by people in the biblical world.[94]

3. A Dialogical Approach to Lukan Theological Intent

It is necessary to delimit the parameters of doctrinal consensus investigated in this section. Omitted from this discussion is a thorough analysis of the contribution made by the 'soteriological' versus 'prophetic' (inspired-speech or charismatic-empowering) Spirit issue to the BHS debate. This section offers American Baptists a path toward BHS doctrinal consensus derived from a dialogue with classical Pentecostal scholarship that is informed by a non-Pentecostal evangelical position. Each scholar in the dialectic follows the

---

[93] Ibid., 40.

[94] Craig L. Blomberg, 'The Globalization of Hermeneutics,' in *JETS* (1995), 582-83.

redaction-critical approach to Luke-Acts and acknowledges the existence of a distinct Lukan pneumatology.

3.1   The Pursuit of Common Ground

Arie W. Zwiep is assistant professor of NT and hermeneutics at Vrije University (Amsterdam, NL).[95] In the autumn 2007 edition of *PentecoStudies*, Zwiep offered an irenic evangelical BHS response to an earlier (2000) thesis presented by Robert Menzies.[96] Zwiep is confessedly 'a former Pentecostal' who completed PhD studies at the University of Durham (UK) under the supervision of James D. G. Dunn.[97] As an evangelical biblical scholar with a special interest in Luke-Acts, Zwiep is not only familiar with the challenge of dialogue and consensus, but is qualified to inform the following sections. He embraces the sentiments of Stronstad[98] and Blomberg[99] who similarly aver in support of 'a mutual willingness to give up one's own opinions for better ones.'[100] From an 'outsider perspective,'[101] Zwiep makes a positive contribution to an American Baptist BHS consensus view; one that militates against a penultimate reading of the Bible to confirm 'what one already believes.'[102]

---

[95] Vrije University, 2012. 'Dr. Arie W. Zwiep,' n.p. Available from: http://home.solcon.nl/ awzwiep/index.htm. [Accessed 20 June 2012].

[96] The article was originally a paper presented at a symposium on the Lukan perspective of BHS at Vrije University (Amsterdam, NL) on 16 February 2006 to mark the 100th anniversary of the Azusa Street Revival. Zwiep refers specifically to the Menzies' 2000 work, *Spirit and Power*, the book under discussion at the symposium. See Arie W. Zwiep, 'Luke's Understanding of baptism in the Holy Spirit,' in *PentecoStudies* (2007), 127-49. See also Arie W. Zwiep, *Christ, the Spirit and the Community of God* (Tübingen: Mohr Siebeck, 2010), 100-19.

[97] Ibid., 127. The reader is by now familiar with James D. G. Dunn and his seminal work, *Baptism in the Holy Spirit: A Re-examination of the New Testament Teaching on the Gift of the Spirit in Relation to Pentecostalism Today, 2nd ed.* ([original work published 1970] London: SCM Press, 2010).

[98] With reference to the doctrine of the Holy Spirit in Luke-Acts, Stronstad writes: '...where it is appropriate, all parties in the current debate must abandon those largely self-serving methodological programs which conspire to either silence or to manipulate Luke's distinctive theology.' See Stronstad, *the Charismatic Theology of St. Luke,'* 12.

[99] Blomberg asserts: '...we have a lot to learn from interpreters of a wide variety of cultures if we are willing to read expositions we might otherwise ignore and raise questions we might otherwise never explore.' See Blomberg, 'The Globalization of Hermeneutics,' 583.

[100] Zwiep, 'Luke's Understanding of baptism in the Holy Spirit,' 127.

[101] Ibid., 128.

[102] This is what Thiselton identifies as the pitfall of socio-pragmatic hermeneutics. See Anthony C. Thiselton, *New Horizons in Hermeneutics* (Grand Rapids: Zondervan Publishing House,

Methodologically, Zwiep begins by stating key points of non-Pentecostal evangelical-classical Pentecostal agreement. These points will be addressed for relevance and applicability to American Baptists.

1) The analyses of the previous sections indicate the general agreement which exists to establish Luke as a historian-theologian. Concurrence of thought on this issue is consistent with the majority of evangelical and classical Pentecostal scholars[103] and stands in contradistinction to the opposing trend of former evangelical scholarship.[104] This is significant to understanding BHS in terms of Lukan pneumatology without making appeals to Pauline didactic literature.

2) It logically follows 'that Luke-Acts must not be read from the angle of Paul's theology or through a Pauline lens: Paul is not the norm for Luke.'[105] Conversely, Luke should not be read into Paul.[106] Conscientious adherence to this rule avoids what in semantics is referred to as the error of 'illegitimate identity transfer.' This semantic fallacy occurs when the sense and referent of Paul's concept of the BHS metaphor is supplied in Luke-Acts (or vice versa).[107]

3) Zwiep's assertion that 'few evangelical scholars would nowadays advocate a traditional dispensationalist or cessationist position' likely reflects his particular theological frame of reference.[108] Elbert's assessment of evangelicalism is altogether different and attributes its

---

1992), 396-98, 529-50, 587-90. See also Larry W. Hurtado, 'Religious Experience and Religious Innovation in the New Testament,' in *JR* (2000), 183-205.

[103] Thiselton, *New Horizons in Hermeneutics*, 29.

[104] Menzies suggests that the rejection of narrative theology was based on 'the more radical expressions of redaction criticism' that minimized the historical intent of the gospel writers in favor of their respective theological message. He cites Ernst Haenchen, *The Acts of the Apostles: A Commentary* (Philadelphia: The Westminster Press, 1971) as exemplary. See also Haenchen, 'The Book of Acts as Source Material for the History of Early Christianity,' in L. E. Keck and J. L. Martyn, eds., *Studies in Luke-Acts* (Nashville: Abingdon Press, 1966), 258-78. A critical review of Ramm, Stott, Fee and Stuart is provided in Menzies and Menzies, *Spirit and Power,* 37-45; 109-19.

[105] Zwiep, 'Luke's Understanding of baptism in the Holy Spirit,' 129.

[106] Atkinson refers to this practice by 'certain Pentecostals' with regard to 1 Cor 12:13 who, 'forgetting that Paul could simply have been using the phrase in a different way from how Luke used it…impose Luke's meaning on Paul's text.' According to Atkinson, an 'independent observer' would otherwise conclude 'that Paul was using the phrase ["baptized by/with one Spirit"] to refer to incorporation into Christ's body, the church.' See Atkinson, 'Worth a Second Look? Pentecostal Hermeneutics,' 54.

[107] James Barr, *The Semantics of Biblical Language* (London: SCM Press, 1961), 217-19.

[108] Zwiep, 'Luke's Understanding of baptism in the Holy Spirit,' 129.

cessationism to 'rationally formatted and traditionally venerated conjectures.'[109] His estimation of evangelicalism[110] includes a vigorous dispensationalism which evinces rationalistic excess by imposing rigid temporal boundaries on the NT text.[111] The result is an evangelical affirmation which holds that 'selected supernatural activities described in the NT should not and could not be expected to occur.'[112] Some evangelicals drive a dispensational wedge between the earthly and heavenly ministry of Jesus. Expectations of the recurrence of the supernatural NT activities performed by Jesus are 'cessationistically filtered' and become rationally unacceptable and/or intellectually incredible.[113] The result is a 'distrust and dismissal of experience' which Elbert repeatedly attributes to a hermeneutical and intellectual 'anti-Lukan concept' known as the 'apostolic age' or the 'Pentecostal age.'[114] This assignment of epochal divisions relegates the experiences depicted in Luke-Acts to a 'once-and-for-all' status having occurred in the 'apostolic age.'[115] Elbert's depiction of cessationist evangelicalism closely approximates the interpretation of the miraculous *charismata* recorded in the book of Acts by many American Baptists, including those previously described in this study (e.g. SBC). He commends (as Blomberg does) an approach which deliberately unsubscribes to the so-called 'apostolic age interpretive methodology' and embraces 'a new paradigm, a new perspective on narrative connectedness and of

---

[109] Paul Elbert, 'Pentecostal/Charismatic Themes in Luke-Acts at the Evangelical Society: The Battle of Interpretive Method,' in *JPT* (2004), 183 n. 7.

[110] Elbert's experience with and among evangelicals includes years of participation in the Evangelical Theological Society, which he describes as 'a group of North American scholars who doctrinally emphasize biblical inerrancy.' See ibid., 187 n. 22 for a detailed accounting of his ETS experience.

[111] Elbert, 'Pentecostal/Charismatic Themes in Luke-Acts at the Evangelical Society,' 183.

[112] Ibid., 184.

[113] Ibid.

[114] Ibid., 184-87.

[115] Elbert characterizes as Lukan portrayals of Spirit-reception remaining 'locked in a frozen paleo-Reformed time capsule, dismissed as nothing more than historical oddities, instigating a "once-for-all" process of osmosis that trickles down through time to other Christians.' See Ibid., 189. Thomas exemplifies this dispensational orientation when he writes: 'Many events in Acts are unrepeatable because they are unique in God's ongoing plan...Acts describes a period of transitions such as those from the law to grace, from Israel's history to the church's history, from an emphasis on the kingdom of Israel to an emphasis on the body of Christ.' See Thomas, 'The Hermeneutics of Noncessationism,' 295.

experiential portrayal as shared by the narrative-rhetorical culture in which the NT was composed.'[116] The issue of dispensationalism is relevant to the degree that it represents an interpretive preunderstanding which precludes the very 'experiential portrayal' that classical Pentecostals assert is integral to properly understanding the phenomena contained in the book of Acts. Classical Pentecostals are not unaffected by dispensationalism, but this influence has not resulted in cessationist approaches to Luke-Acts.[117] The redaction-critical approach, embraced by the scholars under review for this consensus, is interested primarily in how Luke understood the BHS metaphor. The issue of Luke's non-cessationism extends the debate to whether or not he intended the miraculous *charismata* depicted in the book of Acts to be normative for succeeding generations of Christians. The dispensational-cessationist position need not preclude a Lukan understanding of BHS.

4) The relation of first-century Judaism to 'the Spirit of prophecy' conception of the Spirit presented in Luke-Acts is part of the broader debate on the nature of NT prophecy.[118] A brief discussion on the contemporary 'Spirit of prophecy' debate will contextualize an American Baptist response. The term 'Spirit of prophecy' is applied narrowly by Menzies[119] and Cho,[120] more broadly by Levison[121] and

---

[116] Elbert, 'Pentecostal/Charismatic Themes in Luke-Acts at the Evangelical Society,' 214.

[117] For background on the impact of the dispensationalist-fundamentalist movement on classical Pentecostalism, see Gerald T. Sheppard, 'Pentecostals and the Hermeneutics of Dispensationalism: The Anatomy of an Uneasy Relationship,' in *Pneuma* (1984), 5-33.

[118] Zwiep, 'Luke's Understanding of Baptism in the Holy Spirit,' 130.

[119] Menzies, *The Development of Early Christian Pneumatology with Special Reference to Luke-Acts*, 52-112. See also Menzies, *Empowered for Witness*, 48-102.

[120] Youngmo Cho, *Spirit and Kingdom in the Writings of Luke and Paul: An Attempt to Reconcile these Concepts* ([original work published 2005] Eugene: Wipf & Stock Publishers, 2006), 14-51.

[121] Levison contends for a 'diversity of conceptions that co-exist within the writings of individual first-century authors or within a single ancient document...' See John R. Levison, *The Spirit in First-Century Judaism* ([original work published 1997] Boston: Brill Academic Publishers, 2002), 244-54; 'The Spirit in the Gospels: Breaking the Impasse of Early-Twentieth Century Scholarship,' in Amy M. Donaldson and Timothy B. Sailors, eds., *New Testament Greek and Exegesis: Essays in Honor of Gerald F. Hawthorne* (Grand Rapids: William B. Eerdmans, 2003). 55-76. See also his *Filled with the Spirit* (Grand Rapids: William B. Eerdmans Publishing, 2009) which includes extensive analyses of the S/spirit in both Israelite and Jewish literature.

Turner,[122] and contextually by Perry.[123] Hur demonstrates partial reliance upon the first-century Jewish tradition,[124] though not employing the term, 'the Spirit of prophecy.'[125] American Baptist interest in first-century conceptions of the Spirit within Judaism is expressed by Hamilton. However, this only extends to the relation of the Spirit to the Messiah.[126] He endorses the contribution made by first-century Jewish literature to revealing 'the religious milieu' contemporaneous with Jesus.[127] By consulting the Jewish Bible and Jewish literature in conjunction with the NT witness, he deduces the arrival of an eschatological Spirit-anointed Messiah. The Messiah's coming ushers in an unprecedented era characterized by 'a deeper experience of the Spirit.'[128] Hamilton, following a pattern similar to that of Marshall, incorporates 'the Spirit of prophecy' into his three-fold Lukan pneumatological construct.[129] Schreiner does not appeal to Jewish literature in describing 'the prophetic Spirit,' but notes the value of the

---

[122] Turner denies that 'the Spirit of prophecy' is the 'typical' Jewish understanding of the Spirit's role. See Max Turner, 'The Spirit and the Power of Jesus' Miracles in the Lucan Conception,' in *NovT* (1991), 129-36. 'The Spirit of Prophecy and the Power of Authoritative Preaching in Luke-Acts: A Question of Origins,' in *NTS* (1992), 86-88. *The Holy Spirit and Spiritual Gifts, Revised Ed.* (Peabody: Hendrickson Publishers, 1998), 1-18. See also Max Turner, *Power from on High: The Spirit in Israel's Restoration and Witness in Luke-Acts* ([original work published 1996] Sheffield: Sheffield Academic Press, 2000), 86-138.

[123] Perry challenges the 'analytical strategy' which depends 'on a grouping of functionality from the evidence of rabbinic Judaism' to yield 'a dominant concept of the Spirit.' Perry does not discount altogether the 'Spirit of prophecy' concept, only the notion of its dominance. His thesis is that Luke refers to the bestowal of the Spirit 'in terms of the last days of a Jewish Commonwealth and for the purpose of enabling a prophetic mission of deliverance for the renewal of the people.' See Andrew Perry, 'Eschatological Deliverance: The Spirit in Luke-Acts' (PhD diss., University of Durham, 2008), 167-68.

[124] Ju Hur, *A Dynamic Reading of the Holy Spirit in Luke-Acts* (London: T & T Clark International, 2001), 25 n. 35. Hur notes the 'by and large' scholarly acceptance of 'the Spirit of prophecy' to understand the Spirit according to the Jewish tradition (intertestamental or targumic). He contends, however, that by eliminating the Jewish Bible in deference to the Jewish intertestamental literature, scholars risk anachronistically applying the term 'Spirit of prophecy' (which does not appear in Luke-Acts or the Jewish Bible) to pre-Christian Jewish views.

[125] Idid. Hur prefers the term, 'the Spirit of the Lord/God.'

[126] Hamilton, *God's Indwelling Presence,* 101-9.

[127] Ibid., 107.

[128] Ibid., 107-9.

[129] Ibid., 185. See also Marshall, 'The Significance of Pentecost,' 347-69, 55.

contributions of Menzies, Turner, and Shelton[130] to the available scholarship relative to the Spirit in Luke-Acts.[131] Hamilton demonstrates that the relevance of 'the Spirit of prophecy' motif to the distinct pneumatology of Luke-Acts poses no methodological barrier to American Baptists engaging in dialogue with those who make much or little of its derivation from first-century Jewish literature.

5)   Zwiep is correct that to the degree that Stronstad's thesis[132] is sound 'and does justice to Luke's particular view of the Spirit,' the 'power-for-mission'[133] versus 'conversion-initiation' BHS debate diminishes to degree of use (predominate, consistent, or exclusive) rather than kind.[134] Zwiep's further contention is likewise credible, that the equally tenuous polarizing views represented in the debate are not resolved by some 'middle' view, but require a combination of 'both parties' changing course in 'a new direction' in order to gain 'a new perspective' on BHS. This assumes a prioritization of biblical truth over the respective traditions of ecclesiastical identity.[135]

3.2   Systematization and Lukan Intention

Employed respectively by classical Pentecostals and American Baptists, the doctrine of subsequence and separability versus the cessationist and dispensationally-oriented interpretive constructs are based on systematic attempts

---

[130] The relevant works of Turner and Menzies have previously been noted. For Shelton, see James B. Shelton, *Mighty in Word and Deed: The Role of the Holy Spirit in Luke-Acts* ([previous work published 1991] Eugene: Wipf & Stock Publishers, 1999), 15-32.

[131] Schreiner, *New Testament Theology,* 440-43.

[132] Roger Stronstad, *The Charismatic Theology of St. Luke* ([original work published 1984] Peabody: Hendrickson Publishers, 2002). See also Stronstad, *The Prophethood of All Believers: A Study in Luke's Charismatic Theology* ([original work published 1999] Sheffield: Sheffield Academic Press, 2003) and Stronstad, 'The Prophethood of all Believers: A Study in Luke's Charismatic Theology,' in Wonsuk Ma and Robert P. Menzies, eds. *Pentecostalism in Context: Essays in Honor of William W. Menzies* ([original work published 1997] Eugene: Wipf & Stock Publishers, 2008).

[133] By 'power-for-mission' is meant: The role of the Spirit in Luke-Acts is directed toward empowering believers for mission-specific tasks. The work is unrelated to soteriological concerns. The conclusions of Stronstad and Menzies (also Ervin) are anticipated *inter alios* by Schweizer. See Eduard Schweizer, Trans. Geoffrey Bromiley, 'πνεῦμα, πνευματικός,' in Gerhard Kittel and Gerhard Friedrich, eds. *TDNT, Vol. 6* ([original work published 1968] Grand Rapids: William B. Eerdmans Publishing, 1988), 412.

[134] Zwiep, 'Luke's Understanding of baptism in the Holy Spirit,' 130.

[135] Ibid.

to cohere a set of biblically-deduced propositions into doctrinal truth. Zwiep upholds the value of systematic scholarly method, but correctly queries the dominance of method over content in the BHS debate. On his view, it is not apparent that Luke's intention was to present formally an individually-oriented systematic pneumatology.[136] This is supported by Schweizer who cites case studies in Acts to establish the following themes that are strongly emphasized by Luke: (1) the unpredictability of the Spirit's activity, and (2) the freedom of the Spirit.[137] This is especially evident in the non-systematic portrayal of events relating to a particular person's life. Witherington notes the chronological variance of texts in Acts which depict water baptism preceding the reception of the Spirit (8:4-25), water baptism following Spirit reception (10:44-48), and texts where the two appear to occur simultaneously (2:38; 8:38-39).[138] Rather than the normative ordering and individualization of Spirit-related (or other) events, 'Luke intends his audience to know that repentance, faith, baptism, the name of Jesus, and reception of the Spirit were all important elements' to be associated with entering the community of Christ.[139]

Bearing in mind this important individual versus corporate distinction, the manner of discerning Lukan intent becomes central to the BHS debate. Central to the manner of discerning Lukan intent is his interest is in portraying the Spirit's role in the life of individual believers. At issue is whether Luke does so by presenting the predominant and normatively transferrable pattern for all believers of all time, or by portraying the Spirit's corporate role in the life of the new eschatological community from its inception on the Day of Pentecost. Consensus involves discerning the function of BHS, whether derived from individual cases in Luke-Acts which predominately portray the gift of the Spirit as mission-oriented prophetic enabling,[140] and/or the essential character of BHS as an

---

[136] Ibid., 131.

[137] Schweizer, 'πνεῦμα, πνευματικός,' 414. Schweizer cites cases that suggest that the Spirit is not "tied" to baptism (i.e. the water rite): (1) on one occasion the Spirit comes on men prior to baptism, 10:44; (2) on another occasion the Spirit comes without baptism, 2:1-4; and (3) on one occasion the Spirit comes on a disciple who knew only the baptism of JTB (18:25), a baptism which could not, according to 19:3, impart the Spirit to others.

[138] Ben Witherington III, *The Acts of the Apostles: A Socio-Rhetorical Commentary* (Grand Rapids: William B. Eerdmans Publishing, 1998), 154. See Barrett, *A Critical and Exegetical Commentary on the Acts of the Apostles, Vol. 1*, 115.

[139] Ibid., 155.

[140] Robert P. Menzies, 'Luke's Understanding of Baptism in the Holy Spirit: A Pentecostal Perspective,' in *PentecoStudies* (2007), 113.

eschatologically occurring corporate event consisting of present and tangible experience.[141]

It is a contention of this thesis that it would be possible to begin on the path towards BHS convergence, if not total consensus, between American Baptists and those Christians of P/C persuasion by engaging in dialogue within the bounds of the aforementioned parameters. Both traditions coalesce along the following lines of demarcation: (1) approach to Scripture, (2) methods of interpretation, and (3) importance accorded to Luke's writings. Each of these lines are sufficiently basic to conducting a robust debate in a spirit of harmonious enquiry. Independently, these lines do not constitute a direct path to agreement on BHS. Together, they represent a valid and helpful impetus to meaningful and objective dialogue. The following section discusses critical points for investigation if such a dialogue is to occur.

4. BHS and the New Spirit-Empowered Eschatological Community

4.1   Lukan Pneumatological Emphases and the Functional Role of BHS

Classical Pentecostal BHS apologists emphasize the role of the Spirit in exclusive and vocational prophetic empowerment.[142] Soteriological function attributed by Paul to the Spirit is not considered to be in conflict with the doctrine of subsequence advocated by classical Pentecostals according to Luke's distinctive theological perspective.[143] As a theologian 'in his own right,'[144] Luke 'consistently [exclusively][145] portrays the Spirit as a charismatic or, more precisely, a prophetic gift, the source of power for service.'[146] The assertion of a

---

[141] Zwiep, 'Luke's Understanding of baptism in the Holy Spirit,' 132-37.

[142] Stronstad, *The Prophethood of All Believers*, 121.

[143] Menzies, 'Luke's Understanding of Baptism in the Holy Spirit,' 113. Elsewhere, Menzies argues for a process of development in the early church's understanding of the Spirit's work. This is the thesis for *The Development of Early Christian Pneumatology with Special Reference to Luke-Acts* (Sheffield: Sheffield Academic Press, 1991) and *Empowered for Witness: The Holy Spirit in Luke-Acts* (Sheffield: Sheffield Academic Press, 1994). Menzies is preceded by Hermann Gunkel, Trans. Roy A. Harrisville and Philip A. Quanbeck II, *The Influence of the Holy Spirit: The Popular View of the Apostolic Age and the Teaching of the Apostle Paul* (ET Philadelphia: Fortress Press, 1979) and Gonzalo Haya-Prats, Paul Elbert, ed., Trans. Scott A. Ellington, *Empowered Believers: The Holy Spirit in the Book of Acts* (ET Eugene: Cascade Books, 2011).

[144] Stronstad, *The Charismatic Theology of St. Luke*, 11.

[145] Menzies, *Spirit and Power*, 82, 89. See also Robert P. Menzies, 'The Spirit of Prophecy, Luke-Acts and Pentecostal Theology: A Response to Max Turner,' in *JPT* (1999), 52.

[146] Menzies, 'Luke's Understanding of Baptism in the Holy Spirit,' 112.

distinct theology is essential to reconciling Luke with Paul (or even John).[147] Luke's prophetically empowering Spirit reconciles with Paul's soteriologically functioning Spirit by eliciting two Spirit baptisms; one performed by Jesus to empower believers for ministry, and another by the Spirit to place the believer into the body of Christ (1 Cor 12:13).[148]

4.1.1   Reconciling Luke and Paul: A Dual-Functioning Gift of the Spirit

The classical Pentecostal BHS apologetic raises the begging question: 'Can Luke and Paul's alternative theological perspectives reconcile on the basis of a single BHS performed by Jesus?' Exegetical support for this probability is demonstrated in this work by third wave[149] P/C adherents and American Baptists alike.[150] By holding to a distinctive Lukan pneumatology and not interpreting Luke according to Paul, the issue of the nature of the Spirit's BHS function becomes central to the debate.[151] If Luke admits a broader ethical-soteriological function to the role of the Spirit in BHS,[152] then the doctrine of subsequence is invalidated.[153] However, this need not invalidate the Luke-Acts based classical Pentecostal interpretation of the Spirit's function in BHS. The mere admission of a Lukan ethical-soteriological dimension to the Spirit's role in BHS does not abrogate the Spirit's 'prophetic empowering' function in an either/or manner.[154]

---

[147] Positing complementary theologies for Luke and Paul is foundational to the debate. Carson is correct when he writes, 'mutually contradictory theologies cannot both be true, and one cannot even speak of the cannon establishing the allowable range of theologies, since one or more must be false.' See Carson, *Showing the Spirit,* 151.

[148] Menzies, 'Luke's Understanding of Baptism in the Holy Spirit,' 123.

[149] C. Samuel Storms, 'A Third Wave View,' in Wayne A. Grudem, ed., *Are Miraculous Gifts for Today? Four Views* (Grand Rapids: Zondervan, 1996), 179.

[150] B. H. Carroll, *The Holy Spirit: Comprising a Discussion of the Paraclete, the Other Self of Jesus, and Other Phases of the Work of the Spirit of God* (Nashville: Broadman Press, 1939), 30-50.

[151] Menzies, *Spirit and Power,* 48.

[152] Stronstad anticipates the challenge to the 'exclusivity' of the Spirit's empowering role in BHS and cites a variety of Luke-Acts occurrences of Luke reporting 'several kinds of relationships between the Spirit and salvation.' He believes it to be a methodological error to confuse the close relation of the Spirit to salvation with identity of function. See Stronstad, *The Prophethood of All Believers,* 122. Menzies also links the Spirit indirectly with ethical influence. See Menzies, 'The Spirit of Prophecy, Luke-Acts and Pentecostal Theology,' 52-53.

[153] Menzies, *Spirit and Power,* 48.

[154] This is Turner's thesis based on 'the Spirit of prophecy' anticipated prototypically in Judaism to bring about individual and corporate ethical renewal. See Max Turner, *Power from on*

It is possible for the Pentecostal gift of the Spirit to function in a dual capacity. This is a reasonable conclusion drawn from the independently predominant emphases of Luke and Paul regarding the Spirit's functional role in BHS.

Grudem is an example of this approach, noting the discontinuity of the disciples' less-powerful experience of the Spirit prior to Pentecost with more-powerful new covenant experience of the Spirit received on the Day of Pentecost.[155] On his view, the reception of the Spirit (BHS) by the disciples on the Day of Pentecost provided empowerment for Christian living and ministry according to the prediction of Acts 1:8.[156] He describes the new covenant BHS experience of the Spirit as broadly including: (1) increased effectiveness in witness (Acts 1:8; Eph 4:8, 11-13), (2) ethical influence over the presence of sin (Rom 6:11-14; 8:13-14; Gal 2:20; Phil 3:10), (3) power over Satan and demonic forces (2 Cor 10:3-4; Eph 1:19-21; 6:10-18; 1 John 4:4), and (4) possession of ministry gifts (Acts 2:16-18; 1 Cor 12:7, 11; 1 Pet 4:10.[157] The eschatological time of transition from the old covenant to the new covenant work of the Spirit occurred contemporaneously with the tenure of a specific group of disciples (beneficiaries) that received the gift of the Spirit on the Day of Pentecost. If by 'eschatological' is meant a transition in the sense of a one-time occurrence in salvation history, the Pentecostal doctrine of subsequence (in terms of having paradigmatic value for an individualized reception of the Spirit) does not apply to subsequent believers. The nature of the transition precludes repetition because believers today do not receive the Spirit (BHS) having only an old covenant and less-powerful experience of the Spirit (Grudem). Rather, they receive the Spirit in the same manner as those in Corinth; at the moment of their conversion-initiation (1 Cor 12:13).[158] This argument permits the following assertions: Luke reconciles with Paul, the integrity of their independent theological perspectives is maintained, and one BHS is upheld. Thus, Grudem understands the post-Pentecost 'secondary experiences' of the Spirit in Acts (e.g. Samaritans, Cornelius' household, and the Ephesian disciples) to be: (1) providentially intended to

---

High: The Spirit in Israel's Restoration and Witness in Luke-Acts ([original work published 1996] Sheffield: Sheffield Academic Press, 2000), 431-33.

[155] Wayne Grudem, *Systematic Theology: An Introduction to Biblical Doctrine* (Grand Rapids: Zondervan Publishing, 1994), 771.

[156] Grudem, *Systematic Theology,* 771; H. Ray Dunning, *Grace, Faith and Holiness: A Wesleyan Systematic Theology* (Kansas City: Beacon Hill, 1988), 418-24.

[157] Grudem, *Systematic Theology,* 771-72.

[158] Ibid., 773.

consolidate[159] the Christian movement (Samaritans, 8:4-25), (2) a model for how the gospel will go to the ends of the earth (1:8; Cornelius' household, 10:1-48), and (3) insight into the exceptional case of JTB's disciples who believed in the coming Messiah, but required further instruction of his identity and work prior to experiencing genuine conversion (19:1-7).[160]

4.1.2   The Exclusive Charismatic Function of the Spirit in BHS

The above line of argumentation is a non-starter for Menzies due to Luke's portrayal of the Spirit's 'exclusive' charismatic function in BHS. This requires Menzies to posit two BHS occurrences in order to reconcile Luke's independent theology with Paul.[161] He understands BHS constructs such as Grudem's as sympathetic with Luke's 'vocational' emphasis ('empowering for ministry'), but by affirming the BHS received on the Day of Pentecost as 'the essential element of conversion,' such constructs are fatally flawed and in conflict with Luke's exclusive emphasis.[162] Grudem's position stops short of BHS as the means of conversion-initiation. He indicates that the disciples on the Day of Pentecost received the new covenant empowering of the Spirit as the provision of an already existing new covenant.[163] The disciples on the Day of Pentecost are the first to participate in the new covenant empowerment of the Spirit. In response to Ervin,[164] Grudem concedes the realization of the new covenant as coterminous with Jesus' death.[165] On his view, Pentecost is unique because existing (old

---

[159] Perhaps 'validate' is more accurate, lest the Samaritans devolve into a sectarian spur of the Christian movement. Hamilton follows Dunn when he writes, '...it is probably best to think of the Spirit's coming not as an accompaniment of the initial experience of salvation, but as signifying that God has accepted these Samaritans into the church of the Messiah.' See Hamilton, *God's Indwelling Presence*, 190. See Dunn, *Baptism in the Holy Spirit*, 67.

[160] Grudem, *Systematic Theology*, 774-75.

[161] Menzies, *Spirit and Power*, 113.

[162] Menzies, 'Luke's Understanding of Baptism in the Holy Spirit,' 113.

[163] Menzies seems to equate the expression 'new covenant' with conversion (cleansing, justification, moral transformation). Menzies, 'Luke's Understanding of Baptism in the Holy Spirit,' 113. Grudem understands 'new covenant' as additionally referring to a paradigm shift in pneumatological operations. This makes it possible to regard the disciples on the Day of Pentecost as converted, but lacking the fullness of new covenant (more powerful) Spirit endowment (BHS). As a concomitant to the atonement, Pentecost delivers the fullness of new covenant experience.

[164] See also, William P. Atkinson, *Baptism in the Spirit: Luke-Acts and the Dunn Debate* (Eugene: Pickwick Publications, 2011), 52-53.

[165] Grudem, *Systematic Theology*, 771 n. 17. See Howard M. Ervin, *Conversion-Initiation and the Baptism in the Holy Spirit: An Engaging Critique of James D. G. Dunn's Baptism in the Holy Spirit* (Peabody: Hendrickson Publishers, 1984), 14, 15-19.

covenant) believers who lacked the new covenant experience of the Spirit (distinct from conversion), became recipients when the Spirit was eschatologically poured out (BHS) by Jesus on the Day of Pentecost (Acts 2:33).[166] From this programmatic eschatological transition (relative to BHS), it is possible to infer discrete conversion and BHS events within the single eschatological bestowment of the gift of the Spirit; the former is repeatable to individuals so desiring, and the latter is corporately unique and traceable to a one-time epochal event (i.e. Pentecost). Grudem admits this possibility by citing 1 Cor 12:13 as evidence for BHS being 'a distinct element' in the *ordo salutis*.[167] Thus, BHS can be logically separate from personal conversion experience while being chronologically coterminous with conversion. This permits a separate (even deferred) empowering function of the Spirit.[168] This may explain: (1) the 'ambiguity'[169] surrounding the translation of Paul's ἐν ἑνὶ πνεύματι... ἐβαπτίσθημεν construction in 1 Cor 12:13a, (2) the plausibility of the 'awkward' rendering 'in one Spirit...we were baptized,' and (3) the singular agency (Acts 2:33) which coheres with similar BHS references in the Gospels and Acts.[170] If regeneration occurs logically prior to and is a distinct phenomenon separate from BHS, 1 Cor 12:13 presupposes a prior conversion experience and becomes a description of an additional (Pauline) facet of the Spirit's work in BHS. The corporate nature of BHS is indicated by ἡμεῖς πάντες...πάντες ('we all...all'). A testable hypothesis is that BHS accompanies conversion in the sense of making available to the individual the corporate endowment of the Spirit as the means of entrance into the body of Christ and the source of repeated influences necessary for effective Christian living and ministry.[171]

---

[166] Grudem, *Systematic Theology*, 771 n. 17.

[167] The observation is attributed to James Renehan, a student of Grudem. See Ibid., 773 n. 21.

[168] Fee is correct when he avers that according to the combined witness of Luke (Luke-Acts) and Paul (e.g. 1 Cor 12:13), the early believers did not emphasize the differentia represented in 'conversion' and 'Spirit-filled' terminology. See Fee, *Gospel and Spirit*, 114-15.

[169] Ervin, *Conversion-Initiation and the Baptism in the Holy Spirit*, 98-102.

[170] Atkinson opposes this line of argumentation on the grounds that Paul's apparent BHS reference is in fact a reference to an altogether different function of the Spirit, 'incorporation into Christ's body.' See Atkinson, 'Worth a Second Look? Pentecostal Hermeneutics,' 54.

[171] While not endorsing the classical Pentecostal 'second blessing' theology, BHS with evidence of tongues, Carson advocates what he refers to as a 'second-, third-, fourth-, and fifth-blessing theology.' He is not cessationist on the role of tongues in the church, but restricts their function in Acts to 'the inception of the messianic age.' He additionally warns cessationists of the prospect of complacency and the resulting ossification of a merely creedal Christianity.

4.2 The Implications of BHS as a Personally Realized Eschatological Corporate Event

Grudem offers American Baptists a plausible construct for understanding BHS as an experienced reality. However, this dialogical lens requires additional focus away from a common classical Pentecostal and American Baptist assumption; that Luke's pneumatological focus is 'the systematic individualization'[172] of BHS in Luke-Acts.[173] Grudem represents this view when he identifies BHS as an individually experienced phenomenon.[174] Zwiep offers an approach to Luke-Acts which makes it possible to rightly narrow Lukan intention to 'the implications of the work of the Spirit for the new or renewed community of God.'[175] Accordingly, the view does not interpret Luke's particular BHS perspective to be a dogmatic statement which is normative for individual believers. Rather, it spells out 'the implications of the work of the Spirit for the new or renewed community of God.'[176] As an eschatological corporate event, BHS is intrinsic to the community and not a possession of the individual.[177] The BHS event is not repeatable, but individual members of the community are capable of repeatedly realizing its ethical and empowering influence. The epochal occurrence of BHS on the Day of Pentecost effectively places the Spirit's empowering influence readily at the disposal of every believer represented by the corporate body.

4.2.1 BHS as the Eschatological Corporate Gift of the Spirit

Interpreting the gift of the Spirit as an eschatological event occurring on the Day of Pentecost is largely undisputed by American Baptists and classical

---

[172] Dunn and Turner tie Lukan intent to the individual reception of BHS with every conversion. Dunn suggests Acts 2:38 is the norm for 'Christian beginnings' governing each of the 15 conversion accounts in the book of Acts whether BHS is mentioned directly or not. See Dunn, *Baptism in the Spirit,* 90. Turner agrees with Dunn, disputing only the case of the Samaritans which he, contra Dunn, he considers to be exceptional. See Max Turner, *The Holy Spirit and Spiritual Gifts, Revised Ed.* (Peabody: Hendrickson Publishers, 1998), 45. See also Polhill who appears to follow Dunn with reference to the paradigmatic value of Acts 2:38, stating that 'the gift of the Spirit became a normative concomitant of becoming a Christian believer,' *Acts,* 98.

[173] Zwiep, 'Luke's Understanding of baptism in the Holy Spirit,' 135. See also Carson, *Showing the Spirit,* 150-58.

[174] Grudem, *Systematic Theology,* 772-73.

[175] Ibid., 136.

[176] Zwiep, 'Luke's Understanding of baptism in the Holy Spirit,' 136.

[177] Ibid., 136.

Pentecostals. Schreiner considers 'baptism' to be the language of initiation. By performing BHS (Acts 1:5) Jesus commenced an (eschatological) 'new age of the Spirit' (Acts 2:17-18, 33; Joel 2:28).[178] Hamilton refers to the occurrence of BHS on the Day of Pentecost as 'the eschatological gift of the Spirit.'[179] Menzies links 'the eschatological bestowal of the Spirit' and 'the restoration of the Spirit of prophecy' definitively to Luke's use of Joel 3:1-5 LXX (Acts 2:17-21).[180] Stronstad considers the universal gift of the Spirit of God as indicative of 'the age to come.'[181] What is disputed is the programmatic[182] nature of Pentecost and its interpretive (normative) value for individual BHS experience. This section will examine the merits of the evidence in Luke-Acts for interpreting the events of Pentecost to be demonstrative of the corporately received gift of the Spirit (BHS). Further inquiry will identify the implications of an eschatologically occurring corporate gift of the Spirit to the believer's present expectations of BHS experience.

4.2.1.1   Luke's Portrayal of the Pentecostal Gift of the Spirit

Central to the discussion is Luke's portrayal of BHS as a prophetic event associated with the Day of Pentecost. Zwiep suggests that evangelical-classical Pentecostal common ground exists when Pentecost is interpreted to be 'eschatological anticipation' rather than 'eschatological fulfillment.'[183] This distinction considers the latter to emphasize the present over the future (consummative) work of the Spirit.[184] Zwiep understands Pentecost to be an 'anticipation' of eschatological fulfillment. On this view, a proper emphasis on the present 'work of the Spirit in the context of Jesus and the church' is maintained[185] This means that Pentecost has enduring normative value, not in the

---

[178] Schreiner, *New Testament Theology*, 454-55.

[179] Hamilton, *God's Indwelling Presence*, 186-89.

[180] Menzies, *The Development of Early Christian Pneumatology*, 225-26.

[181] Stronstad, *The Charismatic Theology of St. Luke*, 26, 56. Specifically, the increased frequency of prophetic activity evidenced in Luke-Acts is consistent with universal proliferation of prophecy during the messianic age (80-81).

[182] By 'programmatic' is meant the role of Pentecost (the Spirit) in redemptive history. Schreiner traces the activity of 'the prophetic Spirit' in Luke-Acts and concludes that 'the Spirit directed his people in the fulfillment of redemptive history, in the extension of the gospel beyond the confines of the Jewish people.' See Schreiner, *New Testament Theology*, 442-48.

[183] Zwiep, 'Luke's Understanding of baptism in the Holy Spirit,' 133.

[184] Ibid.

[185] Ibid.

sense of repeating the one-time corporate reception of the Spirit, but in the sense of expressing the ongoing functional role of the Spirit in the life of the church (body of Christ).

4.2.1.2   Luke's Portrayal of BHS in Relation to the Winnowing Metaphor

The dynamic nature of this present-future anticipatory fulfillment is expressed by Luke in his portrayal of the relation of BHS to the (Q) winnowing metaphor (Luke 3:17 = Matt 3:12).[186] Luke's depiction of this relation provides an interpretive key for understanding the corporate reception of the Spirit on the Day of Pentecost. It also offers a point of consensus for American Baptists and classical Pentecostals. Following Dunn,[187] Menzies interprets Luke's reference to a baptism ἐν πνεύματι ἁγίῳ καὶ πυρί ('in/with Holy Spirit and fire,' Luke 3:16) to be a unified event conceived by JTB with both positive and negative aspects.[188] Contra Dunn, Menzies denies the relevance of specified Qumranic texts[189] and the allusion to Isa 4:4[190] as indications of Luke's intention to represent the combined metaphors as a personally experienced inner purgative (soteriological) event.[191] Opting contextually ('the winnowing metaphor,' Luke 3:17) to interpret the logion in terms of the eschatological 'sifting of Israel,' the presence of καὶ πυρί ('and fire') is interpreted by Menzies according to the separation motif of the Q metaphor (Luke 3:17 = Matt 3:12).[192] His conclusion does not disavow the purgative element represented by the metaphor (Dunn), but rather its application to the individual.[193] Menzies concludes that the baptism ἐν πνεύματι ἁγίῳ καὶ

---

[186] Ibid., 132.

[187] Dunn, *Baptism in the Holy Spirit,* 13-14. See also James D. G. Dunn, *The Spirit and the Christ: Pneumatology, Vol. 2* (Grand Rapids: William B. Eerdmans Publishing, 1998), 104-6.

[188] Menzies, *The Development of Early Christian Pneumatology,* 137.

[189] Ibid., 138. Menzies dismisses the Qumranic texts cited by Dunn (1QS 3.7-9; 4.21; 1QH 16.12; 7.6; 17.26; frag. 2.9, 13) as irrelevant to the interpretation of JTB's prophecy and the Q metaphor. He does so due to lack of correspondence, but primarily on the basis of Dunn's assertion that 'the Spirit functions to purify the individual and initiate him into the messianic kingdom.' For ET see Florentino García Martínez, *The Dead Sea Scrolls Translated: The Qumran Texts in English, 2nd Ed.* (Grand Rapids: William B. Eerdmans Publishing, 1996).

[190] Ibid. Menzies rejects Isa 4:4 as evidence of the 'inner renewal or moral transformation of the individual' (Dunn's thesis). The passage does affirm Menzies' view of eschatological separation. For ET of the Targum to Isa 4:3-4 cited by Menzies see John F. Stenning, *The Targum of Isaiah* ([original work published 1949] Oxford: The Clarendon Press, 1953).

[191] Ibid.

[192] Ibid., 138-39.

[193] Ibid., 139.

πυρί ('in/with Holy Spirit and fire,' Luke 3:16) refers to a single dual-effect baptism 'experienced by all.' As such, BHS separates the righteous ('grain') from the unrighteous ('chaff') 'by a powerful blast of the Spirit of God'[194] in order to purify the nation (Luke 3:17).[195] The nature of the eschatological separation involves 'sifting and destruction' by means of one baptism with two elements.[196] The righteous are purified, not in the sense of inner personal soteriological cleansing (Dunn), but by virtue of having corporately been separated from the unrighteous.[197]

Menzies' support for this interpretation of Lukan intent is compelling. It finds support in 'messianic and pneumatological views current in Judaism' and derived from the Jewish Bible (Isa 4:4; 11:2, 4; Ps 1:4-5; Job 15:30) and intertestamental texts.[198] There is much to commend in this view which Menzies applies programmatically to the Day of Pentecost. The prophecy of Luke 3:16-17, while undoubtedly conceived to be a unified eschatological event in the mind of JTB, is considered by Luke to be fulfilled in separate and chronologically distinct phases; initial, ongoing, and final.[199] The 'ongoing mission of the church'[200] is a testament to the initial reception of the Spirit occurring on the Day of Pentecost. The final act of separation is eschatologically deferred to a future time when 'the destruction of the unrighteous in the fire of messianic judgment' will occur.[201]

---

[194] See George T. Montague, *The Holy Spirit: Growth of a Biblical Tradition* (New York: Paulist Press, 1976), 38.

[195] Menzies, *The Development of Early Christian Pneumatology,* 139.

[196] Menzies, contra Turner and Webb, identifies the wheat and chaff as collectively the object of messianic sifting, rather than the threshing floor of the post-sifting debris. See Menzies, *Spirit and Power,* 94-95. See also Turner, *The Holy Spirit and Spiritual Gifts,* 26 and Robert L. Webb, 'The Activity of John the Baptist's Expected Figure at the Threshing Floor (Matthew 3.12 = Luke 3.17),' in *JSNT* (1991), 103-11.

[197] Menzies, *The Development of Early Christian Pneumatology,* 139 n. 3.

[198] Ibid., 140. See also Menzies, *Spirit and Power,* 94.

[199] Menzies, *The Development of Early Christian Pneumatology,* 144.

[200] Though placing the emphasis on the present and positive aspects of the unified eschatological baptism prophesied by JTB, Luke does not exclude entirely from the book of Acts elements of the fiery nature of divine judgment (e.g. Acts 5:1-11). It is here that the preaching of JTB differs from the proclamation of Jesus and the early church as well as Luke's unique theological perspective. See Zwiep, 'Luke's Understanding of Baptism in the Holy Spirit,' 133. See also Arie W. Zwiep, *The Association of the Messiah in Lukan Christology* (Leiden: Brill, 1997), 169-171.

[201] Ibid.

4.2.1.3   The Programmatic Nature of Luke 4:16-30

It is important at this point to underscore Menzies' acknowledgement of the baptism ἐν πνεύματι ἁγίῳ καὶ πυρί ('in/with Holy Spirit and fire,' Luke 3:16) to be a corporate phenomenon.[202] According to Menzies, Luke is writing in light of Pentecost and presents the Spirit 'not as the source of cleansing for the individual, but rather as the animating force behind the witness of the church.'[203] Again, Menzies avers, 'it is one thing to assert that the Spirit influences...the ethical life of the Christian community; it is quite another to assert that the Spirit transforms in a direct way the ethical life of each *individual* within the community.'[204] One questions, however, the apparent contradiction of Menzies' programmatic use of Luke 4:18-19 (4:16-30) to establish Luke's intent to present 'Jesus' reception of the Spirit as a model for that of the disciples in Acts and future generations of believers, including his own (Luke 11:13 and Acts 2:17).'[205] The passage recalls Isa 61:1-2 (LXX) and is a 'redactional bridge' that connects Jesus' anointing with the Spirit at his Jordan baptism by JTB (Luke 3:21-22) with his being 'full of the Holy Spirit' during his wilderness temptation encounter (Luke 4:1) and his subsequent return 'in the power of the Spirit' (Luke 4:14). The passage also is prospective and intended by Luke to link Jesus' experience of the Spirit (Luke 3-4) with that of his disciples on the Day of Pentecost (Acts 1-2). According to Menzies, 'this passage [Luke 4:16-30] is crucial for understanding the significance of Jesus' reception of the Spirit and that of his disciples in Acts.'[206] The precise nature of this 'significance' involves the individualization and particularization[207] of the reception of the Spirit by each disciple.[208] For Menzies, it follows that Luke's portrayal of Jesus' pneumatic anointing is 'the

---

[202] Ibid., 140. Menzies writes, '...we search in vain for a reference to a messianic bestowal of the Spirit which purifies and morally transforms the individual.' Again, he writes, 'there are no pre-Christian references to a messianic bestowal of the Spirit that purifies and transforms *the individual.*' See Menzies, *Spirit and Power*, 94. See also Menzies, 'Luke's Understanding of Baptism in the Holy Spirit,' 114-15.

[203] Menzies, *Spirit and Power*, 94.

[204] Ibid., 89.

[205] Menzies, 'Luke's Understanding of Baptism in the Holy Spirit,' 117.

[206] Ibid.

[207] Zwiep, 'Luke's Understanding of baptism in the Holy Spirit,' 134.

[208] Menzies writes, 'Luke's Pentecost account provides what is needed, a promise of missiological power for every believer' (*Spirit and Power*, 101, 114, 155).

means by which [he] was equipped to carry out his divinely appointed task.' This constitutes the anticipated BHS experience of the early church.[209]

Contra Menzies, it is better to recognize the programmatic nature of Luke 4:16-30 without the individualization or particularization of the reception of the Spirit. While it is true that Jesus received the Spirit at the Jordan as an individual, with the exception of some overlapping features, the unique nature of his ministry and mission preclude direct correspondence to others. The emphasis in Luke 4:16-30 (4:18-19) is on the functional role of the Spirit (prophetic empowerment for ministry) and not the individuation of his reception.[210] If the passage is programmatic of Spirit reception, it is best to attribute Lukan intention to acknowledging the functional role of the Spirit coming eschatologically upon the corporate 'body of Christ.' This view tallies with the corporate allusion of Paul's ἡμεῖς πάντες...πάντες ('we all...all') in 1 Cor 12:13.

4.3 Internal Luke-Acts Support for the Corporate Reception of the Spirit

This corporate reception of the Spirit is supported internally[211] in Luke-Acts by the way Luke chooses to describe 'the effects of the coming of Jesus and the Spirit first and foremost in collective and corporate terms.'[212]

1) The announced birth of the Messiah is directed to all people (Luke 2:10).

2) Simeon proclaimed the arrival of the Christ child to acknowledge his provision for both Jew and Gentile (Luke 2:30).

3) The nation of Israel as a whole was the object of the message delivered by John the Baptist (Luke 3:6, 16).

---

[209] Menzies, *The Development of Early Christian Pneumatology*, 144.

[210] See Schreiner, *New Testament Theology*, 441-42.

[211] Nestle-Aland[27] is used for the Acts-related texts. See B. Aland, M. Black, K. Aland, J. Karavidopoulos, C. M. Martini, B. M. Metzger, eds. *Novum Testamentum Graece, 27th Ed.* (Stuttgart: Deutsche Bibelgesellschraft, 1993).

[212] Zwiep, 'Luke's Understanding of baptism in the Holy Spirit,' 134. See Bovon, *Luke the Theologian,* 280. Bovon writes, '...the Holy Spirit, the great eschatological gift announced by the prophets...is however less an individual gift than the gift offered by Christ to his church, with a view toward edification and mission.'

4) The parenthetical reference to 'the crowd of names' in the Bezan text (Acts 1:15) refers to the ancient corporate census of Israel, identified by the metaphorical use of the number 120.[213]

5) The necessity of reconstituting the Twelve is indicative of the imminent arrival of an anticipated corporate event (Acts 1:15-26).

6) The recipients of the Spirit on the Day of Pentecost were a believing community (Acts 2:1-4).[214]

7) The gift of the Spirit is promised to the people as a whole and not to individuals (Acts 2:38).[215]

8) Groups are indicated by the universal filling of Spirit by the disciples (Acts 4:31), the Samaritans receiving the Spirit (Acts 8:14-17), the reception of the Spirit by the Gentile household of Cornelius (Acts 10:44), and the twelve followers of JTB upon whom the Spirit came (Acts 19:1-6).

4.4   Communal Attestation

4.4.1   The View Explained

Stronstad considers the primary difference between the activity of the Spirit throughout Israelite history and the age to come prophesied by JTB to be 'one of magnitude; the gift of the Spirit to individuals and groups will give way to the gift of the Spirit to the community.'[216] Hamilton elaborates in support of this position from an American Baptist perspective. Contra Ladd and Dunn, he considers the BHS group experiences identified in Acts 2, 8, 10, and 19 to be unrelated to conversion.[217] In his view, Luke does not characterize any of the fifteen

---

[213] Josep Rius-Camps and Jenny Read-Heimerdinger, *The Message of Acts in Codex Bezae: A Comparison with the Alexandrian Tradition, Vol. 1* (London: T & T Clark, 2004), 117-18.

[214] Menzies attributes modifications of Joel 3:1-5a (LXX) reflected in Acts 2:17-21 as Luke's redactional intention 'to emphasize that the disciples of Jesus, as recipients of the Spirit of prophecy, are indeed members of this community.' According to Menzies, '...the Spirit of prophecy is a gift given exclusively to the people of God...[it] does not produce faith, it is given to faith.' See Menzies, *The Development of Early Christian Pneumatology*, 215-225.

[215] Rius-Camps and Read-Heimerdinger, *The Message of Acts in Codex Bezae*, 191.

[216] Stronstad, *The Charismatic Theology of St. Luke*, 26.

[217] Hamilton, *God's Indwelling Presence*, 191. See George Eldon Ladd, *A Theology of the New Testament* (Grand Rapids: William B. Eerdmans Publishing, 1974), 384; Dunn, *Baptism in the Holy Spirit*, 70.

conversion accounts recorded in Acts as BHS (2:41, 47; 4:4; 5:14; 6:7; 8:12-13, 36-37[218]; 9:35, 42; 13:48; 16:5, 14, 31-34; 17:11-12; 18:8).[219] He attributes Luke's inclusion of the BHS references in Acts to 'emphatic demonstrations that the eschatological gift of the Spirit has come.'[220] Hamilton concludes (of Luke) that 'the normal pattern of conversion is for believers to receive the indwelling Spirit apart from a dramatic baptism in the Spirit.'[221] This is not to endorse 'a two-stage work of the Spirit' on the basis of an analysis of the four groups receiving the eschatological gift of the Spirit (BHS).[222] Instead, Hamilton interprets Luke's BHS narrative accounts in Acts 2, 8, 10, and 19 as unique, one-time occurrences and without paradigmatic value. Luke's purpose for the BHS occurrences in Acts is to 'show God's approval' of the respective groups.[223]

4.4.2 The View Critiqued

Hamilton is not alone among American Baptists who embrace the BHS 'attestation' view.[224] The view is to be commended to the degree that it reflects Luke's presentation of BHS as an eschatological corporate reception of the gift of the Spirit. The view also explains the partial fulfillment of JTB's prophecy (Luke 3:16) on the Day of Pentecost and the multiple BHS occurrences appearing among distinct groups in Acts. Problematic with the view is its potential overemphasis on 'attestation.' To conclude from the four BHS occurrences detailed by Luke in Acts that they are 'exclusively' meant to 'validate' the group as 'approved by God' is to unnecessarily reduce the narratives to attestation accounts and eliminate the more pronounced ministry-related empowerment which accompanies BHS. Schreiner does not exclude charismatic ministry as a function of BHS. He

---

[218] As a textual note, verse 37 does not appear in many MSS, and in those where it does verse 39 describes the Spirit falling on the eunuch. See Biblical Studies Press, *The NET Bible* (Dallas: Biblical Studies Press, 2007), 2128 n. 14.

[219] Hamilton, *God's Indwelling Presence,* 191.

[220] Ibid.

[221] Ibid., 191, 198 n. 48. Hamilton locates the occasion for the indwelling of the Spirit by the 'believing remnant' as occurring on the day of resurrection (John 20:22). This may be a Johannine reference to Ezek 36:20; 37:9-14 and provides further evidence for a logical separation of the indwelling and BHS functions of the Spirit.

[222] Ibid., 193.

[223] Ibid.

[224] See Carroll, *The Holy Spirit,* 41. See also Schreiner, *New Testament Theology,* 458-59.

concedes that 'equipping for ministry' is a primary function of 'the Spirit of prophecy' received via BHS and depicted in Luke-Acts.[225]

The difference between Schreiner and Hamilton is not the Spirit's role in empowering for ministry, but the relation of the verb 'filled' (πίμπλημι) to the inference of BHS occurring (from Acts 1:4-5) in Acts 2:4. Schreiner includes the verb within the descriptive lexical range of other verbs ('receive/λαμβάνω,' Acts 1:8; 'pour out/ἐκχέω/ἐκχύννωω,' Acts 2:17-18; 'give/δίδωμι,' Luke 11:13; Acts 8:18-19; 11:17; 'come upon/ἔρχομαι/ἐπέρχομαι,' Luke 1:35; Acts 1:8; 'fall upon/ἐπιπίπτω,' Acts 10:44; 11:15; and 'baptize/βαπτίζω,' Luke 3:16; Acts 1:4-5) which uniformly denote the pouring out of the Spirit.[226] Although the verb 'baptize/βαπτίζω' appearing in Luke 3:16 and Acts 1:4-5 is not repeated in Acts 2:4, the Spirit was poured out by Jesus (Acts 2:33) on the 120.[227] Hamilton also considers Luke's use of the verb 'filled' (πίμπλημι) in Acts 2:4 to likewise overlap with the aforementioned verbs 'to show special empowerment.'[228] He (contra Schreiner) further distinguishes the ongoing 'abiding' and 'fruit-bearing' operations of the Spirit (πλήρης/πληρόω)[229] from the iterative[230] and repetitive occasions[231] when 'the ongoing presence of the Spirit' erupts into special empowerment 'for a definite task' (πίμπλημιι, Acts 4:8, 31; 9:17 and 13:9).[232] By making this distinction, Hamilton identifies πίμπλημιι with the corporate eschatological reception of the gift of the Spirit (BHS) in Acts 2:4, but notes that 'empowerment' is Luke's consistent (primary) use of the verb (Acts 4:8, 31; 9:17 and 13:9); the former is intended for identification and the latter for function. This nuance separates BHS and 'filled' (πίμπλημιι) as two separate ministries of the

---

[225] Schreiner, *New Testament Theology*, 454.

[226] Ibid., 450. See Menzies, *The Development of Early Christian Pneumatology*, 212 n. 3. See also Dunn, *Baptism in the Holy Spirit*, 70-72.

[227] Schreiner, *New Testament Theology*, 452-53.

[228] Hamilton, *God's Indwelling Presence*, 201.

[229] Ibid., 194. These terms have 'lifestyle' implications for Luke, or 'the character of the Christian life.'

[230] Turner notes that πίμπλημι is more intensive than πληρόω and 'especially appropriate (in the aorist indicative and participial forms) to denote relatively short events or immediate effects.' See Turner, *Power from on High*, 167.

[231] Ibid., 168. Turner locates two occurrences of πίμπλημι in Luke-Acts which are exceptional and may 'denote the inception of a lasting endowment of the Spirit in exceptional strength' (Luke 1:15 and Acts 9:17). Hamilton also concedes the possibility of this exception for πίμπλημι as a Lukan reference to 'Paul's anointing for ministry.' See Hamilton, *God's Indwelling Presence*, 199 n. 49.

[232] Hamilton, *God's Indwelling Presence*, 201.

Spirit.[233] This is consistent with Hamilton's preference for the more inclusive term 'eschatological gift of the Spirit' over the limiting expression 'Spirit of prophecy.'[234] Menzies also recognizes the two senses of πίμπλημιι used by Luke, but (contra Hamilton) combines them into one 'divine activity' involving 'a permanent promise of pneumatic assistance (either special knowledge or power of speech) for each moment of need.[235]

By separating BHS and ministry empowerment, Hamilton narrows the function of BHS exclusively to attestation, which Menzies also upholds as a non-exclusive function.[236] Hamilton writes, 'each baptism serves to extend the eschatological gift of the Spirit in a new way...each filling, on the other hand, results in power for ministry.'[237] By understanding BHS as solely an eschatological event whereby groups of believers are accredited by God, Hamilton effectively makes ministry empowerment an evidential concomitant to BHS. He writes, 'baptisms and outpourings are emphatic demonstrations that the eschatological gift of the Spirit has come.'[238] They are 'emphatic' due to the corresponding manifestations of the Spirit's ministry. To receive the gift of the Spirit (BHS) is tacitly to possess a non-experiential phenomenon which is distinct from its experienced effects. Receiving the gift of the Spirit (BHS) proximate to and separate from personal conversion experience is non-affective. The empowering operation of BHS, however, involves demonstrative spiritual experience. This is an important distinction, because it does not deny normative value to the evidential character of BHS described in its narrative references (Acts 2, 8, 10, and 19). To suggest that the Acts 2, 8, 10, and 19 BHS accounts are not paradigmatic of what happens at conversion (Hamilton) is exegetically plausible, but it does not follow that the accounts possess no normative value concerning the experience (evidential nature) of BHS demonstrated in the narratives. Hamilton

---

[233] Ibid.

[234] Ibid., 194-95. Contra Turner, Hamilton believes the term 'Spirit of prophecy' is too restrictive given 'that the Spirit also has non-prophetic ministries such as comfort (Acts 9:31) and joy (Acts 13:52). Hamilton, however, does not correctly represent Turner on this point. Turner indicates eight instances in the book of Acts where references to the Spirit activities do not 'immediately fit the categories of gifts we would regard as prototypical of the Spirit of prophecy, including those mentioned by Hamilton. Turner believes that each of these occurrences can be contextually reconciled as 'pertaining to activities of the Spirit of prophecy.' See Turner, *Power from on High*, 349-52.

[235] Menzies, *The Development of Early Christian Pneumatology*, 212.

[236] Ibid., 265.

[237] Hamilton, *God's Indwelling Presence*, 202.

[238] Ibid., 191.

suggests this conclusion when he observes that the differentiated senses of πλήρης, πληρόω, and πίμπλημι in the book of Acts 'do not exhaust...the ministries of the Spirit' conveyed by the verbs.[239] This is an admission to the durative and concomitant role of evidential BHS manifestations by virtue of Spirit-empowered ministry (πίμπλημι). This conclusion can only be drawn from granting normative value to the BHS accounts in Acts.

A corporate reception of 'the gift of the Spirit' (BHS) can be eschatologically unique and unrepeatable, but its effects (in terms of the distinct empowering work of the Spirit it occasions) continue as a boundless resource from which individual members of the corporate body of Christ may draw. This view approximates Menzies' view which interprets 'filled with the Spirit' (Acts 2:4) as fulfilled in the 'momentary and repetitive instances of inspiration' which represent 'concrete realizations' of the promise recorded in Luke 24:49 and Acts 1:8; the equipping of the disciples 'with prophetic power for the mission which lay ahead.'[240] Warrington rightly avers that BHS represents for believers the 'opportunity to interface with the divine via repeated infillings of the Spirit...and [to have] an increasing control of the Spirit being actively enacted in their lives.'[241] This is ultimately related to the character of the eschatological gift of the Spirit ('Spirit of prophecy') received as 'the promise of the father' on the Day of Pentecost.

5. Conclusion

The redaction-critical hermeneutical method represents the best approach for classical Pentecostals and American Baptists to find interpretive commonality concerning Luke-Acts and the discovery of BHS doctrinal consensus. Efforts have been made to qualify the use of redaction-criticism by the contributing scholars of both traditions against charges of 'anti-historical' and 'subjectivizing' by its detractors. Emphasis on the affective nature of BHS in the form of a doctrine of subsequence (two-stage pneumatology) by North American classical Pentecostalism (and some within the neo-Pentecostal/charismatic renewal) impedes progress toward BHS doctrinal consensus with American Baptists. The dialogical approach taken in this chapter includes the addition of an outside non-Pentecostal evangelical voice: (1) to locate common interpretive ground, (2) to remove the identified impasse to convergence/consensus, and (3) to establish BHS

[239] Ibid., 203.

[240] Ibid.

[241] Warrington, *Pentecostal Theology*, 125.

as a phenomenon separate from conversion-initiation and the source for ongoing experiences of the Spirit's empowering for ministry. Areas of general non-Pentecostal evangelical continuity with classical Pentecostals applicable to American Baptists include:

1) The identification of Luke as a historian-theologian.

2) Acceptance of Luke's unique theological contribution to the function and character of BHS presented in his two-volume Luke-Acts corpus.

3) The admission that Luke's non-cessationism, though not widely regarded as normative by dispensational cessationists within the American Baptist tradition, need not preclude redaction-critical conclusions (authorial intent) regarding the BHS metaphor.

4) The contributing role of first-century Judaism to Luke's pneumatological perspective is generally affirmed ('the Spirit of prophecy').

5) Lukan association of 'the gift of the Spirit' with prophetic empowering is generally accepted as a (and not 'the') functional role of BHS.

The dialogical approach to the study of BHS in Luke-Acts has yielded the following points of convergence/consensus.

1) The 'gift of the Spirit' (BHS) is an eschatological event occurring on the Day of Pentecost (Joel 3:1-5 LXX; Acts 2:17-21).

2) The relation of BHS to the (Q) winnowing metaphor (Luke 3:17 = Matt 3:12) provides a Lukan interpretive key for understanding the corporate reception of the Spirit by believers on the Day of Pentecost as the initial fulfillment of a single dual-effect (Spirit-fire) eschatological baptism.

3) The programmatic value of Luke 4:18-19 (16-30) is its emphasis on the functional role of the Spirit (prophetic empowerment for ministry) coming eschatologically upon the corporate body of Christ.

4) Luke-Acts internally supports the way Luke describes the corresponding advents of Jesus and the Spirit in collective and corporate terms (Luke 2:10, 30; 3:6, 16; Acts 1:15-26; 2:1-4).

5) The unique one-time corporate BHS occurrences among the groups described in Acts 2, 8, 10, and 19 are emphatic demonstrations of both the Spirit's coming and of God's approval (attestation).

6) Normative value is ascribed to the non-repeatable corporate BHS occurrences due to the ongoing functional role of the Spirit given via BHS; charismatic equipping for ministry is the primary function of the Spirit of prophecy.

7) The differentiated senses of πλήρης, πληρόω, and πίμπλημι in the book of Acts witness to the durative and concomitant role of evidential BHS manifestations via Spirit-empowered ministry (πίμπλημι).

8) Corporately received, 'the gift of the Spirit' (BHS) is eschatologically unique and unrepeatable. As a boundless resource from which individual members of the corporate body of Christ may draw, it occasions ongoing filling (πίμπλημι) experiences-effects (e.g. empowering work of the Spirit, Acts 4:8, 31; 9:17; 13:9) necessary to Christian life and witness.

-7-

CONCLUSIONS

1. Introduction

This final chapter draws together meaningfully the major findings of the research presented in the previous six chapters with the following objectives in view. First, §2 briefly reexamines the aim of the thesis outlined in the Introduction in order to evaluate and support the effectiveness of its presentation. Second, §3 summarizes by chapter the major findings of the research. Third, §4 details the unique contribution of the thesis to scholarship that is dedicated to the BHS debate. Fourth, §5 suggests for further investigation issues that are not directly addressed in the thesis.

2. Fidelity to the Thesis Aim

Written from an American Baptist point of view, the research contained in this thesis presents the relevant scholarship from two evangelical traditions with opposing BHS views, namely, American Baptist and Pentecostal. The perspective of the charismatic movement appears in the study because it aligns with some classical Pentecostal views though in other ways it is closer to the Baptist BHS position. The purpose of this investigation is to extend the debate beyond the limited parameters of the nature and function of BHS toward the formulation of a consensus view for American Baptist and P/C adherents. This previously unexplored bi-traditional approach to the BHS debate provided a unique focus to the thesis. By placing each tradition within the bounds of centered-set evangelicalism (Chapter 1), American Baptists may root the rationale for BHS doctrinal consensus in the believer's personal conversion experience. This experience is essentially encounter-oriented and is representative of a core spirituality shared with P/C adherents. The core spirituality concerns the ongoing work of the Spirit in the lives of believers (Chapters 2-3). Non-cessationists insist on the normativity of the miraculous *charismata* attached to BHS which is

241

consistent with classical Pentecostals and some within the charismatic renewal movement. This finding emerged from Chapters 4-5 as a significant impasse to American Baptist and P/C consensus. In order to move dialogically toward the formulation of a Luke-Acts based BHS consensus position, the impasse required the introduction of third-party non-Pentecostal evangelical scholar Arie Zwiep (Chapter 6).

3. Summary of the Research Findings

Methodologically, Chapters 1-3 provide context for the respective American Baptist and P/C BHS positions later explored in Chapters 4-5. Ultimately, Chapters 1-3 are foundational to the dialogical approach used in Chapter 6. The result is an encounter-oriented BHS consensus view that informs American Baptist spiritual experience. Chapter 1 adduced personal conversion experience as the essential definitional core of evangelicalism that is common to both American Baptists and P/C adherents. In this strict sense, BHS is an issue of correlative and secondary significance to the debate. Thus, BHS accordance is not essential for evangelical communion. In terms of evangelical orthodoxy, BHS is not a primary doctrine, although it does present the means for personal and dynamic spiritual growth which enhances the definitional center (i.e. personal conversion experience). This makes centered-set evangelicalism a functionally preferable option over bounded-set, or big 'F' Fundamentalism, for American Baptist adherents in pursuit of BHS consensus.

Chapter 2 outlines the full gospel Pentecostal orientation to the Christian life that emphasizes Spirit-based transformational spirituality which is considered antithetical to formal rationalistic Christian traditions. The advance of the Pentecostal experience in its 'second wave' iteration impacted the mainline Christian denominations through the charismatic renewal with its eruption of miraculous *charismata* considered to be normative by members of the movement. This is further demonstrated in the contemporary signs and wonders movement commonly referred to as the 'Third Wave.' Within the tripartite typology of P/C spirituality, BHS is most emphasized by classical Pentecostals and many renewalists as a personally repeatable and Spirit-empowering tactile experience that is subsequent to personal conversion. In addition, BHS is evidenced by glossolalia and is integral to a visibly expressed spirituality. Though differing from classical Pentecostals and renewalists on the timing and evidential nature of BHS, American Baptists, with equal intensity for expressed and ongoing Spirit-based growth, benefit from engaging this opposing BHS apologetic.

Chapter 3 presented voluntarism, or 'soul competency,' as the encounter-oriented root of American Baptist spiritual orientation. Though differing from classical Pentecostals and renewalists on the essential nature of the BHS experience, each tradition shares common ground in the encounter-orientation of spirituality. While American Baptists may shy away from talking about their spiritual experience with the same kind of overt and tactile terms commonly used by P/C adherents, it is clear that from a Baptist perspective Christianity is much more than intellectually assenting to a given set of dogmas. It is likely the historical emphasis on correct doctrine that has produced American Baptist reticence toward articulating spirituality with experiential terms. Nevertheless, American Baptists do grant high value to spiritual experience, not only in their personal and corporate religious life, but also as a guide to their interpretation of Scripture. The Holy Spirit is understood as the channel for this experience.

This common ground of encounter-based spirituality allows for the Pentecostal BHS doctrinal apologetic to inform American Baptist expectations for spiritual experience. Emphasis on the regenerate status of its members places the American Baptist tradition within the definitional parameters of centered-set evangelicalism which anticipates the ongoing work of the Spirit in the lives of believers. This emphasis does not impede communion with other biblically-based spiritual traditions, including many within the P/C tradition. Controversy within the SBC produced models for intra-denominational doctrinal conciliation and even consensus. The modified SBC center-circumference model is transferable to intra-evangelical American Baptist/P/C consensus when matters of circumference (from a Baptist point of view this includes BHS as described within the P/C movement) are debated in light of scriptural authority and on the basis of first-order unity (i.e. where the center is the experience of personal conversion). The implication of these findings is that American Baptists (e.g. SBC) have the methodological means to meaningfully engage P/C spirituality and to move toward BHS consensus. Full agreement may be a distant goal, but this research shows that there is ample ground for American Baptists to engage in dialogue with P/C adherents and to embark on this joint exploration.

Chapter 4 evaluated American Baptist BHS constructs. The research demonstrates that American Baptists generally relate BHS to (or equate it with) personal conversion experience and do not interpret the metaphor as a secondary post-conversion work of the Spirit. The research further indicates that American Baptists do not commonly associate BHS with miraculous *charismata* which are considered, on the contrary, to have ceased with the apostolic era. However, the research did not establish a single BHS conception that is uniformly accepted by the tradition. Instead, it demonstrated the possibility of formulating a unified

American Baptist view from the diverse range of BHS perspectives. This view is stated as follows:

- BHS is the eschatological work initiated by Jesus on the Day of Pentecost (and ultimately completed at the home of Cornelius), whereby the gift of the Spirit functioned to unify and authenticate the body of Christ as empowered witnesses to disseminate the gospel message.

Though largely perceived by American Baptists in Pauline terms as non-affective incorporation into the body of Christ, evaluations of Luke-Acts by Schreiner and Hamilton introduce the Lukan emphasis on 'empowering for service' into their interpretive schema of the BHS metaphor. This admission is the result of the dialectical tension of American Baptist scholarship with P/C articulations of the BHS doctrine. P/C spirituality challenges American Baptists to biblically account for the evidential nature of a repeatable post-Pentecost BHS reception. This challenge is resolved by the proposed consensus detailed in Chapter 6.

Chapter 5 differentiated the diverse BHS views represented in the P/C movement. North American classical Pentecostals and some within the charismatic renewal embrace BHS in Lukan theological terms as a repeatable ministry-related definite experience. This experience is secondary to conversion and is accompanied by glossolalia or some other evidential *charisma* such as are seen in Luke-Acts. Other P/C adherents differ conceptually and semantically, regarding BHS as a later-occurring 'release' of the gift of the Spirit previously received at conversion; these would include, notably, sacramentally-oriented charismatics. Third wave adherents are conceptually similar to non-Pentecostal evangelicals and posit a single-stage pneumatological model that links BHS with personal conversion experience. The two-stage pneumatological BHS model advanced by classical Pentecostals permeates P/C conceptual and semantic differences. Each of the distinct spiritual traditions anticipate profound Spirit-induced endowments of the Spirit subsequent to personal conversion experience. Physical signs bearing witness to the presence and power of the Spirit by BHS recipients is a universally accepted phenomenon within the P/C movement. The research findings focused on the nature of the American Baptist and P/C adherent doctrinal impasse which concerns particular expressions of post-conversional operations of the Spirit in the BHS recipient, namely, the reception of the Spirit (and its association with the miraculous *charismata*).

The steps towards BHS consensus between American Baptist and classical Pentecostal/renewal adherents are presented in Chapter 6. The investigation began methodologically by isolating and adopting redaction-criticism in order to find interpretive commonality for the BHS-related texts in Luke-Acts. Utilizing a third-party and non-Pentecostal evangelical voice (Zwiep), a dialogical approach to consensus aimed at removing the identified impasse in order to conceive BHS as a phenomenon separate from conversion and the source for ongoing encounter-oriented experiences of the Spirit's empowering for ministry. The three traditions concur on several factors relative to Luke's unique theological contribution to the BHS debate. With agreement on these foundational points, examination of the BHS-related Luke-Acts texts resulted in a range of conclusions:

1. BHS is a one-time corporate and eschatological reception of the Spirit by the body of Christ on the Day of Pentecost.

2. BHS programmatically fulfilled the initial functional/empowerment stage of a Spirit/fire eschatological baptism.

3. Repeated occasions of BHS, described narratively by Luke, are for purposes of divine attestation of diverse Christian groups.

4. The ongoing personal role of the Spirit as 'charismatic equipping for ministry' is anticipated by the previously-received corporate BHS occurrence.

5. The durative sense of the Spirit's empowering is evidenced by the differentiated senses of πλήρης, πληρόω, and πίμπλημι used by Luke in the book of Acts.

6. BHS manifestations via displays of the Spirit's empowering for ministry attest to the ongoing filling/πίμπλημι (i.e. empowering work of the Spirit, Acts 4:8, 31; 9:17; 13:9) necessary to Christian life and witness.

A most important outcome of this research is that BHS common ground is approached when the metaphor is conceived as an eschatologically unique and unrepeatable corporate reception of the Spirit by the body of Christ on the Day of Pentecost, one that provides ongoing evidential charismatic equipping for Christian life and ministry.

4. The Unique Contribution of the Thesis to BHS-Related Scholarship

The research presents apologetic articulations of BHS positions by American Baptists and P/C adherents. It is not, however, a theological or exegetical investigation into the interpretive merits of these views. Instead, the research formulates a dialogical BHS construct. The construct is a consensus view comprised of existing points of agreement between two spiritually diverse theological traditions informed by a neutral third. The thesis represents, therefore, a non-partisan/non-sectarian approach to BHS scholarship, one that informs the essential spiritual core of one tradition (American Baptist) by the essential spiritual core of another (P/C movement).

5. Remaining Issues for Investigation

The importance of the thesis, especially for American Baptists, is outlined in the Introduction of this study. Yet, two discernible questions remain which are not probed in-depth by this research and represent additional areas for scholarly enquiry. The first area of enquiry concerns the Lukan 'Spirit of prophecy' versus Pauline 'soteriological Spirit' debate relative to the nature and function of BHS. This debate is documented abundantly in the works of Turner and Menzies and reflected upon briefly in the works of Hamilton and Schreiner. A more robust American Baptist scholarly appraisal of the Luke-Paul pneumatological debate would provide further insight into the nature and function of BHS. To illustrate, Darrell L. Bock, an influential evangelical scholar among American Baptists, is research professor of NT studies at Dallas Theological Seminary (Dallas, TX). Of the 492 pages in his *A Theology of Luke and Acts* (2012), Bock devotes only 16 pages to Lukan pneumatology, mentioning the works of Turner and Menzies in his bibliography.[1] A second area of enquiry for American Baptists concerns non-cessationism as an implication of the consensus BHS view advanced by this study. As the evidential byproduct of a once-and-for-all eschatological event, charismatic expressions (*charismata*) of the Spirit's ongoing role in the body of Christ, including to so-called 'miraculous gifts,' directly relate to prior BHS reception. A revisiting of non-cessationism by American Baptists in light of the findings of this research will prove valuable to BHS expectations while improving relations with P/C adherents.

---

[1] Darrell L. Bock, *A Theology of Luke and Acts* (Grand Rapids: Zondervan, 2012), 211-26.

BIBLIOGRAPHY

ABBOTT-SMITH, G. 1964. *A Manual Greek Lexicon of the New Testament.* Edinburgh: T & T Clark.

AIKEN, Daniel L. (ed). 2007. *A Theology of the Church.* Nashville: B & H Academic.

AKIN, Daniel L. 2011. The Future of the Southern Baptist Convention. *In:* David S. DOCKERY, Ray VAN NESTE, and Jerry TIDWELL, (eds). *Southern Baptists, Evangelicals, and the Future of Denominationalism*, Nashville: B & H Academic, pp.261-78.

ALAND, B., Black, M., ALAND, K., KARAVIDOPOULOS, J. et al. (eds). 1993. *Novum Testamentum Graece, 27th Ed.* Stuttgart: Deutsche Bibelgessellschraft.

ALBRECHT, Daniel E. 1992. Pentecostal Spirituality: Looking through the Lens of Ritual. *Pneuma.* **14**(2), pp.107-25.

ALBRECHT, Daniel E. 1997. Pentecostal Spirituality: Ecumenical Potential and Challenge. *Cyberjournal for Pentecostal-Charismatic Research.* **2**(1), pp.1-52.

ALBRECHT, Daniel E. 1999. *Rites in the Spirit: A Ritual Approach to Pentecostal/Charismatic Spirituality.* Sheffield: Sheffield Academic Press.

ALFORD, Dean. 2006. Tongues Tied. *Christianity Today*, 15 February, p.21.

ALLIANCE, Baptist World. 2010. *BWA to Explore Talks with Orthodox and Pentecostals.* [online]. [Accessed 26 September 2011]. Available from World Wide Web: <http://www.bwanet.org/bwa.php?m=news&p=news _item&id =503>

AMERICA, Conservative Baptists of. 2011. *Doctrinal Statement.* [online]. [Accessed 30 August 2011]. Available from World Wide Web: <http://www. cbamerica.org/cba_Resources/Doctrinal_Statement.php>

AMERICA, First Baptist Church in. 2011. *History.* [online]. [Accessed 19 December 2011]. Available from World Wide Web: <http://www.firstbaptist churchinamerica.org/?page_id=60>

Bibliography

AMMERMAN, Nancy Tatom. 1990. *Baptist Battles: Social Change and Religious Conflict in the Southern Baptist Convention*. London: Rutgers University Press.

AMMERMAN, Nancy Tatum. 2002. *Bible Believers: Fundamentalists in the Modern World*. Chapel Hill: Rutgers University Press.

ANDERSON, Alan. 2004. *An Introduction to Pentecostalism*. Cambridge: Cambridge University Press.

ANDERSON, Alan. 2007. *Spreading Fires: The Missionary Nature of Early Pentecostalism*. London: SCM Press.

ANDERSON, Alan. 2010. Varieties, Taxonomies, and Definitions. *In*: Alan ANDERSON, Michael BERGUNDER, André DROOGERS, and Cornelius VAN DER LAAN, (eds). *Global Pentecostalism: Theories and Methods*, Berkley: University of California Press, pp.13-29.

ANDERSON, Allan H. and HOLLENWEGER, Walter J. (eds). 1999. *Pentecostals after a Century: Global Perspectives on a Movement in Transition*. Sheffield: Sheffield Academic Press.

ANDERSON, Gordon L. 1994. Pentecostal Hermeneutics, Part 1. *Paraclete*. **28**(1), pp.1-11.

ANDERSON, Gordon L. 2005. *Baptism in the Holy Spirit, Initial Evidence, and a New Model*. [online]. [Accessed 10 November 2011]. Available from World Wide Web: <Baptism in the Holy Spirit, Initial Evidence, and a New Model>

ANDERSON, Neil T. 1990. *Victory Over the Darkness: Realizing the Power of Your Identity in Christ*. Ventura: Regal Books.

APOSTLES, International Coalition of. 2011. *About ICA*. [online]. [Accessed 12 November 2011]. Available from World Wide Web: <http://www.coalitionof apostles.com/about-ica/>

ARCHER, Kenneth J. 1996. Pentecostal Hermeneutics: Retrospect and Prospect. *Journal of Pentecostal Theology*. **8**(1), pp.63-81.

ARCHER, Kenneth J. 2001. Early Pentecostal Biblical Interpretation. *Journal of Pentecostal Theology*. **18**(1), pp.32-71.

ARCHER, Kenneth J. 2004. *Hermeneutics for the Twenty-First Century: Spirit, Scripture and Community*. London: T&T Clark.

ARCHIVES, Southern Baptist Historical Library and. 2010. *Edgar Young Mullins*. [online]. [Accessed 15 December 2011]. Available from World Wide Web: <http://www.sbhla.org/bio_eymullins.htm>

ARRINGTON, French L. 1981. The Indwelling, Baptism, and Infilling with the Holy Spirit. *Pneuma*. **3**(1), pp.1-10.

ARRINGTON, French L. 1988. Hermeneutics. *In*: Stanley BURGESS and Gary B. MCGEE, (eds). *Dictionary of Pentecostal and Charismatic Movements*, Grand Rapids: Zondervan Publishing, pp.376-89.

ARRINGTON, French L. 1988. Hermeneutics, Historical Perspective on Pentecostal and Charismatic. *In*: Stanley M. BURGESS and Gary MCGEE, (eds). *Dictionary of Pentecostal and Charismatic Movements*, Grand Rapids: Zondervan Publishing House, p.382.

ARRINGTON, French L. 1994. The Use of the Bible by Pentecostals. *Pneuma*. **16**(1), pp.101-7.

ARRINGTON, French L. 1994. *Christian Doctrine: A Pentecostal Perspective, Vol. 1*. Cleveland: Pathway Press.

ASSEMBLIES OF GOD, General Council. 2011. *AG Position Papers and other Statements*. [online]. [Accessed 10 November 2011]. Available from World Wide Web: <http://ag.org/top/Beliefs/Position_Papers/index.cfm>

ASSEMBLIES OF GOD, General Council. 2011. *Our 16 Fundamental Truths*. [online]. [Accessed 10 November 2011]. Available from World Wide Web: <http://www.ag.org/top/beliefs/statement_of_fundamental_truths/sft_full.cfm#7>

ATKINSON, William P. 1995. Pentecostal Responses to Dunn's Baptism in the Holy Spirit: Luke-Acts. *Journal of Pentecostal Theology*. **6**(1), pp.87-131.

ATKINSON, William P. 1995. Pentecostal Responses to Dunn's Baptism in the Holy Spirit: Pauline Literature. *Journal of Pentecostal Theology*. **7**(1), pp.49-72.

ATKINSON, William P. 2003. Worth a Second Look? Pentecostal Hermeneutics. *Evangel*. **21**(2), pp.49-54.

Bibliography

ATKINSON, William P. 2011. *Baptism in the Spirit: Luke-Acts and the Dunn Debate*. Eugene: Pickwick Publications.

AUTRY, Arden C. 1993. Dimensions of Hermeneutics in Pentecostal Focus. *Journal of Pentecostal Theology*. **3**(1), pp.29-50.

BADIA, Leonard F. 1980. *The Qumran Baptism and John the Baptist's Baptism*. Lanham: University of America Press.

BAER, Jr. Richard A. 1976. Quaker Silence, Catholic Liturgy, and Pentecostal Glossolalia: Some Functional Similarities. *In*: Russell P. SPITTLER, (ed). *Perspectives on the New Pentecostalism*, Grand Rapids: Baker Book House, pp.150-64.

BAINTON, Roland H. 1955. *Here I Stand: A Life of Martin Luther*. New York: Meridian.

BANCROFT, Emery. 1977. *Elemental Theology*. Grand Rapids: Zondervan Publishing.

BARNES, William H. 2002. Brownsville Revival. *In*: Stanley M. BURGESS and Eduard M. VAN DER MAAS, (eds). *New International Dictionary of Pentecostal and Charismatic Movements*, Grand Rapids: Zondervan, pp.445-47.

BARR, James. 1961. *The Semantics of Biblical Language*. London: SCM Press.

BARRETT, C. K. 1975. *The Holy Spirit and the Gospel Tradition*. London: S.P.C.K.

BARRETT, C. K. 1994. *A Critical and Exegetical Commentary on the Acts of the Apostles, Vol. 1*. Edinburgh: T&T Clark.

BARRETT, C. K. 2006. *Acts 1-14*. London: T & T Clark.

BARRETT, C. K. 2006. *Acts 15-28*. London: T & T Clark.

BARRETT, David B., George T. KURIAN, and Todd M. JOHNSON. 2001. World Summary. *In*: David B. BARRETT, George T. KURIAN, and Todd M. JOHNSON, (eds). *World Christian Encyclopedia: A Contemporary Survey of Churches and Religions in the Modern World, 2nd ed., Vol. 1*, New York: Oxford University Press, pp.741-50.

Bibliography

BARRETT, David B. and Todd M. JOHNSON. 2002. Global Statistics. *In*: Stanley M. BURGESS and Eduard VAN DER MAAS, (eds). *The New International Dictionary of Pentecostal and Charismatic Movements*, Grand Rapids: Zondervan, pp.284-302.

BARTH, Karl and Trans. Gabriel VAHANIAN. ET 1960. *The Faith of the Church: A Commentary on the Apostle's Creed According to Calvin's Catechism*. London: Fontana Books.

BAUER, Walter, William F. Arndt, F. Wilbur Gingrich, and Frederick W. Danker. 1979. *A Greek-English Lexicon of the New Testament and Other Early Christian Literature, 2nd ed*. Chicago: The University of Chicago Press.

BEASLEY-MURRAY, G. R. 1962. *Baptism in the New Testament*. London: Macmillan & Co., Ltd.

BEBBINGTON, D. A. 2005. *Evangelicalism in Modern Britain: A History from the 1730s to the 1980s*. London: Routledge.

BENNETT, Dennis. 1970. *Nine O'Clock in the Morning*. Plainfield: Bridge Publishing.

BENNETT, Dennia and Rita BENNETT. 1971. *The Holy Spirit and You: A Study Guide to the Spirit-Filled Life*. Plainfield: Logos.

BERENDS, Kurt O. 1999. Social Variables and Community Response. *In*: Edith L. BLUMHOFER, Russell P. SPITTLER, and Grant A. AND WACKER, (eds). *Pentecostal Currents in American Pentecostalism*, Chicago: University of Illinois Press, pp.68-89.

BITTLINGER, Arnold. 1981. Charismatic Renewal: An Opportunity for the Church? *In*: Arnold BITTLINGER, (ed). *The Church is Charismatic: The World Council of the Churches and the Charismatic Renewal* , Geneva: World Council of Chburches, p.10.

BLACKABY, Henry. 2008. *Experiencing God: Knowing and Doing the Will of God, Revised and Expanded*. Nashville: B & H Books.

BLASS, F. and A. DEBRUNNER. 1961. *A Greek Grammar of the New Testament and Other Early Christian Literature*. Chicago: The University of Chicago Press.

251

BLOESCH, Donald G. 1978. *Essentials of Evangelical Theology: God, Authority, & Salvation, Vol. 1*. New York: Harper & Row.

BLOESCH, Donald G. 1992. *A Theology of Word & Spirit: Authority & Method in Theology*. Downers Grove: InterVarsity Press.

BLOMBERG, Craig L. 1992. Matthew. *In*: David S. DOCKERY, (ed). *The New American Commentary: An Exegetical and Theological Exposition of Holy Scripture*, Nashville: Broadman Press, pp.71-80.

BLOMBERG, Craig L. 1994. 1 Corinthians. *In*: Terry MUCK, (ed). *The NIV Application Commentary*, Grand Rapids: Zondervan Publishing House, p.252.

BLOMBERG, Craig L. 1995. The Globalization of Hermeneutics. *Journal of the Evangelical Theological Society*. **38**(4), pp.581-93.

BLOMBERG, Craig L. 2006. *From Pentecost to Patmos: An Introduction to Acts through Revelation*. Nashville: B & H Publishing Group.

BLOMBERG, Craig L. 2009. *Jesus and the Gospels: An Introduction and Survey, 2nd Ed.* Nashville: B & H Academic.

BLUE, Ken. 1987. *Authority to Heal*. Downers Grove: InterVarsity Press.

BLUMHOEFER, Edith L. 1993. *Restoring the Faith: The Assemblies of God, Pentecostalism, and American Culture*. Chicago: University of Illinois Press.

BLUMHOFER, Edith L., SPITTLER, Russell P., and WACKER, Grant A. (eds). 1999. *Pentecostal Currents in American Protestantism*. Chicago: University of Illinois Press.

BLUMHOEFER, Edith L. and C. R. Armstrong. 2002. Assemblies of God. *In*: *The New International Dictionary of Pentecostal Charismatic Movements*, Grand Rapids: Zondervan Publishing House, pp.333-40.

BLUNT, John Henry. 1874. *Dictionary of Sects, Heresies, Ecclesiastical Parties, and Schools of Religious Thought*. London: Rivingtons.

BOARD, International Mission. 2006. *Policy on Tongues and Prayer Language*. [online]. [Accessed 28 June 2011]. Available from World Wide Web: <http://www.imb.org/main/news/details.asp?LanguageID=1709&StoryID=3834>

BOARD, International Mission. 2007. *Guidelines on Tongues and Prayer Language.* [online]. [Accessed 28 June 2011]. Available from World Wide Web: <http://www.gofbw.com/news.asp?ID=7358>

BOARD, International Mission. 2007. *IMB Trustees Adopt Revised Baptism, Prayer Language Guidelines.* [online]. [Accessed 28 June 2011]. Available from World Wide Web: <http://www.imb.org/main/news/details.asp?LanguageID= 1709&Story ID=5581>

BOARD, North American Mission. 2011. *Self-Assessment.* [online]. [Accessed 28 June 2011]. Available from World Wide Web: <http://www.namb.net/self-assessment/>

BOARD, International Mission. 2012. *Position Paper Concerning the IMB Policy on Glossolalia.* [online]. [Accessed 6 April 2012]. Available from World Wide Web: <http://www.imb.org/main/news/details.asp?LanguageID= 1709& StoryID =3839>

BOCK, Darrell L. 2006. Luke 1:1-9:50. *In*: Moisés SILVA, (ed). *Baker Exegetical Commentary on the New Testament*, Grand Rapids: Baker Book House, p.345.

BOCK, Darrell L. 2012. *A Theology of Luke and Acts.* Grand Rapids: Zondervan.

BORCHERT, Jerald L. 1996. John 1-11. *In:* E. Ray Clendenen, (ed). *the new American Commentary: An Exegetical and Theological Exposition of the Holy Scripture, Vol. 25a,* Nashville: Broadman Press, p. 138.

BOTTOMLY, Kirk. 1993. Coming out of the Hanger: Confessions of an Evangelical Deist. *In*: Gary S. GREIG and Kevin N. SPRINGER, (eds). *The Kingdom and the Power: Are Healing and the Spiritual Gifts Used by Jesus and the Early Church Meant for the Church Today?*, Ventura: Regal Books, pp.258-74.

BOVON, Fançois. 2006. *Luke the Theologian.* Waco: Baylor University Press.

BRAND, Chad Owen (ed). 2004. *Perspectives on Spirit Baptism.* Nashville: B & H Publishing.

BRAND, Chad Owen. 2004. Introduction. *In*: Chad Owen BRAND, (ed). *Perspectives on Spirit Baptism: Five Views* , Nashville: Broadman & Holman Publishers, pp.1-14.

BRESHEARS, Gerry. 1998. *Deliverance Ministry: A Consensus Statement from Pentecostal, Charismatic and Historic Evangelicals.* [online]. [Accessed 11 April 2012]. Available from World Wide Web: <http://www.raystedman.org/rrf/ delivera. html>

BROADUS, John A. 1886. Commentary on the Gospel of Matthew. *In*: Alvah HOVEY, (ed). *An American Commentary on the New Testament*, Philadelphia: Amwerican Baptist Publication Society, pp.31-52.

BROOKS, James A. 1991. Mark. *In*: David S. DOCKERY, (ed). *The New American Commentary: An Exegetical and Theological Exposition of Holy Scripture, Vol. 23* , Nashville: Broadman Press, pp.37-42.

BROWN, Colin. 1985. *That You May Believe: Miracles and Faith Then and Now.* Grand Rapids: William B. Eerdmans Publishing.

BROWN, Michael L. 1996. *Holy Fire: America on the Edge of Revival.* Shippensburg: Destiny Image Publishers.

BRUMBACK, Carl. 1947. *What Meaneth This?* Springfield: The Gospel Publishing House.

BRUNER, Frederick Dale. 1970. *A Theology of the Holy Spirit: Pentecostal Experience and the New Testament Witness.* London: Hodder and Stoughton.

BRUNER, Frederick Dale. 2004. *The Christbook: Matthew 1-7.* Grand Rapids: William B. Eerdmans Publishing.

BULTMANN, Rudolf. 1964. Is Exegesis without Presupposition Possible? *In*: S. M. OGDEN, (ed). *Existence and Faith: Shorter Writings of Rudolf Bultmann*, London: Collins, pp.342-52.

BUNDY, D. D. 2002. Bibliography and Historiography. *In*: Stanley M. BURGESS and Edward M. VAN DER MASS, (eds). *The New International Dictionary of Pentecostal and Charismatic Movements*, Grand Rapids: Zondervan, pp.382-417.

BUNDY, D. D. 2002. Keswick Higher Life Movement. *In*: Stanley M. BURGESS and Eduard VAN DER MAAS, (eds). *The New International Dictionary of Pentecostal Charismatic Movements*, Grand Rapids: Zondervan, pp.820-21.

BURGESS, Stanley M. and VAN DER MAAS, Eduard M. (eds). 2002. *The New International Dictionary of Pentecostal and Charismatic Movements*. Grand Rapids: Zondervan.

BURGESS, Stanley M. 2002. Neocharismatics. *In*: Stanley M. BURGESS and Eduard M. VAN DER MASS, (eds). *New International Dictionary of Pentecostal and Charismatic Movements*, Grand Rapids: Zondervan, p.928.

BURLESON, Wade. 2005. *Open Letter to the SBC*. [online]. [Accessed 31 August 2011]. Available from World Wide Web: <http://www.puritanboard.com/f24/ southern-baptist-convention-new-ruling-10624/>

BURROWS, Robert. 1986. Americans Get Religion in the New Age: Anything is Permissible if Everything is God. *Christianity Today*, 16 May, pp.17-23.

BUSH, L. Russ and Tom J. NETTLES. 1995. *Baptists and the Bible*. Nashville: B&H Academic.

BYRD, Joseph. 1993. Paul Ricoeur's Hermeneutical Theory and Pentecostal Proclamation. *Pneuma*. **15**(2), pp.213-14.

CADBURY, Henry J. 1927. *The Making of Luke-Acts*. New York: Macmillan.

CANER, Emir. 2006. Southern Baptists, Tongues, and Historical Policy. *The Center for Theological Research*, October, pp.1-9.

CANNISTRACI, David. 1998. *Apostles and the Emerging Apostolic Movement: A Biblical Look at Apostleship and How God is using it to Bless His Church Today*. Ventura: Regal Books.

CARGAL, Timothy B. 1993. Beyond the Fundamentalist-Modernist Controversy: Pentecostals and Hermeneutics in a Post-Modern Age. *Pneuma*. **15**(2), pp.163-87.

CARNELL, Edward J. 2007. *The Case for Biblical Christianity*. Eugene: Wipf & Stock Publishers.

CARR, Anne E. 1988. *Transforming Grace*. San Francisco: Harper & Row.

Bibliography

CARROLL, B. H. 1939. *The Holy Spirit: Comprising a Discussion of the Paraclete, the Other Self of Jesus, and Other Phases of the Work of the Spirit of God*. Nashville: Broadman Press.

CARSON, D. A. 1983. Redaction Criticism: On the Legitimacy and Illegitimacy of a Literary Tool. *In*: D. A. CARSON and J. D. WOODBRIDGE, (eds). *Scripture and Truth*, Grand Rapids: Zondervan, pp.119-42, 376-81.

CARSON, D. A. 1984. Matthew. *In*: Frank E. GAEBELEIN, (ed). *The Expositor's Bible Commentary, Vol. 8*, Grand Rapids: Zondervan Publishing House, pp.98-106.

CARSON, D. A. 2003. *Showing the Spirit: A Theological Exposition of 1 Corinthians 12-14*. Grand Rapids: Baker Book House.

CARSON, D. A. 2005. *Becoming Conversant with the Emerging Church: Understanding a Movement and its Implications*. Grand Rapids: Zondervan.

CARSON, D. A. and Douglas J. MOO. 2005. *An Introduction to the New Testament, 2nd Ed.* Grand Rapids: Zondervan.

CARTLEDGE, Mark J. 2000. The Nature and Function of New Testament Glossolalia. *Evangelical Quarterly* **72**(2), pp. 135-50.

CENTRAL, Sermon. 2010. *2008 The Outreach 100*. [online]. [Accessed 27 June 2011]. Available from World Wide Web: <http://www.sermoncentral.com/articleb.asp?article=top-100-largest-churches>

CERILLO, August. 1999. The Beginnings of American Pentecostalism: A Historiographical Overview. *In*: Edith L. BLUMHOFER, Russell P. SPITTLER, and Grant A. WACKER, (eds). *Pentecostal Currents in American Protestantism*, Chicago: University of Illinois Press, pp.229-59.

CHAFER, Lewis Sperry. 1980. *Systematic Theology, Vol. 7*. Dallas: Dallas Seminary Press.

CHAN, Simon. 1997. The Language Game of Glossolalia, or Making Sense of the Initial Evidence. *In*: Wonsuk MA and Robert MENZIES, (eds). *Pentecostalism in Context: Essays in Honor of William W. Menzies*, Sheffield: Sheffield Academic Press, pp.80-95.

CHAN, Simon. 1999. Evidential Glossolalia and the Doctrine of Subsequence. *Asian Journal of Pentecostal Studies*. **2**(2), pp.195-211.

Bibliography

CHAN, Simon. 2003. *Pentecostal Theology and the Christian Spiritual Tradition.* Sheffield: Sheffield Academic Press.

CHAPMAN, Morris H. 2009. Axioms of a Cooperating Southern Baptist. *In:* David S. DOCKERY, (ed). *Southern Baptist Identity: An Evangelical Denomination Faces the Future,* Wheaton: Crossway Books, pp.159-73.

CHO, Youngmo. 2006. *Spirit and Kingdom in the Writings of Luke and Paul: An Attempt to Reconcile these Concepts.* Eugene: Wipf & Stock.

CHRISTENSON, Larry. 1968. *Speaking in Tongues and its Significance for the Church.* Minneapolis: Bethany House.

CHRISTENSON, Larry. 1976. *The Charismatic Renewal Among Lutherans.* Minneapolis: Lutheran Charismatic Renewal Service.

CHRISTENSON, Larry. 1987. *Welcome, Holy Spirit: A Study of Charismatic Renewal in the Church.* Minneapolis: Augsburg Fortress Publications.

CHURCH, Pentecostal Free Will Baptist. 2011. *History of the Pentecostal Free Will Baptist Church.* [online]. [Accessed 27 June 2011]. Available from World Wide Web: <http://www.pfwb.org/ history.htm>

CHURCHES, General Association of Regular Baptist. 2011. *Articles of Faith.* [online]. [Accessed 30 August 2011]. Available from World Wide Web: <http:// www.garbc.org/about-us/our-beliefs/doctrinal-statement/>

CLARK, Stephen. 1969. *Confirmation and the Baptism of the Holy Spirit.* Benet Lake: Dove.

CLARK, Stephen. 2003. *Baptized in the Holy Spirit.* East Lansing: Tabor.

COLLE, Ralph Del. 2004. Spirit Baptism: A Catholic Perspective. *In:* Chad Owen BROWN, (ed). *Perspectives on Spirit Baptism,* Nashville: Broadman & Holman Publishers, pp.241-89.

COLLEGE, Trinity Theological. 2012. *Faculty.* [online]. [Accessed 21 May 2012]. Available from World Wide Web: <http://www.ttc.edu.sg/index.php? option=com_ content&task=view&id=22&Itemid=30>

COLLINS, Adela Yarbro. 2007. Mark: A Commentary. *In:* Harold W. ATTRIDGE, (ed). *Hermeneia: A Critical and Historical Commentary on the Bible* , Minneapolis: Augsburg Fortress Press, p.130.

Bibliography

COMBS, William W. 2010. Book Review: John R. Levison, Filled with the Spirit. *Themelios*. **35**(1), pp.57-58.

CONFERENCE, Baptist General. 2011. *Affirmations of Faith*. [online]. [Accessed 30 August 2011]. Available from World Wide Web: <http:// www.convergeworld wide.org/about/values/affirmation-faith>

CONFERENCE, European Pentecostal Charismatic Research Association. 2009. *Cracked or Broken: Pentecostal Unity*. [online]. [Accessed 28 June 2013]. Available from the World Wide Web: < http://www.epcra.ch/papers_pdf/oxford/ keith_ warrington.pdf >

CONN, Charles W. 1956. *Pillars of Pentecost*. Cleveland: The Pathway Press.

CONNER, W. T. 1937. *Christian Doctrine*. Nashville: Broadman Press.

CONVENTION, Southern Baptist. 2011. *About the Southern Baptist Convention*. [online]. [Accessed 21 June 2011]. Available from World Wide Web: <http://www. sbc.net/aboutus/default.asp>

CONVENTION, Southern Baptist. 2011. *Baptist Faith and Message*. [online]. [Accessed 30 August 2011]. Available from World Wide Web: <http:// www.sbc.net /bfm/default.asp>

CONVENTION, Southern Baptist. 2011. *Comparison of 1925, 1963 and 2000 Baptist Faith and Message*. [online]. [Accessed 28 June 2011]. Available from World Wide Web: <http://www.sbc.net/bfm/bfmcomparison.asp>

CONVENTION, The Southern Baptist. 2012. *Soul Competency*. [online]. [Accessed 4 April 2012]. Available from World Wide Web: <http:// www.sbc. net/aboutus/ pssoul.asp>

CONZELMANN, Hans and Trans. Geoffrey BUSWELL. ET 1961. *The Theology of Luke*. New York: Harper & Row.

COOK, W. Robert. 1979. *The Theology of John*. Chicago: Moody Press.

CORDES, Paul. 1997. *Call to Holiness: Reflections on the Catholic Charismatic Renewal*. Collegeville: Liturgical Press.

COULTER, Dale. 2001. What Meaneth This? Pentecostals and Theological Inquiry. *Journal of Pentecostal Studies*. **10**(1), pp.38-64.

COX, Raymond. 1969. *The Foursquare Gospel*. Los Angeles: Foursquare Publications.

COX, Harvey. 1995. *Fire from Heaven: The Rise of Pentecostal Spirituality and the Reshaping of Religion in the Twenty-First Century*. New York: Addison-Wesley Publishing Company.

CREEMERS, Jelle. 2011. The Intertwined Problems of Representation and Reception in Pentecostal Ecumenical Involvement: A Case Study. *One in Christ* **46**(1), pp. 1-21.

CRISP, Oliver D. 2010. Faith and Experience. *In*: Gerald R. MCDERMOTT, (ed). *The Oxford Handbook of Evangelical Theology*, Oxford: Oxford University Press, pp.68-80.

CRISWELL, W. A. 1966. *The Holy Spirit in Today's World*. Grand Rapids: Zondervan Publishing.

CRISWELL, W. A. 1973. *The Baptism, Filling & Gifts of the Holy Spirit*. Grand Rapids: Zondervan Publishing.

CULTURE, Encyclopedia of Arkansas History &. 2011. *Lawrence Brooks Hays*. [online]. [Accessed 19 December 2011]. Available from World Wide Web: <http:// encyclopediaofarkansas.net/encyclopedia/entry-detail.aspx? entryID=506>

CUTTER, George B. 1927. *Speaking with Tongues*. New Haven: Yale University Press.

DALE, James W. 1912. *Classic Baptism: An Inquiry into the Meaning of the Word BAPTIZW as Determined by the Usage of Classical Greek Writers*. Philadelphia: Presbyterian Board of Publication and Sabbath School Work.

DALMAN, Gustav. 1964. *Arbeit und Sitte in Palästina, Vol. 3*. Hilescheim: George Olma.

DANA, H. E. and Julius R. MANTEY. 1957. *A Manual Grammar of the Greek New Testament*. New York: The Macmillan Company.

DAVIDS, Peter H. 1993. A Biblical View of the Relationship of Sin and the Fruits of Sin: Sickness, Demonization, Death, Natural Calamity. *In*: Gary S. GREIG and Kevin N. SPRINGER, (eds). *The Kingdom and the Power: Are Healing and the Spiritual Gifts Used by Jesus and the Early Church Meant for the Church Today?* , Wheaton: Regal Books, pp.111-32.

DAVIES, W. D. and A. C. ALLISON. 1988. *Matthew, Vol. 1*. London: T & T Clark, Ltd.

DAWSON, John. 2001. *Taking our Cities for God: How to Break Spiritual Strongholds*. Lake Mary: Charisma House.

DAYTON, Donald W. 1991. Some Doubts about the Usefulness of the Category "Evangelical". *In*: Donald W. DAYTON and Robert K. JOHNSON, (eds). *The Variety of American Evangelicalism*, Knoxville: The University of Tennessee Press, pp.245-51.

DAYTON, Donald W. 2000. *Theological Roots of Pentecostalism*. Peabody: Hendrickson Publishers.

DEARTEAGA, William. 1992. *Quenching the Spirit: Examining Centuries of Opposition to the Moving of the Holy Spirit*. Lake Mary: Creation House.

DEERE, Jack. 1993. *Surprised by the Power of the Spirit: A Former Dallas Seminary Professor Discovers that God Speaks and Heals Today*. Grand Rapids: Zondervan Publishing.

DEERE, Jack. 1996. *Surprised by the Voice of God: How God Speaks Today through Prophecies, Dreams, and Visions*. Grand Rapids: Zondervan Publishing House.

DICKASON, C. Fred. 1987. *Demon Possession and the Christian*. Chicago: The Moody Bible Institute.

DISTINCTIVES, Baptist. 2010. *Baptist Distinctives Articles List*. [online]. [Accessed 14 December 2011]. Available from World Wide Web: <http://www. baptistdistinctives.org/articles_list.shtml>

DISTINCTIVES, Baptist. 2010. *What Makes a Baptist a Baptist?* [online]. [Accessed 14 December 2011]. Available from World Wide Web: <http://baptist distinctives.org/artpdf/article2_0105.pdf>

DOCKERY, David S. 1989. Millard J. Erickson: Baptist and Evangelical Theologian. *Journal of the Evangelical Theological Society.* **32**(4), pp.519-32.

DOCKERY, David S. 1992. Baptism. *In*: Joel B. GREEN and Scot MCKNIGHT, (eds). *Dictionary of Jesus and the Gospels*, Downers Grove: InterVarsity Press, pp.55-58.

DOCKERY, David S. 2001. Looking Back, Looking Ahead. *In*: Timothy GEORGE and David S. DOCKERY, (eds). *Theologians of the Baptist Tradition, Revised Ed.*, Nashville: B & H Publishing, pp.338-60.

DOCKERY, David S. 2001. The Broadus-Robertson Tradition. *In*: Timothy GEORGE and David S. DOCKERY, (eds). *Theologians of the Baptist Tradition, Revised Ed.*, Nashville: B & H Publishing, pp.90-114.

DOCKERY, David S. and GEORGE, Timothy (eds). 2001. *Theologians of the Baptist Tradition*. Nashville: B & H Publications.

DOCKERY, David S. 2008. *Southern Baptist Consensus and Renewal: A Biblical, Historical, and Theological Proposal*. Nashville: B & H Academic.

DOCKERY, David S. 2009. Southern Baptists in the Twenty-First Century. *In*: *Southern Baptist Identity: An Evangelical Denomination Faces the Future*, Wheaton: Crossway Books, pp.13-21.

DOCKERY, David S. 2011. So Many Denominations: The Rise, Decline, and Future of Denominationalism. *In*: Davis S. DOCKERY, Ray VAN NESTE, and Jerry TIDWELL, (eds). *Southern Baptists, Evangelicals, and the Future of Denominationalism*, Nashville: B & H Academic, pp.3-34.

DOCKERY, David S. (ed). 2011. *Southern Baptist Identity: An Evangelical Denomination Faces the Future*. Wheaton: Crossway Books.

DODS, Marcus. 1912. *The Bible: Its Origin and Nature*. New York: Charles Scribner's Sons.

DONAHUE, John R. and Daniel J. HARRINGTON. 2002. The Gospel According to Mark. *In*: Daniel J. HARRINGTON, (ed). *Sacra Pagina*, Collegeville: The Liturgical Press, p.62.

DROOGERS, André. 2010. Essentialist and Normative Approaches. *In*: Alan ANDERSON, Michael BERGUNDER, André DROOGERS, and Cornelius VAN DER LAAN, (eds). *Global Pentecostalism: Theories and Methods*, Berkley: University of California Press, pp.30-50.

DU PLESSIS, David. 2004 Reprint. *The Spirit Bade Me Go: The Astounding Move of God in the Denominational Churches*. Gainesville: Bridge-Logos Publishers.

DUNN, James D. G. 1972. Spirit and Fire Baptism. *Novum Testamentum*. **14**(2), pp.81-92.

DUNN, James D. G. 1993. Baptism in the Spirit: A Response to Pentecostal Scholarship on Luke-Acts. *Journal of Pentecostal Theology*. **3**(1), pp.3-27.

DUNN, James D. G. 1997. *Jesus and the Spirit: A Study of the Religious and Charismatic Experience of Jesus and the First Christians as reflected in the New Testament*. Grand Rapids: William B. Eerdmans Publishing.

DUNN, James D. G. 1998. Baptism in the Holy Spirit...Yet Once More. *Journal of the European Theological Association*. **18**(1), pp.3-25.

DUNN, James D. G. 1998. *The Christ and the Spirit: Christology, Vol. 1*. Grand Rapids: William B. Eerdmans Publishing.

DUNN, James D. G. 1998. *The Christ & The Spirit: Pneumatology, Vol. 2*. Grand Rapids: William B. Eerdmans Publishing.

DUNN, James D. G. 2003. *Christianity in the Making: Jesus Remembered, Vol. 1*. Grand Rapids: William B. Eerdmans Publishing.

DUNN, James D. G. 2010. Baptism in the Holy Spirit, Yet Once More...Again. *Journal of Pentecostal Theology*. **19**(1), pp.23-43.

DUNN, James D. G. 2010. *Baptism in the Holy Spirit: A Re-examination of the New Testament Teaching on the Gift of the Spirit in relation to Pentecostalism Today, 2nd ed.* Philadelphia: The Westminster Press.

DUNNING, H. Ray. 1988. *Grace, Faith and Holiness: A Wesleyan Systematic Theology*. Kansas City: Beacon Hill.

DUPREE, Sherry S. 2002. Church of God in Christ. *In*: Stanley M. BURGESS and Eduard M. VAN DER MAAS, (eds). *New International Dictionary of Pentecostal and Charismatic Movements*, Grand Rapids: Zondervan, pp.535-36.

DURNBAUGH, Donald. 1968. *The Believers' Church: The History and Character of Radical Protestantism*. New York: Macmillan.

EDGAR, Thomas R. 1996. *Satisfied by the Promise of the Spirit: Affirming the Fullness of God's Provision for Spiritual Living*. Grand Rapids: Kregel Resources.

EDWARDS, Jonathan. 1984. A Narrative of Surprising Conversions. *In*: *Jonathan Edwards on Revival*, Carlisle: Banner of Truth, p.14.

EDWARDS, James R. 2002. The Gospel According to Mark. *In*: D. A. CARSON, (ed). *The Pillar New Testament Commentary*, Grand Rapids: William B. Eerdmans Publishing, p.29.

EERDMAN, Charles R. 1956. *The Gospel of Mark*. Philadelphia: The Westminster Press.

ELBERT, Paul. 2004. Pentecostal/Charismatic Themes in Luke-Acts at the Evangelical Society: The Battle of Interpretive Method. *Journal of Pentecostal Theology*. **12**(2), pp.181-215.

ELLINGSEN, Mark. 1988. *The Evangelical Movement: Growth, Impact, Controversy, Dialogue*. Minneapolis: Augsburg Press.

ELLIOTT, Hannah. 2007. *Study: Half of SBC Pastors Believe in Prayer Languages*. [online]. [Accessed 23 June 2011]. Available from World Wide Web: <http://www. abpnews.com/content/view/2556/120/>

ELLIS, E. Earl (ed). 1977. *New Century Bible: The Gospel of Luke*. London: Thomas Nelson & Sons Ltd.

ERICKSON, Millard J. 1986. *Christian Theology*. Grand Rapids: Baker Book House.

ERVIN, Howard M. 1969. *These are not Drunken as Ye Suppose*. Plainfield: Logos International.

ERVIN, Howard M. 1981. Hermeneutics: A Pentecostal Option. *Pneuma*. **3**(1), pp.16-23.

ERVIN, Howard M. 1984. *Conversion-Initiation and the Baptism in the Holy Spirit: An Engaging Critique of James D. G. Dunn's Baptism in the Holy Spirit.* Peabody: Hendrickson Publishers.

ERVIN, Howard M. 1987. *Spirit Baptism: A Biblical Investigation.* Peabody: Hendrickson Publishers.

ESTEP, Jr. William R. 1958. A Baptist Reappraisal of Sixteenth Century Anabaptists. *Review and Expositor.* **55**(1), pp.55-58.

ESTEP. JR., William R. 1963. *The Anabaptist Story.* Nashville: Broadman Press.

ESTEP, Jr. William R. 1996. *The Anabaptist Story: An Introduction to Sixteenth-Century Anabaptism, Third Edition.* Grand Rapids: William B. Eerdmans Publishing.

EVANGELICALS, Institute for the Sudy of American. 2008. *Lewis Sperry Chafer.* [online]. [Accessed 19 March 2012]. Available from World Wide Web: <http://isae. wheaton.edu/hall-of-biography/lewisschafer/>

FAITH, Yale Center for Christian. 2009. *Loving God and Loving Neighbor: A Christian Response to A Common Word Between Us and You.* [online]. [Accessed 26 September 2011]. Available from World Wide Web: <http:// www.yale.edu/ faith/acw/acw.htm>

FARNELL, F. David. 2003. The Montanist Crisis: A Key to Refuting Third-Wave Concepts of New Testament Prophecy. *The Master's Seminary Journal.* **14**(2), pp.235-62.

FAUPEL, D. William. 1989. *The Everlasting Gospel: The Significance of Eschatology in the Development of Pentecostal Thought.* PhD Dissertation: University of Birmingham.

FAUPEL, D. William. 1993. Whither Pentecostalism? *Pneuma.* **15**(1), pp.9-27.

FEE, Gordon D. 1976. Hermeneutics and Historical Precedent: A Major Problem in Pentecostal Hermeneutics. *In*: Russell P. SPITTLER, (ed). *Perspectives in the New Pentecostalism,* Grand Rapids: Baker Book House, pp.118-32.

FEE, Gordon D. 1985. Baptism in the Holy Spirit: The Issue of Separability and Subsequence. *Pneuma.* **7**(2), pp.87-99.

FEE, Gordon D. 1987. *The First Epistle to the Corinthians*. Grand Rapids: William B. Eerdmans Publishing.

FEE, Gordon D. 1991. *Gospel and Spirit: Issues in New Testament Hermeneutics*. Peabody: Hendrickson Publishers.

FEE, Gordon D. 1995. *God's Empowering Presence: The Holy Spirit in the Letters of Paul*. Peabody: Hendrickson Publishers.

FEE, Gordon D. 2002. *New Testament Exegesis: A Handbook for Students and Pastors, 3rd Ed.*. Westminster: John Knox Press.

FINN, Nathan A. 2009. Priorities for a Post-Resurgence Convention. *In*: David. S. DOCKERY, (ed). *Southern Baptist Identity: An Evangelical Denomination Faces the Future*, Wheaton: Crossway Books, pp.257-80.

FINN, Nathan A. 2011. Southern Baptists and Evangelicals: Passing on the Faith to the Next Generation. *In*: David S. DOCKERY and with Ray VanNeste and Jerry TIDWELL, (eds). *Southern Baptists, Evangelicals, and the Future of Denominationalism*, Nashville: B & H Academic, pp.231-59.

FINNEY, Charles G. 1908 reprint. *An Autobiography*. Westwood: Fleming H. Revell Co.

FITZMYER, Joseph A. 1989. *Luke the Theologian: Aspects of His Teaching*. New York: Paulist Press.

FLOKSTRA, III Gerald J. 1999. Sources for the Initial Evidence Discussion: A Bibliographic Essay. *Asian Journal of Pentecostal Studies*. **2**(2), pp.243-59.

FORD, Josephine. 1972. Pentecostal Catholicism. *In*: Christian DUQUOC and Claude GEFFRÉ, (eds). *The Prayer Life*, London: Burns and Oates, pp.85-90.

FOSTER, Richard. 1978. *Celebration of Disciplines: The Path to Spiritual Growth*. San Francisco: Harper & Row.

FOX, George. 1975. George Fox, The Great Mystery of the Great Whore unfolded; And Antichrist's Kingdom, Vol. 3. *In*: *The Works of George Fox*, New York: AMS Press, p.13.

FRANCE, R. T. 2002. *The New International Greek Testament Commentary: The Gospel of Mark*. Grand Rapids: William B. Eerdmans Publishing.

Bibliography

FREEMAN, Curtis W. 1997. Can Baptist Theology Be Revisioned? *In: Perspectives in Religious Studies 24*, pp. 288-92.

GAFFIN, Jr. Richard B. 1979. *Perspectives on Pentecost: New Testament Teaching on the Gifts of the Holy Spirit.* Phillipsburg: Presbyterian and Reformed Publishing.

GARLAND, David E. 1996. Mark. *In*: Terry MUCK, (ed). *The NIV Application Commentary*, Grand Rapids: Zondervan Publishing House, pp.41-47.

GARLAND, David E. 2007. 1 Corinthians. *In*: Robert W. YARBROUGH and Robert H. STEIN, (eds). *Baker Exegetical Commentary on the New Testament*, Grand Rapids: Baker Academic, p.591.

GARRETT, Jr. James Leo (ed). 1969. *The Concept of the Believers' Church: Addresses from the 1967 Louisville Conference.* Scottdale: Herald Press.

GARRETT, Jr., James Leo, HINSON, E. Glenn, and TULL, James E. (eds). 1983. *Are Southern Baptists Evangelicals?* Macon: Mercer University Press.

GARRETT, Jr. James Leo. 1983. Who are the Evangelicals? *In*: Jr. James Leo GARRETT, Glenn E. HINSON, and James E. TULL, (eds). *Are Southern Baptists Evangelicals?*, Macon: Mercer University Press, pp.31-63.

GARRETT, Jr. James Leo. 1990. *Systematic Theology: Biblical, Historical, and Evangelical, Vol. 2.* Grand Rapids: William B. Eerdmans Publishing.

GARRETT, Jr. James Leo. 2008. The Roots of Baptist Beliefs. *In*: Davis S. DOCKERY, (ed). *Southern Baptist Identity: An Evangelical Denomination Faces the Future*, Wheaton: Crossway Books, pp.139-53.

GARRETT, Jr. James Leo. 2009. *Baptist Theology: A Four-Century Study.* Macon: Mercer University Press.

GAUSE, R. Hollis. 1976. Issues in Pentecostalism. *In*: Russell P. SPITTLER, (ed). *Perspectives on the New Pentecostalism*, Grand Rapids: Baker Book House, pp.108-109.

GAUSTAD, Edwin S. 1952. Baptists and Experimental Religion. *Chronicle: The Journal of the American Baptist Historical Society*, July, pp.110-11, 115-16.

GAUSTAD, Edwin S. 1978. *Baptist Piety: The Last Will and Testimony of Obadiah Holmes.* Washington: Christian College Consortium.

GEE, Donald. 1967. *Wind and Flame*. Croydon: Heath Press Ltd.

GEE, Donald. 1972. *Now that You've Been Baptized in the Spirit*. Springfield: Gospel Publishing House.

GELPI, Donald. 1971. *Pentecostalism: A Theological Viewpoint*. New York: Paulist Press.

GELPI, Donald. 1976. *Charism and Sacrament: A Theology of Christian Conversion*. New York: Paulist Press.

GELPI, Donald L. 1992. The Theological Challenge of Charismatic Spirituality. *Pneuma*. **14**(2), pp.185-97.

GELPI, Donald L. 2001. *The Gracing of Human Experience: Rethinking the Relationship between Nature and Grace*. Collegeville: The Liturgical Press.

GOATLEY, David. 1997. The Charismatic Movement Among Baptists Today. *Review and Expositor*. **94**(1), p.36.

GOFF, Jr. J. R. 1988. *Fields White Unto Harvest: Charles F. Parham and the Missionary Origins of Pentecostalism*. Fayetteville: University of Arkansas Press.

GOFF, James R. 1991. Initial Tongues in the Theology of Charles Fox Parham. *In*: Gary B. MCGEE, (ed). *Initial Evidence: Historical and Biblical Perspectives on the Pentecostal Doctrine of Spirit Baptism* , Peabody: Hendrickson Publishers, pp.57-74.

GOHR, Glenn W. 2002. Kansas City Prophets. *In*: Stanley M. BURGESS and Eduard M. VAN DER MAAS, (eds). *New International Dictionary of Pentecostal and Charismatic Movements*, Grand Rapids: Zondervan, pp.816-17.

GORDON, A. J. 1882. *The Ministry of Healing: Miracles of Cure in All Ages*. Chicago: Flemming H. Revell Co.

GORDON, A. J. 1884. *The Two-Fold Life*. Boston: Howard Gamett.

GORDON, A. J. 1895. Ministry of Women. *Truth; or Testimony for Christ*, February, pp.87-92.

GORDON, A. J. 1950. *The Ministry of the Spirit*. Philadelphia: The Judson Press.

GRADY, J. Lee, 2010. *The Holy Spirit is Not for Sale.* Grand Rapids: Chosen Books.

GREEN, Michael. 1977. *I Believe in the Holy Spirit.* Grand Rapids: William B. Eerdmans Publishing Company.

GREEN, Joel B. 1995. *The Theology of the Gospel of Luke.* Cambridge: Cambridge University Press.

GREEN, Bradley G. 2001. Millard J. Erickson. *In*: Timothy GEORGY and David S. DOCKERY, (eds). *Theologians of the Baptist Tradition, Revised Edition*, Nashville: Broadman & Holman Publishers, pp.317-37.

GREIG, Gary S. and SPRINGER, Kevin N. (eds). 1993. *The Kingdom and the Power: Are Healing and the Spiritual Gifts Used by Jesus and the Early Church Meant for the Church Today?* Ventura: Regal Books.

GREIG, Gary S. and Kevin N. SPRINGER. 1993. Introduction. *In*: Gary S. GREIG and Kevin N. SPRINGER, (eds). *The Kingdom and the Power: Are Healing and the Spiritual Gifts Used by Jesus and the Early Church Meant for the Church Today?* , Wheaton: Regal Books, p.20.

GREIG, Gary S. 1993. The Purpose of Signs and Wonders in the New Testament. *In*: Gary S. GREIG and Kevin N. SPRINGER, (eds). *The Kingdom and the Power: Are Healing and the Spiritual Gifts Used by Jesus and the Early Church Meant for the Church Today?*, Ventura: Regal Books, pp.133-74.

GRENZ, Stanley J. 1993. *Revisioning Evangelical Theology: A Fresh Agenda for the 21st Century.* Downers Grove: InterVarisity Press.

GRENZ, Stanley J. 1994. *Theology for the Community of God.* Nashville: Broadman & Holman Publishers.

GRENZ, Stanley J. and John R. FRANKE. 2001. *Beyond Foundationalism: Shaping Theology in a Postmodern Context.* Louisville: Westminster John Knox Press.

GRENZ, Stanley J. 2006. *Renewing the Center: Evangelical Theology in a Post-Theological Era, 2nd Edition.* Grand Rapids: Baker Academic.

GRIEND, Alvin J. Vander. 1996. *Discover Your Gifts and Learn How to Use Them.* Grand Rapids: CRC Publications.

268

Bibliography

GROMACKI, Robert. 1999. *The Holy Spirit.* Nashville: Word Publishing.

GROSSMANN, Siegfried. 1981. *Stewards of God's Grace.* Exeter: Paternoster Press.

GRUDEM, Wayne A. 1994. *Systematic Theology: An Introduction to Biblical Doctrine.* Grand Rapids: Zondervan Publishing.

GRUDEM, ed. Wayne A. 1996. *Are Miraculous Gifts for Today?: Four Views.* Grand Rapids: Zondervan Publishing House.

GRUDEM, Wayne A. 1996. Preface. *In*: Wayne A. GRUDEM, (ed). *Are Miraculous Gifts for Today? Four Views*, Grand Rapids: Zondervan Publishing, pp.9-20.

GRUDEM, Wayne. 2005. Forward. *In*: M. James SAWYER and Daniel B. WALLACE, (eds). *Who's Afraid of the Holy Spirit: An Investigation into the Ministry of the Spirit of God Today*, Dallas: Biblical Studies Press, pp.iv-v.

GUELICH, Robert A. 1982. The Beginning of the Gospel. *Biblical Research.* **27**(1), pp.5-15.

GUELICH, Robert A. 1989. Mark 1-8:26. *In*: Bruce M. METZGER, (ed). *Word Biblical Commentary*, Dallas: Word, p.18.

GUNDRY, Robert H. 1967. *The Use of the Old Testament in St. Matthew's Gospel with Special Reference to the Messianic Hope.* Boston: E. J. Brill.

GUNDRY, Robert H. 1993. *Mark: A Commentary on His Apology of the Cross.* Grand Rapids: William B. Eerdmans Publishing.

GUNKEL, Hermann, Trans. Roy A. Harrisville and Philip A. Quanbeck II. ET 1979. *The Influence of the Spirit: The Popular View of the Apostolic Age and the Teaching of the Apostle Paul.* Philadelphia: Fortress Press.

HABETS, Myk. 2010. *The Anointed Son: A Trinitarian Spirit Christology.* Eugene: Pickwick Publications.

HAENCHEN, Ernst. 1966. The Book of Acts as Source Material for the History of Early Christianity. *In*: L. E. KECK and J. L. MARTYN, (eds). *Studies in Luke-Acts*, Nashville: Abingdon Press, pp.258-78.

Bibliography

HAENCHEN, Ernst. 1971. *The Acts of the Apostles: A Commentary*. Philadelphia: The Westminster Press.

HALLFORD, R. F. 1960. Distinctive Doctrines of Baptists. *Central Bible Quarterly*. 3(4), pp.39-42.

HAMILTON, Jr. James M. 2006. God's Indwelling Presence: The Holy Spirit in the Old & New Testaments. *In*: E. Ray CLENDENEN, (ed). *NAC Studies in Bible & Theology*, Nashville: B&H Academic, pp.183-203.

HAMMETT, John S. 2005. *Biblical Foundations for Baptist Churches: A Contemporary Ecclesiology*. Grand Rapids: Kregel Publications.

HAMON, William S. 1997. *Apostles, Prophets and the Coming Moves of God: God's End-Time Plans for His Church and Planet Earth*. Shippensburg: Destiny Image Publishers.

HANSEN, Collin. 2011. Introduction. *In*: David NASELLI and Collin HANSEN, (eds). *Four Views on the Spectrum of Evangelicalism*, Grand Rapids: Zondervan, pp.9-18.

HARRIS, Brian. 2008. Beyond Bebbington: The Quest for Evangelical Identity. *Churchman*. **122**(3), pp.201-19.

HARRIS, Murray J. ET 1978. Appendix. *In*: Colin BROWN, (ed). *The New International Dictionary of New Testament Theology, Vol. 3*, Grand Rapids: Zondervan Publishing House, pp.1171-1214.

HARRISON, Paul M. 1959. *Authority and Power in the Free Church Tradition*. Carbondale: Southern Illinois University Press.

HART, Larry. 1978. Problems of Authority in Pentecostalism. *Review and Expositor*. **75**(1), p.261.

HART, Larry. 2004. Spirit Baptism: A Dimensional Charismatic Perspective. *In*: Chad Owen BRAND, (ed). *Perspectives on Spirit Baptism: Five Views*, Nashville: Broadman & Holman Publishers, pp.105-69.

HARTWICK, A. Reuben. 1995. Speaking in Tongues: The Initial Physical Evidence of the Baptism in the Holy Spirit. *Paraclete*. **29**(3), pp.9-15.

HATHAWAY, Malcolm R. 1998. The Elim Pentecostal Church: Origins, Development and Distinctives'. *In*: Keith WARRINGTON, (ed). *Pentecostal Perspectives*, Carlisle: Paternoster Press, pp.6-8.

HAUGHEY, John C. (ed). 1979. *Theological Reflections on the Charismatic Renewal*. Ann Arbor: Servant Books.

HAWTHORNE, Gerald F. 1991. *The Presence and the Power: The Significance of the Spirit in the Life and Ministry of Jesus*. Dallas: Word Publications.

HAYA-PRATS, Gonzalo, Elbert, Paul, ed., Trans. Ellington, Scott A. ET 2011. *Empowered Believers: The Holy Spirit in the Book of Acts*. Eugene: Cascade Books.

HAYFORD, Jack W. 1996. *The Beauty of Spiritual Language: Unveiling the Mystery of Speaking in Tongues*. Nashville: Thomas Nelson Publishers.

HAYKIN, A. G. and Kenneth J. STEWART. 2008. Preface. *In*: A. G. HAYKIN and Kenneth J. STEWART, (eds). *The Advent of Evangelicalism: Exploring Historical Continuities*, Nashville: B&H Academic, pp.17-20.

HAYS, Lawrence Brooks. 1963. *The Baptist Way of Life*. Englewood Cliffs: Prentice Hall.

HEADQUARTERS, Apostolic Faith Mission. 1965. *A Historical Account of the Apostolic Faith: Trinitarian-Fundamental Evangelistic Organization*. Portland: Apostolic Faith Mission Headquarters.

HENDERSON, Trennis. 2006. *Rankin Talks Candidly About Private Prayer Language, Recent IMB Action*. [online]. [Accessed 28 June 2011]. Available from World Wide Web: <http://www.abpnews.com/content/view/951/119/>

HENRY, Carl. F. H. 1947. *The Uneasy Conscience of Modern Fundamentalism*. Grand Rapids: William B. Eerdmans Publishing.

HENRY, Carl F. H. 1976. *God, Revelation, and Authority, Vol. 1*. Waco: Word Books.

HENRY, Carl F. H. 1983. *God, Revelation and Authority, Vol. 6*. Waco: Word Books.

HENRY, Carl F. H. 1986. *Confessions of a Theologian: An Autobiography*. Waco: Word Publications.

HEWETT, James A. 2002. Baptist Pentecostals and Charismatics. *In*: Stanley M. BURGESS and Eduard M. VAN DER MAAS, (eds). *The New International Dictionary of Pentecostal and Charismatic Movements*, Grand Rapids: Zondervan Publishing House, pp.363-64.

HIEBERT, Paul G. 1978. Conversion, Culture and Cognitive Categories. *Gospel in Context*. 1(4), pp.24-28.

HILL, David. 1979. *New Testament Prophecy*. London: Marshall, Morgan, and Scott.

HINSON, E. Glenn. 1983. A Response to Professor Garrett. *In*: Jr. James Leo GARRETT, Glenn E. HINSON, and James E. TULL, (eds). *Are Southern Baptists Evangelicals?*, Macon: Mercer University Press, pp.209-14.

HINSON, E. Glenn. 1983. Baptists and Evangelicals: What is the Difference? *In*: Jr. James Leo GARRETT, E. Gless HINSON, and James E. TULL, (eds). *Are Southern Baptists Evangelicals?*, Macon: Mercer University Press, pp.165-83.

HINSON, E. Glenn. 1983. In Search of Our Baptist Identity. *In*: Jr. James Leo GARRETT, E. Gless HINSON, and James E. TULL, (eds). *Are Southern Baptists Evangelicals?*, Macon: Mercer University Press, pp.131-45.

HINSON, E. Glenn. 1983. The Future of the Baptist Tradition. *In*: Jr. James Leo GARRETT, E. Gless HINSON, and James E. TULL, (eds). *Are Southern Baptists Evangelicals?*, Macon: Mercer University Press, pp.185-94.

HOBBS, Herschel H. 1996. *An Exposition of the Four Gospels: The Gospel of Matthew and the Gospel of Mark, Vol. 1*. Grand Rapids: Baker Books.

HOCKEN, Peter D. 1981. The Pentecostal-Charismatic Movement as Revival and Renewal. *Pneuma*. 3(1), pp.33-47.

HOCKEN, Peter D. 1994. *The Glory and the Shame: Reflections on the 20th Century Outpouring of the Holy Spirit*. Wheaton: Harold Shaw Publishers.

HOCKEN, Peter D. 2002. Charismatic Movement. *In*: Stanley M. BURGESS and Edward M. VAN DER MASS, (eds). *The New International Dictionary of Pentecostal and Charismatic Movements*, Grand Rapids: Zondervan, pp.478-519.

HOCKEN, Peter D. 2009. *The Challenges of the Pentecostal, Charismatic and Messianic Jewish Movements: The Tensions of the Spirit.* Farnham: Ashgate Publishing, Ltd.

HOLDER, Frank. 1966. *The Holy Spirit.* Kisummu: Evangel Publishing House.

HOLLENWEGER, Walter J. 1972. *The Pentecostals: The Charismatic Movement in the Churches.* Minneapolis: Augsburg Publishing House.

HOLLENWEGER, Walter J. 1986. After Twenty Years' Research on Pentecostalism. *International Review of Mission.* **75**(297), pp.3-12.

HOLLENWEGER, Walter J. 1992. The Critical Tradition of Pentecostalism. *Journal of Pentecostal Theology.* **1**(1), pp.14-38.

HOLLENWEGER, Walter J. 1997. *Pentecostalism: Origins and Developments Worldwide.* Peabody: Hendrickson Publishers.

HOLMAN, Charles L. 1998. *Luke Vis A Vis Paul.* Orlando, FL.

HORTON, Stanley. 1955. *Into all Truth: A Survey of the Course and Content of Divine Revelation.* Springfield: Gospel Publishing House.

HORTON, Stanley M. 1981. *The Book of Acts.* Springfield: Gospel Publishing House.

HORTON, Stanley M. 1982. The Pentecostal Explosion: How the Fire Fell in 1906 and Spread. *Assemblies of God Heritage.* **2**(3), pp.2-8.

HORTON, Stanley M. 1999. *I and II Corinthians.* Springfield: Gospel Publishing House.

HORTON, Stanley M. 2004. Spirit Baptism: A Pentecostal Perspective. *In*: Chad Owen BRAND, (ed). *Perspectives on Spirit Baptism: Five Views*, Nashville: Broadman & Holman, pp.47-94.

HOSKYNS, Edwyn Clement and Francis Noel DAVEY. 1956. *The Fourth Gospel, 2nd Ed.* London: Faber & Faber.

HOVEY, Alvah. 1885. *Commentary on the Gospel of John.* Philadelphia: American Baptist Publication Society.

HOVEY, Alvah. 1982. *Restatement of Denominational Principles*. Philadelphia: American Baptist Publication Society.

HOWARD-BROWNE, Rodney M. 1991. *Flowing in the Holy Ghost: A Practical Handbook on the Gifts of the Spirit*. Louisville: RHBEA Publications.

HOWE, Jr. Claude L. 1978. The Charismatic Movement in Southern Baptist Life. *Baptist History & Heritage*. **21**(1), pp.121-22.

HOYLE, Lydia Huffman. 2006. Baptist Americanus. *In*: W. Glenn, Jr. JONAS, (ed). *The Baptist River: Essays on Many Tributaries of a Diverse Tradition*, Macon: Mercer University Press, pp.269-84.

HUDSON, Winthrop Still. 1953. Baptists Were Not Anabaptists. *The Chronicle*. **16**(1), pp.171-79.

HUDSON, Winthrop Still. 1956. Who Were the Baptists? *Baptist Quarterly*. **16**(1), pp.303-12.

HUDSON, Winthrop Still. 1957. Who Were the Baptists? *Baptist Quarterly*. **17**(1), pp.53-55.

HUGHES, Ray H. 1963. *What is Pentecost?* Cleveland: Pathway Press.

HUGHES, Ray H. 1976. The New Pentecostalism: Perspective of a Pentecostal Administrator. *In*: Russell P. SPITTLER, (ed). *Perspectives on the New Pentecostalism*, Grand Rapids: Baker Book House, pp.166-80.

HUGHES, Richard T. 1991. Are Restorationists Evangelicals? *In*: Donald W. DAYTON and Robert K. JOHNSTON, (eds). *The Variety of American Evangelicalism*, Knoxville: The University of Tennessee Press, pp.109-34.

HULL, William E. 1970. John. *In*: Clifton J. ALLEN, (ed). *The Broadman Bible Commentary: Luke-John*, Nashville: Broadman Press, pp.221-24.

HUMPHRIES, Fisher. 2001. Edgar Young Mullins. *In*: Timothy GEORGE and David S. DOCKERY, (eds). *Theologians of the Baptist Tradition, Revised Ed.* , Nashville: B & H Publications, pp.181-201.

HUNTER, Harold D. 1983. *Spirit-Baptism: A Pentecostal Alternative*. Lanham: University Press of America.

HUNTER, Harold D. and HOCKEN, Peter D. (eds). 1993. *All Together in One Place: Theological Papers from the Brighton Conference on World Evangelization*. Sheffield: Sheffield Academic Press.

HUNTER, Harold D. 2008. *Cyberjournal for Pentecostal-Charismatic Research #17*. [online]. [Accessed 10 November 2011]. Available from World Wide Web: <http://www.pctii.org/cyberj/cyberj17/Irenaeus.html>

HUR, Ju. 2001. *A Dynamic Reading of the Holy Spirit in Luke-Acts*. London: T & T Clark International.

HURST, Randy. 2003. Power for Purpose. *Today's Pentecostal Evangel*, 8 June, p.13.

HURTADO, Larry W. 1991. Normal, but not the Norm: "Initial Evidence" in the New Testament. *In*: Gary B. MCGEE, (ed). *Initial Evidence: Historical and Biblical Perspectives on the Pentecostal Doctrine of Spirit Baptism*, Peabody: Hendrickson Publishers, pp.189-200.

HURTADO, Larry W. 2000. Religious Experience and Religious Innovation in the New Testament. *The Journal of Religion*. **80**(2), pp.183-205.

HYATT, Eddie L. 2002. *2000 Years of Charismatic Christianity: A 21st Century Look at Church History from a Pentecostal/Charismatic Perspective*. Lake Mary: Charisma House.

ISRAEL, Richard D., Daniel E. ALBRECHT, and Randal G. MCNALLY. 1993. Pentecostals and Hermeneutics: Texts, Rituals and Community. *Pneuma*. **15**(2), pp.137-61.

JAICHANDRAN, Rebecca and B. D. MADHAV. 2003. Pentecostal Spirituality in a Postmodern World. *Asian Journal of Pentecostal Studies*. **6**(1), pp.39-61.

JEFFREYS, George. 1929. *The Miraculous Foursquare Gospel, Vol. 1*. London: Elim Publishing.

JENSEN, Richard A. 1975. *Touched by the Spirit: One Man's Struggle to Understand His Experience of the Holy Spirit*. Minneapolis: Augsburg Press.

JEREMIAS, Joachim. 1971. *New Testament Theology: The Proclamation of Jesus*. New York: Charles Scribner's Sons.

JERVELL, Jacob. 1996. *The Theology of the Acts of the Apostles*. Cambridge: Cambridge University Press.

JOHNSON, James E. 1985 reprint. Spurgeon, Charles Haddon. *In*: Walter A. ELWELL, (ed). *Evangelical Dictionary of Theology*, Grand Rapids: Baker Book House, p.1051.

JOHNSON, Robert K. 2000. Evangelicalism. *In*: Adrian HASTINGS, Alistair MASON, and Hugh S. PYPER, (eds). *Oxford Dictionary of Christian Thought*, Oxford: Oxford University Press, pp.217-20.

JOHNSON, Todd M., David B. BARRETT, and Peter CROSSING. 2011. Status of Global Mission, 2011, in Context of 20th and 21st Centuries. *International Bulletin for Missionary Research*. **35**(1), pp.36-37.

JOHNSTON, Robert K. 1984. Pentecostalism and Theological Hermeneutics: Evangelical Options. *Pneuma*. **6**(1), pp.51-67.

JONES, Philip L. 1909. *A Restatement of Baptist Principles*. Philadelphia: Griffith and Rowland.

JONES, C. E. 1983. *A Guide to Pentecostalism, 2 Vols*. Metuchen: Scarecrow Press.

JOSEPHUS and Trans. WILLIAM WHISTON. 1987. The Antiquities of the Jews. *In*: *The Works of Josephus*, Peabody: Hendrickson Publishers, p.484.

JOY, John. 2005. The Outpouring of the Holy Spirit in the Catholic Charismatic Renewal: Theological Interpretation of Experience. *Antiphon*. **9**(2), pp.141-65.

KANTZER, Kenneth. 1980. The Charismatics Among Us. *Christianity Today*, 22 February, pp.25-29.

KÄRKKÄINEN, Veli-Matti. 1998. *Spiritus ubi vult spirat: Pneumatology in Catholic-Pentecostal Dialogue (1972-1989)*. Helsinki: Luther Agricola Society.

KÄRKKÄINEN, Veli-Matti. 2002. *Pneumatology: The Holy Spirit in Ecumenical, International, and Contextual Perspective*. Grand Rapids: Baker Academic.

KÄRKKÄINEN, Veli-Matti. 2010. Pneumatologies in Systematic Theology. *In*: Alan ANDERSON, Michael BERGUNDER, André DROOGERS, and Cornelius VAN DER LAAN, (eds). *Studying Global Pentecostalism: Theories and Methods*, Berkley: University of California Press, p.224.

KEATHLEY, Hampton IV. 1999. *Are Miraculous Gifts for Today?* [online]. [Accessed 20 June 2011]. Available from World Wide Web: <http://bible.org/ seriespage/are-miraculous-gifts-today>

KECK, Leander E. 1970. The Spirit and the Dove. *New Testament Studies*. **17**(1), pp.41-67.

KEENER, Craig S. 1999. *A Commentary on the Gospel of Matthew*. Grand Rapids: William B. Eerdmans Publishing.

KELLSTEDT, Lyman A. and Corwin L. SMIDT. 1991. Measuring Fundamentalism: An Analysis of Different Operational Strategies. *The Journal of the Scientific Study of Religion*. **30**(1), pp.259-78.

KERR, D. W. 1921. Not Ashamed. *Pentecostal Evangel*, April, p.5.

KIRTLEY, James S. 1926. *The Baptist Distinctives and Objective*. Valley Forge: Jusdon Press.

KLEIN, William W., Craig L. BLOMBERG, and Robert L. Jr. HUBBARD. 2004. *Introduction to Biblical Interpretation*. Nashville: Thomas Nelson Publishers.

KLIEVER, Lonnie D. 1962. General Baptist Origins: The Question of Anabaptist Influence. *Mennonite Quarterly Review*. **36**(1), pp.291-321.

KOENIG, John. 1981. Documenting the Charismatics. *Word & World* **1**(3), pp. 287-90.

KOMONCHAK, Joseph A., COLLINS, Mary, and LANE, Dermot A. (eds). 1990. *The New Dictionary of Theology*. Collegeville: The Liturgical Press.

KÖSTENBERGER, Andreas J. 2006. Baptism in the Gospels. *In*: Thomas R. SCHREINER and Shawn D. WRIGHT, (eds). *Believer's Baptism: Sign of the New Covenant*, Nashville: B & H Academic, pp.11-34.

KRAFT, Charles H. 1979. *Christianity and Culture*. Maryknoll: Orbis Books.

KRAFT, Charles H. 2005. *Appropriate Christianity*. Pasadena: William Carey Library.

KRAFT, Charles H. and KRAFT, Marguerite G. 1993. Communicating and Ministering the Power of the Gospel Cross-Culturally. *In*: Gary S. GREIG and Kevin N. SPRINGER, (eds). *The Kingdom and the Power: Are Healing and the Spiritual Gifts Used by Jesus and the Early Church Meant for the Church Today?*, Ventura: Regal Books, pp. 345-56.

KYDD, Ronald A. N. 1984. *Charismatic Gifts in the Early Church: An Exploration into the Gifts of the Spirit During the First Three Centuries of the Christian Church*. Peabody: Hendrickson Publishers.

LADD, George Eldon. 1952. *Crucial Questions about the Kingdom of God*. Grand Rapids: William B. Eerdmans Publishing.

LADD, George Eldon. 1971. *The Gospel of the Kingdom: Scriptural Studies in the Kingdom of God*. Grand Rapids: William B. Eerdmans Publishing.

LADD, George Eldon. 1974. *A Theology of the New Testament*. Grand Rapids: William B. Eerdmans Publishing.

LAMPE, G. W. H. 1951. *The Seal of the Spirit: A Study in the Doctrine of Baptism and Confession in the New Testament and the Fathers*. London: Longmans, Green and Co.

LAND, Steven J. 2001. *Pentecostal Spirituality: A Passion for the Kingdom*. Sheffield: Sheffield Academic Press.

LAURENTIN, René. 1977. *Catholic Pentecostalism*. Garden City: Doubleday.

LEDERLE, Henry I. 1988. *Treasures Old and New: Interpretations of Spirit-Baptism in the Charismatic Renewal Movement*. Peabody: Hendrickson Publishers.

LEDERLE, Henry I. 1991. Initial Evidence and the Charismatic Movement: An Ecumenical Appraisal. *In*: Gary B. MCGEE, (ed). *Initial Evidence: Historical and Biblical Perspectives on the Pentecostal Doctrine of Spirit Baptism*, Peabody: Hendrickson Publishers, pp.131-41.

LEDERLE, Henry I. 1994. Life in the Spirit and Worldview: Some Preliminary Thoughts on Understanding Reality, Faith and Providence from a Charismatic Perspective. *In*: Mark W. WILSON, (ed). *Spirit and Renewal: Essays in Honor of J. Rodman Williams* , Sheffield: Sheffield Academic Press, pp.22-33.

LEONARD, Bill J. 2003. *Baptist Ways: A History*. Valley Forge: Judson Press.

LEONARD, Bill J. 2010. *The Challenge of Being Baptist: Owning a Scandalous Past and an Uncertain Future*. Waco: Baylor University Press.

LEVADA, Cardinal William J. 1996. *Pentecostal Catholics: A History of the Catholic Charismatic Renewal*. [online]. [Accessed 10 November 2011]. Available from World Wide Web: <http://www.sfspirit.com/renewal-history.html>

LEVISON, John R. 2000. Holy Spirit. *In*: Craig A. EVANS and Stanley E. PORTER, (eds). *Dictionary of New Testament Background*, Downers Grove: InterVarsity Press, pp.509-11.

LEVISON, John R. 2002. *The Spirit in First-Century Judaism*. Boston: Brill Academic Publishers.

LEVISON, John R. 2003. The Spirit in the Gospels: Breaking the Impasse of Early-Twentieth Century Scholarship. *In*: Amy M. DONALDSON and Timothy B. SAILORS, (eds). *New Testament Greek and Exegesis: Essays in Honor of Gerald F. Hawthorne* , Grand Rapids: William B. Eerdmans Publishing, pp.55-76.

LEVISON, John R. 2009. *Filled with the Spirit*. Grand Rapids: William B. Eerdmans Publishing.

LIEFELD, Walter L. 1996. *Interpreting the Book of Acts*. Grand Rapids: Baker Book House.

LIFE, The Pew Forum on Religion & Public. 2007. *U.S. Religious Landscape Survey: Affiliations*. [online]. [Accessed 7 July 2011]. Available from World Wide Web: <http://religions.pewforum.org/affiliations>

LIM, David. 1999. A Reflection on the "Initial Evidence" Discussion from a Pentecostal Pastor's Perspective. *Asian Journal of Pentecostal Studies*. **2**(2), pp.223-32.

LINDBERG, Carter. 1983. *The Third Reformation? Charismatic Movements and the Lutheran Tradition*. Macon: Mercer University Press.

LINDSELL, Harold. 1976. *The Battle for the Bible: The Book that Rocked the Evangelical World*. Grand Rapids: Zondervan Publishing.

LINDSELL, Harold. 1979. *The Bible in the Balance*. Grand Rapids: Zondervan Publishing House.

LING, Tan May. 1998. A Response to Frank Macchia's "Groans too Deep for Words: Towards a Theology of Tongues as Initial Evidence. *Asian Journal of Pentecostal Studies*. 1(2), pp.1-8.

LITFIN, Duane. 2011. The Future of Evangelicalism (and Southern Baptists). *In*: David S. DOCKERY, Ray VAN NESTE, and Jerry TIDWELL, (eds). *Southern Baptists, Evangelicals, and the Future of Denominationalism*, Nashville: B & H Academic, pp.97-111.

LOVELACE, Richard. 1985. Baptism in the Holy Spirit and the Evangelical Tradition. *Pneuma*. 7(2), pp.101-23.

LOVETT, Loenard. 1975. Black Origins of the Pentecostal Movement. *In*: Vinson SYNAN, (ed). *Aspects of Pentecostal-Charismatic Origins*, Gainesville: Bridge-Logos, pp.125-40.

LOYD-JONES, D. Martin. 1984. *Joy Unspeakable: Power & Renewal in the Holy Spirit*. Wheaton: Harold Shaw Publishers.

LUMPKIN, William L. 1959. *Baptist Confessions of Faith*. Philadelphia: The Judson Press.

MA, Wonsuk. 1997. A "First Waver Look at the "Third Wave": A Pentecostal Reflection on Charles Kraft's Power Encounter Terminology. *Pneuma*. 19(2), pp.189-206.

MACARTHUR, Jr. John F. 1980. *The Charismatics: A Doctrinal Perspective*. Grand Rapids: Zondervan Publishing.

MACARTHUR, Jr. John F. 1984. *The MacArthur New Testament Commentary: 1 Corinthians*. Chicago: The Moody Bible Institute.

MACARTHUR, Jr. John F. 1987. *The MacArthur New Testament Commentary: Galatians*. Chicago: The Moody Bible Institute.

MACARTHUR, Jr. John F. 1992. *Charismatic Chaos*. Grand Rapids: Zondervan Publishing.

MACARTHUR, John F. 2003. Does God Still Give Revelation? *The Master's Seminary Journal*. **14**(2), pp.217-34.

MACARTHUR, John F. 2013. *Strange Fire: The Danger of Offending the Holy Spirit with Counterfeit Worship*. Nashville: Nelson Books.

MACCHIA, Frank D. 1992. Sighs too Deep for Words: Toward a Theology of Glossolalia. *Journal of Pentecostal Theology*. **1**(1), pp.47-73.

MACCHIA, Frank D. 1993. The Question of Tongues as Initial Evidence: A Review of Initial Evidence, Edited by Gary B. McGee. *Journal of Pentecostal Studies*. **2**(1), pp.117-27.

MACCHIA, Frank D. 1993. Tongues as a Sign: Towards a Sacramental Understanding of Pentecostal Experience. *Pneuma*. **15**(1), pp.61-76.

MACCHIA, Frank D. 1996. God Present in a Confused Situation: The Mixed Influence of the Charismatic Movement on Classical Pentecostalism in the United States. *Pneuma*. **18**(1), pp.33-54.

MACCHIA, Frank D. 1998. Groans too Deep for Words: Toward a Theology of Tongues as Initial Evidence. *Asian Journal of Pentecostal Studies*. **1**(2), pp.1-20.

MACCHIA, Frank D. 2002. Theology, Pentecostal. *In*: Stanley M. BURGESS and Eduard VAN DER MAAS, (eds). *The New International Dictionary of Pentecostal and Charismatic Movements*, Grand Rapids: Zondervan, pp.1120-41.

MACCHIA, Frank D. 2006. *Baptized in the Spirit: A Global Pentecostal Theology*. Grand Rapids: Zondervan.

MACDONALD, William G. 1964. *Glossolalia in the New Testament*. Springfield: Gospel Publishing House.

MACDONALD, William. 1976. Penteciostal Theology: A Classical Viewpoint. *In*: *Perspectives on the New Pentecostalism*, Grand Rapids: Baker Book House, p.60.

MACDONALD, William G. 1976. Pentecostal Theology: A Classical Perspective. *In*: Russell P. SPITTLER, (ed). *Perspectives on the New Pentecost*, Grand Rapids: Baker Book House, pp.59-74.

MACGORMAN, Jack W. 1974. *The Gifts of the Spirit: An Exposition of 1 Corinthians 12-14*. Nashville: Broadman Press.

MACINTOSH, Douglas Clyde. 1919. *Theology as an Empirical Science*. New York: Macmillan.

MAHAN, Asa. 1870. *The Baptism of the Holy Ghost*. New York: Hughes and Palmer.

MANDRYK, Jason. 2010. *Operation World: The Definitive Prayer Guide to Every Nation, 7th ed*. Colorado Springs: Biblica Publishing.

MANDRYK, Jason. 2010. *Operation World: Glossary*. [online]. [Accessed 5 July 2011]. Available from World Wide Web: <http://www.operationworld.org/glossary>

MANTEY, Julius R. 1952. On Causal Eis Again. *Journal of Biblical Literature*. **70**(2), pp.309-11.

MANTEY, Julius R. 1952. The Causal Use of Eis in the New Testament. *Journal of Biblical Literature*. **70**(1), pp.45-58.

MARCUS, Ralph. 1952. On Causal Eis. *Journal of Biblical Literature*. **70**(1), pp.129-30.

MARCUS, Ralph. 1953. The Elusive Eis. *Journal of Biblical Literature*. **71**(1), p.44.

MARCUS, Joel. 1999. *The Way of the LORD: Christological Exegesis of the Old Testament in the Gospel of Mark*. Edinburgh: T & T Clark.

MARCUS, Joel. 2000. *The Anchor Bible: Mark 1-8*. New York: Doubleday.

MARING, Norman H. 1958. Notes from Religious Journals. *Foundations*. **1**(1), pp.91-95.

MARSDEN, George M. 1980. *Fundamentalism and American Culture: The Shaping of Twentieth-Century Evangelicalism, 1870-1925*. Oxford: Oxford University Press.

MARSDEN, George M. 1991. *Understanding Fundamentalism and Evangelicalism*. Grand Rapids: William B. Eerdmans Publishing.

MARSHALL, I. Howard. 1971. *Luke: Historian and Theologian*. Grand Rapids: Zondervan Publishing House.

MARSHALL, I. Howard. 1977. The Significance of Pentecost. *Scottish Journal of Theology*. **30**(1), pp.347-69.

MARSHALL, I. Howard. 1978. *The Gospel of Luke: A Commentary on the Greek Texts*. Grand Rapids: William B. Eerdmans Publishing.

MARSHALL, I. Howard. 1986. *The Acts of the Apostles: An Introduction and Commentary*. Leicester: InterVarsity Press.

MARSHALL, I. Howard. 1991. Luke and His Gospel. *In*: Peter STUHLMACHER, (ed). *The Gospel and the Gospels*, Grand Rapids: William B. eerdmans Publishing, pp.273-82.

MARSHALL, I. Howard and PETERSON, David (eds). 1998. *Witness to the Gospel: The Theology of Acts*. Grand Rapids: William B. Eerdmans Publishing.

MARTIN, Dan. 1987. Lewis Named President of the Home Mission Board. *Baptist Press*, 14 April, pp.1-10.

MARTÍNEZ, Florentino García. 1996. *The Dead Sea Scrolls Translated: The Qumran Texts in English, 2nd Ed.*. Grand Rapids: William B. Eerdmans Publishing.

MARXSEN, Willi. 1969. *Mark the Evangelist: Studies on the Redaction History of the Gospel*. New York: Abington Press.

MASSEY, Richard D. 1998. The Word of God: Thus Saith the Lord. *In*: Keith WARRINGTON, (ed). *Pentecostal Perspectives*, Carlisle: Paternoster Press, pp.64-79.

MAUSER, Ulrich. 1963. *Christ in the Wilderness: The Wilderness Theme in the Second Gospel and Its Basis in the Biblical Tradition*. London: SCM Press.

MAYHUE, Richard L. 2003. Cessationism: The Gifts of Healings and Divine Healing. *The Master's Seminary Journal*. **14**(2), pp.263-86.

Bibliography

MCBETH, H. Leon. 1987. *The Baptist Heritage: Four Centuries of Baptist Witness.* Nashville: B & H Academic.

MCCLYMOND, Michael J. (ed). 2004. *Embodying the Spirit: New Perspectives on North American Revivalism.* Baltimore: Johns Hopkins University Press.

MCCUNE, Rolland D. 1998. The Formation of the New Evangelicalism: Historical and Theological Antecedents, Part One. *Detroit Baptist Seminary Journal.* 3(1), pp.3-32.

MCCUNE, Rolland D. 1999. The Formation of the New Evangelicalism: Historical Beginnings, Part Two. *Detroit Baptist Seminary Journal.* 4(1), pp.110-51.

MCDONNELL, Kilian. 1972. Baptism in the Holy Spirit as an Ecumenical Problem. *In*: Kilian MCDONNELL and Arnold BITTLINGER, (eds). *The Baptism in the Holy Spirit as an Ecumenical Problem*, Notre Dame: Catholic Renewal Services, p.33.

MCDONNELL, Kilian and Arnold BITTLINGER. 1972. *The Baptism in the Holy Spirit as an Ecumenical Problem.* Notre Dame: Catholic Renewal Services.

MCDONNELL, Kilian. 1974. The Distinguishing Characteristics of the Charismatic-Pentecostal Spirituality. *One in Christ.* 10(2), pp.117-28.

MCDONNELL, Kilian. 1975. *The Holy Spirit and Power: The Catholic Charismatic Renewal.* Garden City: Doubleday.

MCDONNELL, Kilian (ed). 1980. *Presence, Power, Praise: Documents on the Charismatic Renewal, 3 Vols.* Collegeville: Liturgical Press.

MCDONNELL, Kilian. 1980. Theological and Pastoral Orientations on the Catholic Charismatic Renewal: Malines Document I. *In*: Kilian MCDONNELL, (ed). *Presence, Power, Praise: Documents on the Charismatic Renewal, Vol. 3*, Collegeville: Litugical Press, p.32.

MCDONNELL, Kilian and George T. MONTAGUE. 1991. *Fanning the Flame: What Does Baptism in the Holy Spirit Have to Do with Christian Initiation?* Collegeville: The Order of St. Benedict.

MCDONNELL, Kilian and George T. MONTAGUE. 1994. *Christian Initiation and Baptism in the Holy Spirit: Evidence from the First Eight Centuries*. Collegeville: Liturgical Press.

MCDONNELL, Kilian. 1995. Five Defining Issues: The International Classical Pentecostal/Roman Catholic Dialogue. *Pneuma*. **17**(2), pp.175-88.

MCDOUGALL, Donald G. 2003. Cessationism in 1 Cor 13:8-12. *The Master's Seminary Journal*. **14**(2), pp.177-213.

MCGEE, Gary B. (ed). 1991. *Initial Evidence: Historical and Biblical Perspectives on the Pentecostal Doctrine of Spirit Baptism*. Peabody: Hendrickson Publishers.

MCGEE, Gary B. 2002. Initial Evidence. *In*: Stanley M. BURGESS and Eduard M. VAN DER MAAS, (eds). *New International Dictionary of Pentecostal and Charismatic Movements*, Grand Rapids: Zondervan, pp.784-91.

MCINTIRE, C. T. 1985. Fundamentalism. *In*: Walter A. ELWELL, (ed). *Evangelical Dictionary of Theology*, Grand Rapids: Baker Book House, pp.433-35.

MCKISSIC, William Dwight. 2007. *The IMB Tongues Policy: Emotional Prejudice or Exegetical Precision?* [online]. [Accessed 29 June 2011]. Available from World Wide Web: <http://dwightmckissic.wordpress.com/2007/05/25/the-imb-tongues-policy-emotional-prejudice-or-exegetical-precision/>

MCNAMEE, J. J. 1974. *The Role of the Spirit in Pentecostalism: A Comparative Study*. PhD diss.: Eberhard Karls University.

MEISTER, Chad and J. B. STUMP. 2010. *Christian Thought: A Historical Introduction*. New York: Routledge.

MENZIES, William W. 1971. *Anointed to Serve*. Springfield: Gospel Publishing House.

MENZIES, William W. 1985. The Methodology of Pentecostal Theology: An Essay in Hermeneutics. *In*: Paul ELBERT, (ed). *Essays on Apostolic Themes: Studies in Honor of Howard M. Ervin*, Peabody: Hendrickson Publishers, pp.1-14.

Bibliography

MENZIES, Robert P. 1991. *Empowered for Witness: The Spirit in Luke-Acts.* Sheffield: Sheffield Academic Press.

MENZIES, Robert P. 1991. *The Development of Early Christian Pneumatology with Special Reference to Luke-Acts, JSNTS 54.* Sheffield: Sheffield Academic Press.

MENZIES, Robert P. 1991. The Distinctive Character of Luke's Pneumatology. *Paraclete.* **25**(1), p.18.

MENZIES, Robert P. 1992. The Essence of Pentecostalism: Forum Conducted at the Asia Pacific Theological Seminary Chapel. *Paraclete.* **26**(3), pp.1-13.

MENZIES, Robert P. 1999. The Spirit of Prophecy, Luke-Acts and Pentecostal Theology: A Response to Max Turner. *Journal of Pentecostal Theology.* **15**(1), pp.49-74.

MENZIES, William W. and Robert P. Menzies. 2000. *Spirit and Power: Foundations of Pentecostal Experience.* Grand Rapids: Zondervan.

MENZIES, William W. and Stanley M. HORTON. 2000. *Bible Doctrines: A Pentecostal Perspective.* Springfield: Logion Press.

MENZIES, Robert P. 2007. Luke's Understanding of Baptism in the Holy Spirit. *PentecoStudies.* **6**(1), pp.108-26.

MILLER, Perry. 1953. *Roger Williams: His Contribution to the American Tradition.* Cleveland: Bobbs-Merrill.

MILLER, Donald E. 1997. *Reinventing American Protestantism: Christianity in the New Millennium.* Berkley: University of California Press.

MINISTRIES, Catholic Renewal. 2008. *About Life in the Spirit Seminars.* [online]. [Accessed 5 November 2011]. Available from World Wide Web: <http://www. crmweb.org/ftf/FTF5.html>

MINISTRIES, Aldersgate Renewal. 2011. *Life in the Spirit Seminar and Life in the Spirit Experience.* [online]. [Accessed 5 November 2011]. Available from World Wide Web: <http://aldersgaterenewal.org/update-newsletter-news/183-life-in-the-spirit-seminar-and-life-in-the-spirit-experience>

MINISTRIES, Holy Spirit Renewal. 2011. *Roots*. [online]. [Accessed 23 June 2011]. Available from World Wide Web: <http://www.hsrm.org/ index.php? option=com_content&view=article&id=50&Itemid=72>

MITTELSTADT, Martin William. 2010. *Reading Luke-Acts in the Pentecostal Tradition*. Cleveland: CPT Press.

MOHLER, Jr. R. Albert. 1994. A Call for Baptist Evangelicals & Evangelical Baptists: Commonalities of Faith and a Common Quest for Identity. *In*: David S. DOCKERY, (ed). *Southern Baptists and American Evangelicals*, Nashville: Baptist Sunday School Board, p.238.

MOHLER, Jr. R. Albert. 2000. Reformist Evangelicalism: A Center without a Circumference. *In*: Michael S. HORTON, (ed). *A Confessing Theology for Post-Modern Times*, Wheaton: Crossway Books, pp.131-53.

MOHLER, Jr. R. Albert. 2009. Southern Baptist Identity: Is There a Future? *In*: David. S. DOCKERY, (ed). *Southern Baptist Identity: An Evangelical Denomination Faces the Future*, Wheaton: Crossway Books, pp.25-42.

MOHLER, Jr. R. Albert. 2011. Confessional Evangelicalism. *In*: Andrew David NASELLI and Collin HANSEN, (eds). *Four Views on the Spectrum of Evangelicalism* , Grand Rapids: Zondervan, pp.68-96.

MOHLER, Jr. R. Albert. 2011. Southern Baptists, Evangelicals, and the Future of Denominationalism. *In*: David S. DOCKERY, Ray VAN NESTE, and Jerry TIDWELL, (eds). *Southern Baptists, Evangelicals, and the Future of Denominationalism*, Nashville: B & H Academic, pp.279-91.

MOLTMANN, Jürgen. 1993. The Spirit Gives Life: Spirituality and Vitality. *In*: Harold D. HUNTER and Peter D. HOCKEN, (eds). *All Together in One Place: Theological Papers from the Brighton Conference on World Evangelization* , Sheffield: Sheffield Academic Press, pp.22-37.

MONTAGUE, George T. 1976. *The Holy Spirit: Growth of a Biblical Tradition*. New York: Paulist Press.

MONTAGUE, Kilian McDonnell and George T. 1994. *Christian Initiation and Baptism in the Holy Spirit*. Collegeville: Liturgical Press.

MOODY, William Revell. 1900. *The Life of Dwight L. Moody*. Chicago: Flemming H. Revell Co.

Bibliography

MOODY, Dale. 1976. *Spirit of the Living God: What the Bible Says about the Holy Spirit*. Nashville: Broadman Press.

MORIARITY, Michael G. 1992. *The New Charismatics: A Concerned Voice Responds to Dangerous New Trends*. Grand Rapids: Zondervan Publishing House.

MORELAND, J. P. 2007. *Kingdom Triangle*. Grand Rapids: Zondervan.

MORRIS, Leon. 1960. *Spirit of the Living God: The Bible's Teaching on the Holy Spirit*. London: InterVarsity Press.

MOSTELLER, James D. 1957. Baptists and Anabaptists. *The Chronicle*. **20**(1), pp.3-27.

MOSTELLER, James D. 1957. Baptists and Anabaptists. *The Chronicle*. **20**(2), pp.100-14.

MOULTON, James Hope and Nigel TYRNER. 1963. *A Grammar of New Testament Greek: Syntax, Vol. 3*. Edinburgh: T & T Clark.

MULLINS, E. Y. 1915. Baptism of the Holy Spirit. *In*: James ORR, (ed). *The International Standard Bible Encyclopedia*, Chicago: The Howard-Severance Company, pp.399-401.

MULLINS, E. Y. 1917. The Testimony of Christian Experience. *In*: R. A. TORREY and A. C. DIXSON, (eds). *The Fundamentals, Vol. 4*, Los Angeles: Bible Institute of Los Angeles, pp.314-23.

MULLINS, E. Y., 1917. *The Christian Religion in its Doctrinal Expression*. Philadelphia: Roger Williams Press, 1917.

MULLINS, E. Y., 1923. The Contribution of Baptists to the Interpretation of Christianity *IN: The Hibbert Journal*. **21**(3), pp. 344-44.

MULLINS, E. Y., 1925. *Baptist Beliefs*. Valley Forge: Judson Press.

MULLINS, Edgar Y. 2010. *The Axioms of Religion*. Macon: Mercer University Press.

MURRAY, Ian H. 1998. *Pentecost Today?: The Biblical Basis for Understanding Revival*. Carlisle: The Banner of Truth Trust.

NASELLI, David and HANSEN, Collin (eds). 2011. *The Spectrum of Evangelicalism*. Grand Rapids: Zondervan.

NATHAN, Rich and Ken WILSON. 1995. *Empowered Evangelicals: Bringing Together the Best of the Evangelical and Charismatic Worlds*. Ann Arbor: Servant Publications.

NETTLES, Thomas J. 1999. E. Y. Mullins: Reluctant Evangelical. *Southern Baptist Theological Journal*. 3(1), pp.24-42.

NEWBIGIN, Lesslie. 1954. *The Household of God: Lectures on the Nature of the Church*. New York: Friendship Press.

NEWMAN, A. H. 1933. *A Manual of Church History, Vol. 1*. Philadelphia: American Baptist Publication Society.

NEWMAN, Larry Vern. 2009. *The Ultimate Evidence: Rethinking the Evidence Issues for Spirit Baptism*. Eugene: Wipf & Stock.

NIENKIRCHEN, Charles W. 1993. *A. B. Simpson and the Pentecostal Movement*. Peabody: Hendrickson Publishers.

NOLL, Mark A. 2003. *The Rise of Evangelicalism: The Age of Edwards, Whitefield and the Wesleys*. Downers Grove: InterVarsity Press.

NOLL, Mark. 2010. What is an Evangelical? *In*: Gerald R. MCDERMOTT, (ed). *The Oxford Handbook of Evangelical Theology*, Oxford: Oxford University Press, pp.21-32.

NOLLAND, John. 1993. Luke 9:21-18:34. *In*: Bruce M. METZGER, (ed). *Word Biblical Commentary*, Dallas: Word, p.632.

NORMAN, R. Stanton. 2005. *The Baptist Way: Distinctives of a Baptist Church*. Nashville: Broadman and Holman Publishers.

NORMAN, R. Stanton. 2011. Souther Baptist Identity: A Theological Perspective. *In*: David S. DOCKERY, (ed). *Southern Baptist Identity: An Evangelical Denomination Faces the Future*, Wheaton: Crossway Books, pp.43-63.

O'BRIEN, Robert J. 1975. *Baptist Press: New Service of the Southern Bpatist Convention*. [online]. [Accessed 28 June 2011]. Available from World Wide Web: <http://media.sbhla.org.s3.amazonaws.com/4080,03-Nov-1975.pdf>

Bibliography

O'BRIEN, Robert J. 1975. Five Baptist Churches Plan National Charismatic Meet. *Baptist Press News Service*, 3 November, pp.1-5.

OCKENGA, Harold John. 1959. *Power through Pentecost*. Grand Rapids: William B. Eerdmans Publishing.

O'CONNOR, Edward. 1971. *The Pentecostal Movement in the Catholic Church*. Notre Dame: Ave Maria Press.

OLSON, Roger E. 1995. Postconservative Evangelicals Greet the Postmodern Age. *The Christian Century*, 3 May, pp.480-83.

OLSON, Roger E. 2004. *The Westminster Handbook to Evangelical Theology*. Louisville: Westminster John Knox Press.

OLSON, Roger E. 2006. Confessions of a Post-Pentecostal Believer in the Charismatic Gifts. *Criswell Theological Review*. 4(1), pp.31-40.

OLSON, Roger E. 2011. Postconservative Evangelicalism. *In*: David NASELLI and Collin HANSEN, (eds). *Four Views on the Spectrum of Evangelicalism* , Grand Rapids: Zondervan, pp.161-87.

O'NEILL, J. C. 1961. *The Theology of Acts in its Historical Settings*. London: S.P.C.K.

PACKER, J. I. 1993. The Empowered Christian Life. *In*: Gary S. GREIG and Kevin N. SPRINGER, (eds). *The Kingdom and the Power: Are Healing and the Spiritual Gifts Used by Jesus and the Early Church Meant for the Church Today?*, Ventura: Regal Books, pp. 207-15.

PACKER, J. I. 2002. *Keep in Step with the Spirit*. Grand Rapids: Fleming H. Revell.

PALMA, Anthony D. 2001. *The Holy Spirit: A Pentecostal Perspective*. Springfield: Gospel Publishing House.

PALMA, Anthony D. 2005. Spirit Baptism: Before and After. *Enrichment Journal*. 10(1), pp.90-101.

PALMER, Phoebe Worrall. 1965. *Four Years in the Old World*. Boston: Forster & Palmer.

PALMERVILLE, Paul A. 1985. *The Third Force in Missions*. Peabody: Hendrickson Publishers.

PARHAM, Sarah. 1969. *The Life of Charles F. Parham, Founder of the Apostolic Faith Movement*. Joplin: Hunter Publishing House.

PARKER, Danielle. 2007. *The Legacy of Howard M. Ervin*. [online]. [Accessed 24 December 2011]. Available from World Wide Web: <http://www.oru.edu/news/alumni_news/20090923_legacy_howard_ervin.php>

PATTERSON, W. M. 1969. *Baptist Successionism: A Critical View*. Valley Forge: Judson Press.

PATTERSON, Paige. 2011. Learning from the Anabaptists. *In*: David S. DOCKERY, (ed). *Southern Baptist Identity: An Evangelical Denomination Faces the Future*, Wheaton: Crossway Books, pp.123-37.

PATTERSON, James A. 2011. Reflections on 400 Years of the Baptist Movement: Who we Are, What we Believe. *In*: David S. DOCKERY, Jerry TIDWELL, and Ray VAN NESTE, (eds). *Southern Baptists, Evangelicals, and the Future of Denominationalism (Nashville: B&H Academic, 2011), 193*, Nashville: B & H Academic, pp.191-230.

PAWSON, J. David. 1989. *The Normal Christian Birth: How to Give New Believers a Proper Start in Life*. London: Hodder & Stoughton.

PAWSON, J. David. 1993. *Fourth Wave: Charismatics and Evangelicals -are we Ready to Come Together?* London: Hodder and Stoughton.

PAYNE, Ernest Alexander. 1944. *The Free Church Tradition in the Life of England*. London: SCM Press.

PAYNE, Ernest Alexander. 1947. *The Baptist Movement in the Reformation and Onwards*. London: Carey Kingsgate.

PAYNE, Ernest Alexander. 1949. *The Anabaptists of the 16th Century and Their Influence in the Modern World*. London: Carey Kingsgate.

PAYNE, Ernest Alexander. 1956. Who are the Baptists? *Baptist Quarterly*. **16**(1), pp.339-32.

PEARLMAN, Myer. 1937. *Knowing the Doctrines of the Bible*. Springfield: Gospel Publishing House.

Bibliography

PENNEY, John Michael. 1997. *The Missionary Emphasis of Lukan Pneumatology*. Sheffield: Sheffield Academic Press.

PENTECOST, J. Dwight. 1963. *The Divine Comforter: The Person and Work of the Holy Spirit*. Westwood: Fleming H. Revell.

PERRY, Andrew. 2008. *Eschatological Deliverance: The Spirit in Luke-Acts*. PhD diss.: University of Durham.

PETTS, David. 1987. *The Baptism in the Holy Spirit in Relation to Christian Initiation*. MA thesis: University of Nottingham.

PETTS, David. 1998. The Baptism in the Holy Spirit: The Theological Distinctive. *In*: Keith WARRINGTON, (ed). *Pentecostal Perspectives*, Carlisle: Paternoster Press, pp.101-15.

PIERARD, R. V. 1984. Evangelicalism. *In*: Walter A. ELWELL, (ed). *Evangelical Dictionary of Theology*, Grand Rapids: Baker Book House, pp.382-84.

PINNOCK, Clark H. 1976. The New Pentecostalism: Reflections of an Evangelical Observer. *In*: Russell P. SPITTLER, (ed). *Perspectives on the New Pentecostalism*, Grand Rapids: Baker Book House, pp.182-92.

PINNOCK, Clark H. 1996. *Flame of Love: A Theology of the Holy Spirit*. Downers Grove: InterVarsity Press.

PIPER, John. 1990. *Are Signs and Wonders for Today*. [online]. [Accessed 22 June 2011]. Available from World Wide Web: <http://www.desiringgod.org/resource-library/sermons/are-signs-and-wonders-for-today>

PIPER, John. 1990. *You will be Baptized with the Holy Spirit*. [online]. [Accessed 20 March 2012]. Available from World Wide Web: <http:// www. desiringgod.org/ resource-library/sermons/you-will-be-baptized-with-the-holy-spirit>

PIPER, John. 2008. *This is He Who Baptizes with the Holy Spirit*. [online]. [Accessed 18 August 2013]. Available from World Wide Web: <http:// www. desiringgod.org/resource-library/sermons/this-is-he-who-baptizes-with-the-holy-spirit>

292

PLÜSS, Jean-Daniel. 1993. Azusa and Other Myths: The Long and Winding Road from Experience to Stated Belief and Back Again. *Pneuma.* **15**(2), pp.189-201.

PLÜSS, Jean-Daniel. 1999. Initial Evidence or Evident Initials? A European Point of View on a Pentecostal Distinctive. *Asian Journal of Pentecostal Studies.* **2**(2), pp.213-222.

POLHILL, John B. 1992. Acts. *In*: David S. DOCKERY, (ed). *The New American Commentary: An Exegetical and Theological Exposition of Holy Scripture, Vol. 26*, Nashville: Broadman Press, p.54.

POLOMA, Margaret M. 1986. Pentecostals and Politics in North and Central America. *In*: Jeffrey K. HADDEN and Anson SHUPE, (eds). *Prophetic Religions and Politics*, New York: Paragon, p.330.

POLOMA, Margaret M. 1998. Inspecting the Fruit of the "Toronto Blessing": A Sociological Perspective. *Pneuma.* **20**(1), pp.43-70.

POLOMA, Margaret M. 2003. *Main Street Mystics: The Toronto Blessing & Reviving Pentecostalism.* New York: AltaMira Press.

PRESS, Healing and Revival. 2004. *Equipping the Saints.* [online]. [Accessed 11 April 2012]. Available from World Wide Web: <http:// healingandrevival. com/BioJWimber.htm>

PRESS, Biblical Studies. 2007. *The NET Bible.* Dallas: Biblical Studies Press.

QUEBEDEAUX, Richard. 1974. *The Young Evangelicals: The Story of the Emergence of a New Generation of Evangelicals.* New York: Harper & Row.

RAMM, Bernard. 1959. *The Pattern of Religious Authority.* Grand Rapids: William B. Eerdmans Publishing.

RAMM, Bernard. 1960. *The Witness of the Spirit: An Essay on the Contemporary Relevance of the Internal Witness of the Holy Spirit.* Grand Rapids: William B. Eerdmans Publishing Company.

RAMM, Bernard. 1984. *Protestant Biblical Interpretation, 3rd Ed.* Grand Rapids: Baker Book House.

RANAGHAN, Kevin and Dorothy. 1983. *Catholic Pentecostals Today.* South Bend: Renewal Services.

Bibliography

RAYBURN, Robert S. 1985. Christian, Names of. *In*: Walter A. ELWELL, (ed). *Evangelical Dictionary of Theology*, Grand Rapids: Baker Book House, pp.216-18.

READ-HEIMERDINGER, Jenny. 2002. *The Bezan Text of Acts: A Contribution of Discourse Analysis to Textual Criticism* New York: Sheffield Academic Press.

READER, The Reformed. 1999. *Historic Baptist Documents*. [online]. [Accessed 14 December 2011]. Available from World Wide Web: <http://www.reformedreader .org/ccc/hbd.htm>

REDDIN, Opal. 1993. Letter to the Editor. *Advance*, November, p.42.

RENEWAL, Catholic Charismatic. 2011. *National Service Committee*. [online]. [Accessed 5 November 2011]. Available from World Wide Web: <http://www.nsc-chariscenter.org/index.asp>

RESEARCH, International Bulletin of Missionary. 2011. *Status of Global Mission, 2011, in Context of 20th and 21st Centuries*. [online]. [Accessed 22 June 2011]. Available from World Wide Web: <http://www.gordonconwell.edu/sites/ default/ files/ StatusOfGlobalMission.pdf.>

RICHARDSON, Suzy. 2006. Pastor Faces Removal for Tongues Challenge. *Charisma*, 31 March, p.28.

RICHTER, Philip J. 2004. God is Not a Gentleman! *In* Michael J. MCCLYMOND, (ed). *Embodying the Spirit: New Perspectives on North American Revivalism*, Baltimore: Johns Hopkins University Press, pp. 153-72.

RIDDERBOS, Herman. 1997. *The Gospel of John: A Theological Commentary*. Grand Rapids: William B. Eerdmans Publishing.

RIGGS, Ralph M. 1949. *The Spirit Himself*. Springfield: Gospel Publishing House.

ROBECK, Cecil M. 1992. The Nature of Pentecostal Spirituality. *Pneuma*. **14**(2), pp.103-106.

ROEBECK, Jr. Cecil. 1996. Pentecostal Origins from a Global Perspective. *In*: Harold D. HUNTER and Peter D. HOCKEN, (eds). *All Together in One Place: Theological Papers from the Brighton Conference on World Evangelization*, Sheffield: Sheffield Academic Press, pp.166-80.

ROBERTSON, A. T. 1930. *Word Pictures in the New Testament, Vol. 1.* Nashville: Sunday School Board of the Southern Baptist Convention.

ROBERTSON, A. T. 1930. *Word Pictures in the New Testament, Vol. 3.* Nashville: Sunday School Board of the Southern Baptist Convention.

ROBERTSON, A. T. 1947. *A Grammar of the Greek New Testament in Light of Historical Research.* Nashville: B & H Academic.

ROBERTSON, A. T. 1977. *Luke the Historian in Light of Research.* Grand Rapids: Baker Book House.

RUIS-CAMPS, Josep and Jenney READ-HEIMERDINGER. 2004. *The Message of Acts in Codex Bezae: A Comparison with the Alexandrian Tradition, Vol. 1.* London: T & T Clark.

RUSHBROOKE, James A. 1926. *Protestant of the Protestants: The Baptist Churches, Their Progress, and Their Spiritual Principle.* London: Kingsgate.

RUTHVEN, Jon. 2005. *Can Charismatic Theology Be Biblical? Foundations for a Charismatic Theology.* [online]. [Accessed 20 June 2011]. Available from World Wide Web: <http://www.tffps.org/docs/ Foundations%20for%20a%20 Charismatic%20Theology.pdf>

RUTHVEN, Jon. 2005. *The 'Foundational Gifts' of Ephesians 2:20.* [online]. [Accessed 20 June 2011]. Available from World Wide Web: <http://www. tffps.org/docs/ The%20Foundational%20Gifts%20of%20Ephesians% 202,20. pdf>

RUTHVEN, John. 2011. *On the Cessation of the Charismata: The Protestant Polemic on Postbiblical Miracles, Revised and Expanded.* Tulsa: Word & Spirit Press.

RYKEN, Leland. 1974. *The Literature of the Bible.* Grand Rapids: Zondervan Publishing House.

RYRIE, Charles C. 1965. *The Holy Spirit.* Chicago: Moody Press.

RYRIE, Charles C. 1972. *A Survey of Bible Doctrine.* Chicago: Moody Press.

RYRIE, Charles C. 1986. *Basic Theology: A Popular Systematic Guide to Understanding Biblical Truth.* Wheaton: Victor Books.

Bibliography

RYRIE, Charles C. 1995. *Dispensationalism*. Chicago: Moody Bible Institute.

SAMARIN, William J. 1976. Religious Goals of a Neo-Pentecostal Group in a Non-Pentecostal Church. *In*: Russell P. SPITTER, (ed). *Perspectives on the New Pentecostalism*, Grand Rapids: Baker Book House, pp.134-49.

SCHENKEL, Albert Frederick. 1999. New Wine and Baptist Wineskins: American and Southern Baptist Denominational Responses to the Charismatic Renewal. *In*: Edith BLUMHOEFER, Russell P. SPITTLER, and Grant A. WACKER, (eds). *Pentecostal Currents in American Protestantism*, Chicago: University of Illinois Press, pp.152-67.

SCHNEIDER, Herbert. 1975. Baptism in the Holy Spirit in the New Testament. *In*: Kilian MCDONNELL, (ed). *The Holy Spirit and Power*, Garden City: Doubleday, p.49.

SCHOOL, Duke Divinity. 1997. *Re-envisioning Baptist Identity: A Manifesto for Baptist Communities in North America*. [online]. [Accessed 16 December 2011]. Available from World Wide Web: <http://divinity.duke.edu/sites/ default/files/ documents/faculty-freeman/reenvisioning-baptist-identity.pdf>

SCHOOL, The Henry Center of Trinity Evangelical Divinity. 2007. *The Life of Carl F. H. Henry*. [online]. [Accessed 29 June 2011]. Available from World Wide Web: <http://www.henrycenter.org/about/carl-f-h-henry/life/>

SCHOOL, Trinity Evangelical Divinity. 2012. *Donald A. Carson, Ph.D.* [online]. [Accessed 26 December 2012]. Available from World Wide Web: <http://web.tiu. edu/divinity/academics/faculty/carson>

SCHREINER, Thomas R. 2006. Baptism in the Epistles: An Initiation Rite for Believers. *In*: E. Ray CLENDENEN, (ed). *Believer's Baptism: Sign of the New Covenant in Christ*, Nashville: B & H Academic, pp.67-96.

SCHREINER, Thomas R. 2008. *New Testament Theology: Magnifying God in Christ*. Grand Rapids: Baker Academic.

SCHWEIZER, Eduard and Trans. Geoffrey W. BROMILEY. 1988. Pneuma, Pneumatikos. *In*: Gerhard KITTEL and Gerhard FRIEDRICH, (eds). *Theological Dictionary of the New Testament, Vol. 6*, Grand Rapids: William B. Eerdmans Publishing, pp.332-455.

SEMINARY, Bethel. 2010. *The Baptist Pietist Clarion.* [online]. [Accessed 26 December 2011]. Available from World Wide Web: http://www.bethel.edu/cas/dept/history/Baptist_Pietist_Clarion_Issues/BPC_May_2011.pdf>

SEMINARY, Fuller. 2008. *Cecil M. Robeck, Jr.* [online]. [Accessed 1 August 2013]. Available from World Wide Web: , http://www.fuller.edu/academics/faculty/cecil-robeck.aspx>

SHELLEY, Bruce. 1967. *Evangelicalism in America.* Grand Rapids: William B. Eerdmans Publishing.

SHELTON, James B. 1994. A Reply to James D. G. Dunn's Baptism in the Spirit: A Response to Pentecostal Scholarship on Luke-Acts. *Journal of Pentecostal Theology.* **4**(1), pp.139-43.

SHELTON, James B. 1999. *Mighty in Word and Deed: The Role of the Holy Spirit in Luke-Acts.* Eugene: Wipf and Stock Publishers.

SHEPPARD, Gerald T. 1984. Pentecostals and the Hermeneutics of Dispensationalism. *Pneuma.* **6**(1), pp.5-33.

SHURDEN, Walter B. 1998. The Baptist Idenity and the Baptist Manifesto. *Perspectives in Religious Studies.* **25**(4), pp.321-40.

SIMPSON, A. B. 1896. *Power from on High: An Unfolding of the Doctrine of the Holy Spirit in the Old and New Testaments, Part Two: The New Testament.* Harrisburg: Christian Publications.

SIMPSON, A. B. 1905. The Baptism of the Holy Spirit: a Crisis or an Evolution? *Living Truths*, December, pp.705-15.

SIMPSON, A. B. 1925. *The Fourfold Gospel.* New York: Gospel Alliance Publishing.

SMAIL, Thomas A. 1975. *Reflected Glory: The Spirit in Christ and Christians.* London: Hodder and Stoughton.

SMIDT, Corwin E., Lyman A. KELLSTEDT, John C. GREEN, and James L. GUTH. 1996. The Spirit-Filled Movements and American Politics. *In*: John Clifford GREEN, (ed). *Religion and the Culture Wars: Dispatches from the Front*, London: Rowman & Littlefield Publishers, pp.219-39.

SMIDT, Corwin E., Lyman A. KELLSTEDT, John C. GREEN, and James L. GUTH. 1999. The Spirit-Filled Movements in Contemporary America: A Survey Perspective. *In*: Edith L. BLUMHOFER, Russell P. SPITTLER, and Grant A. WACKER, (eds). *Pentecostal Currents in American Protestantism*, Chicago: University of Illinois Press, pp.111-30.

SMITH, Christian. 1998. *American Evangelicalism: Embattled and Thriving.* Chicago: University of Chicago Press.

SOULEN, Richard N. and R. Kendall SOULEN. 2001. *Handbook of Biblical Criticism*. Louisville: Westminster John Knox Press.

SPENCER, Michael. 2011. *Southern Baptists and Charismatics: What a Long, Strange Trip It's Been*. [online]. [Accessed 23 June 2011]. Available from World Wide Web: <http://www.internetmonk.com/archive/what-a-long-strange-trip-its-been>

SPENER, Philip Jacob, Trans. Theodore G. Tappert. 1964. *Pia Desideria.* Minneapolis: Fortress Press.

SPITTLER, Russell P. (ed). 1976. *Perspectives on the New Pentecostalism.* Grand Rapids: Baker Book House.

SPITTLER, Russell P. 1999. Corinthian Spirituality: How a Flawed Anthropology Imperils Authentic Christian Existence. *In*: Edith L. BLUMHOFER, Russell P. SPITTLER, and Grant A. AND WACKER, (eds). *Pentecostal Currents in American Protestantism*, Chicago: University of Illinois Press, pp.3-19.

SPITTLER, Russell P. 2002. Glossolalia. *In*: Stanley M. BURGESS and Eduard M. VAN DER MAAS, (eds). *The New International Dictionary of Pentecostal and Charismatic Movements*, Grand Rapids: Zondervan, pp.670-76.

SPITTLER, Russell P. 2002. Spirituality, Pentecostal and Charismatic. *In*: Stanley M. BURGESS and Edward M. VAN DER MASS, (eds). *The New International Dictionary of Pentecostal and Charismatic Movements*, Grand Rapids: Zondervan, pp.1096-1102.

SPIVEY, James. 2001. Benajah Harvey Carroll. *In*: Timothy GEORGE and David S. DOCKERY, (eds). *Theologians of the Baptist Tradition, Revised Ed.* , Nashville: B & H Publications, pp.163-80.

298

SPURGEON, C. H. 1858. *The Outpouring of the Holy Spirit*. [online]. [Accessed 27 June 2011]. Available from World Wide Web: <http://www. spurgeongems.org/vols 4-6/chs201.pdf>

STAGG, Frank. 1969. Matthew. *In*: Clifton J. ALLEN, (ed). *The Broadman Bible Commentary: General Articales, Matthew-Mark*, Nashville: Broadman Press, pp.89-93.

STAGG, Frank. 1969. *The Broadman Bible Commentary: General Articles, Matthew-Mark*. Nashville: Broadman Press.

STAGG, Frank, E. Glenn HINSON, and Wayne E. OATES. 1967. *Glossolalia: Tongue Speaking in Biblical, Historical, and Psychological Perspective*. Nashville: Abington Press.

STANFORD, Miles J. 1996. *Demon Possession and the Christian*. [online]. [Accessed 11 April 2012]. Available from World Wide Web: <http://withchrist. org/MJS/dickasonf.pdf>

STANTON, Graham N. 1992. Presuppositions in New Testament Criticism. *In*: I. Howard MARSHALL, (ed). *New Testament Interpretation: Essays on Principles and Methods* , Grand Rapids: William B. Eerdmans Publishing, pp.60-71.

STASSEN, Glenn H. 1962. Anabaptist Influence in the Origin of Particular Baptists. *Mennonite Quarterly Review*. **36**(1), pp.322-48.

STATISTICS, National and World Religion. 2004. *Largest Religious Groups in the USA*. [online]. [Accessed 21 June 2011]. Available from World Wide Web: <http:// www.adherents.com/rel_USA.html>

STEIN, Robert H. 1992. Luke. *In*: David S. DOCKERY, (ed). *The New American Commentary: An Exegetical and Theological Exposition of Holy Scripture, Vol. 24* , Nashville: Broadman Press, p.135.

STEIN, Robert H. 2008. Mark. *In*: Robert W. YARBROUGH and Robert H. STEIN, (eds). *Baker Exegetical Commentary on the New Testament*, Grand Rapids: Baker Academic, pp.38-53.

STEIN, Robert H. 2011. *The Basic Guide to Interpreting the Bible: Playing by the Rules, 2nd Ed.* Grand Rapids: Baker Academic.

STENNING, John F. 1953. *The Targum of Isaiah*. Oxford: The Clarendon Press.

STITZINGER, James F. 2003. Spiritual Gifts: Definitions and Kinds. *The Master's Seminary Journal.* **14**(2), pp.143-76.

STOEFFLER, F. Ernest. 1965. *Rise of Evangelical Pietism.* Leiden: E. J. Brill.

STORMS, C. Samuel. 1996. A Third Wave View. *In*: Wayne A. GRUDEM, (ed). *Are Miraculous Gifts for Today? Four Views*, Grand Rapids: Zondervan, pp.175-223.

STORMS, C. Samuel. 2007. *Signs of the Spirit: An Interpretation of Jonathan Edwards' Religious Affections.* Wheaton: Crossway Books.

STRONG, A. H. 1909. *Systematic Theology: A Compendium and Commonplace Book Designed for the Use of Theological Students, Vol. 3.* Philadelphia: The Griffith & Rowland Press.

STRONSTAD, Roger. 1988. The Hermeneutics of Lucan Historiography. *Paraclete.* **22**(4), pp.5-17.

STRONSTAD, Roger. 1988. Trends in Pentecostal Hermeneutics. *Paraclete.* **22**(3), pp.1-12.

STRONSTAD, Roger. 1989. The Holy Spirit in Luke-Acts. *Paraclete.* **23**(1), p.26.

STRONSTAD, Roger. 1992. Pentecostal Experience and Hermeneutics. *Paraclete.* **26**(1), pp.14-30.

STRONSTAD, Roger. 1992. Pentecostal Experience and Hermeneutics. *Paraclete.* **15**(1), pp.18-30.

STRONSTAD, Roger. 2002. *The Charismatic Theology of St. Luke.* Peabody: Hendrickson Publishers.

STRONSTAD, Roger. 2003. *The Prophethood of All Believers: A Study in Luke's Charismatic Theology.* Sheffield: Sheffield Academic Press.

STRONSTAD, Roger. 2008. The Prophethood of all Believers: A Study in Luke's Charismatic Theology. *In*: Wonsuk MA and Robert P. MENZIES, (eds). *Pentecostalism in Context: Essays in Honor of William W. Menzies*, Eugene: Wipf & Stock Publishers, pp.60-77.

STRONSTAD, Roger. 2010. Forty Years On: An Appreciation and Assessment of Baptism in the Holy Spirit by James D. G. Dunn. *Journal of Pentecostal Theology.* **19**(1), pp.3-11.

STROZIER, Charles B. 1994. *Apocalypse: On the Psychology of Fundamentalism in America.* Boston: Beacon Press.

STUART, Douglas and Gordon D. FEE. 1982. *How to Read the Bible for All its Worth: A Guide to Understanding the Bible.* Grand Rapids: Zondervan Publishing House.

SUENENS, Léon, Trans. Francis. ET 1974. *A New Pentecost?* New York: Seabury.

SULLIVAN, Francis. 1974. Baptism in the Holy Spirit: A Catholic Interpretation of the Pentecostal Experience. *Gregorianum.* **55**(1), pp.46-66.

SULLIVAN, Francis. 1982. *Charisms and Charismatic Renewal: A Biblical Theological Study.* Ann Arbor: Servant Publications.

SUURMOND, Jean-Jacques, Trans. John Bowden. ET 1995. *Word and Play: Towards a Charismatic Theology.* Grand Rapids: William B. Eerdmans Publishing Company.

SWANSON, Dennis M. 2003. Bibliography of Works on Cessationism. *The Master's Seminary Journal.* **14**(2), pp.311-27.

SWETE, H. B. 1902. *The Gospel According to St. Mark: The Greek Text with Introduction, Notes, and Indices.* London: MacMillan and Co.

SYNAN, Vinson. 1971. *The Holiness-Pentecostal Movement in the United States.* Grand Rapids: William B. Eerdmans Publishers.

SYNAN, Vinson. 1974. *Charismatic Bridges.* Ann Arbor: Word of Life.

SYNAN, Vinson. 1994. The Role of Tongues as Initial Evidence. *In*: Mark W. WILSON, (ed). *Spirit and Renewal: Essays in Honor of J. Rodman Williams*, Sheffield: Sheffield Academic Press, pp.67-82.

SYNAN, Vinson. 2001. Charismatic Renewal Enters the Mainline Churches. *In*: Vinson SYNAN, (ed). *The Century of the Holy Spirit: 100 Years of Pentecostal and Charismatic Renewal, 1901-2001*, Nashville: Thomas Nelson Publishers, pp.149-76.

SYNAN, Vinson. 2001. *In the Latter Days: The Outpouring of the Holy Spirit in the Twentieth Century*. Fairfax: Xulon Press.

SYNAN, Vinson. 2001. *The Century of the Holy Spirit: 100 Years of Pentecostal and Charismatic Renewal*. Nashville: Thomas Nelson Publishers.

SYNAN, Vinson. 2001. The Charismatics: Renewal in Major Protestant Denominations. *In*: Vinson SYNAN, (ed). *The Century of the Holy Spirit: 100 Years of Pentecostal and Charismatic Renewal, 1901-2001*, Nashville: Thomas Nelson Publishers, pp.177-208.

SYNAN, Vinson. 2001. The Pentecostal Century: An Overview. *In*: Vinson SYNAN, (ed). *The Century of the Holy Spirit: 100 Years of Pentecostal and Charismatic Renewal, 1901-2001*, Nashville: Thomas Nelson Publishers, pp.1-13.

SYNAN, Vinson. 2002. Fundamentalism. *In*: Stanley M. BURGESS and Eduard VAN DER MAAS, (eds). *The New International Dictionary of Pentecostal Charismatic Movements*, Grand Rapids: Zondervan, pp.655-58.

The Holy Bible: English Standard Version. 2001. Wheaton: Crossway.

The Holy Bible: New International Version. 1984. Grand Rapids: Zondervan.

THISELTON, Anthony C. 1992. *New Horizons in Hermeneutics*. Grand Rapids: Zondervan Publishing House.

THOMAS, John C. 1994. Women, Pentecostals and the Bible: An Experiment in Pentecostal Hermeneutics. *Journal of Pentecostal Theology*. 5(1), pp.41-56.

THOMAS, Robert L. 2002. *Evangelical Hermeneutics: The New Versus the Old*. Grand Rapids: Kregel Publications.

THOMAS, Robert L. 2003. The Hermeneutics of Noncessationism. *The Master's Seminary Journal*. 14(2), pp.287-310.

THOMAS, Robert L. and FARNELL, David (eds). 1998. *The Jesus Crisis: The Inroads of Historical Criticism into Evangelical Scholarship*. Grand Rapids: Kregel Publications.

THOUGHT, The Royal Aal Al-Bayt Institute for Islamic. 2007. *A Common Word Between Us and You.* [online]. [Accessed 26 September 2011]. Available from World Wide Web: <http://www.acommonword.com/index.php?lang= en&page =option1>

TIDWELL, Jerry N. 2011. Awakenings and Their Impact on Baptists and Evangelicals: Sorting Out the Myths in the History of Missions and Evangelism. *In*: Davis S. DOCKERY, Ray VAN NESTE, and Jerry TIDWELL, (eds). *Southern Baptists, Evangelicals, and the Future of Denominationalism,* Nashville: B & H Academic, pp.135-45.

TIPPETT, Alan. 1987. *Introduction to Missiology.* Pasadena: William Carey Library.

TODAY, Christianity. 2006. *The Top 50 Books that have Shaped Evangelicals.* [online]. [Accessed 21 November 2011]. Available from World Wide Web: <http:// www.christianitytoday.com/ct/2006/october/23.51.html>

TODAY, Life. 2011. *James and Betty Robison.* [online]. [Accessed 31 August 2011]. Available from World Wide Web: <http://lifetoday.org/about-life/james-and-betty-robison/>

TOLBERT, M. A. 1989. *Sowing the Gospel: Mark's World in Literary-Historical Perspective.* Philadelphia: Fortress Press.

TORBET, Robert G. 1993. *A History of the Baptists.* Valley Forge: Judson Press.

TORREY, R. A. 1895. *The Baptism with the Holy Spirit.* New York: Flemming H. Revell & Company.

TORREY, R. A. 1974. *The Person & Work of the Holy Spirit.* Grand Rapids: Zondervan Publishing House.

TORREY, R. A. 1996. *What the Bible Teaches.* New Kensington: Whitaker House.

TORREY, R. A. 2008. *The Holy Spirit: Who He is and What He Does.* Alachua: Bridge-Logos.

TORREY, R. A. and Charles L. FEINBERG. 1958. *The Fundamentals: The Classic Sourcebook of Foundational Biblical Truths.* Grand Rapids: Kregel Publications.

TOWNS, Elmer. 1996. *Putting an End to the Worship Wars*. Nashville: B & H Publishers.

TRADITION, Christian Thought &. 2011. *About Nathan A. Finn*. [online]. [Accessed 16 December 2011]. Available from World Wide Web: <http://www. nathanfinn.com/about>

TRAVIS, William G. 2004. Pietism and the History of American Evangelicalism. *In*: Millard J. ERICKSON, Paul Kjoss HELSETH, and Justin TAYLOR, (eds). *Reclaiming the Center: Confronting Evangelical Accommodation in Postmodern Times*, Wheaton: Crossway Books, pp.251-79.

TROELSCH, Ernst E., Olive Wyon, Trans. 1992. *The Social Teaching of the Christian Churches, Vol. 1*. Louisville: Westminster John Knox Press.

TROELTSCH, Ernst E., Olive Wyon, Trans. 1931. *The Social Teaching of the Christian Churches, Vol. 2*. London: George Allen & Unwin.

TUGWELL, Simon. 1972. *Did You Receive the Spirit?* New York: Paulist Press.

TULL, James E. 1983. Evangelicals and Baptists: The Shape of the Question. *In*: Jr. James Leo GARRETT, E. Gless HINSON, and James E. TULL, (eds). *Are Southern Baptists Evangelicals?*, Macon: Mercer University Press, p.28.

TURLINGTON, Henry E. 1969. Mark. *In*: Clifton J. ALLEN, (ed). *The Broadman Bible Commentary: General Articles, Matthew-Mark* , Nashville: Broadman Press, pp.266-69.

TURNER, Max. 1980. *Luke and the Spirit: Studies in the Significance of Receiving the Spirit in Luke-Acts*. PhD diss.: University of Cambridge.

TURNER, Max. 1981. Jesus and the Spirit in Lucan Perspective. *TynBul*. **32**(1), p.40.

TURNER, Max. 1989. Ecclesiology in the Major Apostolic Restorationist Churches in the United Kingdom. *Vox Evangelica*. **19**(1), pp.83-108.

TURNER, Max. 1991. The Spirit and the Power of Jesus' Miracles in the Lucan Conception. *Novum Testamentum*. **33**(2), pp.124-52.

TURNER, Max. 1992. The Spirit of Prophecy and the Power of Authoritative Preaching in Luke-Acts: A Question of Origins. *New Testament Studies*. **38**(1), pp.66-88.

TURNER, Max. 1994. The Spirit of Prophecy and the Ethical/Religious Life of the Christian Community. *In*: Mark W. WILSON, (ed). *Spirit and Renewal: Essays in Honor of J. Rodman Williams*, Sheffield: Sheffield Academic Press, pp.166-90.

TURNER, Max. 1998. *The Holy Spirit and Spiritual Gifts in the New Testament Church and Today, Revised Ed.* Peabody: Hendrickson Publishers.

TURNER, Max. 1998. The Spirit of Prophecy as the Power of Israel's Restoration and Witness. *In*: I. Howard MARSHALL and David PETERSON, (eds). *Witness to the Gospel: The Theology of Acts*, Grand Rapids: William B. Eerdmans Publishing, pp.327-48.

TURNER, Max. 2000. *Power from on High: The Spirit in Israel's Restoration and Witness in Luke-Acts.* Sheffield: Sheffield Academic Press.

TURNER, Max. 2005. Luke and the Spirit: Renewing Theological Interpretation of Biblical Pneumatology. *In*: Craig G. BARTHOLOMEW, Joel B. GREEN, and Anthony C. THISELTON, (eds). *Reading Luke: Interpretation, Reflection, Formation*, Grand Rapids: Zondervan, pp.267-92.

TURNER, Max. 2010. James Dunn's Baptism in the Holy Spirit: Appreciation and Response. *Journal of Pentecostal Theology.* **19**(1), pp.25-31.

TURNER, David L. 2008. Matthew. *In*: Robert W. YARBROUGH and Robert H. STEIN, (eds). *Baker Exegetical Commentary on the New Testament*, Grand Rapids: Baker Academic, pp.104-16.

UNDERWOOD, Alfred Clair. 1947. *A History of the English Baptists*. London: Carey Kingsgate.

UNGER, Merrill F. 1944. The Baptism with the Holy Spirit, Part 1. *Bibliotheca Sacra.* **101**(402), pp.232-47.

UNGER, Merrill F. 1952. *Biblical Demonology: A Study of the Spiritual Forces Behind the Present World Unrest.* Wheaton: Van Kampen Press.

UNGER, Merrill F. 1974. *The Baptism & Gifts of the Holy Spirit.* Chicago: Moody Press.

UNGER, Merrill F. 1991. *What Demons Can Do To Saints.* Chicago: The Moody Bible Institute.

UNIONE, Centro Pro. 2012. *Pentecostal-Roman Catholic Dialogue.* [online]. [Accessed 20 April 2012]. Available from the World Wide Web: <http://www.prounione.urbe.it/dia-int/pe-rc/e_pe-rc-info.html>

UNIVERSITY, Cornerstone. 2012. *David Turner.* [online]. [Accessed 20 April 2012]. Available from World Wide Web: <http://assets1.mytrainsite.com/501431/turner_vitae.pdf?r=1536>

UNIVERSITY, Mercer. 2012 *William E. Hull.* [online]. [Accessed 20 April 2012]. Available from World Wide Web: <http://www.mupress.org/contributorinfo.cfm?ContribID=641>

UNIVERSITY, Vanguard. 2012. *Frank D. Macchia.* [online]. [Accessed 21 May 2012]. Available from World Wide Web: <http://religion.vanguard.edu/faculty /frank-macchia>

USA, Assemblies of God. 2010. *Baptism in the Holy Spirit: The Initial Experience and Continuing Evidences of the Spirit-Filled Life.* [online]. [Accessed 17 November 2011]. Available from World Wide Web: <http://ag.org/top/Beliefs /Position_Papers/pp_downloads/PP_Baptism_In_the_Holy_Spirit.pdf>

USA, Assemblies of God. 2010. *Our 16 Fundamental Truths.* [online]. [Accessed 21 October 2011]. Available from World Wide Web: <http://ag.org/top/Beliefs/ Statement_of_Fundamental_Truths/sft_full.cfm#8>

USA, Vineyard. 2010. *Statement of Faith.* [online]. [Accessed 17 November 2011]. Available from World Wide Web: <http://www.vineyardusa.org/ site/files/about/_Vineyard%20USA%20Statement%20of%20Faith.pdf>

USA, American Baptist Churches. 2011. *10 Facts You Should Know About American Baptists.* [online]. [Accessed 23 June 2011]. Available from World Wide Web: <http://www.abc-usa.org/portals/0/ABC10FactsBrochure.pdf>

USA, Vineyard. 2011. *Vineyard History.* [online]. [Accessed 11 November 2011]. Available from World Wide Web: <http://www.vineyardusa.org/site/about /vineyard-history>

VAN DUSEN, Henry P. 1955. Caribbean Holiday. *The Christian Century.*, pp.946-48.

VAN DUSEN, Henry P. 1958. The Third Force in Christendom. *Life Magazine.*, pp.113-21.

VAN NESTE, Ray and TIDWELL, Jerry (eds). 2011. *Southern Baptists, Evangelicals, and the Future of Denominationalism.* Nashville: B & H Publications.

VEDDER, Henry C. 1907. *A Short History of the Baptists.* Philadelphia: American Baptist Publication Society.

VINES, Jerry. 1999. *Spirit Works: Charismatic Practices and the Bible.* Nashville: Broadman & Holman Publishers.

VOLF, Miroslav. 1998. *After our Likeness: The Church as the Image of the Trinity.* Grand Rapids: William B. Eerdmans Publishing.

VON BUSEK, Craig. 2007. *Southern Baptists Struggle with the Holy Spirit.* [online]. [Accessed 23 June 2011]. Available from World Wide Web: <http://www. cbn.com/spirituallife/churchandministry/vonbuseck_southern baptist_holyspirit.aspx?mobile=false>

WACKER, Grant. 1984. The Functions of Faith in Primitive Pentecostalism. *Harvard Theological Review.* 77(1), pp.353-75.

WACKER, Grant. 1990. Wild Theories and Mad Excitement. *In*: Harold B. SMITH, (ed). *Pentecostals from the Inside Out*, Wheaton: Victor Press, p.21.

WACKER, Grant A. 1999. Travail of a Broken Family: Radical Evangelical Responses to the Emergence of Pentecostalism in America. *In*: Edith L. BLUMHOFER, Russell P. SPITTLER, and Grant A. AND WACKER, (eds). *Pentecostal Currents in American Protestantism*, Chicago: University of Illinois Press, pp.23-49.

WACKER, Grant. 2003. *Heaven Below: Early Pentecostals and American Culture.* Cambridge: Harvard University Press.

WAGNER, C. Peter. 1983. The Third Wave? *Pastoral Renewal*, July-August, pp.1-5.

WAGNER, C. Peter (ed). 1987. *Signs & Wonders Today: The Story of Fuller Theological Seminary's Remarkable Course on Spiritual Power.* Altamonte Springs: Creation House.

Bibliography

WAGNER, C. Peter. 1988. *The Third Wave of the Holy Spirit: Encountering the Power of Signs and Wonders*. Ann Arbor: Servant Publications.

WAGNER, C. Peter. 1992. *Warfare Prayer*. Ventura: Regal Books.

WAGNER, C. Peter. 1993. *Breaking Strongholds in Your City*. Ventura: Regal Books.

WAGNER, C. Peter. 1997. Contemporary Dynamics of the Holy Spirit in Missions: A Personal Pilgrimage. *In*: C. Douglas MCCONNELL, (ed). *The Holy Spoirit and Mission Dynamics*, Pasadena: William Carey Library, pp.107-22.

WAGNER, C. Peter. 1998. The New Apostolic Reformation. *In*: C. Peter WAGNER, (ed). *The New Apostolic Churches: Rediscovering the New Testament Model of Leadership and Why it is God's Desire for the Church Today* , Ventura: Regal Books, pp.13-27.

WAGNER, C. Peter. 1999. *Churchquake! The Explosive Dynamics of the New Apostolic Reformation*. Ventura: Regal Books.

WAGNER, C. Peter. 2002. New Apostolic Reformation. *In*: Stanley M. BURGESS and Eduard M. VAN DER MAAS, (eds). *New International Dictionary of Pentecostal and Charismatic Movements*, Grand Rapids: Zondervan, p.930.

WAGNER, C. Peter. 2002. Third Wave. *In*: Stanley M. BURGESS and Eduard M. VAN DER MAAS, (eds). *New International Dictionary of Pentecostal and Charismatic Movements*, Grand Rapids: Zondervan, p.1141.

WAGNER, C. Peter. 2006. *Apostles Today*. Ventura: Regal Books.

WAGNER, C. Peter. 2008. *The Book of Acts: A Commentary*. Ventura: Regal Books.

WALDVOGEL, Edith Lydia. 1977. *The Overcoming Life: A Study in the Reformed Evangelical Origins of Pentecostalism*. PhD diss.: Harvard University.

WALLACE, Daniel B. 1996. *Greek Grammar Beyond the Basics*. Grand Rapids: Zondervan.

WALLACE, Daniel B. 2005. Who's Afraid of the Holy Spirit? An Investigation into the Ministry of the Spirit of God Today. *In*: Daniel B. WALLACE and M. James SAWYER, (eds). *Introduction: Who's Afraid of the Holy Spirit? The Uneasy Conscience of a Non-Charismatic Evangelical*, Dallas: Biblical Studies Press, pp.1-13.

WALLACE, Daniel B. and SAWYER, James M. (eds). 2005. *Who's Afraid of the Holy Spirit? An Investigation into the Ministry of the Spirit of God Today.* Dallas: Biblical Studies Press.

WALVOORD, John F. 1958. *The Holy Spirit: A Comprehensive Study of the Person and Work of the Holy Spirit.* Findlay: Dunham Publishing Company.

WARD, Wayne E. 1970. What is a Baptist? Personal Religious Freedom. *Western Recorder*, 4 April , p.2.

WARFIELD, Benjamin B. 1976. *Counterfeit Miracles: The Cessation of the Charismata.* Carlisle: The Banner of Truth Trust.

WARRINGTON, Keith (ed). 1998. *Pentecostal Perspectives*. Paternoster Press: Carlisle.

WARRINGTON, Keith. 1999. A Window on Wimber and Healing. *Churchman*. **113**(1), pp.1-11.

WARRINGTON, Keith. 2000. *Jesus the Healer: Paradigm or Unique Phenomenon?* Carlisle: Paternoster Press.

WARRINGTON, Keith. 2008. *Pentecostal Theology: A Theology of Encounter.* London: T & T Clark.

WARRINGTON, Keith. 2009. The Message of the Holy Spirit: The Spirit of Encounter. *In*: Derek TIDBALL, (ed). *The Bible Speaks Today*, Downers Grove: Inter-Varsity Press, p.63.

WATTS, Rikki E. 2000. *Isaiah's New Exodus in Mark.* Grand Rapids: Baker Academic.

WEAVER, C. Douglas. 2008. *In Search of the New Testament Church: The Baptist Story.* Macon: Mercer University Press.

309

WEBB, Robert L. 1991. The Activity of John the Baptist's Expected Figure at the Threshing Floor (Matthew 3.12 = Luke 3.17. *Journal for the Study of the New Testament.* **43**(1), pp.103-11.

WEBB, Robert L. 2006. *John the Baptizer and Prophet: A Socio-Historical Study.* Eugene: Wipf and Stock Publishers.

WEBORG, John C. 1991. Pietism: Theology in Search of Living Toward God. *In*: Donald W. DAYTON and Robert K. JOHNSON, (eds). *The Variety of American Evangelicalism*, Downers Grove: InterVarsity Press, pp.161-183.

WELKER, Michael, Trans. John F. Hoffmeyer. ET 1994. *God the Spirit.* Minneapolis: Fortress Press.

WELLS, David F. and WOODBRIDGE, John D. (eds). 1975. *The Evangelicals.* New York: Abingdon Press.

WERNLE, Paul. 1903. *The Beginnings of Christianity, Vol. 1.* Oxford: Williams and Norgate.

WESLEY, John. 1938. *The Journal of the Rev. John Wesley A.M., Vol. 1.* London: Epworth Press.

WESLEY, John. 1938. *The Journal of the Rev. John Wesley A.M., Vol. 2.* London: Epworth Press.

WESLEY, John. 1952. *A Plain Account of Christian Perfection.* London: The Epworth Press.

WHITE, Barrington R. 1971. *The English Separatist Tradition: From the Marian Martyrs to the Pilgrim Fathers.* London: Oxford University Press.

WHITE, Barrington R. 1983. *A History of the English Baptists, Vol. 1.* London: Baptist Historical Society.

WHITE, John. 1988. *When the Spirit Comes with Power: Signs & Wonders Among God's People.* Downers Grove: InterVarsity Press.

WILLIAMS, Ernest S. 1991. *Systematic Theology, Vol. 3.* Springfield: Gospel Publishing House.

WILLIAMS, Don. 1993. Following Christ's Example: A Biblical View of Discipleship. *In*: Gary S. GREIG and Kevin N. SPRINGER, (eds). *The Kingdom and the Power: Are Healing and the Spiritual Gifts Used by Jesus and the Early Church Meant for the Church Today?* , Ventura: Regal Books, pp.175-96.

WILLIAMS, George Huntston. 1957. *Spiritual and Anabaptist Writers*. Philadelphia: Westminster Press.

WILLIAMS, J. Rodman. 1971. *The Era of the Spirit*. Plainfield: Logos International.

WILLIAMS, J. Rodman. 1972. *The Pentecostal Reality*. Plainfield: Logos.

WILLIAMS, J. Rodman. 1976. Pentecostal Theology: A Neo-Pentecostal Viewpoint. *In*: Russell P. SPITTLER, (ed). *Perspectives on the New Pentecostalism*, Grand Rapids: Baker Book House, pp.76-85.

WILLIAMS, J. Rodman. 1980. *The Gift of the Holy Spirit Today*. Plainfield: Logos.

WILLIAMS, J. Rodman. 1996. *Renewal Theology: Systematic Theology from a Charismatic Perspective, 3 Vols*. Grand Rapids: Zondervan.

WILLIAMS, J. Rodman. 2003. *A Theological Pilgrimage*. [online]. [Accessed 22 September 2011]. Available from World Wide Web: <http:// www.cbn.com/ spiritual life/BibleStudyAndTheology/DrWilliams/bk _theopilgrim_ch03.aspx>

WILLIAMS, J. Rodman. 2012. *Renewal Theology featuring the works of theologian J. Rodman Williams*. [online]. [Accessed 5 May 2012]. Available from World Wide: Web <http://www.renewaltheology.net>

WILLIAMS, Roger. 1863. *Experiments of Spiritual Life & Health and their Preservatives in which the Weakest Child of God may get Assurance of his Spiritual Life and Blessedness and the Strong may find Proportionate Discoveries of his Christian Growth, and the Means of it*. Providence: Sidney S. Rider.

WILLS, Gregory A. 2003. Progressive Theology and Southern Baptist Controversies of the 1950s and 1960s. *Southern Baptist Journal of Theology*. 7(1), pp.12-31.

WILLS, Gregory A. 2009. Southern Baptist Identity: A Historical Perspective. *In*: David S. DOCKERY, (ed). *Southern Baptist Identity: An Evangelical Denomination Faces the Future*, Wheaton: Crossway Books, pp.69-87.

WILLS, Gregory A. 2009. *Southern Baptist Theological Seminary, 1859-2009.* Oxford: Oxford University Press, 2009.

WILSON, Mark W. (ed). 1994. *Spirit and Renewal: Essays in Honor of J. Rodman Williams.* Sheffield: Sheffield Academic Press.

WIMBER, John and Kevin SPRINGER. 1986. *Power Evangelism.* San Francisco: Harper & Row Publishers.

WIMBER, John and Kevin SPRINGER. 1987. *Power Healing.* San Francisco: Harper San Francisco.

WIMBER, John. 1991. *Power Points.* San Francisco: Harper Collins.

WINER, George Benedict. 1874. *A Grammar of the Idiom of the New Testament: Prepared as a Solid Basis for the Interpretation of the New Testament.* Andover: Warren F. Draper.

WINGFIELD, Mark. 2000. Mohler Criticizes Mullins' Influence and Doctrine of Soul Competency. *The Baptist Standard*, 17 April, pp.17-20.

WITHERINGTON, III Ben. 1998. *The Acts of the Apostles: A Socio-Rhetorical Commentary.* Grand Rapids: William B. Eerdmans Publishing.

WYCKOFF, John W. 1994. The Baptism in the Holy Spirit. *In*: Stanley M., Jr. HORTON, (ed). *Systematic Theology: A Pentecostal Perspective*, Springfield: Logion Press, pp.423-55.

YARNELL, III Malcolm B. 2006. Are Southern Baptists Evangelicals?: A Second Decadal Reassessment. *Ecclesiology.* **2**(2), pp.211-12.

YARNELL, III Malcolm B. 2006. The Heart of a Baptist. *Criswell Theological Review.* **4**(1), pp.73-87.

YARNELL, III Malcolm B. 2007. The Person and Work of the Holy Spirit. *In*: Daniel L. AKIN, (ed). *A Theology for the Church*, Nashville: B & H Academic, pp.604-84.

YONG, Amos. 2005. *The Spirit Poured Out on all Flesh: Pentecostalism and the Possibility of Global Theology*. Grand Rapids: Baker Academic.

YUN, Koo Dong. 2003. *Baptism in the Holy Spirit: An Ecumenical Theology of Spirit Baptism*. Lanham: University Press of America.

ZIMMERMAN, Thomas F. 2006. The Reason for the Rise of the Pentecostal Movement. *In*: Grant MCCLUNG, (ed). *Azusa Street and Beyond: 100 Years of Commentary on the Global Pentecostal/Charismatic Movement*, Gainesville: Bridge-Logos, pp.89-96.

ZONDERVAN. 2012. *Robert P. Menzies*. [online]. [Accessed 21 May 2012]. Available from World Wide Web: <http://zondervan.com/menziesr>

ZWIEP, Arie W. 1997. *The Association of the Messiah in Lukan Christology*. Leiden: Brill.

ZWIEP, Arie W. 2007. Luke's Understanding of Baptism in the Holy Spirit. *PentecoStudies*. **6**(2), pp.127-49.

ZWIEP, Arie W. 2010. *Christ, the Spirit and the Community of God*. Tübingen: Mohr Siebeck.

ZWIEP, Arie W. 2012. [online]. [Accessed 20 June 2012]. Available from World Wide Web: <http://home.solcon.nl/awzwiep/index.htm>